D1765349

320

Occidentalis Americæ partis,
vel earum Regionum quas Chri
stophorus Columbus primũ detexit
Tabula Chorographica multorum
Auctorum ſcriptis, præſertim verò ex
Hieronymi Benzonij (qui totis xiiii
annis eas Provinciã diligenter
perluſtravit)
Hiſtoria,
conflata & in æs inciſa a
Theodoro de Bry Leod.
Anno M D XCIIII

Marraſou

Hanocorouſſouau

Sorrochas
Sorrochas

Iucayonoque ſiue maior

om Caniaueral
de Sanct Hellena

LVCAYA

Bahama

Maris pars plena eſt Inſulis,
breulibus & puluinis valdè inſidiofis

Plumachary

Mayn guana

Inſ S Tome

Mont Chri
ſti

Portus Regius
HAYTI
STVE SPANIOLA Iſabella
Lago ſal
Port plati
Rio de luna

Hanc Inſulam ſecunda Navigatione obtinuit Columbus,
et Hiſpaniolam appellavit

Lago dolce

Capus

S.Iuana

Rio de luxa

Dominica
Rio delphin

Rio d'Orana S Catelina
Hiſpani magna ex parte tenent
inatuq maximam uim tranſmittunt.

S.Germam BORICHEN
Virgines S Ioanns
INSVLAS IOANIS DE PORTV DEVIT

Dorthricus Virginda

Anguilla Bene

In hanc Inſulam prima Navigatione ap
pulit Columbus, Deſideratam nominauit,
et, in, Chriſtiani nominis memoria Crucem
fixit.

Antigua Boricua
Saba
S.Lucia
S Crux Estazia
Cubucheta
Guadalupe S Dominica

Marigalente

Mons Serrut S Vincentz

Margarita Domica Baruodos

Granada Cubucheira
y de S.B

Mantinen

Pichibaroa
Amba
Cap de uele
Bucare
Diaues
La roca
Putaguari
Tortaga

Curiana
Rio Hondo
Coſta de Giorgeprata
Valle D'ametico Taſte
R.de bordones Maracapana
CVMANA
Tacaris
Iumbi
Nebert
Benezuela

Cariaco
Chirubichi P. de galea
Coſta de Narro
Rio dolce CVBAGVA
Camari

Paria

R.Dolce

In iſtam Inſulam delatus eſt tertia Navigatione
Columbus, cui nomen indidit ab Omonibus, quaru
foripana quinta pars Regi cedit

Monte eſpeco

Puntabox

Ancon

AVREA

CARIBANA

REG

Rio Negro

Circulus Aequnoctialis

Aldea de arpol edos

Auapari
R.Verde
R.Salado

Auapari
R de S.Vincente Pinço

315 320 325 330

West Indian Nations
A NEW HISTORY

West Indian Nations

A NEW HISTORY

Philip Sherlock

ST. MARTIN'S PRESS NEW YORK

AFFILIATED PUBLISHERS: Macmillan Limited, London —
also at Bombay, Calcutta, Madras and Melbourne
Printed by C.T.P.S. Hong Kong

Acknowledgements

The author and publisher wish to acknowledge the following sources of illustrations:

Barbados Tourist Board	p. 137
British Museum	p. 197
Institute of Jamaica	p. 268
Jamaica Information Service	pp. 277, 287
Mansell Collection	pp. 10, 203
Radio Times, Hulton Picture Library	pp. 13, 24, 29, 213
Camera Press Ltd	p. 280
Office of the Prime Minister of Trinidad and Tobago	p. 297
The University of Wisconsin Press (By the Regents of The University of Wisconsin).	pp. 126, 127, 129, 239

Cover illustration courtesy of NASA

Cover photographs:
Simon Bolivar and Toussaint L'Ouverture,
courtesy of Mansell collection;
José Martí, courtesy of Radio Habana Cuba;
Marcus Garvey, courtesy of Jamaica Information Service.

TO

EDNA MANLEY

Peace and Love, Regardless

Introduction

In many respects this book is a companion to *The Short History of the West Indies* in which the aim was the study of the West Indies in its own right. The emphasis here is also on ' the accumulated experience of the people of the West Indies ' but with this difference, that attention is directed especially to the experience of the black and brown people who comprise the large majority of the West Indian people; and an attempt is made also to indicate the importance of that inner world of the folk, the ' inscape ' in Edward Brathwaite's phrase, which we have for so long either disregarded or disowned.

Today's West Indian scholars begin, very properly, with the basic assumption that Caribbean history exists in its own right, and Dr. Elsa Goveia's *Slave Society in the British Leeward Islands* is a brilliant example of what is being achieved. I, in common with others of my generation, reached this conclusion through hard years of doubt, questioning, discovery, certainty. I acknowledge my debt to those who led the way, including Mr. C. L. R. James, Dr. Eric Williams and Dr. John Parry; and to the many artists who set about the task of portraying and interpreting the West Indian experience, giving us in the process a literature and theatre, schools of dance, music, painting and sculpture.

In many instances the sources on which I have drawn appear in the text. I am grateful to all the authors concerned. In addition I acknowledge my indebtedness to Dr. Lloyd Best's study *A Model of Pure Plantation Economy*; Dr. Mary Reckord's paper on *Chinese Contract Labour in Cuba 1847–64*; a paper on *Factors involved in immigration and movements in the working force of British Guiana in the Nineteenth Century* by G. W. Roberts and H. A. Johnson; *The Experience of African Immigrants in 19th Century Jamaica* by M. Schuyler; and a paper entitled *Puerto Rico* by Dr. Ben Stephansky.

Contents

Contents (*continued*)

CHAPTER 1

The First Islanders

The story of the people of the Caribbean begins with the nature of the region itself, with its prevailing winds, its soils, mountain ranges, valleys, rivers, harbours, its ocean currents, its periods of rainfall and of drought. The physical surroundings, the climate, the indigenous plants and the marine life influenced the pattern of exploration and settlement. They set the limits within which the Amerindian gathered his food, built his home and established a way of life. The dweller on the coastlands and in the islands carried on man's age-long struggle to manipulate his environment, striving to break through the limits nature imposed on him by developing a technology that added strength to his arm, speed to his feet, that enabled him to tame animals and to use the power of wind and water for his own purposes. In order to survive, the Amerindian felled forest trees with implements of stone and made clearings for planting maize and cassava. In order to preserve his meat he found a way of getting rid of tho prussic acid from cassava and making casareep. In order to cross the sea that barred him from islands visible on the horizon he made dug-outs and found paths across the Caribbean by the stars. The setting influenced his way of life, and the setting itself was shaped by events that took place when the surface of our planet was cooling to its present form.

Asia first discovered and settled America. It may have been as much as 35,000 years ago that the first straggling parties of Mongoloid people, under the pressure of hunger perhaps, began

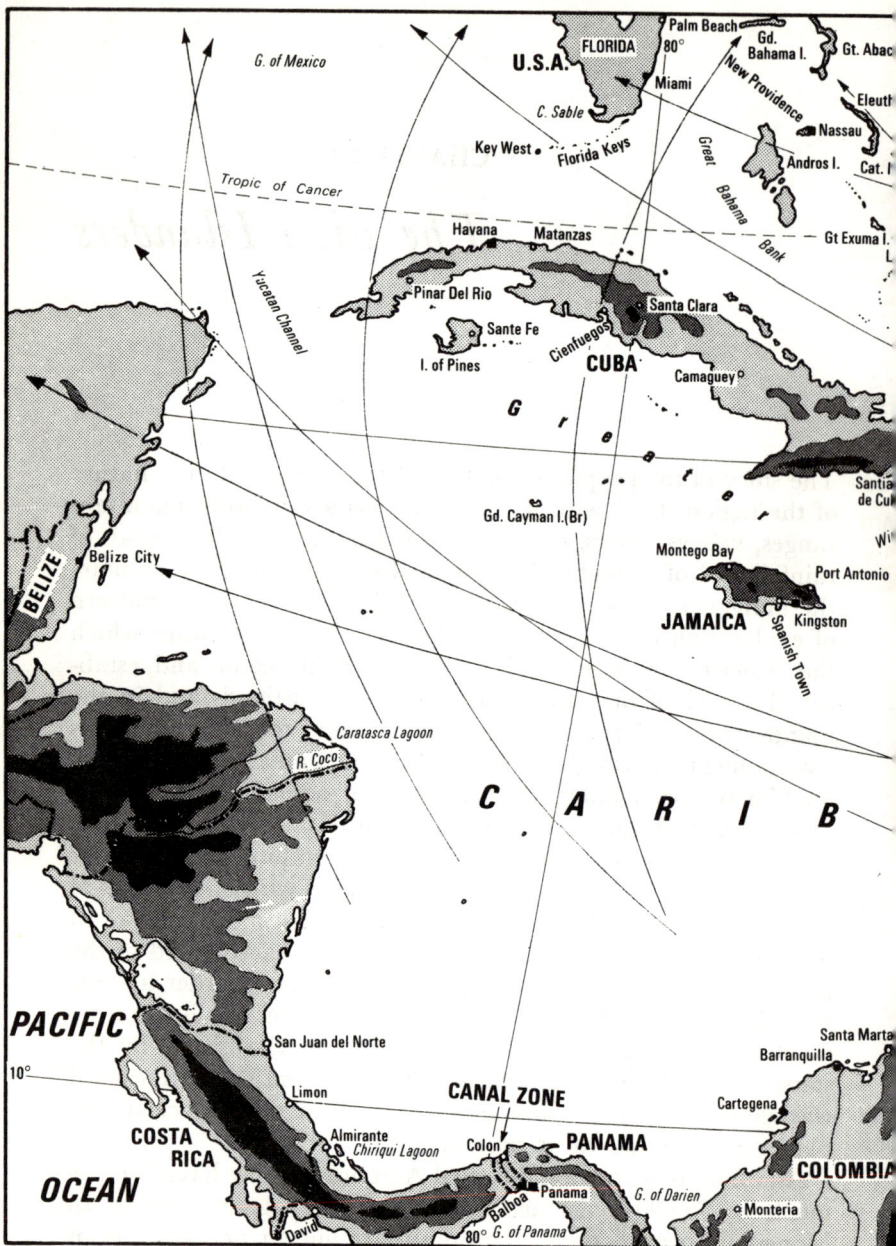

The Caribbean 1973

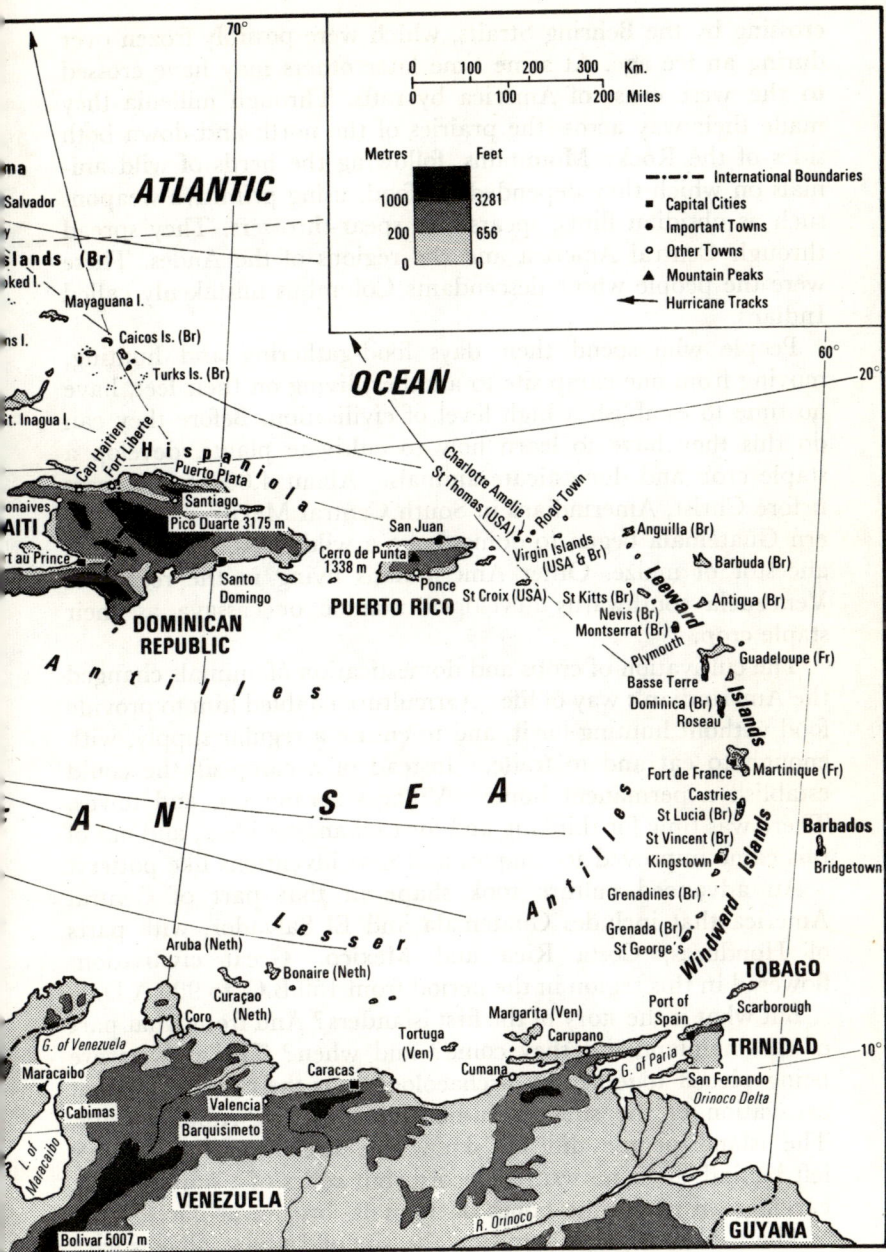

70°

ATLANTIC

Km.
0 100 200 300
0 100 200 Miles

Metres	Feet
1000	3281
200	656
0	0

-·-·- International Boundaries
■ Capital Cities
● Important Towns
○ Other Towns
▲ Mountain Peaks
← Hurricane Tracks

ma

Salvador

y

lands (Br)

ked I.

Mayaguana I.

ns I.

Caicos Is. (Br)

Turks Is. (Br)

t. Inagua I.

OCEAN

60°

20°

Cap Haitien
Fort Liberté

H i s p a n i o l a

Puerto Plata

onaives

Santiago

AITI

Pico Duarte 3175 m

t au Prince

Charlotte Amelie
St Thomas (USA)

Road Town

Anguilla (Br)

Barbuda (Br)

San Juan

Virgin Islands
(USA & Br)

Cerro de Punta
1338 m

Santo
Domingo

Ponce

PUERTO RICO

St Croix (USA)

St Kitts (Br)

Antigua (Br)

Nevis (Br)

DOMINICAN
REPUBLIC

Montserrat (Br)

Plymouth

Guadeloupe (Fr)

A

n

t

i

l

l

e

s

Basse Terre

Dominica (Br)

Roseau

Fort de France

Martinique (Fr)

Castries

St Lucia (Br)

L

e

e

w

a

r

d

Islands

F

A

N

S

E

A

St Vincent (Br)

Kingstown

Barbados

Bridgetown

Antilles

Grenadines (Br)

L

e

s

s

e

r

Grenada (Br)

St George's

W

i

n

d

w

a

r

d

Islands

TOBAGO

Aruba (Neth)

Bonaire (Neth)

Curaçao
(Neth)

Coro

Margarita (Ven)

Port of
Spain

Scarborough

G. of Venezuela

Tortuga
(Ven)

Carupano

TRINIDAD

10°

Maracaibo

Caracas

Cumana

G. of Paria

San Fernando

Orinoco Delta

Cabimas

Valencia

L. of
Maracaibo

Barquisimeto

VENEZUELA

R. Orinoco

GUYANA

Bolivar 5007 m

3

crossing by the Behring Straits, which were possibly frozen over during an ice age. At some time later others may have crossed to the west coast of America by rafts. Through millenia they made their way across the prairies of the north and down both sides of the Rocky Mountains, following the herds of wild animals on which they depended for food, using primitive weapons such as obsidian flints, spears and spear-throwers. They spread through Central America and the regions of the Andes. These were the people whose descendants Columbus mistakenly called Indians.

People who spend their days food-gathering and hunting, moving from one camp site to another, living on their feet, have no time to establish a high level of civilisation. Before they can do this they have to learn how to cultivate plants, develop a staple crop and domesticate animals. About 4,000–5,000 years before Christ, Amerindians in South Central Mexico and Northern Guatemala began to domesticate a wild grass, teocintle, the ancestor of maize. Other Amerindians living in the region of Venezuela southwards developed manioc or cassava as their staple crop.

The cultivation of crops and domestication of animals changed the Amerindian's way of life. Agriculture enabled him to provide food without hunting for it, and to ensure a regular supply, with enough to eat and to trade. Instead of a camp-site he could establish a permanent home. Villages sprang up, and towns. There was time for thinking and for exchanging ideas, and out of this came improved techniques and new inventions like pottery.

An advanced culture took shape in that part of Central America that includes Guatemala and El Salvador, with parts of Honduras, Costa Rica and Mexico. Great civilisations flowered in this region in the period from 150 B.C. to 900 A.D.

But what is the story of the first islanders? And from what part of the mainland did they come? and when? The answers are being pieced together by archaeologists, as the result of patient excavation of the sites of Indian villages and rubbish heaps. The island people did not know the art of writing so they left behind them no written record, but relics of a simpler kind, carvings on rocks, the bones of animals, broken artifacts.

The rubbish dumps found on the site of Indian villages vary

in size according to the size of the village and the length of settlement. They are given the name of 'middens', a Danish word for kitchen refuse, because the importance of these mounds was first recognised in Denmark. Amerindian middens are found throughout the archipelago and in the Bahamas. They date back to different periods but generally they contain the shells of molluscs, the bones of fish, aguti or conies and turtle, and very occasionally of birds, along with pottery, implements of stone and shell, and ashes. Skeletons have been found in some middens.

Since the early 1950's scientists have been able to date relics like these with a considerable degree of accuracy. All organic matter contains carbon, and among the various compounds of carbon there is one radio-active isotype whose age can be estimated by the use of radiation counters. Carbon-dating indicates that some of the islands, such as Cuba, Hispaniola and Trinidad were settled at a much earlier period than was thought at first. Some of the relics found at Palo Seco in Trinidad are about 2,500 years old. Relics found near Fort Liberté in north-eastern Haiti are even older. Some archaeologists suggest that they date back about 5,000 years. This means that migration into the islands lasted over a long period and the relics show that people of three culture periods, were involved. Earliest are the ancient or palaeo-Indians who used very simple tools of stone. They did not know how to grind and polish their artifacts of stone. They were food-gatherers, not growers of food. Ancient Indian sites dating from this first period have been identified in Florida, Cuba and Hispaniola.

There followed groups of Indians who were more advanced, the middle-period Indians. Meso-Indian sites have been found in the Greater Antilles, and in islands off the coast of Venezuela, but as yet no meso-Indian sites have been found in the Lesser Antilles. Neither the palaeo-Indian nor the meso-Indian sites contain pottery. This is found only in the late-Indian or neo-Indian sites, along with beautifully polished tools, such as stone axes, ground smooth and hafted.

Some of the most important Indian sites in the Caribbean have been found in Hispaniola; in north-eastern Haiti, at Ile à Vache and other nearby places, and in an area not far north of Port au Prince. Carbon dating shows that relics found on these sites belong to a period 2,000 or 3,000 years before the birth of Christ.

The people who inhabited the islands at the time when Columbus arrived were the late or neo-Indians; some speaking Arawakan, and others Cariban. They migrated from Venezuela, and their kinsmen survive in the basin of the Orinoco and in parts of Guyana. The Arawaks who lived in the Greater Antilles were wiped out in the first century of Spanish occupation. The Amerindians of Trinidad survived until the early 19th

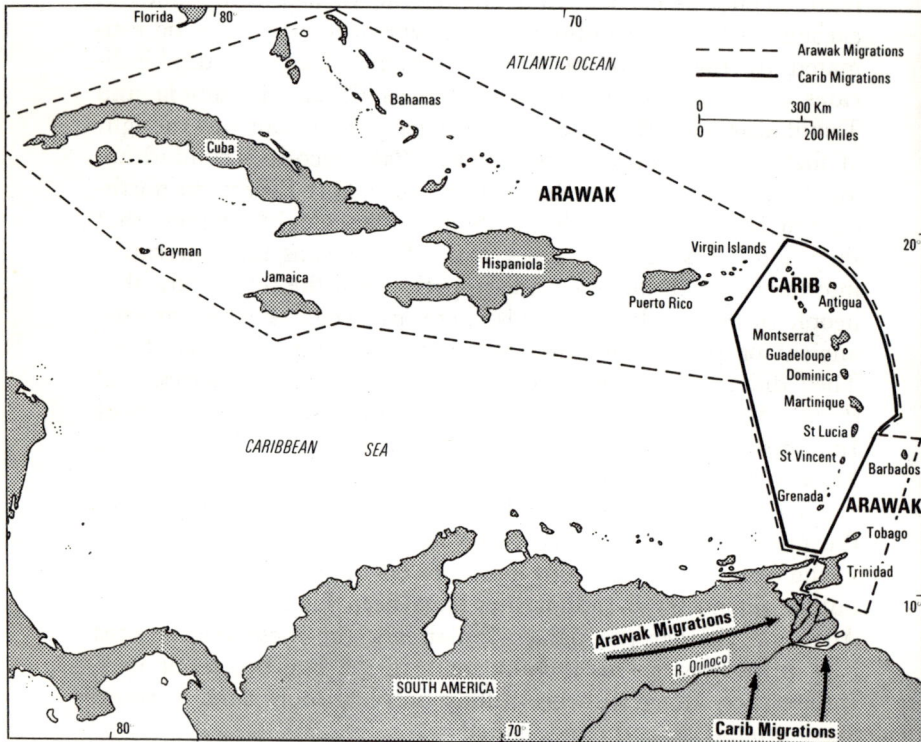

Arawak and Carib Areas of Caribbean

century and we still use many of their place names. The only Amerindians left in the islands are in the Carib Reserve on the windy north-east coast of Dominica. In their mythology the Caribs consider themselves the first of the Indian tribes. They speak of themselves as ' the ' people, and of their language as ' the ' language.

In his *Journal* Columbus gave a vivid description of the Indians he met:

> All those whom I did see were youths, so that I did not see one who was over the age of thirty; they were very well built with very handsome bodies and fine faces. Their hair is coarse almost like the hair of a horse's tail and short... Some of them are painted black and they are the colour of the people of the Canaries—neither black nor white—and some of them are painted white and some red and some in any colour they can find. They do not bear arms or know of them, for I showed them swords and they took them by the blade and cut themselves through ignorance. They have no iron. Their spears are certain reeds, without iron, and some of these have a fish tooth at the end, while others are pointed in various ways... Their legs are very straight, all alike; they have no great bellies but very good figures. They came to the ship in boats which are made of tree trunks like long boats all of one piece. They are very wonderfully carved... and large, so that in some forty or fifty men came... They row them with a paddle, and they travel wonderfully fast...

One of the remarkable things about this early period of European conquest and exploration is the extent to which it is documented. A number of the Spanish explorers and missionaries wrote accounts of the lands and people of the New World and Spanish historians recorded the events that took place, describing the Indians, their conquest, the establishment of Spanish rule, the introduction of a new system of trade and the emergence of a new society. In her study of the historiography of the West Indies, Dr Elsa Goveia points out that these writers recorded an historic process which they knew at first hand and for this reason they were able to make a unique contribution to our knowledge of the islands. Three of the most detailed and most important accounts are those by Peter Martyr, Las Casas and Oviedo. Peter Martyr was an Italian priest who lived at the court of the Spanish sovereigns and was a tutor to the royal princes. He wrote letters commenting on the happenings of his time and when news came about the discovery of the Indies he turned eagerly to those who could tell him about the new-found lands and people. The period in which Peter Martyr lived was one of enquiry and of curiosity, and the *Letters* or *Decades* he wrote between 1493 and 1526, the year of his death, helped to excite and to maintain Europe's interest in the Americas. He never saw the lands or people he described but he was able to build up a remarkably accurate picture on the basis of eye-witness accounts given by those who had visited the Indies.

The historian Fernandez de Oviedo, on the other hand, knew the islands and the mainland, Terra Firme. His first book, *Summary of the Natural History of the Indies*, published in 1626, dealt chiefly with the mainland. The second book, his famous *Natural and General History of the Indies*, written in part in Santo Domingo, was based on statements made to him by some of the early colonists as well as on his own observations.

Bartholomew Las Casas spent most of his long life in the Indies and few if any rivalled him in his knowledge of the Indians and of the lands of the Caribbean. His father was with Columbus on the voyage of 1493 and it is reported that he returned to Spain in 1498 with an Arawak slave. The son, Bartholomew, accompanied Ovando on his trans-Atlantic voyage of 1502 and took part in the conquest of both Hispaniola and Cuba. At a later point we will consider the work Las Casas did on behalf of the Indians. Here we are concerned with him as a historian, a man who saw that he was living in a period of dramatic change, and recognised the importance of preserving all the documents that he could find, and of writing down accounts of the lands he visited, their climate and fauna and flora and their inhabitants. He spent some forty years working on his history of the Spanish New World up to the year 1520; but he is most widely known for his devastating attack on the Spanish colonial system in a much shorter work, his *Brief Account of the Destruction of the Indians*, written at a time when Spain was preparing its New Laws in an effort to safeguard the Indians.

Our age thinks of the Arawak world which Columbus found as primitive. Yet these people, working within the limits of a stone age technology, without the art of writing, wholly dependent on muscle power, developed a culture that won the respect of the European newcomers, who remarked on their lack of guile, their happiness, their ready gift for friendship, and their highly organised society, hierarchic in character, the line of authority running from the local chief or noble to the caciques who ruled over districts and to the greater caciques whose rank was that of king. Las Casas and others noted also their well-developed system of agriculture. They cleared tracts of land and cultivated them by making a number of mounds like large yam-hills, knee high and several feet across. In these they planted their root crops; cassava, which provided them with a supply of starchy food year after year; sweet potatoes which the Spaniards also came to prize; ground nuts; yautia, still one of the widely used root crops of Puerto Rico; and along with these maize and squash. The other two essential plants, cotton and tobacco were not included in the conucos, as the Spaniards called the cultivated tracts of land. The name survives in some of the Spanish-speaking islands. The Arawaks supplemented their diet of starchy food and beans with land animals and rodents like the coney and manicou and with shell-fish, turtles, manati and fish. In the winter months when ducks migrated from the north they ate these also.

The island Indian touches our lives most closely through the crops in our fields. These are his memorial. But in any case his system of agriculture is of interest because it so efficiently sustained man without destroying nature. In his work on *The Early Spanish Main*, Sauer emphasises that 'the white man never fully appreciated the excellent combination of plants that were grown in conucos.'

There were two forms of handicraft in which the island people excelled. They made beautifully carved canoes. It is clear from accounts by Columbus and others that the canoes were fast, seaworthy and that they responded quickly to skilled handling. The other craft that was highly regarded was the making of ceremonial seats of wood, called *dubos*, richly carved and highly polished. The greater the caicque the larger

West Indian Canoe (from a woodcut made in 1563)

his stock of *dubos*. Thus they appear to have been more highly valued than gold, for as one of the early Spanish colonists remarked, the Arawaks thought nothing of gold as wealth, but valued it only ' for good appearance '.

The Arawaks called their houses *bohios*. Las Casas speaks of them as being well-swept and clean, with ten to fifteen people living in each with their wives and children. ' In a single house of thatch which will be thirty to forty feet across and circular and lacks separate rooms ten to fifteen vecinos will live happily '. This means that a village of 15 houses would have about 250 inhabitants. Near by would be the conuco, the leaves covering the mounds and protecting them from soil erosion. On the fringe of the village were the rubbish heaps that now yield so much information to the archaeologist. Usually the houses were grouped around an open space, the great houses of the cacique standing out prominently; and in this open space the festivities, meetings and ceremonies took place.

For many centuries these people lived a settled life in the islands of the archipelago and in the Bahamas. Suddenly without warning, a hurricane of culture broke upon them.

CHAPTER 2

Two Old Worlds Meet

To the Arawaks and Caribs of the islands the Caribbean was world enough, the Atlantic a barrier impassable for their pirogues. God rose in the east each morning, a burning fountain whence issued light and life. That was the region from which one day the gods might visit the earth.

To the European the Mediterranean was the centre of the world, the Atlantic a barrier beyond which lay nothing, a region of mystery. His world-picture began to change in the fifteenth century. Enquiry marked the age and a search began for wider horizons through knowledge, travel and exploration, one of the chief purposes being to find a sea-route to the East.

Two powerful motives spurred Europe forward toward expansion. One was religious. It sprang out of the long war of the Cross against the Crescent. The other motive was that of self-interest, of riches through a profitable trade in silks, spices and gold. Portugal and Spain were drawn by the prospect. Spain was still engaged in a Crusade, a war of Christian against Arab that did not end until the capture of Grenada in Spain in 1492. Portugal had gained its national independence as the result of an earlier victory in that same struggle. In both countries the religious appeal was strong, and each was interested in trade. Portugal had a long rugged sea coast and a tradition for seamanship gained through its trade in wine, salt and fish. The question was whether it was possible to find a way to the East round the coast of Africa, and thereby at one and the same time defeat the Muslim and win a lucrative trade.

Under the leadership of Prince Henry the Navigator, Portugal soon became the centre for a new science of navigation. At the beginning of the century the European navigator usually hugged the shore because, once out of sight of land, he had the greatest difficulty in telling where he was. By the end of the century however an easy way was found by which sailors using the sun's declination were able to calculate the position of their ship. The sailor made use of an agreed estimate, a degree of latitude being eighteen Portuguese leagues; and he had a chart on which to plot his observations. This achievement was due to an unprecedented combination of sea-experience and academic knowledge; and the methods really worked, as Vasco de Gama showed in the course of his great voyage to India, by the accuracy of his navigation and of his first landfall on the South African coast.

Profits soon flowed from the West African trade. By the middle of the century the Portuguese had a brisk trade with Guinea in gold, ivory, pepper, slaves. The thrust south continued. A trading post was established at El Mina. Fernando Po was discovered. By 1489 Portuguese sailors had reached the Congo. But in Lisbon and other centres there was speculation also about another route to the East. Assuming that the world was a sphere, why not reach the East by sailing west across the Atlantic?

For so great an enterprise it was necessary to have ships suited to oceanic voyages. Just such a vessel had been developed by Portuguese and Spanish ship-builders, who combined features in the design of the Mediterranean caravel with those of the square-rigged Northern European ship, thus getting the best of both worlds by combining the square rig and the lateen rig in a new type of ship, the caravela redonda. The foremast and the mainmast were square rigged, and the mizzen mast was lateen-rigged. The lateen sails could be furled when they proved a handicap. Since the ship carried a larger area of sail it could be built bigger. Here was a ship that gave Europe the capacity to transport men and goods across an ocean.

While these things were happening Christopher Columbus, a Genoese by birth, had moved to Lisbon because he wished to be at the centre of activity in cartography and navigation. His studies convinced him that it was possible to find an ocean route to the Indies by sailing west. He calculated the distance he would have to cover and he prepared with great care a proposal which was turned down by one European ruler after another. Finally in 1492 Queen Isabella decided to finance his expedition. Columbus was given letters to the Great Khan of Cathay, and was made Admiral and also Governor of any lands he discovered.

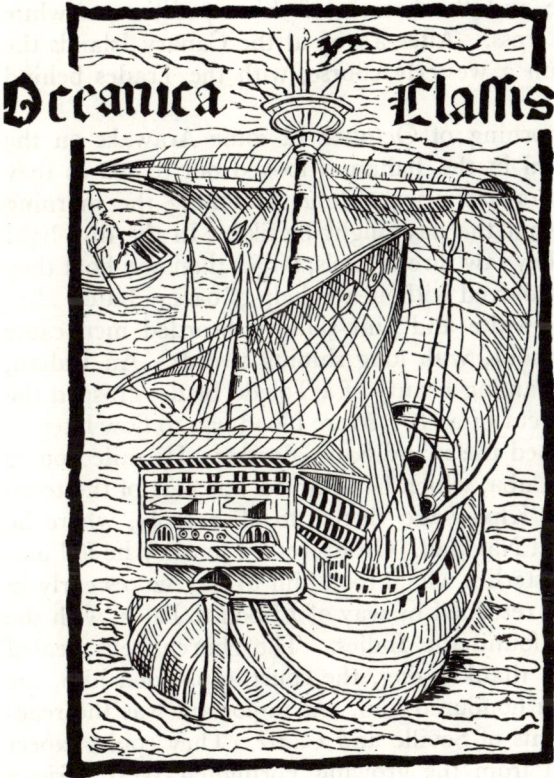

Spanish Caravel in which Columbus discovered America (from a drawing attributed to Columbus)

The fleet with which Columbus set out in 1492 consisted of a sailing ship of the new pattern, the *Santa Maria*, and two light fast caravels, the *Niña* and *Pinta*. He had ninety men with him, most of them from Cadiz and neighbouring ports.

Before daybreak on the morning of Friday August 2, 1492, the ships weighed anchor and moved from the mouth of the Rio Tinto to the waters of the Atlantic. As dawn broke and the ships left the shelter of the harbour they came to life with creaking timbers and swelling sails. The morning breeze lifted the flags that hung from the mast; among them the royal flag of Isabella of Castile and the banner of the expedition, a white field with a green cross. After a stop at the Canary Islands the little fleet set off on a westerly course, with the Trades behind them.

Early in the morning of October 12 some Arawaks on the island of Guanahani in the Bahamas looked out to sea as they and their forefathers had always done, searching the morning sky for a sign of what the day might be like. In the dim light of early morning they saw three vessels, larger than any boat they had ever seen, that moved without the help of oars. Later, after the sun had risen, white and pink-skinned bearded men came ashore, clad in armour, with long shining swords. An Indian, attracted by the gleaming beauty of a Toledo blade, grasped the naked weapon and cut himself. More blood was to flow later.

Columbus renamed the island San Salvador. He sailed on to the north coast of Cuba, which he assumed was part of the territories of the Great Khan, and thence to Hispaniola, where he established a base at Navidad. On his return journey he fell into the path of the Westerlies which took him to the Azores early in January 1493. He returned by way of Lisbon to Palos, with the news that he had found the Indies. The church bells pealed their welcome and thanksgiving, the court applauded him, the Sovereigns of Spain honoured him. As important was the reaction of the merchants of Seville and Cadiz. They could expect little or no benefit from the growing Portuguese-West African trade; but now Columbus had opened up a way to the wealth of the East by a route free from Portuguese control. Nothing was too good for him.

The Spanish Sovereigns acted quickly to make their claim secure. They obtained from Pope Alexander VI a grant, by Papal decree of all lands not held by a Christian Prince on

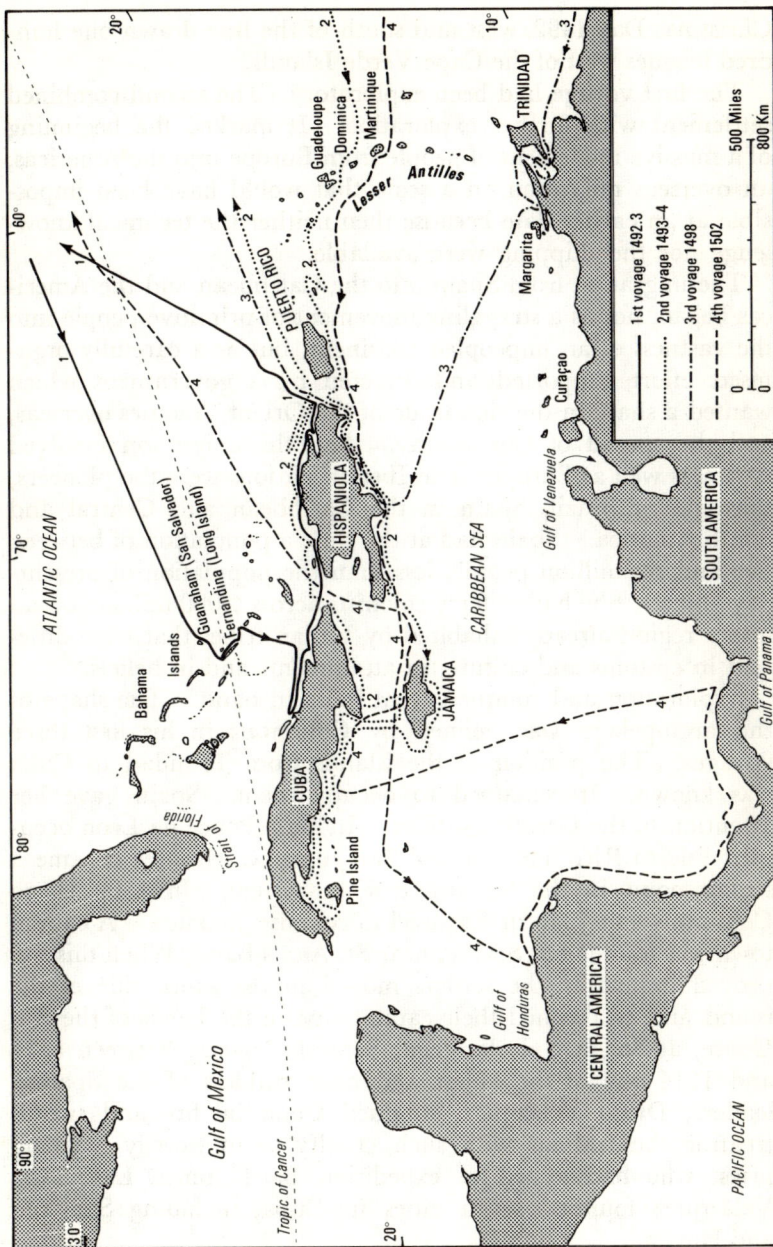

Columbus' voyages of discovery

Christmas Day 1492, west and south of the line drawn one hundred leagues west of the Cape Verde Islands.

The first voyage had been exploratory. The second combined settlement with further exploration. It marked the beginning of a massive movement of people from Europe into the Americas, an overseas migration on a scale that would have been impossible at an earlier date because then neither the technical knowledge nor the shipping were available.

The migration from Spain into the Caribbean and the Americas began, not as a straggling movement of primitive people into the vastness of an unpeopled continent, but as a carefully organised effort supported and directed by a government which wanted a share in the rich trade of the Orient, colonies overseas, and the spread of Christianity. And this migration involved Africa as well as Europe. The Iberian nations were the pioneers, Portugal in Brazil, Spain in the Caribbean and Central and South America. Spain had at the time a population of between five and six million people, less than the population of present-day Cuba. She had to ferry colonists across 4,000 miles of ocean into a region already inhabited by Indian tribes that were different in customs and culture, in attainments and in beliefs.

Exploration and conquest went hand in hand. The shape of the archipelago was defined by Columbus in his first three voyages. The position of the islands from Trinidad to Cuba was known. It remained to occupy them. Spain gave her attention to the Greater Antilles. In 1508 Ponce de Leon occupied Puerto Rico and founded San Juan, which later became a strong point in the Spanish defence system. In 1509 Diego Columbus sent Juan de Esquivel to colonise Jamaica. A capital town was founded at Seville, near St. Ann's Bay. When this site proved unhealthy the settlers moved to the south side of the island and established their capital city on the banks of the Rio Cobre, at St. Jago de la Vega, Spanish Town. Between 1511 and 1514 one of the ablest and most ruthless of the Spanish leaders, Diego Velázquez, subdued Cuba by fire and sword, treating the Indians with such cruelty as to horrify a young priest who had joined his expedition, Bartholomew Las Casas. Velázquez founded seven cities in Cuba, including Santiago and Havana.

On his third voyage in 1498, Columbus entered the Caribbean by way of the Gulf of Paria which separates Trinidad and Venezuela. In the following year Alonso de Ojeda coasted along the Venezuelan shoreline from the Gulf of Paria to the entrance of the Gulf of Maracaibo. Rodrigo de Bastides followed in 1500, exploring from the Gulf of Paria to the Isthmus of Panama, to a harbour later called Nombre de Dios. One of those who sailed on this expedition with Ojeda was Vasco Nuñez de Balboa, who returned later to the Isthmus to find glory and death there. The voyage which Solis and Pinzon made in 1506 down the Yucatan peninsula to Nombre de Dios completed the exploration of the Caribbean coastline. Three later voyages revealed the outline of the Gulf of Mexico: those of Cordoba in 1518 to the west coast of the peninsula of Yucatan; of Grijalva in 1519 almost to Vera Cruz; and of Pineda who in 1519 sailed along the coastline of the Gulf to the mouth of the Mississippi and to the west coast of Florida.

Cuba and Hispaniola were bases from which to explore and conquer other islands and the mainland; and the conquistadors soon widened the circle of Spanish power, creating other bases on the mainland. The first was on the Isthmus of Panama. Two expeditions were sent out, one to Veragua under Nicuesa, another to the north coast of Colombia under Ojeda. More than a thousand men set off in 1509 under these two leaders. Fever, factiousness and Indian attacks frustrated the attempt. The Spaniards were almost completely wiped out. The survivors chose as leader Vasco Nuñez de Balboa, now recognised as one of the greatest of the conquistadors. He took command and established friendly relations with some of the Indians. From them he learned about rich nations on the other side of the forest, and a great sea, and a country where they stored gold like grains of corn. Fired with hope, Balboa organised a small expedition and crossed the Isthmus, after a march in which every day brought new dangers and difficulties. On the morning of September 29, 1513, he saw from a high hill the Pacific spread before him like a silver shield. In the small company that stood with him on the shore of the Pacific and set about founding the city of Darien were Pizarro, and a negro, Olano.

Balbao's time of triumph was brief. He dreamed of linking

the east and west coasts of the Isthmus by trail; but it was his rival Pedrarias who did this. A crafty unscrupulous old man of seventy, he arrived at the Isthmus in charge of reinforcements sent out by Ferdinand, armed with the authority of Governor. He had Balboa executed on a flimsy charge of treason, founded the city of Panama, linked it with Nombre de Dios by a rough road, and then turned to the exploration of the north whence reports had reached him of a rich King called Nicaragua. Pedrarias sent his lieutenants, De Cordoba and De Soto, to explore Nicaragua's kingdom. With these the exploration and conquest of Central America got under way.

A second centre of power was Mexico City. Mexico was colonised from Cuba. Like many of the Spaniards on the islands, Velázquez had begun to turn his eyes to the mainland. After sending out two small parties of reconnaissance into the Bay of Honduras he fitted out a larger expedition of fifteen ships and 600 men and put his secretary, Hernan Cortés, in command. Whispers reached him about Cortés that led the Governor to revoke the appointment but it was too late. Cortés was not the man to give up command. In defiance of the Governor, he sailed from the landlocked harbour of Santiago to the open sea bound for Yucatan, setting out on a journey that was to take him from the Gulf of Mexico to Tenoctitlan, Mexico City, and thence by way of Guatemala to the Bay of Honduras. Making for the peninsula of Yucatan, Cortés stopped briefly at Cozumel where he rescued a priest, Father Geronimo, from the Indians. The priest spoke Mayan. Further on, inside the Gulf, Cortés landed at Tabasco, defeated the Indians and captured Dona Marina, who knew the language of the Aztecs. With the help of these two, Cortés was able to communicate with Mayas and Aztecs.

Vera Cruz was part of the Aztec empire over which the emperor Montezuma ruled. The emperor tried to bribe Cortés to leave by sending him rich gifts: pearls, two large plates of silver and gold, and grains of gold enough to fill a helmet. Cortés burnt his ships, and set off on a long difficult march to Mexico City.

The odds against Cortés appeared overwhelming. He had to lead his men through difficult unknown country, inhabited by tribes subject to the Aztecs. He had as enemy a highly organised government and a disciplined people with a long military tradition, and with a sophisticated civilisation centred on their capital city, Mexico City. Advanced though their culture was, their weapons were mostly of wood, stone and bone. Cortés, in contrast, had weapons of steel and cannon. Also the horses he had brought from Cuba terrified the Indians, who had never seen animals of this kind.

In the course of a dramatic march from Vera Cruz to Mexico City, Cortés won over as allies some tribes which resented Aztec rule. He was aided also by the religious fears of the Aztec emperor Montezuma, in whose mind there was a growing uncertainty, a fear that Cortés might be the god Quetzalcoatl, the benefactor of man.

The Aztecs believed that Quetzalcoatl would return some day from the East to dwell with them and it happened that the period predicted by the priests for his return coincided with the year in which Cortés arrived. Montezuma opened the gates of Mexico City to the Spaniards and Cortés had very nearly achieved his aim when he received news of the arrival at Vera Cruz of an expedition sent out by Velázquez to apprehend him. He set off for the coast at full speed, won over the new troops with his honeyed tongue, and returned to find the Aztecs enraged by the brutality of his soldiers. He made Montezuma prisoner, but the Aztecs rose under a new chief Cautemoc, and in a ferocious night attack forced the Spaniards to retreat from the city with heavy loss of life. The end was near however. Cortés took and sacked the city. Montezuma was stoned to death by his people and Cortés became master of the Aztec empire.

Cortés lost no time in using Mexico City as a base from which to explore and settle regions to the west and south; by 1524 the Spaniards were on the Pacific coast around the Santiago River. In this way, by thrusts from Panama and from Mexico, the *conquistadors* brought Central America under Spanish rule.

By 1550 the *conquistadors* had done their work. With scanty resources they had made their way to the Indies, adventurers taking a chance in a world of fantasy and myth that had suddenly been opened up before them. Many died in squalour; others, like de Quesada, Pizarro, Cortés, put vast regions and immense wealth into the hands of the Spanish Crown, bringing into

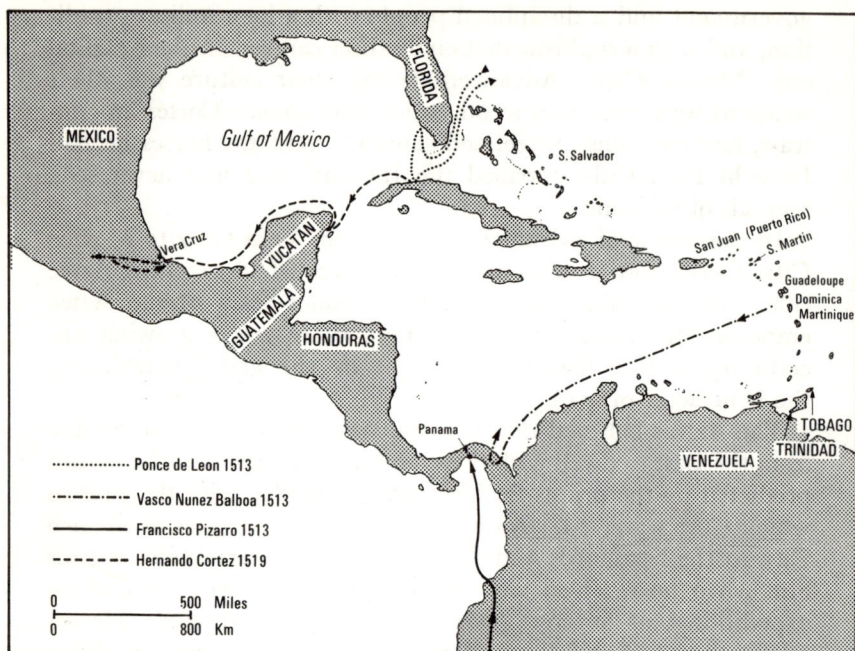

Routes of the Conquistadors

existence kingdoms like Nueva España, New Granada, Castillo de Oro. The Crown authorised their journeys of conquest but gave to few the authority of Governor or Viceroy, being suspicious of subjects who might become too powerful.

The expansion of Spanish power on the mainland and the discovery of rich mineral resources in Mexico and Peru created an acute population problem in the island colonies. In 1532 the Bishop of Santo Domingo complained bitterly of the emigration to the mainland and of the encouragement the expeditions gave to adventurers in search only of what they could steal, who never settled down but set off in the hope of finding another New Spain. Those who remained, even those with deepest roots in the island, prayed nightly ' May God take me to Peru '.

CHAPTER 3

Spain's Island Colonies

The first permanent European settlement in the Americas was in Hispaniola where the city of Santo Domingo was founded in what is now the Dominican Republic. Beyond it, on a bluff overlooking the Ozama River, stands the restored Alcazar Palace. Originally it was built in the period 1511–1514 by the son of Christopher Columbus, Diego Columbus, Viceroy and Governor General. Despite the rapidly growing importance of the mainland provinces this palace remained the seat of the Spanish Court in the Americas for the first half of the sixteenth century.

Within the city, on a quiet corner of the Calle Padre Billini, stands an old Dominican monastery. It was in this monastery that Bartholomew Las Casas wrote some of his most passionate protests against the enslavement and exploitation of the Indian. The Alcazar Palace and the monastery may be taken as representing the two most powerful forces in the Spanish colonisation of the Caribbean, the State and the Church.

Bartholomew Columbus founded the city in 1496. It was destroyed by hurricane in 1502 and rebuilt by Nicholas Ovando on the western bank of the Ozama River. The founding of a town was an important occasion, representing the establishment of Spanish rule and so was attended with considerable ceremony, followed by the setting up of a city council or *cabildo* to exercise authority over the town and the surrounding countryside. The town became the stronghold of Spanish settlement, the place of residence of merchants, government officials and of the landed aristocracy. Most of the Spanish colonial towns of America are laid out after the fashion of Santo Domingo, but nowhere else in the archipelago do the walls and buildings breathe such a sense of the past as do the stone houses and narrow streets of old Santo Domingo, and the forts of Santa Barbara and San Gil that were part of the city's defences. Here Pizarro, Cortés, Balboa, Velázquez, Ojeda, Alvarado, Ponce de Leon and other *conquistadors* planned their expeditions, fitted out their ships, and recruited their men.

And there are memories of the Arawak people. Arawak blood manifests itself now and then in the broad cheekbones, sturdy short figures and lank black hair of some who move through the streets or along the country roads. In the modern city the neon signs flash the old Arawak names; Quisqueya, Caonabo, the great Cacique Guarionex, Enriquillo and Anacaona. Today the events that took place in Hispaniola during that first period of Spanish colonisation seem remote and the persons involved appear unreal. But history has to do with man, and yesterday's themes recur in our time, in Viet Nam, Indo-China, Angola, South Africa. West Indians looking at the events of that period in Hispaniola see the exploitation of the Arawak as similar to the exploitation of the African. The rationalisations justifying Arawak slavery were of the same kind as those used to justify African slavery. The resistance of the Arawak, like the resistance of the African, was evidence of that passion for freedom of which the Spanish priest Las Casas was one of America's earliest and most eloquent advocates.

Hispaniola was the most developed Arawak island of the period. As the first Spanish colony and the chief base for the conquest of the mainland it became the stage where the tragic events of the first period of European colonisation were played out between 1492 when Columbus arrived, and the decade of the 1520's when the Isthmus of Panama, Mexico, Guetemala and Honduras became the chief centres of conflict and exploitation. The principles that guided Spain were formulated first for Hispaniola. It was there that the political problems, and the moral issues involved in the European colonisation of the Caribbean and Americas, first became manifest.

Four basic principles guided Spain in the establishment and rule of her Empire. The first was that the Crown was supreme, and that the Indies and all the Americas were the property of the Crown; not of any Spanish *Cortes* or any other authority, but of the Spanish sovereign. It was also a basic principle that the native people of the colony should supply the labour needed for making the colony self-sustaining and a source of wealth to the mother-country. When the Spanish invaders occupied the Greater Antilles the Indians became subjects of the Spanish Crown. As such they were entitled to the Crown's protection. It also became the responsibility of the Church to convert and protect them. At the same time however, they formed the labour force; and though they were in theory free they were not in fact free to withhold their labour. And the colonists on the spot had no intention of giving up their right to the labour of the Indian. The result was the degradation of the Indian to serfdom, his enslavement and destruction, and a search for new sources of labour.

A third principle was that trade had to be exclusively with the mother country. This was in keeping with the mercantile theory of the time, by which colony and mother country were treated as a unit, the colony existing for the benefit of the mother country, supplying it with the raw materials it needed and buying its manufactured goods.

To these three principles there was added a fourth, that the Church was a partner in the colonial enterprise. It supported established authority, saw to the spiritual welfare of colonists and subject peoples, and had the duty of converting, protecting and training the Indians.

In the light of these basic principles a structure of empire was gradually created. But up to 1498 Columbus, under his contract with the Crown, had sweeping powers. He and his heirs were to be Governors of all the lands he found, in perpetuity; and the proceeds from the newly discovered lands were to be shared between the Crown and himself. As Governor of Hispaniola, Columbus was determined to exercise his full authority over the colonists and the Indians; and he was determined to put the island's economy on a profit-yielding base as quickly as possible. He saw the two chief sources of revenue as gold and a trade with

An Indian Cacique addressing Columbus

Spain in Arawak slaves. Looking forward from this point, we find that colonisation meant death for the Arawaks of Hispaniola, Jamaica, Puerto Rico and of Cuba. Columbus, at his first encounter with the welcoming Indians on Guanahani, had written words of doom; ' they should be good servants and of quick intelligence...and I believe they would easily be made Christians.'

Twelve years after his landing on Guanahani, Columbus, looking at what had happened to the Indian, was horrified. It is reported that he said that six out of every seven had died since he left the island. Columbus may have got his numbers wrong, but there is no doubt that even in the relatively short time of twelve years the Arawak population had been greatly reduced in numbers through forced labour and enslavement, repressive acts of great cruelty, and new diseases such as smallpox and measles against which it had little or no immunity. What took place in Hispaniola happened in other places where European colonisation was in process.

When Columbus returned to Hispaniola from Jamaica in 1494 he found the Arawaks desperate. They rose in rebellion. Columbus organised a punitive expedition, hunted down the rebels with armed men and dogs, and took a number of them captive. Some he distributed to the colonists. About 500 were shipped to Spain for sale. Only half survived the voyage and many of those were sick. Very soon those who survived were sent back to Hispaniola by order of the Queen; and so the hope of a prosperous slave trade in Indians withered away.

Following the suppression of the rising, Columbus set out for the interior of the island on a mission of pacification. The great cacique Guarionex, and the lesser chiefs, submitted to him; and he imposed a poll-tax of gold dust on the population.

The Spaniards, by weakening the power of the caciques, were destroying the social and economic structure of Indian society. Some colonists returned to Spain with accounts of the severity and incompetence of Columbus. Most of those who remained lived off the Indians. In 1496 Columbus returned to Spain to answer complaints that had been made against him, leaving his brother Bartholomew in charge. Some disaffected colonists, led by Francisco Roldan, established themselves in the western part of the island. The Indians were harried and their leaders Mayobanex and Guarionex imprisoned. Arawak leadership was liquidated and the structure of Arawak society destroyed; and this made the collection of tribute all the more difficult.

When Columbus returned from Spain in 1498 he brought orders to distribute lands to colonists *repartimentos* for growing food-crops, laying out fields of sugar-cane, and building houses and sugar-mills *ingenios*. These grants represented the recognition of private ownership and a first attempt at a land policy and they were conditional on colonists remaining in the island for four years. The Crown reserved for itself all brazilwood, which was valued for its red dye and all metal-producing land. But what happened was not the establishment of farms worked by European settlers. The *repartimento* became a distribution of Indians to Spanish colonists, for use as their labour force. Back in Hispaniola the Admiral had to find sources of revenue other than gold, the supply of which was diminishing.

By 1500 the first phase of Spanish colonisation in Hispaniola had come to an end. The Crown, according to Peter Martyr, had grown weary of the stream of complaints from the island. A new governor, Francisco de Bobadilla, was sent out. He arrived in Santo Domingo to find the island torn apart by a rising of colonists against Columbus. Enraged, Bobadilla sent the three Columbus brothers back to Spain in chains. The crown began to grant licences to others to explore and settle the Indies. These licences or *capitulaciones* were at first issued by Juan Rodriguez de Fonseca, who in 1503 set up in Seville the *Casa de Contratación*, to manage all the affairs of the Indies. Bobadilla was recalled after two years and a new governor appointed. He was Nicholas de Ovando, an experienced administrator and military commander. In 1502 he arrived in Santo Domingo with a large fleet of thirty ships and 2500 settlers. His arrival marked the beginning of settled Spanish rule in the Indies.

Ovando lost no time in asserting his authority. He brought Roldan and his truculent faction under control. Then he turned his attention to the Arawaks of the western part of the island, which up to that time had been Arawak country. The justification for his conduct was the classic one in the imperial vocabulary; it was preventive action, to forestall an attack that was being planned by Anacaona, the most powerful queen in the region. The purpose was ' pacification '. The methods were treachery and murder. Anacaona, attended by more than forty lesser caciques and other people, welcomed Ovando, his chief lieutenant Diego Velázquez, and a well-armed force of Spaniards. She feasted them in the royal dwelling, her *bohio*. Ovando's men watched him. They knew what to do. At a sign they turned on their hosts, massacred them, set the buildings ablaze, burned some of the Indians to death, and carried Anacaona away to Santo Domingo where she was hung in the public square.

At the close of his first two years in office Ovando could claim to have pacified Hispaniola and to have brought the whole island under Spanish rule. To keep it that way, and ensure that the diminishing Indian labour force was used efficiently, he expanded and supervised the use of the *encomienda*. He was no stranger to the system of forced labour through the *encomienda*. He had known it in Spain. He saw to it that the apportionment of the Indians was linked with the ' efficiency ' of the *encomendero*, his efficiency being measured by the amount of gold and of food that his work-gang produced.

One of Ovando's most important undertakings was the establishment of settlements. The Spanish settlement became a *villa*, the Indian settlement a *pueblo*. The *villa* had its council or *cabildo* elected, in theory at least, by the citizens.

Laws were passed in Spain to encourage settlement in the Indies. Concessions were offered to those who opened up new settlements. Husbands were required to send back to Spain for their wives. Artisans and tradesmen were sent out. Supplies of cattle, plants and seeds were carried across the Atlantic. It is estimated that just over 20,000 persons emigrated from Spain to the Indies in the first half of the sixteenth century, most of them going to the mainland.

Most of the Spanish colonists were after gold and land; but the driving purpose was gold, and Pizarro put the matter bluntly when he said that he had not gone to Peru to convert the Indians but to take their gold from them. The attempt to establish Hispaniola as a colony based on gold and slave-trading having failed, the colonists turned to ranching, to the management of herds of horses and cattle, of swine and sheep, and to the acquisition of large estates.

Domestic animals are so much a part of our world that it is difficult to realise that they were absent from the Arawak world. The only beast of burden available to the Indian on the mainland before the coming of Columbus was the llama of Peru; elsewhere the Indian carried his own burdens on land, and his radius of movement was restricted to what his body could sustain for he had not discovered the wheel. The Arawak of Hispaniola, Jamaica, Cuba and Puerto Rico found his world transformed by the introduction of horses and mules, of cattle, swine, sheep, goats. For the first time he saw the wheel, and saw also how much easier it made the transportation of people and of goods; and while he saw the supply of food greatly increased by the addition of beef, pork and mutton he found that his own cultivations, his conucos, were ravaged and destroyed by herds of horses, cattle and hogs that roamed in large numbers over the savanna.

Ranching flourished. The management of herds and flocks was in the Spanish tradition and the ownership of large estates carried social prestige. It was natural therefore that the Spanish colonists should have turned to ranching. The environment favoured it, for the islands were clean of stock diseases; and there was ample grass. The method was open range. Horses, cattle and pigs were turned out to graze on the savanna. By 1507 Ovando was able to say that Hispaniola had enough breeding mares and there was no need to import more. The hogs increased in numbers. Many went wild, and as early as 1508 licences were issued for hunting wild pigs. From this early period also comes the use of the word *cimarrones* which was applied to the herds of wild horses and cattle that lived in mountainous regions, around the summits, the *cima*. The word came to be applied also to those Africans who escaped to the refuge of the mountains, the *cimarrones* or ‘ maroons ’. It became a sport to organise hunting expeditions, monteria, to round up the *hatos* for branding and to kill cattle for meat; and the word *hato* was transferred from the herd to the savanna, so that we find on old maps of Jamaica the *hato* of Ayalas (Yallahs) or of Liguanea. In Jamaica this periodic killing of cattle for hides and tallow or lard, *manteca*, gave the island its chief export. Indeed so much *manteca* was exported from a north-coast harbour that it was named Manteca Bahia, Montego Bay.

For some years it seemed as if sugar production would become, along with ranching, a source of wealth for the colonists in Hispaniola. This old world crop had given Cyprus a flourishing sugar industry in the middle ages and had been transplanted to the Atlantic islands of Madeira and the Canaries after their discovery, with such good results that it was transported thence to the Caribbean, by Columbus. Oviedo the historian says that the first man to start sugar production in Hispaniola was a physician of Santo Domingo, Gonzalo Velosa. He was clearly well-to-do for he ‘ at his own cost brought sugar masters to the island ’, built a horse-mill *trapeche* and introduced the technicians and art of making sugar from the Canary Islands. Oviedo recounts

how he took to Spain and delivered to dying King Ferdinand
the first boxes of sugar made in the island. The industry, says
Oviedo, grew and multiplied.

Sixteenth Century Sugar Factory engraved after Stradanus

While these events were unfolding, two developments took
place that portended the social and economic transformation of
the Caribbean. One was the entry of Africa into the region.
Another, disregarded at the time, was the unforeseen unplanned
emergence in Cuba of a resident farming community, a Cuban
community, rooted in the soil of Cuba. What happened was
that after Velázquez had decimated and subdued the Indians,
the island remained sparsely settled. Velázquez made few grants
of land because there was practically no demand. After his
death the practice developed for *cabildos* to make land
grants, it being discreetly provided that they did so without

29

prejudice to the rights of the Crown. The grants were of two kinds; large areas of land to men who wished to establish ranches, *hatos*; and small tracts of land to men of modest means who established small holdings, *estancias*. Cuba had landroom, so as the Cuban historian Guerra y Sanchez points out, the growth of the large estates did not block the development at the same time of small farms. ' In Cuba the foundations were laid for a new and original nationhood, the fruit of three centuries of settlement '.

Jamaica, set inside the rim of the archipelago, attracted few settlers when it became clear that the island had no gold. In 1512 there was a proposal for abandoning the island and moving the settlers to Cuba. The Arawak population perished swiftly, wiped out by famine, smallpox and other diseases. In order to save the Indians from complete extermination the Governor Melgarejo proposed in 1598 that land should be specially reserved for them, but the colonists objected. By 1655, when the English took Jamaica, the native people had been almost completely wiped out.

Jamaica was not a key-point in the Caribbean defence system like Puerto Rico or Cuba; but it had value as a bread-basket. It lay on the return route for ships sailing from Cartagena to Havana, and it built up a trade in hides and tallow and salted meat, importing in exchange olive oil, wine, wheaten flour, clothing and hardware. The economy was based on cattle and on a few crops. Sugar cane was cultivated in patches and some sugar made for local use. Cotton and tobacco were grown. In addition to the capital Spanish Town, there were small settlements at points along the coast, such as Puerto Anton, Esquival (Old Harbour), Morante and Las Chorrerras (Ocho Rios). The most important reinforcement to the Spanish population came in 1580 when a number of Portuguese Jews arrived in the island.

Trinidad, the only Spanish colony in the Eastern Caribbean, was the most neglected of all. There is no record of a ship visiting the island before 1510, when a slave raiding party arrived, captured 200 Indians and carried them off to Puerto Rico and Santo Domingo for sale. Various Spanish leaders contended for the island, and made occasional attacks on the Indians; but it was a hard-bitten Spanish conquistador, Antonio de Berreo, who, having come to Venezuela late in life, and having been taken captive by the legend of El Dorado, saw the importance of Trinidad as a base for the exploration of the Orinoco. His dream, and that of his rival Walter Raleigh, ended in disaster. Trinidad languished for 250 years, wholly neglected.

CHAPTER 4

The Structure of Empire

Migration and settlement carry with them the transplanting of customs, attitudes, institutions. In our time we have seen West Indian migrants to Britain take with them a liking for their typical dishes, for their own music, their vivid mode of expression which Naipaul, Selvon and Lamming recapture in their works. In the process of time these customs and attitudes are modified by the new environment and by the native English culture that surrounds them like a sea.

In the same way the Spanish migrant to the Caribbean carried with him his traditions, customs and institutions. But he did not go simply as a migrant. He went as conqueror, taking with him his technology; the wheel, the use of iron and other metals, the printing press, the wind-driven ship, the compass, sword, gunpowder, and the plough; and with these, crops and animals, swine, horses, cattle, sheep. The Indian of the islands played little part in the slow blending of customs and traditions, for he was destroyed; but on the mainland there sprang up a Creole culture in which the American-born Spaniard, the *Criollo*, felt himself different from the Spaniard born in Spain, the *Gachupine*. In the islands it was the African who gave a distinctive character to the new communities that were to come into existence.

During the years between 1500 and 1530 Spain established a system of government in the Indies. The undertaking was a difficult one, largely because four thousand miles of ocean lay between her and her empire, and the only means of communication was the sailing ship. Nevertheless institutions were set up, the officials appointed and the machinery of government set in motion.

The details about the functioning of *Audiencias* and *Cabildos*, and about the duties of *Oidores* and *Corregidores* may appear dull and remote; but in fact they shaped the life of the majority of the Caribbean people, who speak Spain's language and who inherited and modified these institutions. The lawyers who drew up the regulations and laws for the Indies were transferring to the Caribbean institutions that were born out of the experience and needs of the Spanish people. The setting up of *Cabildos* and the laying out of towns represented the transplanting of a political institution and pointed to an intermeshing of Spanish and Indian cultures.

The system of government that was established in the Indies was more judicial than administrative in character. This concept of political power as the expression of justice had been carried over from the age of feudalism and to this mediaeval concept there was added a growing trend toward an absolute highly centralised monarchy. The lawyers who served the Spanish Crown knew that the reconquest of Spain has been made possible by the unification of Spain under Ferdinand and Isabella. They had seen the dangers to authority that could come from the over-powerful noble, and they set about fashioning a system that would provide for direct control by the Crown and that would have institutions powerful enough to control over-mighty subjects like the *conquistadors*.

At first the King consulted the Council of Castile about Indian problems and policies but the ever increasing volume of business led in 1524 to the establishment of the Council of the Indies; the most important institution in the system. The Council had judicial as well as administrative and advisory functions. It was the Supreme Court of appeal for the cases from the Higher Courts in the Colonies. It advised the Crown on policy and directed and supervised a wide range of imperial activities; appointing officials including those of the Church, directing the conversion of the Indians, controlling the settlement of new colonies, deciding in what circumstances foreigners might be permitted to enter the Indies, and prescribing the way in which towns were to be laid out. Every sphere of colonial life came within the jurisdiction of the Council. It oversaw the collection and expenditure of royal revenue in colonial undertakings, and it required all explorers and *conquistadors* to keep diaries and to make detailed reports.

In the Indies the most powerful official was the Viceroy. He was given authority by the Crown to deal with every aspect of government. The office was not created until after the conquest of Mexico when the King appointed a Viceroy to exercise royal authority. He exercised supreme military authority in his kingdom and over neighbouring waters. He appointed officials and ecclesiastics to office within the Vice-royalty, supervised the collection of taxes through a superintendent of the Treasury, and oversaw the development and administration of industries. So extensive was the territory included in a Vice-royalty that it had to be split into smaller parts. These divisions were administered by an *Audiencia* which consisted of from three to fifteen persons, who advised the Viceroy and carried out his orders. The *Audiencia* also had judicial powers, functioning as a supreme court. The Viceroy could impose his will in political matters but in judicial affairs an *Audiencia* had the right to deal directly with the Crown.

As there were checks on the Viceroy so there were checks on the *Audiencia*. Members could not marry without royal permission, nor engage in business, nor own real estate.

The *Audiencia* of Santo Domingo, the first to be established, was set up in 1524. At that time it had authority over the coastal region from Venezuela to Mexico. With the growth of the empire other *Audiencias* were established; that of Mexico in 1527 and at a later date those of Northern Mexico, Guatemala, Lima and Bogota.

The Viceroy appointed Governors in each province who collected the taxes, were on the alert against rebellions, and made sure that the laws and regulations handed down from the centre were observed. He, in turn, appointed *Alcaldes* and through them the Governor, and through him, the *Audiencia* and Viceroy kept in touch with small remote districts.

The Crown gave power and the Crown limited power by an

elaborate system of checks and balances. These were institutionalised, the most effective being the *Residencia* and the *Visita*.
The *Residencia* was a court made up of three judges from Spain,
which investigated the rule of the Viceroy and Governor. It sat
toward the end of an official's term of office and heard complaints
against him, and he was not allowed to leave his territory until
the investigation was completed. The *Visita* was carried out by
an Inspector or *Visitador*, specially sent out by the Crown, often
without advance notice, to look into the rule of a Viceroy or
Audiencia. He was of high rank and was given great authority
by the Crown, so much that on his arrival he outranked the
Viceroy.

These institutions were parts of the central government. Local
government was a function of the city or municipality. This was
in the Spanish tradition, which derived in turn from the Romans
and the Iberians.

In principle, the *Cabildo* or town council was an elective or
representative body, with members called *Regidores* who were
elected each year; but in fact the commander of a settlement
often appointed the first set, and then, at the end of the year, the
outgoing *Regidores* picked others to succeed them, and so the
Cabildo became oligarchic in character. This tendency toward
oligarchic rule was strengthened by the Crown's practice of selling certain urban offices in perpetuity. Though the members of
the *Cabildo* were not paid they had ample opportunity for looking after their interests and those of their friends, since they had
authority over a wide range of matters such as the distribution of
land, fixing of prices and the distribution of the Indian labour
force.

In the early period of colonisation some cities requested meetings of parliamentary assemblies, *Cortes*, but the Crown refused
this. It was through the municipal authorities, acting in the
name of the people of the city that representations were often
made to the Viceroys, and even to the Crown itself through the
Procuradores.

In matters of trade, as we have seen, it was accepted that the
mother country and her colonies formed a single trading unit.
This monopoly was weakened in practice because Spain did not
have the shipping to supply all the goods that her colonies re-

quired and the American coastline was too long to be regularly patrolled. In times of peace smugglers breached the monopoly. In times of war it was modified by the granting of special licences.

The Caribbean was central to the Spanish colonial trading system. Spain kept pushing back the western frontier of her empire, continuing the search for her own trade route to the East. She found this in 1542 when she occupied the Phillipines, and acquired Manila and began the development of Lima and Acapulco. The Manila galleon carried oriental goods, spices, silks, Indian muslin, cotton, porcelain and plants such as mango and tamarind to Acapulco, and the goods moved on to Spain by way of Vera Cruz and Havana. Though the Manila galleon only sailed every two years the oriental trade became important. Of greater value was the cargo that the Peruvian armada took to Panama whence it was trans-shipped to Spain by way of Nombre de Dios and Havana.

Even at this distance in time it is possible to catch something of the eager excitement with which settlers in the Indies looked forward to the arrival of the ships from Seville. Owners of ranches prepared their products; killing cattle, curing hides, salting meat, preparing lard for the candlemakers and shipwrights of Europe. On the haciendas, planters ground their sugar-cane and prepared sugar for shipment. Others cultivated indigo, tobacco and cotton. In exchange the colonists imported household utensils, machinery and other hardware, weapons, tools of iron and steel, textiles of wool and cotton.

Spain drew on Italian experience for controlling her expanding imperial trade when she set up the *Casa de Contratación* in 1503. It superintended all trade and commerce between Spain and her colonies, regulated the sailings of merchantmen and warships and dictated the trade routes. It had several functions. It performed the work of the courts through judges and it took charge of the property of owners who died on their way to the colonies until the rights of their heirs were established. It collected the revenue due to the Crown and supervised all expenditure authorised by the Council of the Indies. It supervised communication and mail between the colonies and Spain. It built up a monumental collection of charts, maps and diaries of navigation through a specially appointed cosmographer.

The Casa de Contratación was transferred from Seville to Cadiz in 1717. It lost much of its importance after that date through administrative changes made by Charles III who used Special Secretaries to perform many of its functions.

Private enterprise had a role to play through the *Consulados*, or Guilds of Merchants. These were given the duty of dealing with cases caused by bankruptcy settling disputes over trade and commercial transactions before a judge and officials, deciding claims for small amounts, and hearing claims for large amounts in which there was a right of appeal to an *Audiencia*.

The trade routes dictated by the House of Trade for ships bound for the Indies were those that Columbus had pioneered. They made use of the North East Trades and ocean currents on the outward journey, and of the more northerly Westerlies when returning. In 1543 shipping to the Indies was organised in two fleets, each sailing in convoy, since the wealth of the cargoes attracted pirates.

In the 1540's the total tonnage of ships sailing for the Indies from Seville each year was of the order of 7,000 to 8,000 tons; by the 1580's the annual tonnage had increased to 20,000 tons. That quantity could be carried today by one oil tanker. To keep the picture in scale, we should remember that the population of Spain at that period was of the order of four or five million. Today it is thirty million.

The first fleet, the *flota*, usually set out in May from Seville, and entered the Caribbean by the Mona Passage between Hispaniola and Puerto Rico. Some ships fell out and made for Jamaica and Honduras. The main fleet sailed south of Hispaniola and Cuba to Vera Cruz by way of the Yucatan Channel. There it remained until the following February, when it sailed to Havana to await the galleons.

The second fleet, the galleons, set out in August and being bound for Nombre de Dios on the Isthmus of Panama, took a more southerly route. It entered the Caribbean through the Windward Islands, and sailed along the coast of South America under the protection of the *Armada de Barlovento*, the Windward Fleet, which patrolled these waters. At Nombre de Dios the galleons unloaded their cargoes for Panama and Peru, took on board gold, silver and agricultural products for Spain, and set out by way of the Yucatan Channel for Havana. There both fleets took on supplies and made ready for the long return journey. The journey out and back extended over a period of a year.

The Church was of primary importance in supporting the authority of the Crown and in unifying the empire. The Cathedral in Santo Domingo and the Cathedrals and churches of Central and South America show how deep and enduring was the work that began with a group of twelve priests who sailed from Spain to Hispaniola with Columbus on his second voyage in 1493.

Organized in Spain, the church in the Indies had bishops in charge of dioceses, priests who worked in the towns and villages, and orders of nuns and friars, notably the Dominicans, Franciscans, Jesuits and Augustinians. In settled areas and beyond the frontiers of the colonies they established Missions that served as churches, trade schools and cultural centres all in one. To the Indian larder based on potatoes, maize, beans and peppers, the Mission added such new crops as the climate and soil allowed: rice, sugar-cane, wheat, figs, lemons, limes, olives, oranges and peaches. To the old Indian skills in making houses of adobe and thatch, the Church added new skills, carpentry, the making of tiles and bricks, iron work, including the making of locks, keys, bells and the like; the tanning of hides and making of tallow, butter, soap and wine. In the Greater Antilles and on the mainland from Mexico and Florida to Chile in the far south the Missions extended their work; and since they became centres for the teaching of Spanish they helped to give the Indies a common language as well as a common faith.

With the passing of the years the Church became powerful and rich. The evangelising zeal cooled. Self-sacrifice tended to become self-indulgence. Priests and bishops committed many abuses. Notwithstanding all this, the Church continued its work of protecting the Indians, founding schools, hospitals, asylums and orphanages.

During the latter part of the sixteenth century the Inquisition or Holy Office was transferred to the Indies. It was an ecclesiastical court to put down heresy and punish heretics, and it heard and tried cases of heresy, bigamy, Judaism, blasphemy and witchcraft and inflicted penalties including burning at the stake. It appears however that in the West Indies unavowed Jews could live in comparative safety from the Inquisition. The Holy Office was used to regulate opinion and belief, and like all institutions charged with suppressing freedom of opinion, it was at times guilty of hideous cruelties.

CHAPTER 5

Heritage of Empire

While Spain was shaping the structure of her empire, her rivals were getting ready to challenge her right to prohibit them from founding empires and from developing monopolies of their own. Others, French, Dutch, English, Portuguese, followed in ever growing numbers, for the claim to monopoly bred conflict. The outcome for the Caribbean was a tradition of competition and rivalry which was engendered by the parochialism and cutthroat rivalry of contending European nations.

Opposition to Spain's monopoly showed itself in her rivals efforts to found colonies and to establish their own monopolies. Their seaman and traders engaged in smuggling and piracy; and in proportion as these intensified, the harshness of Spain's prohibition increased. But the Indies beckoned to every seagoing trader, to every adventurer. The Portuguese, against whom Spain did not generally apply her restrictions, led the way in smuggling, taking Africans, manufactured goods and cloth to Brazil and moving them by boat up the Plate River, and by mule caravans across the Andes to the mines of Potosi and the cities of Cuzco and Lima.

In 1520 Jean Ango, a privateer in the pay of a French merchant of Dieppe, lying off the Azores, captured two of the ships that Cortés had despatched from Vera Cruz with some of the treasure from Montezuma's palace. Instead of the usual cargo of dyewoods and hides, Ango and his men found jewels and gold. The effect was electric. When in the 1530's the Incas were conquered and the wealth of Peru was added to that of Mexico, the Indies, Potosi and Peru became synonyms for fabulous wealth. Our age, which has known the excitement of space ships and moon landings can understand the eager interest with which the seaports of Western Europe, Nantes, Dieppe, Bristol, Plymouth, Amsterdam received each returning ship; and in the pages of Shakespeare and his contemporaries we see the impact on European imagination of the marvels of the Americas. As for the seaman and traders, which of them could resist the magnetic pull of silver and gold? The venture could always be justified as a blow at Spanish power, or as a blow for Protestantism against the hated Papist.

Besides, the Spanish colonists were ready to trade. Spain insisted on her exclusive rights but she did not have the shipping to supply the colonists with the goods they needed. Nor did she have the industrial capacity to supply her steadily expanding American market. Committed by Philip and the Emperor Charles to expansion and war in Europe, she was carrying an intolerable burden of debt, was spending her manpower in Italy and the Netherlands, and was at the same time attempting to govern and to police her empire in the Americas. Often her colonists were in despair. They complained bitterly about the shortage of Spanish shipping. Some Spanish colonies were short of settlers; Trinidad notably, for when the Bishop of Puerto Rico visited the island in 1634 he informed the King of Spain that there were no more than forty destitute Spanish settlers there.

The first foreigner to attempt to develop trade with the Indies openly and systematically was John Hawkins. His father William Hawkins had sailed from England to the Guinea coast, then across to Brazil and finally back to England, anticipating the triangular trade which his son pioneered and which became one of the world's largest trading systems. John Hawkins showed that it was good business to include the Guinea coast and the Caribbean in one trading venture. In doing this he infringed the Spanish monopoly, for he had no licence from the Spanish Crown. Hawkins formed a syndicate to finance his voyage and set out with three small ships on his first triangular trading voyage. He called in at Teneriffe, took on a Spanish pilot, sent messages to Hispaniola to possible purchasers to tell them of his coming, then sailed to Sierra Leone where he secured 300 Africans, some by force, others by purchase from the Portuguese. With these he set off by the middle passage to Hispaniola. There he paid the fees required, got written statements from the officials saying how correctly he had behaved, and made for home. The profits were exceptionally good. Hawkins immediately made preparations for a second voyage. The Queen and some of her advisers took shares; but quietly. Again he cajoled and bullied the local authorities along the coast of Venezuela, and returned to England without hindrance. The voyage paid handsomely. A foreigner, Hawkins had entered the Indies without Spain's permission, had traded there without proper licence and had taken to the Indies goods that had not been cleared through Seville. On the credit side he had conducted himself correctly, protesting that he was ' a great servitor of the majesty of King Philip ', one who did not desire to ' offend or occasion difficulties '; but one also who meant to get his way.

But those Spanish officials who had granted permits to Hawkins or turned a blind eye to his trading were being prosecuted in Spain. The Caribbean defences were being put in order. Queen Elizabeth, anxious not to provoke Spain too far, forbade Hawkins to return to the Indies. In 1567 he persuaded the Queen to allow him to make another venture and this time things went badly. The middle passage took seven weeks before Dominica came into sight. From Hispaniola he went on to other ports, persuading and inducing the Spaniards to trade, until at last he came to Rio de la Hacha where an old opponent of his, the King's Treasurer, Castellanos, bade him be gone. The English landed, took the town and made off with its treasure.

John Hawkins finally came to the port of San Juan de Ulloa in the Gulf of Mexico. His ships needed overhauling and provisioning. It was the middle of the hurricane season and the *Jesus* in particular was in bad shape, ' the leaks so big as the thickness of a man's arm, the living fish did swim upon the ballast as in the sea...' A low reef ran in front of the coast, about a third of a mile from it. On this a few guns were planted so that whoever held this bank was in control of the shipping. Fifteen miles further up the coast lay the town of Vera Cruz where most of the Spaniards on the coast lived.

Hawkins took possession of the island. Next morning the Spanish fleet came into sight. It consisted of eleven merchantmen with two war ships, all under the command of Francisco de Luxan. With the fleet was the newly appointed Viceroy of New Spain, Don Martin Enriquez. He obtained Hawkins' consent that the Spanish fleet might enter the port while the English were to go ahead with overhauling their ships and were to keep control of the island until they left. Hostages were given, but the English remained alert. Robert Barrett, an English seaman said Hawkins noticed that guns were being put in position and trained on his ships and that he sent him twice on the afternoon of September twenty third to the Viceroy,

> and the second time the general seized him, and threw him below hatches, tied hand and foot, and in chains and in about an hour the battle occurred in which the Spanish fleet broke up the English fleet and the said John Hawkins fled in a shallop with the Vice Admiral.

Only the tiny *Judith* of fifty tons and the *Minion* escaped. Of the English survivors who were in Spanish hands some were sent to Spain where two were burnt alive by the Inquisition at Seville, some were made galley slaves and others were imprisoned for a time in Mexico.

The disaster at San Juan de Ulloa indicated that the Hawkins formula was not acceptable. Spain did not intend to compromise as far as trade or settlement were concerned. She had underlined that by attacking and destroying a French settlement in Florida even though the Spanish admiral Menendez de Aviles said he had wiped out the Huguenots, not because they were Frenchmen but as Lutheran heretics. Henceforth those who traded should be prepared to fight. Smuggling continued; and as need arose the smugglers turned to raiding.

French corsairs were among the earliest of the raiders. In the 1530's France and Portugal made a pact, the Treaty of Lyon, by which France agreed not to permit her subjects to attack Portuguese shipping and not to interfere with Portuguese traders on the West African coast. The French corsairs thereupon began to prey on Spanish shipping in the Caribbean or on the way to Europe. There were many suitable bases from which to operate in the Bahama Islands. In the winter of 1536 Jean Ango, captured a number of Spanish ships making their way through the Florida Channel. This was the route by which Spanish ships sailed in convoy from the Isthmus of Panama heavily laden with rich cargo. Jean Ango's men attacked the Spanish fleet, captured nine ships out of more than twenty or more, sacked some ports in Hispaniola, failed in an attempt on Santiago, and returned to Dieppe laden with plunder.

There now began a long series of attacks on Spain in the Indies. The record is written in part on the Caribbean landscape; in fortifications like those that command the harbours of Havana, San Juan and Cartagena and in the ruins of strong points along the Caribbean coastline. In addition, after the middle of the century, every outbreak of war between Spain and France, England or the rebellious low Countries found European naval forces entering the Caribbean. Just as commerce had become trans-oceanic, following on the voyages of Columbus, Magellan and Vasco de Gama, so naval warfare, hitherto limited to the Mediterranean and coastal waters, also took on a new character. The new technology of shipbuilding, cannon, gunpowder and compass which had enabled Columbus to span the Atlantic also transformed naval warfare. Hawkins, Drake and Menendez de Aviles were among the first to see the strategic importance of the Caribbean in relation to European conflicts and to develop strategic plans of attack on the one hand, of defence on the other.

The chief events in the challenge to the Spanish monopoly can be set out briefly. In 1553 a French privateer, Francois de Clerc, nicknamed Timberleg, entered the Caribbean with a fleet of French warships, sacked some coastal towns and in 1554 took the city of Santiago in Cuba. A year later his lieutenant Jacques Sores took Havana, held it for three weeks, and departed only when the ransom money had been paid.

Drake brought a larger perspective to the conflict. He had some experience of the Caribbean, gained while serving with Hawkins on the disastrous third voyage, and on two voyages in 1570 and 1571, when he traded slaves for hides and silver. On his 1571 voyage he probed along the coast of the Isthmus and made contact with native Indians and with bands of runaway slaves. When relationships between England and Spain became strained in 1572 Drake set out for the Caribbean with seventy-two men and two small ships; a highly mobile force designed for actions involving surprise and speed. He struck quickly at Nombre de Dios and got back to Plymouth in 1573 laden with booty.

During the ten years that followed, Anglo-Spanish relations were somewhat easier, and Drake became involved elsewhere. Between 1577–80 he made his celebrated voyage around the world. By the time he returned to England it was becoming clear that war between England and Spain was inevitable, and in 1585 Drake set out on his Indies voyage with a large fleet of some twenty ships and a force of 2,500 men. The attempt was partially successful. He took Santo Domingo and Cartagena, but fever and casualties cut his fighting force to 800, and he abandoned the idea of an attack on the Isthmus. Hoping to capture the Spanish treasure fleet he lay in wait at Cape San Antonio where he refitted his ships; but the armada slipped by and made its way safely to Havana. Drake, concluding that his force was not strong enough for a successful attack on Havana, returned to England.

Drake's last voyage to the Indies was in 1595 when he shared the command of a large fleet with Hawkins. The voyage went badly. The attack on San Juan failed. Hawkins died off Puerto Rico. An attempt on the Isthmus proved ineffective. Drake died off the coast of Veragua, and Baskerville, who succeeded to the command, had difficulty in fighting his way through a Spanish fleet in the Florida Channel.

Like Drake, Pedro Menendez de Aviles, the chief architect of the Spanish Caribbean defence system, saw strategy in large terms. An experienced seaman and commander, he had been in charge of two Spanish fleets, one homeward bound from the Indies in 1555, the other outward bound from Cadiz in 1562. In the two years following this second voyage Menendez developed a strategy of Caribbean defence that was both regional and Atlantic in scope. Inevitably, he was primarily concerned with the imperial interests of Spain, not with the welfare of the colonists. He saw the need for looking at the region as a whole, and for putting its defence under one commander, responsible for coordinating and directing the measures that had to be taken. Just as Drake had aimed at defeating Spain by hamstringing her in the Indies so Menendez recommended striking at privateers and raiders before they got across the Atlantic by establishing a base in the Scilly Isles. He understood also that trade might lead to settlement, and he recognised the importance of the Florida Channel to the Spanish Indies. As a result, after he was made responsible for creating the defence system and was appointed *adelantado* of Florida, he destroyed the small Huguenot colony that had been founded on the coast, and established in its place the fortified post of St. Augustine.

Menendez established a defence system in which the three chief elements were the use of a convey system for all ships moving between Spain and the Caribbean, except for light fast vessels on urgent business; cruiser squadrons based in the Caribbean to patrol the shipping-routes and undertake search-and-destroy missions against interlopers; and the fortification and permanent garrisoning of key ports. In the convoy system of the Indies, the homeward bound Spanish fleet that gathered each year in Nombre de Dios sailed for Havana in January, rounding Cape San Antonio and making its way in the teeth of the Trades along the north-west coast of Cuba. In February the ships assembled at Vera Cruz set sail for Havana, beating their way for three or four weeks against the wind. Havana, then a small town, almost burst its seams during the boisterous months when the ships were revictualling and making ready for the trans-Atlantic haul. They sailed in early summer, well ahead of the hurricane season. The first part of the homeward voyage lay through the narrow Florida Channel, where every seaman was on the alert, knowing that the numerous cays and islets provided perfect bases for pirates; and the ships held to a northerly course until the Westerlies began to fill their sails and they could turn east toward Spain. Spain retained the system for 150 years. During that time she lost only three fleets sailing in convoy, one to the English, and two to the Dutch.

The system was costly, however, and it tied up shipping when Spain was short of ships and the colonists were clamouring about the shortage of supplies and the high cost of imports. The colonists were in a dilemma. Forbidden to trade with foreigners they were unable to get adequate supplies from Spain because she was short of shipping. However, as far as Menendez was concerned, the treasure fleets had the priority. He gave priority also to fortifying Havana, which he transformed into a fortress, and equipped with a dockyard for refitting ships and making small vessels. He died in 1574, before completing his work. The cruiser squadrons of the Windward fleet were not created until 1582, one fleet being based on Cartagena, the other on Santo Domingo. The fortification of San Juan was carried out in the 1590's, so that by the time Drake invaded the Caribbean in 1595 he found the Spaniards ready for him.

The defences were sorely needed for in 1595 France, England and the Netherlands, in the Treaty of the Hague, combined in an alliance against Spain. A fleet made up of English and Dutch ships wiped out a Spanish convoy fleet waiting in Cadiz harbour, and by this single blow stopped Spanish-American trade for two years. The French backed out in 1598, the English under James in 1604. But Spain paid a price. The English recognised Spain's monopoly in territories she had occupied, but did not recognise her right to land she had not occupied. Spain kept silent on the point, knowing that her enemies might regard silence as consent. When she made peace with the Dutch in the Treaty of Antwerp in 1509, she not only recognised Holland as an independent nation but also accepted the inclusion of a clause that could be interpreted as admitting the principle of settlement by other powers in lands not held by her.

CHAPTER 6

Entry of Africa

Although under compulsion, Africa also entered the Caribbean and the Americas. This came about through the Portuguese voyages of exploration down the coast of West Africa and their establishment of a monopoly of the West African trade; and through Spain's need for a labour force in the Indies, the Arawaks having been destroyed. Spain first established a sugar industry in the Caribbean but it was from Brazil that the methods and techniques of the sugar-and-slave plantations were taken to Barbados, St. Kitts, and Martinique. From the Caribbean point of view this transfer of a system of trade and production is important; but the central fact is that it involved Africa; that the system depended on Africans who were moved across the Atlantic; that though they endured unmentionable agonies they created a way of life in lands once alien to them; that they contributed to the growth of societies with unique identifiable characteristics; that throughout this extensive region of variety and contrast Africa survives and the African origin constitutes a common bond.

There had long been a trade in slaves across the Sahara from the interior of Africa to the North African coast. Portugal opened up an alternative route when, after the capture of Ceuta in 1415, her seamen began to probe down the West African coast. By 1481 Portuguese explorers had reached the Congo and in 1497, five years after Columbus made his way to the Caribbean, Vasco de Gama rounded the Cape of Good Hope and opened up an ocean route to the true Indies. By 1513, the year in which Balboa discovered the Pacific, the Portuguese were in the true spice islands, the Moluccas. In 1445, almost half a century before Columbus landed in Hispaniola, the Portuguese took their first cargo of Africans to Lisbon for sale as slaves. The trade in ivory, pepper, gold and slaves grew steadily, and the Guinea coast became an essential part of Portugal's economy. Her ships moved along the African coast from the Senegal and Gambia rivers south to the Sherbro River, past mountains where frequent electric storms set the valleys echoing with thunder like the growling of lions, whence the name Sierra Leone; and on by way of the Ivory Coast and the dreaded Bight of Biafra to the Congo, Luanda and Benguela.

Portugal, in order to preserve and protect her trading monopoly along this 5,000 mile stretch of coast, negotiated with a local ruler for the right to build a fortified trading station about half way between Sekondi and Cape Coast Castle. This stretch of coast was called El Mina de Ouro, the Mine of Gold, probably because the Portuguese hoped to find there the mines whence the Africans obtained the gold with which they traded. The fort was called El Mina, the Castle of the Mine. Built in 1482 on dark grey cliffs, with battlements, courtyards, sunlit parapets and dark dungeons, protected on the landward side by the fort of St. Jago, El Mina symbolised Portuguese power and the Portuguese monopoly for 150 years, until the Dutch took it in 1637.

Off shore there were islands that Spain and Portugal colonised. Isabella of Spain had settled the Canaries and developed a system of agriculture thereby sharing out the land and granting large areas to Spaniards who had some capital. A thriving sugar industry had been established in the islands. Portugal had in Madeira, Sao Tomé and the Cape Verde Islands bases of strategic value, which were of use in maintaining her trading monopoly and as stopping places for ships bound for the Americas or trading along the African coast. The pattern of colonisation and exploitation which Spain and Portugal established in these islands and in the Americas, was in marked contrast with that which they followed in West Africa. This is understandable, for the effort at colonising America was in itself an almost intolerable burden for Spain with its five million people; while Portugal was extended to the limit or beyond it in the East Indies and in Brazil. As far as trade with West Africa went, it could be obtained only through local middlemen and chiefs. Also, along the coast there were deadly fevers. The physical barriers were formidable, and added to these were people with a reputation for courage and martial ability.

The perspectives of history change with time and place. To the Spanish colonist in Santo Domingo in 1511 the arrival of a slave ship with a party of fifty Africans for sale as slaves direct from West African must have seemed of little more than passing interest. He had seen Africans at work as slaves in his homeland, and he had seen them at work in Hispaniola also. To him the realities were the development that had taken place in Hispaniola under Ovando, the transformation of the destitute settlement of 1502 into a prosperous centre of administration in the Indies, inhabited by some 4000 colonists. We who are West Indians, looking back across four and a half centuries, point to the arrival of the slave ship direct from West Africa as a turning point in our history. It opened up a trade route between the African and American coasts of the Atlantic, serving as pioneer for thousands of ships that in the course of four centuries transported ten million Africans or more to the Americas and changed the history of Europe, Africa and America.

Africa's presence in America was confirmed by the grant of an *Asiento*, a permit or import licence which Charles II made in 1518 to one of his favourites, Gouvernot, Governor of Bresa. The licence was for the importation of 4,000 Africans. Bresa sold his permit to some Genoese merchants, for the Genoese were on hand wherever trade was stirring. The colonists welcomed the prospect of a steady supply of Africans as slaves. Their attitude was described by Las Casas who said that when he pleaded for the liberation of the Indians of Hispaniola the colonists said they would set their Indians free if he would get them a licence from the King to import a dozen African slaves from Castile.

Spain succeeded in her attempt to establish a sugar industry in Hispaniola, but, as we have seen, Mexico and Peru drew settlers away from the islands, ranching competed with sugar, and in the end it was the Brazilian example that was to transform Barbados and St. Kitts into sugar islands. The time sequence

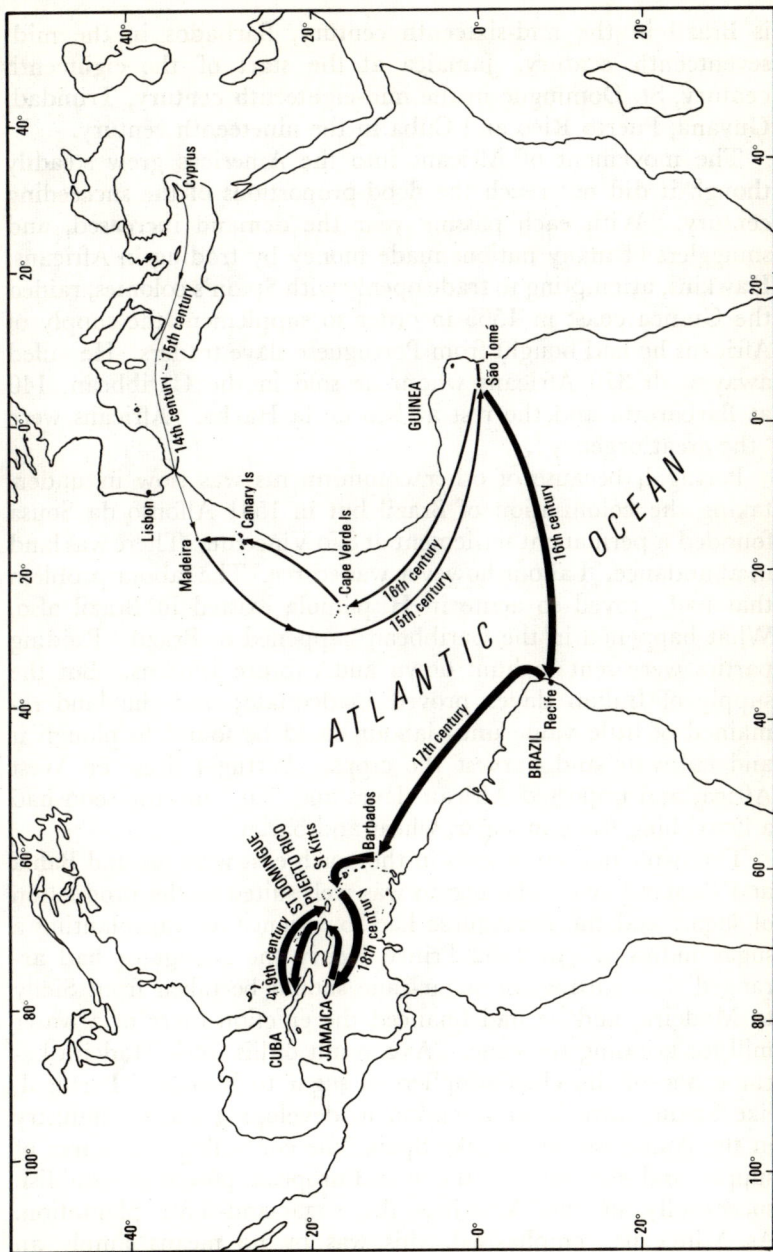

Mid Atlantic showing the movement of the Sugar Industry

Cyprus

14th century – 15th century

Lisbon

Madeira

Canary Is

Cape Verde Is

São Tomé

GUINEA

16th century

15th century

16th century

ATLANTIC   OCEAN

17th century

Recife

BRAZIL

Barbados

St Kitts

PUERTO RICO

ST DOMINGUE

4 19th century

18th century

CUBA

JAMAICA

is Brazil in the mid-sixteenth century, Barbados in the mid seventeenth century, Jamaica at the start of the eighteenth century, St. Domingue in the mid-eighteenth century, Trinidad, Guyana, Puerto Rico and Cuba in the nineteenth century.

The movement of Africans into the Americas grew steadily though it did not reach the flood-proportions of the succeeding century. With each passing year the demand increased, and smugglers of many nations made money by trading in Africans. Hawkins, attempting to trade openly with Spain's colonies, raided the Guinea coast in 1565 in order to supplement the supply of Africans he had bought from Portuguese slave traders. He sailed away with 370 Africans whom he sold in the Caribbean, 140 at Barbarotta and the rest at Rio de la Hacha. Africans were ' the great urgency '.

Portugal, because of other commitments was slow in undertaking the colonisation of Brazil but in 1531 Alfonso da Sousa founded a permanent settlement at São Vincente. There was land in abundance. Labour however was scarce. The labour problem that had proved so acute in Hispaniola existed in Brazil also. What happened in the Caribbean happened in Brazil. Raiding parties were sent to hunt down and capture Indians. But the supply of Indian slaves proved inadequate; and the land remained of little value until labour could be found to plough it and cultivate and harvest the crops. Portugal drew on West Africa, and imported African slaves and São Vincente soon had a flourishing trade in sugar, wheat and barley.

The two chief settlements in the north-east were around Bahia and Pernambuco. The region was well suited to the production of sugar, and the Portuguese had experience in transplanting a sugar industry. In 1452 Prince Henry the Navigator had arranged that cuttings of sugar-cane should be taken from Sicily to Madeira, and he had financed the erection there of a water mill for grinding the cane. As a result of his work Madeira became one of the chief suppliers of sugar to Europe. Portugal, like Spain, turned her attention to developing a sugar industry in the Americas; but unlike Spain, she controlled the source of supply and she became the first European power to establish successfully in the Americas the sugar-and-slave plantation. As Mintz has emphasised, this was by no means simply an innovation in agriculture. Rather 'the plantation was an absolutely unprecedented social, economic and political institution '. It was organised to produce a single crop to satisfy large-scale demand, and since free men will not work as employed agricultural labourers if they have access to land which they can cultivate for themselves, the labourers had to be supplied by force. The sugar-and-slave plantation rapidly made Brazil a large sugar producer. When Portugal was united with Spain in 1580 she was exposed to attack from Spain's enemies, the most implacable of whom was Holland. In 1630 the Dutch captured Recife which was the key to the valuable sugar area of Pernambuco, holding it until the Brazilians drove them out in 1654.

The unit of production was the large estate, and the unit of colonisation was the family. The labour force consisted of some Indians and an ever-increasing number of Africans. The prosperity of the aristocrats and of the country rested on the sugar estate and the sugar estate rested on the muscle and skill of the African. It is estimated that by 1585 about one third of the population of Brazil was African. The estate was a self-contained world, with its own labour force, artisans, craftsmen, cattlemen, cart drivers, sugar makers and distillers. The centre of this world was the Great House. A Brazilian scholar, Gilberto Freyre, has described the Big House and the slave shack as representing an entire economic, social and political system.

> The Big House was at one and the same time a fortress, a bank, a cemetery, a hospital, a school, and a house of charity giving shelter to the aged, the widow and the orphan...
> The rich were in the habit of protecting their dwellings and manor houses by a powerful row of stakes, in the manner of the natives, and these stockades were manned by domestics, retainers, and Indian slaves and also served as a refuge for the neighbours when they were unexpectedly attacked by the savages...

The defences were necessary, as the history of the black state of Palmares showed. The Portuguese colonists settled along the coast from the Rio São Francisco north to Filipeia, establishing their homesteads and laying out plantations of sugar-cane. The industry brought prosperity to the region and as the industry expanded the number of Africans imported into Pernambuco increased. In the early years many of these Africans came from the region of the Upper Guinea, with increasing numbers from the Bight of Biafra in the second half of the 16th century and with the largest numbers coming from the tribes of Angola in the 17th century. Like the Portuguese at this period, the blacks had to adjust to a new country; but unlike the Portuguese they came from many different peoples and represented a wide spread of cultures. Numbers of them fled from the plantations and established settlements in the sparsely populated region between the coastal lands and the arid interior. They survived largely because the palm trees that abounded in the region provided them with food, whence the name Palmares. These black communities, *mocambos*, created a state that was self-sufficient, resolute in defending itself, capable of managing its own affairs, committed to unity notwithstanding many cultural differences. These things the blacks achieved on their own, without the resources and weapons of the whites, and in the face of Portuguese hostility. The Portuguese raided their settlements but were unable to destroy them. After the Dutch gained control of north-east Brazil in 1624 the flow of black fugitives from the plantations grew, and the Dutch also failed in their efforts to break the stubborn black state. In 1650 the blacks proclaimed Palmares an independent republic, with an elected Head of State and a system of courts and magistrates. The land was parcelled out, and surplus foodcrops traded with the Indians and with some of the settlements on the coast.

In 1654 the Portuguese retook north-east Brazil from the Dutch, and after consolidating their position they attempted to reduce Palmares. Failing in this, they recognised the independence of the black republic in 1678 in a treaty which never became effective. The Portuguese Crown objected to it. So did an insurgent group in Palmares which would not agree to any act of fealty to Portugal. Zumbi, the leader of the Palmares insurgents, gained control of the state, and developed a strategy of retaliatory raids against the Portuguese. In the last decade of the century the Portuguese, with the help of colonists from São Paulo, embarked on a carefully planned campaign against Palmares. They lost more than 6,000 captured or killed. The people of Palmares

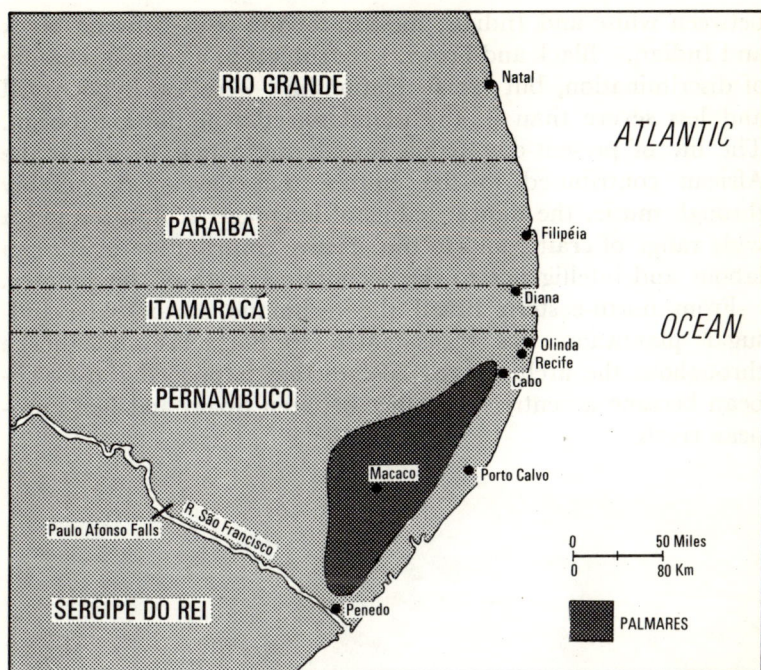

Palmares Republic late seventeenth century

suffered heavily. More than 20,000 were killed. On February 6, 1694 the Portuguese took the last stronghold of Palmares, Macaco, in the interior of Alagoas, after a siege that lasted forty-two days. Two years later they tracked Zumbi to his place of refuge and killed him. But the destruction of Palmares did not signify an end to the struggle of new world blacks for the right to stand on their own feet and make their own way in the world. Some sixty years after the Portuguese treaty with Palmares, the English signed a treaty recognising the independence of the Maroons of Jamaica. A century after Zumbi was killed the blacks of Haiti were entering on their successful struggle for freedom.

In contrast, the north witnessed the growth of a society in which a significant characteristic was the intermingling of Portuguese and black or Indian. There were three categories; mulatto for the cross between white and black; mameluco for the cross between white and Indian; mestizo for the cross between black and Indian. Black and brown were subject to a certain measure of discrimination, but racial relationships were less hypocritical and less severe than in the island societies of the Caribbean. The life of present-day Bahia reveals the extent to which the African contributed to the culture that developed, notably through music, the dance, habits of language, sculpture, and a wide range of crafts; and to the massive contribution of African labour and intelligence to the economic growth of the country.

From north-eastern Brazil the technique of the slave-and-sugar plantation was transplanted to Barbados and thence throughout the archipelago. Before that happened the Caribbean became a centre of conflict between Spain and her European rivals.

CHAPTER 7

African Perspective

What was the background of the African people who were taken from their homelands to Brazil, the islands of the Caribbean and the Deep South? What was the history of the tribes and nations to which they belonged? And what is the African past?

These questions are important for us for many reasons. One is that the African past is a part of the heritage of the people of the Caribbean archipelago. We live in that part of the Americas where people of African origin are in the majority, govern themselves, and are citizens of sovereign states. In Jamaica, for example, the population consists for the most part of black and brown people. Three out of four persons are black, and only one out of every twenty is European, East Indian, Chinese or Syrian. The structure of the population of Barbados, Antigua, St. Kitts and Montserrat is much the same. About 85 out of every 100 persons in Antigua are black, and 12 out of every 100 are brown. St. Kitts and Montserrat have an even larger proportion of blacks, 86 per cent and 92 per cent respectively. In Trinidad and Guyana the two largest groups are non-European. Trinidad has 46 per cent black and Guyana 38 per cent. The proportion of East Indians in these two countries, is 36 per cent and 45 per cent respectively. Whites form 2·75 per cent and 2·93 per cent of the population of these two countries. Demographically, the map of the islands can be drawn in black and brown; and because people of African origin are dominant it is essential that they should be concerned with Africa and African history. Besides, knowledge of this kind will help to free us from the misconceptions that we inherited from the colonial period through a school system which either neglected Africa altogether or presented Africa as a primitive, barbarous place. Traditionally many European historians either neglected African history or undervalued it.

There was a substantial mythology about Africa which was accepted and taught because it appeared to justify, or at least to explain, the enslavement of the African, or his exclusion from the full rights of citizenship, or simply in order to satisfy that bigotry which identifies skin-colour with merit. Much of the history taught in our schools was European-centred, and in the past there were many European and American historians who held the view that African history really began with the exploration and colonisation of Africa by Europeans; and more especially by the English and French. In the same way that Caribbean history was treated as a footnote to European history so African history was treated as beginning with the arrival of Europeans; or, in other words, the history of Africa was treated as if it were the same as the history of the European colonisation of Africa.

Up to recent years relatively little was known about the history of Africa. During the last quarter of a century, however, archaeologists and anthropologists have made a number of exciting discoveries that throw new light on the past of Africa, and as a result historians are taking a new approach to the study of African history. These discoveries indicate that any scientific study of man's past, of the way in which man evolved and learned to use and to make implements and weapons, must include a study of the past of Africa, because the evidence indicates that man had his origins in Africa.

This chapter can do no more than point to some of these discoveries and refer to one or two well-known books that are examples of the new understanding of what Africa means in the history of man. One such book is Basil Davidson's *Mother Africa*; another is Davidson's anthology of writings about Africa, *The African Past*. Alongside these are three books by Melville Herskovits, an American sociologist who devoted his life to a study of the West African peoples of Dahomey and Ashanti and of African survivals in the Americas; *The Myth of the Negro Past*, *Life in a Haitian Valley* and *Trinidad Village*. Two widely read books about the African in our part of the world are Eric Williams' *Negro in the Caribbean* and Lerone Bennet's account of the African in the United States, published under the title *Before the Mayflower*. The title emphasises the fact that Africans were taken to North America in 1619, a year before the Pilgrim Fathers landed at Plymouth in New England. Lerone Bennet reminds us that Africa, long thought of as the Dark Continent, is now regarded as the place where man first received light; that ancient Africans, long regarded as primitive and ignorant, are now known to have contributed significantly to Egyptian civilisation and to have created powerful highly organised states and empires.

Up to the 1920's scientists thought that man originated in Central Asia. In 1924 they were astonished at the discovery of fossil bones in South Africa which belonged to a much earlier period than those found anywhere else in the world. As recently as 1959 Dr. Luis Leakey found much older remains in the Olduvai Gorge in Tanganyika, now Tanzania, in the region of Lake Victoria. The gorge is a 25 mile canyon, and its walls contain layer upon layer of the ancient shores of the lake. The lowest beds contained crude tools fashioned from pebbles while the higher beds contained tools that were better made; so as the anthropologist moved up the layers he was able to trace the evolution of stone tools up to the more advanced implements of stone-age man. Leaky's discoveries of bones and tools established the fact that Africa was the cradle of man. In 1967 a fragment of jawbone was found in deposits on Lothagm Hill in Kenya where other important finds had already been made; and up to the present this fragment represents the oldest member of the human family ever found. It provides evidence that dates back more than five million years. There are many gaps in the story of the development of early man, of how he adopted his ground-living habit and an upright posture which freed his arms to use tools, but there is now abundant evidence that the history of early Africa is inseparably bound up with the history of man himself. The discoveries that have been made change the perspectives of human history as well as the perspectives of African history.

There is convincing evidence also of the development of advanced cultures in various parts of Africa. Scholars working in the Sudan have found around Khartoum and in the Nile Valley, evidence that negroid people contributed to the growth of Egyptian civilisation. These discoveries, which are very much nearer to us in time, include fragments of beautifully made pottery which are older than any found in the earliest city known to man. Evidence points to the fact that negroid people in that region were using tools and planting grain some six thousand years ago; that by 4000 years before Christ African people in lands bordering the West Africa forest area had developed a system of agriculture based on cereals, and that another system based on stock-raising had been developed in the highlands of East Africa. Much more work remains to be done before the history of these early periods can be sketched even tentatively,

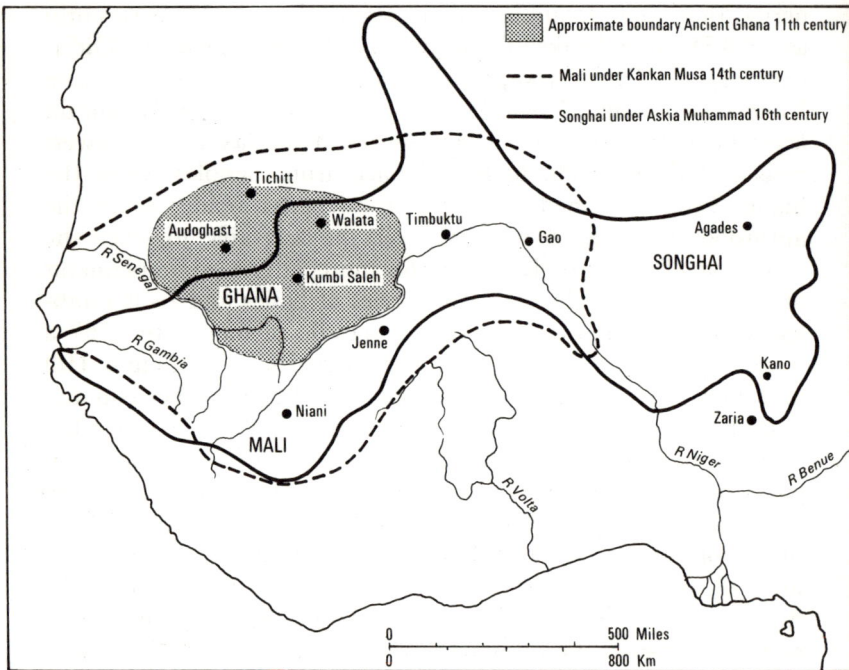

West Africa showing ancient empires of Ghana, Mali and Songhai

but what has been found establishes that African people played an important part in the development of civilisation.

There followed an important period in the early history of Africa when African peoples learned how to smelt iron and make iron tools and weapons. The knowledge spread from some of the people of the Eastern Mediterranean, such as the Phoenecians, to the Egyptians of the Nile Valley and into the regions of northern Ethiopia. From these regions it spread gradually through other parts of Africa. During the same period there was trade between East Africa and lands across the Indian Ocean, possibly as far as parts of Indonesia. This trade added the banana and yam to the stock of foods used by the African. Davidson, in *The African Past* points out that:

> these two factors, better tools and new types of food, appear to have promoted just that ' population explosion ' which the old ecology had failed to produce; and ' the explosion is closely associated with the emergence of the Bantu-speaking family of African people who now dominate the whole central and southern region of the continent '.

As a result the primitive social organisation of the Stone Age period began to break up, and more complex societies emerged with clearly defined political systems.

The rock carvings and engravings that have been found south of the Zambesi provide further evidence of the growth of an artistic tradition that dates back perhaps 8000 years before the Birth of Christ. This rock forms a valuable record of early man's use of religious ritual and ceremony, of his dances, hunting expeditions and wars.

A West Indian, visiting Africa, is almost overwhelmed by the size of the continent and by the impact of the past. Coming from a region where the islands, large or small, look much alike he finds desert and tropical rainforest, rolling upland country and towering mountains; and he finds also great cultural diversity, the Arab north, the Bushmen of the south, Bantu, Ibo, Yoruba, the peoples of Ethiopia, a bewildering range of languages and cultures spread out across vast distances. In contrast with his own brief history of three or four centuries, and with the separateness imposed by the sea and enforced by history, he finds cultures and traditions rooted in the distant past. A blacksmith working with bellows and charcoal fire in a village on the bank of the Benue River is linked by his craft with workers in terra cotta and iron who learned how to smelt iron ore and make implements of iron in that region two centuries before the birth of Christ. He finds in the Western Sudan reminders that rice was grown there more than 1000 years before Christ. In Ethiopia and the Nile Valley he sees work in copper and bronze that had its origins with the Hittites who lived more than 1500 years before Christ. Present and past run together, modern factories for making textiles and a village weaver stretching his long threads, and threading his shuttle in the way his ancestors did five centuries ago.

Notwithstanding this diversity it is possible to pick out certain characteristics that are shared by many African peoples. One is a capacity for political organisation. John Hope Franklin, in his history of Negro Americans, *From Slavery to Freedom*, remarked that ' wherever one observes the peoples of Africa he finds some form of political organisation. They were not all highly organised kingdoms—to be sure, some were simple, isolated family states—but they all seem to indicate the normal capability and desire of establishing governments to solve the problems which every community of people encountered '. There were family states, village states, small kingdoms and at times great empires. Procedures were worked out for an orderly transfer of authority when a ruler died; this was not simply by the automatic succession of the eldest son, since he might not make the best ruler. Though the king had great power he ruled with the help of advisers and ministers, so that he and members of the nobility functioned as a kind of parliament. Below the king there were local rulers or kings who had considerable power in local affairs. Our West Indian visitor, moving through the countries of West Africa, becomes aware of this tradition of established authority, and of the subtle ways in which power is limited in the interests of the tribe or nation. Seeing this, he understands how rebellious African slaves in north-eastern Brazil established an independent republic that withstood Portuguese attacks for forty years; how rebellious African slaves set up their own free communities in the mountains of Jamaica; how rebellious African slaves in Haiti organised armies that defeated Napoleon's forces and established a free republic; how at the time of emancipation, newly freed blacks set up well-organised free villages of their own on the coastlands of Guyana and in the hill country of Jamaica.

Another aspect of the African way of life is the strength of the family and of the ties of kinship. Among some peoples descent was traced through the mother, in others through the father; but whatever the system, whether matriarchal or patriarchal, the family was made up of all living descendants of the same ancestor. As time went on and the number of families increased they made up a clan. Religion enforced the strong ties of family and kinship for when a man died his spirit lived on and took an active interest in the affairs of the family. The spirits of the most ancient ancestors were the most powerful, and separation from their care and oversight was a disaster. As we come to understand the powerful cohesive force of the African family and kinship group and the pervading influence of a religion based on ancestor worship and on the presence of ancestral spirits in certain familiar rocks and trees and in the sky above, we recognise that the physical agonies of slavery were less than the extreme mental anguish of those who were torn away from family, from the kinship group, and from the protection of the ancestral spirits. Not only were they torn away, but on the plantations of the Caribbean they were denied any opportunity of recreating either family or kinship group, save in so far as one might make kinsmen of those who crossed the Atlantic on the same ship or of those who worked on the same estate.

Our visitor, moving through bustling modern cities like Accra, Lagos and Ibadan, or through villages in the interior, would note immediately the liveliness of the markets with their women-traders, and alongside the movement of people into the towns, the attachment of the countryman to the land and to tilling the soil. The land has always been the life of the people, and though an individual or a group might be granted the use of specific pieces of land this does not mean that they have the right to alienate it. When they stop using it the land reverts to the collective ownership of the tribe. And because the land bears food, tilling the soil was one of the noblest callings. There was a high degree of specialisation, both in the growing of special crops and in the manufacture of goods and the production of works of art. This specialisation encouraged trade; international trade like that between the old empires of Ghana and Mali and the Berber traders who lived to the north of them, and with the cities of north Africa and the Middle East; and local trade between villages and townships. As Franklin reminds us, Africa was ' never a series of isolated self-sufficient communities, but an area which had far-flung interests, that were based on agriculture, industry and commerce '. The effect of such contacts on the culture was immeasurable. It can only be said that these routes of commerce were the highways over which civilisation as well as goods travelled, and that Africa gave much of her own civilisation to others and received a good deal in return '. Thinking of his Caribbean homeland, our West Indian in Africa finds a link with this African past in the West Indian tilling his ' ground ', in the women traders of every West Indian market, and in the ' higgler women ' who for generations supplied the island markets.

CHAPTER 8

The Settlement of the
Eastern Caribbean

To return to the Caribbean. One of the difficulties that we as West Indians have with our early history is that we do not feel involved. The initiatives and the decisions lie elsewhere. The heroes are not ours, neither Drake nor his opponent Menendez, nor Cortes nor the Aztec Cautemoc. Hatuey is nearer to us, and Queen Anacaona, because they fought for independence, for freedom, but they are not ours. As a result we do not claim our past. Few of our novelists turn to this early period, or indeed to the later period of which the memories are bitter. The outstanding exceptions are Mittelholzer with his *Kaywana's Children* and *Kaywana Blood*, Naipaul with his account of *The Loss of El Dorado*, and Vic Reid with *New Day;* and of the poets, A. J. Seymour with *Kyk-Over-All* and *Clouds Over Guiana*.

The land however is ours, and through the land the conflicts that shaped our destiny and the scattered groups of transplanted people who began to make their homes on the savannahs and who found a refuge in the mountains; poor smallholders tilling the Cuban soil, Maroons in Jamaica and Hispaniola, in these we find and recognise a kinship. And, however remote they may appear, the closing years of the 16th century and the first quarter of the 17th century are important for us. In this period we discern signs of change; gathering forces that enabled the Dutch to break both the Spanish and Portuguese trading monopolies, that put it in the power of the French and the English to settle in the Eastern and Central Caribbean, that saw the Dutch transporting Africans to Brazil, and Africans and the technique of the sugar-and-slave plantation to the Eastern Caribbean.

These forces were generated largely by the expansion of Holland, France and England across the Atlantic, with these three nations seeking trade and territory in parts of America not effectively occupied by Spain and Portugal. Men with capital to invest were looking overseas. Hawkins had shown by his first two Caribbean voyages that there was good money to be made from trade as apart from piracy. North America produced commodities in urgent demand in Western Europe and the volume of trade increased rapidly.

In the tropical belt there were areas that were within reach of Spain's arm but were not in her hands. The islands of the Eastern Caribbean were inhabited by the indigenous people. Trinidad, a Spanish colony, was wholly defenceless. To the south, the Wild Coast, which extended from the mouth of the Orinoco to the region of the Amazon, offered prospects of a trade in tobacco. There dream and reality ran together; El Dorado and tobacco trading.

Raleigh is the name with which we begin. He gave a new direction to English effort in tropical America. He was not much taken with the views of Drake and others that the capture of the Isthmus of Panama would stop the flow of treasure to Spain. For him the wise thing was to find new sources of wealth for England, greater even than Spain's ' Indian gold that endangereth and disturbeth all the nations of Europe '. For this new source he turned to the region running from Cumana to Brazil, and he fixed his hopes on the valley of the Orinoco, for he had learned from explorers like Captain Jacob Whiddon and the Spanish prisoner of war Pedro Sarmiento that ' there was the rich and beautiful Empire of Guiana, and that great and golden city which the Spaniards call El Dorado and the Indians Manoa'. He set out in 1595 to conquer this kingdom as Cortés had conquered Mexico; but six months after arriving at the Orinoco he was back in England, having failed. In 1617, released from the Tower so that he might make another attempt, Raleigh set off to find mines of gold, called at Trinidad where he stayed with half his force of fourteen ships and 1,000 men to guard the mouth of the Orinoco. The Spaniards at São Tomé were on the look out. Keymis, who led the advance, and his 400 men took São Tomé by storm. In the fighting one of Raleigh's two sons was killed. The English had to withdraw, making their way down river back to Raleigh in Trinidad. Keymis reported to Raleigh what had happened, went to his cabin and hanged himself. In England Raleigh found prison and execution awaiting him; yet although his attempt ended in failure it attracted attention to Guiana, and English settlements in the Eastern Caribbean sprang out of early efforts to establish trading and planting settlements on the Wild Coast.

In this tropical region there were commodities from which a man might take a fortune. One was sugar. That was out of the question for adventurers and poachers. They had neither the technical experience nor the access to land where they could count on being secure. But dyewoods were in demand, especially those woods which, like logwood, yielded a rich red dye. The manufacturers of cloth in the Netherlands used it for dyeing cloth; and when they found out how to make the dye fast the market in Europe and in England expanded to the point where a ton of logwood might fetch as much as £100. It was little wonder that traders sailed for Brazil and remote places of the Caribbean coast, set up camps, and cut and loaded their cargoes of dyewood. Tobacco also was in demand. Dutch traders and those of other nations made their way to the Caribbean to exchange cloth and pots and pans for hides and for tobacco; ' freighting smoke ' they called the tobacco trade. It soon became clear that the trade could be made easier and more profitable if planting settlements were established; so, toward the close of the 16th century Dutchmen, and some English and French were to be found along the Wild Coast and on the banks of the rivers of Guiana, teaching the Indians to grow tobacco and exchanging trinkets, axes and knives for tobacco and cotton. The French set up a colony at Cayenne in 1607 and the Caribs wiped it out. Then they tried further south near the Amazon. The English tried in 1604, under Leigh, and failed. An attempt under Robert Harcourt petered out in 1613, after four years. Roger North tried for two years, from 1619 to 1621, and failed. The Dutch finally, after several failures, succeeded when Captain Groenewegen founded a settlement of men from Zeeland on the Essequibo in 1616. From this date up to the middle of the 17th century the Dutch gained and held the ascendancy in the Caribbean. They became the carriers of the region. Their ships frequented every coast, trading with the colonists in the face of Spanish prohibition.

They seized and held the sugar region of Brazil for twenty years, from 1634 to 1654. There they gained an insight into the techniques of sugar production so that they were able to advise the French and English colonists in the Eastern Caribbean when they ran into difficulties in the 1640's. Their naval forces controlled the waters of the Caribbean from the middle of the 1620's and as a result, behind the screen of Dutch naval power, the French and English founded colonies in the Caribbean.

The conflict between Holland and Spain began in 1568 when the Northern provinces of the Low Countries rebelled against Spanish rule. Strongly Calvinist, accustomed to the exercise of ancient privileges, they resented the highly centralised government of Spain and objected to her penal decrees against heretics. They feared also the introduction of the Inquisition. In 1579 they formed the Union of Utrecht and in 1581 they declared their independence from Spain. This independence Spain virtually recognised when she agreed to a twelve years truce in 1609. By the time that she resumed her attempt to crush the Dutch in 1621 they had grown too powerful, so after thirty more years of fruitless struggle she formally recognised Dutch independence in the Treaty of Westphalia in 1648.

The details of that long war of independence, its triumphs and disasters, belong to the history of Europe. The results, however, changed Caribbean history, and made possible the establishment of new societies in the Caribbean. The Dutch, through their East India and West India Companies waged war in both hemispheres, but we are more closely concerned with their activities in the Atlantic and the Caribbean.

Spain, attempting to maintain her monopoly, had decreed that trade in the Indies should be carried on only by Castilians; but in practice other Spanish subjects, the Dutch especially, shared in the trade by carrying the products of the Indies from Seville to other European ports. After the Dutch declared their independence in 1581, Philip, King of Spain, seeking to break them, forbade all Spanish trade with the Netherlands and seized all Dutch ships in Spanish ports. In turn the Netherlands forbade their subjects to trade with Spain. Shut out from the Iberian peninsula, in which direction were Dutch traders and investors to look? And where were they to find the salt which previously they had obtained from Portugal and which they needed desperately for their herring trade? Many turned to the Far East, while others came in steadily increasing numbers to the Caribbean.

Philip's decree was not rigidly enforced until 1598, when the Dutch were barred from Portugal. They found an important supply of salt, however, in the Araya lagoon on the coast of Venezuela, near Cumana. Araya became a centre for smuggling, and the Dutch built up so large a trade in tobacco that the price on the European market fell. Spain had to cut back production and at the same time she tried to put brakes on the illicit trade by forbidding her colonists on the mainland of America to grow tobacco. She took other desperate measures also. In 1605 her armada, under Luis Fajardo, captured twelve Dutch ships in a surprise attack on Araya, and closed the port for some years. The Governors of Venezuela caught and hanged a number of smugglers. In order to destroy the salt trade her brilliant military engineer Antonelli advised that the Araya lagoon should be flooded by letting in the sea. In north-western Hispaniola she embarked on a scorched earth policy, compelling her colonists to leave Puerto Plata, Yaguana and Monte Christi, destroying their crops and depopulating the region. Some colonists fled to Cuba. Others withdrew to Santo Domingo. Others became buccaneers. The cattle and swine ran wild. The forest returned to cover the fields. The buccaneers moved in, and after them the French.

During these years the Dutch, English and French also began their attempts at colonisation, following a policy that William Usselinx, a Calvinist refugee from Antwerp, had advocated; that Protestant settlements should be established to serve as bases for smuggling and raiding, sources of supply of ships' provisions and for tropical staples. The Dutch intensified their attacks on Spain and Portugal after 1621, when the Twelve Years Truce came to an end, and at this time they founded the

Dutch West India Company, a course that Usselinx had urged also. But the Company was not organised only for settlement and trade as Usselinx had proposed, nor was it simply an association of partners who were bent on making money from smuggling and raiding. Rather, it was a powerful corporation to which the Dutch States granted the power to maintain its own warships, and to settle, build, administer and defend colonies. It was to make war against Spain and Portugal and to make profits out of them at the same time. It was to hold a monopoly of trade on the coasts of West Africa and the Americas, for the Dutch, shrewd traders with international experience, understood well the essential and complementary relation between Africa and the West Indies. They already had a trading post at Goree on the West African coast and they were rapidly becoming slave traders on a large scale. At the same time they threw their strength into an attack on Spain in the Caribbean. Their fleets gained the mastery in the Caribbean after 1625, the supreme triumph being the capture of a Spanish treasure fleet in Matanzas Bay in 1627. That blow destroyed Spain's credit in Europe and left her soldiers in the Low Countries without pay. The Dutch Admirals, notably Pater and De Ruyter, kept up the pressure by constant raids on Cuba, Santo Domingo and Puerto Rico. Spanish shipping, with the exception of the treasure fleets, were swept from the Caribbean. In 1634 they took and settled Cura-çao, which had an excellent harbour, Aruba and Bonaire. The scale of the Dutch effort was world wide, including the expulsion of the Portuguese from Ceylon and the Moluccas, the founding of a settlement at the Cape of Good Hope in 1652 and the establishment of an empire in north eastern Brazil from 1634 to 1654.

The English and French gained footholds in the Eastern Caribbean in the years 1625–1650. The two first attempts by the English were unsuccessful. In 1605 the Caribs of St. Lucia beat off some Englishmen who tried to establish themselves there and four years later the Caribs of Grenada did the same. Success came at last when Thomas Warner, on his way back from Guiana, where he had been with Thomas North, called at the island of St. Christopher. ' He well viewing the island thought it would be a very convenient place for planting of tobacco, which was ever a rich commodity.' Warner secured financial backing in England and founded a settlement in the island in 1625. Barbados came next. John Powell, on his way back to England from Brazil, landed on the island in 1624, found it uninhabited, claimed it for the King of England, and went on to London to find support. William Courteen, a London merchant with Dutch connections, found the money for establishing a settlement. The first few years were very difficult, and in 1627 when there was a severe shortage of food, Groenewegen came to the rescue with supplies. By 1630 however Barbados was attracting settlers, and was entering on a period of swift growth as a tobacco island. There followed the settlement from St. Kitts of some of the neighbouring islands; Nevis in 1628; Montserrat in 1632; Antigua also in the same year. A second attempt to settle St. Lucia during the years 1638–41 was defeated by the Caribs.

Shortly after Warner founded his first settlement in St. Kitts a battered French ship limped into Basseterre harbour seeking succour. Warner welcomed the newcomers, de Roissy, d'Esnambuc and their men, largely because relationships with King Tegreman were deteriorating. On hearing that the Caribs were planning an attack Warner and d'Esnambuc struck first in a night attack, massacred the king and a number of his people, and drove the survivors from the island.

Spain had always tried to keep the Caribbean a closed sea, and, though she had been gravely weakened by the Dutch, she viewed the settlements in the islands with concern. In 1629 Don Fabrique Toledo was sent from Spain with a fleet to destroy the new settlements and to protect the treasure fleet. He attacked St. Kitts and Nevis, compelled the colonists to surrender, took a number of them prisoners, destroyed the crops and burnt the dwellings and then continued on his way to convoy the Spanish treasure fleet from Cartagena and Vera Cruz. Warner was in England at the time. He returned to the island with supplies in 1630, and gradually the English and French settlers drifted back to make a new beginning.

It was beyond Spain's strength to follow up Toledo's blow. Exhausted by decades of war in Europe and in the Indies, impoverished and weakned by defeats at the hands of the Dutch, she was forced to concentrate on protecting her treasure fleet. Miraculously she managed to do this, save for the disaster at

Matanzas Bay. But she could no longer maintain control of the Caribbean.

Through d'Esnambuc France had gained a footing in the islands in 1625. Richelieu came to power in that year and embarked on his task of making France a great power. D'Esnambuc appealed to the Cardinal through some of his friends, informing him of the fertility and richness of the Antilles, and His Eminence decided to form a company which might meet the expense of a first expedition. The Company of St. Christopher, which Richelieu founded, did little for the colony. It collapsed in · 1635, when it was superseded by the Company of the Isles of America. In that year the French settled in the islands of Martinique and Guadeloupe.

In these various ways it came about that between 1625 and 1640 Holland, France and England established themselves firmly in the Eastern Caribbean. The French and English colonies were founded primarily to produce tropical crops for the mother country. These ventures cost money, as the Spanish and Portuguese knew only too well. As we have seen, the Spanish and Portuguese Crowns took the initiative in founding colonies, encouraging those with capital to participate by offering large grants of land. Holland set up two great trading companies and gave them powers of a kind that the Spanish Crown had jealously kept to itself. France used the chartered company as an agent, the company usually being formed on the initiative of the Crown. In the case of England, the initiative for forming the Company generally came from the private sector. The period was one in which the tightly organised financial institutions of the Middle Ages, such as the Guilds of Merchants, were giving way to institutions that were more flexible, like the joint stock company in which anyone with the money could buy shares. The Crown gave its support, chartered the company, even took shares in it; but the initiative and the bulk of the capital came from private enterprise. On occasion also the Crown made use of a practice that derived from feudal times, granting territory to a nobleman who in this way became the proprietor and had the right to appoint the governor and other officials. Carlisle for example was made proprietor of Barbados by Charles I. The ease with which these grants were made underlines the fact that at this period the Crown attached relatively little importance to the business of colonisation.

In the 1630's the profits from the settlements came chiefly from tobacco. In 1627, two years after landing on St. Kitts, Thomas Warner sent his first crop of tobacco to London, ten tons in weight. In the following year a report to the Earl of Carlisle put the total export of tobacco from St. Kitts and Barbados from the time of settlement at 100,000 lbs. Indigo, cotton and some ginger were also produced but tobacco was the money maker; so much so that a tract-writer of the period wished that the Caribbees might come to be called the Unfortunate Islands ' in that they produce nothing but stinking tobacco '.

The proprietors and companies turned to England for their labour force. There were good reasons why at that time Englishmen and, to a lesser degree Frenchmen, should wish to emigrate. A measure of inflation had set in early in the 17th century in England, prices were rising, and the country with its four million people appeared to have too many people and too few jobs. Jobs and land were to be found across the Atlantic. There also one might find refuge from religious persecution or from the debtors prison or from harsh landlords. West Indians know from their own experience how powerful is the urge to self-betterment by emigration. In the 1880's they began to migrate to Panama. In the decades that followed they made their way to Costa Rica to work on the banana plantations that were being established there and in the 1920's they went to Cuba to work on the sugar plantations. In the same period they emigrated to the cities of the United States and in the decade of the 1950's more than 150,000 went to Britain. These people all found the money to meet the costs of migration. But each year there are also those farm-workers who go on contract, to work at some specified task for a limited period of time. In the middle years of the last century large numbers of East Indians came to the West Indies in this way, under a system of contract or indenture. In the 17th century it was the Englishman who came to the islands under contract, as an indentured servant; but in that period there were few safeguards for the man who signed a form of indenture. What he did in fact was to sell himself for a period of years, usually five in the case of the English, three years or less in the case of a Frenchman. The system of indenture was widely used to provide the islands and the North American colonies with a labour force and a population; for at the end of the period of indenture the servant received a small sum of money and a grant of land. It is estimated that during the thirty years from 1654 to 1684 as many as 10,000 indentured servants sailed from the port of Bristol alone to the mainland and the Caribbean, and that about one-half of all who migrated from England to the mainland went as indentured servants. The terms are set out in an early description of Barbados:

> It is the custom for a Christian servant to serve four years, and to enjoy his freedom; and (which he hath dearly earned) £10 sterling or the value of it in goods if his master be so honest as to pay...

The system was wide open to abuse, for many masters took the view that they should get all they could out of the servant for the time they had him. Ligon, writing of Barbados in the 1650's, said that the slaves and their posterity, being subject to their masters for ever, were preserved with greater care than the servants who are theirs for five years. This savage treatment led some servants, Henry Morgan for example, to run away. Others rebelled.

At the end of his period of indenture the servant became both landholder and labourer, working in his field of tobacco or indigo with such help as he could afford. The picture in the 1640's is that of island communities that were predominantly white, made up of some merchants, some large landholders and a very large number of small-holders. In 1645 there were in Barbados, the most developed of the colonies at that time, 11,200 property holders out of a total population of 46,000. By then clouds were gathering. Quality tobacco from Virginia was taking the market away from the islands. Tobacco prices fell. In the island of St. Kitts, which had been divided between the English and French, the danger of over production was so great that in 1639 Warner and de Poincy, the governor of the French part, agreed that all tobacco plants on that island and on other islands under their control should be destroyed, and that no new planting should take place for 18 months. The slump in tobacco was a severe blow, for a small patch of tobacco could keep a small-holder. For a brief period indigo offered some hope as an alternative crop but it yielded small profit. Colonists began to move out to other islands. Some turned to privateering or joined ventures elsewhere, in Tortuga and later in Jamaica.

CHAPTER 9

Pirates' Nests and Plantations

In the Caribbean at this time (1600–1660) colonisation wore many faces. The new faces in the eastern islands were those of the white smallholders making homes and planting tobacco, indigo, cotton. Tentative lines of communication ran from the patches and clearings around Basseterre and Bridgetown to Dieppe and Nantes, to London and Bristol, to the counting houses of merchants who had put money into the venture and to the departments of government where companies were given their charters and bankrupt noblemen given islands from which to extract an income. Very different were the new faces in Hispaniola and on desolate shores in the western Caribbean. Among these the 'cowcatchers' were on their own. Their support lay in partnership with other men who served no interest but their own, kept no code but that which they made, established their right to territory with a cutlass and musket. These in an unplanned disorderly way rooted themselves in Tortuga and in parts of Hispaniola, establishing the foundations of the French colony of St. Domingue. Out of camps on the coast of Campeachy and Honduras came the colony of British Honduras.

One of the great historians of the Caribbean, Jean Baptiste du Tertre, described the cowcatchers and buccaneers of Hispaniola in his *General History of the French Antilles*, two volumes of which were published in Paris in 1667. He had been soldier and sailor before becoming a priest, and although he concentrated chiefly on the French Antilles he described the ways in which a new kind of society began to take shape in our lands. In Dr Elsa Goveia's words:

> His book vividly recreates the turbulent precarious life of the early colonisers; their physical environment and the changes wrought by them in the new lands which they occupied; the extraordinary events by which their fortunes were changed...The whole tremendous work...is in fact a kind of encyclopaedia in which the attempt is made to explain a strange new society, where colonists, free Indians, indentured servants, slaves, buccaneers, Catholics, 'heretics' and Jews mingled in a fascinating exoticism under tropical skies.

Du Tertre says that the buccaneers were so called from the word *boucan*, a sort of wooden grid-iron made of several sticks placed on four forks, on which the *boucaniers* grilled their hogs. They inhabited parts of the northern and western coasts of Hispaniola which the Spaniards had depopulated.

> The greater part had sought refuge in these places and were reduced to this way of life to avoid the punishments due for the crimes which they had committed in Europe and which could be proved against many of them. In general they were without any habitation or fixed abode, but only rendez-voused where the cattle were to be found. They bartered hides and smoked meat for wine, brandy, gunpowder and bullets.

The Spanish governors in Hispaniola made occasional raids against these outlaws, using mobile lancer squadrons, and they tried to starve them out by destroying the wild animals or driving them away. Action provoked reaction, and Spain became the most hated enemy of the buccaneers. As they became more established they developed a code of regulations of their own, to which they adhered. By 1630 Tortuga, a small rock-bound island off the coast of Hispaniola, was becoming known as one of their chief bases.

At this point the buccaneers became associated with Puritans who were attempting to found a colony in the south west of the

Caribbean. The promoters had been concerned with the colonisation of Virginia, and the Bermudas. Among the leaders was Robert Rich, Earl of Warwick, who had also been a party to privateering raids against the Spaniards, and who aimed at making profits from founding a colony that would serve for planting tobacco and as a base for raiding Spanish shipping. Warwick, his associate John Pym and others chose for their purpose an uninhabited island which they called Providence, off the coast of Honduras. In the hands of an enemy, Providence threatened Spain's nerve centre on the Isthmus of Panama and the main Spanish shipping route from Cartagena and Porto Bello to Havana. That the English were able to hold this base for even a few years indicates how weakened Spain had been by her war with the Dutch. Warwick and his group planned to settle Providence as a Puritan colony, but it proved difficult to attract Puritan settlers. Instead, disgruntled colonists from the Bermudas moved in, and privateering became as important as planting.

Links were soon formed between the two foreign strongholds in the Central Caribbean, Providence and Tortuga. The relationship was established by Anthony Hilton, who had been with Warner in St. Kitts, and who later, finding Warner's authority too oppressive, led a group of colonists to Nevis. After the Spaniards attacked Nevis in 1629 Hilton and a party of adventurers moved to Tortuga. He got financial backing for his enterprise from Warwick, and as a result of their agreement Tortuga came under the control of the Providence Company. In 1635 a Spanish force captured Tortuga and wiped out most of its inhabitants. At the same time another Spanish naval force failed in an attack on Providence, which rapidly became popular with privateers and smugglers. By 1636 Warwick and his group were actively pressing a design against Spain in the form of a West India Association which was to include all the English colonies in the Caribbean. Sea captains from Boston and Salem frequented the island, there was a brisk trade with Indians on the Honduras coast, and a Dutch Captain Blauvelt, whose name survives in the Gulf of Honduras as Bluefields, brought back encouraging reports of a possible route to the Pacific by way of the Lake of Nicaragua. On the island black slaves produced cotton and tobacco for export. With the arrival of Governor Nathanial Butler in 1637 Providence became more committed to raids against Spanish cities than to agriculture. In 1638 colonists from Providence established small settlements in the Bay Islands, including Ruatan. From other parts of the Caribbean the news was reassuring. The cowcatchers who had taken refuge from a Spanish attack against Tortuga in 1635 were returning to the island from their hiding places in the forests of Hispaniola. But in 1640 Providence saw the English lose their ascendancy in Tortuga to the French under Le Vasseur, an expert military engineer who had taken a party of Huguenots from St. Kitts to the island, which he brought under his control and governed up to the time of his assassination in 1653. Providence was left in an exposed position. The colony was given a respite in 1639 when Admiral Martin Tromp smashed a large Spanish fleet in English waters in the Downs, a roadstead by the Goodwin Sands, and again in 1640 when a Dutch fleet from Pernambuco defeated a Spanish fleet in four days of fighting off Itamaracas. In 1639 Providence defeated a Spanish force under the Governor of Cartagena, but in the following year, 1640, Don Pimienta attacked the island and compelled the colonists to surrender.

Tortuga, on the other hand, survived its disasters. In 1640 de Poincy, the French governor of St. Kitts, solved the problem of keeping peace between the Huguenots and Catholic factions on the island, by sending Le Vasseur and a party of Huguenots, as we have seen, to establish French ascendancy there. He succeeded in making himself Governor, thus securing a second strategically valuable base on the northern rim of the Caribbean. The Spaniards took the island by storm after Le Vasseur's death, and stationed a garrison there. With Providence and Tortuga retaken, Spain had repaired the great breach that her enemies had opened up in the Central Caribbean.

But not for long. Cromwell had his eyes fixed on the Indies as a step toward empire and also toward making London a centre for world trade, supplanting Amsterdam. There was popular appeal in the proposal to attack Spain in the Indies. There was advocacy and public support enough, so in 1654 preparations were put in hand. At the close of the year 2,500 men were hurried to Portsmouth as recruits for an expedition that was in many respects a strange combination of planning and improvisation, involving seasoned sailors and an undisciplined soldiery, divided authority and confusion of purpose. Early in 1655 the fleet dropped anchor in Bridgetown, and without delay the commanders, Admiral Penn and General Venables, set about ' eating up the island '; a pleasant pastime since Barbados had declared for the Royalists. Venables drafted 4,000 men and another 1,200 men were taken aboard in the Leeward Islands. The instructions given to the commanders were that they should attack first either Puerto Rico or Hispaniola, and then either Cartagena or Havana ' which is the back door of the West Indies and will obstruct the passing of the Spaniards Plate Fleet into Europe.' Santo Domingo was selected as the objective; and the Spaniards in their anxiety to bolster the city's defences withdrew the small garrison from Tortuga, leaving it free yet again to the buccaneers. At Santo Domingo the English commanders made a disastrous mistake in landing the soldiers at too great a distance from the city, some thirty miles or so. No thought had been given to supplying them with water and food. The troops, ill-equipped and poorly trained, were soon thrown into a panic by small bands of Spanish lancers and cowcatchers. Only the landing of a party of sailors to cover the retreat prevented a massacre.

Cromwell was not the kind of man to whom one returned with a report of failure. The expedition sailed on to Jamaica which at the time had about 1,500 Spanish settlers. Morale was low in the island. There had been a series of quarrels between governors and the church authorities. The coastal settlements had suffered so frequently from pirates' raids that the sight of a sail at sea spread fear. Twice the capital, Spanish Town, had been sacked. When Cromwell's ships appeared off Passage Fort on May 10, 1655 they found the Spaniards ready to negotiate. The island became an English colony. But it had not yet been conquered. Cristobel Isasi, a resolute Spanish leader, organised the black people, most of whom had been slaves, into guerilla bands. They fought from bases in the St. John's district of St. Catherine, where a mountain bears the name of one of the leaders, Juan de Bolas; from Vera-Mahollis, and from forested heights on the north coast. Cuba and Mexico sent help, but too little. Spain could not intervene because her navy had been virtually destroyed by Blake at Santa Cruz in the Canaries in 1657. But the blacks and the handful of Spaniards held out for five years. Not until Juan de Bolas saw that the struggle was futile did the guerilla war come to an end and Jamaica pass under English rule. The skill and courage of the blacks foreshadowed what was to come in the Maroon wars, in which black people of the new world gained their first independence struggle.

Jamaica did not begin as a planting colony like Barbados and St. Kitts. During a century and a half of Spanish rule it had attracted few Spanish colonists, so that the total population at the time of the English conquest was of the order of 2,500, including women, children and slaves as well as colonists. According to the Abbot of Jamaica most of the year was taken up with killing wild cattle to get the hides and fat. There were large herds of swine also, common to all who wished to hunt them for lard and pork which, when dried in the sun, was called 'jerk pork'. The English soldiers had to learn how to catch their food and how to adjust to the climate; otherwise, as one put it, they ran the risk of 'starving in a cooks shop'. Of the original 7,000 about one half died in the first six months and the island gained a bad reputation as a place of deadly fevers and dysentery. Also, there was the risk of swift night raids by the Maroons. In 1661 generous grants of land were offered to anyone who would undertake to plant them but there were few takers. Such settlers as came were mostly from Barbados and the Leeward Islands. The flow from the Eastern Caribbean increased after 1664, when a Barbados planter, Thomas Mody-ford, was made Governor of Jamaica, and was given powers to ratify the original grants and to throw open very nearly half a million acres that had been reserved to the Crown ' for the better encouragement of the planters and those who will plant within five years...' Just over 200,000 acres of land were granted by letters patent over a five year period, but little of it was planted.

It is of interest to compare the development of Jamaica and of the French colony in Hispaniola during these years. The appointment of the Barbados planter Thomas Modyford to the Governorship of Jamaica in 1664 is parallelled by the appointment of an unsuccessful sugar planter of Martinique, Bertrand d'Ogeron as Governor of Tortuga in 1665. Modyford aimed at making Jamaica a centre for trade in goods and in slaves with Spanish America and a base for privateering. D'Ogeron, in keeping with Colbert's policy of developing and expanding French power in the Caribbean, was instructed to use Tortuga as a base for establishing a French Colony in Hispaniola. He reported to Colbert that the seven or eight hundred Frenchmen in the island were scattered in remote inaccessible places in small groups, recognising no authority, committing 'a thousand brigandages'. He succeeded in attracting numbers of the French filibusters back to Tortuga, while many of the English moved to Port Royal, with the result that these two places became notorious as centres of buccaneering. At the same time he developed a number of orderly settlements on Hispaniola itself, at places on the west coast such as Petit Goave and Leogane. At about the same period therefore permanent settlements began to take hold in Jamaica and in what was to become St. Domingue, while buccaneering was centred on Port Royal and Tortuga. Each Governor, carrying out his government's policy, used the buccaneers as allies. This was all very well when the common enemy was Spain, but the policy became yet another cause of division in the already fragmented Caribbean when France, Holland and English got at each other's throats in the 1660's. This aspect of Caribbean history indicates how at every point separatism and rivalry were engendered in the Caribbean as a consequence not only of national but even of sectional interests.

The buccaneers based on Port Royal had their heyday in the 1660's especially in the years following 1664 when the second Dutch war broke out between England and Holland. Charles II knew that Louis XIV was likely to join the Dutch, and in order to enlist the help of the buccaneers in the Caribbean Modyford was given the power to grant commissions of reprisal to buccaneer captains, their pay being the plunder they got. This meant that the burden of defending the English islands rested mainly on white militias with the buccaneers used as a striking force at sea. But the buccaneers could not easily be fitted into policies and purposes that were not of their making and offered them little loot. They proved useless in St. Kitts where the French colonists, aided by Irish white servants who hated their English masters, won possession of the island in 1666. More than 8,000 English settlers became displaced persons, refugees seeking shelter and land in Jamaica, Virginia and even in Nevis. The buccaneers took St. Eustatius from the Dutch but lost it a few months later to the French. They refused to attack Curaçao. The English retrieved the situation in the Eastern Caribbean after losing all their colonies save Nevis and Barbados, not through the buccaneers but through the arrival in 1667 of a small naval squadron under Berry. This enabled the Barbadians to take the offensive and to recapture Antigua and Monserrat. In contrast, in 1667 the buccaneers undertook and carried out with great efficiency—and with great brutality also—a campaign in Central America in which they penetrated far up the San Juan river and took the town of Granada. In 1688 Morgan, a Welsh indentured servant who had run away from bondage in Barbados, raided Cuba. He sailed to the Isthmus where he took strongly fortified Puerto Bello, then returned to Port Royal with a quarter of a million pieces of eight. His desperadoes recounted horrifying tales of how Morgan locked up the Spanish garrison in a fort and blew them to pieces. In 1669 Morgan sailed from Port Royal with ten ships and 1,000 men, bypassed Cartagena which had been his first objective, took Maracaibo and on his way back to Port Royal captured three Spanish warships carrying treasure. In 1671 he set out with an even larger force, including French buccaneers from Tortuga, made a nine-days march across the Isthmus to the city of Panama, plundered and utterly destroyed the city and returned with rich booty and pieces of eight. But English merchants were beginning to see that buccaneering was the death of trade and that the great rivals were the Dutch and the French, not the Spaniards. After protracted negotiations both countries signed the Treaty of Madrid in 1671, each agreeing to abstain from pillage and to revoke all letters of marque and reprisal. For the first time Spain acknowledged the presence of the English in the Caribbean. Modyford was recalled and a new Governor, Thomas Lynch, sent out to ensure that the new policy was carried out. Raiding continued, but the peak period was over for the buccaneers of Port Royal, and in 1680 even Morgan turned policeman, offering his old associates the choice between a grant of land and a gibbet on which to swing at Port Royal.

Tortuga, however, remained a centre of buccaneering up to the end of the century. The French government used them during the Third Dutch War from 1672–1678 and kept them as a striking force, backed up by a strong French fleet, as a way of pressurizing Spain to recognise the French colony of St. Domingue. Some of Morgan's old comrades joined the French on Tortuga, serving under buccaneers whose name filled the Caribbean with terror; de Grammont who established himself near Maracaibo for six months; de Maintenon who plundered the Margarita pearl fisheries and invested the profits in a sugar plantation and factory in Martinique; van Horn and de Graaf who took and sacked Vera Cruz in 1683. To the protests of Spain against open robbery and murder were added those of Holland and England, for no shipping was safe from the buccaneers. In 1673 the Dutch had agreed with Spain in the Treaty of the Hague to stop raiding. The English had agreed the same in 1680 in the Treaty of Windsor. Finally France in the Treaty of Ratisbon agreed that all hostilities should cease on both sides ' within Europe and without, both on this side of and beyond the Line '. A new Governor, du Cusse, was sent to Saint Domingue to carry out the new policy. He did this by buying out the leaders. De Graaf, like Morgan, was bribed into the royal service and like Morgan he took a hand in putting down his former associates. And from Saint Domingue he went on to become a founder of the French colony of Louisiana in the early 18th Century.

In these two colonies of Jamaica and Saint Domingue piracy gave way to planting; but to a new kind of planting, that of the slave and sugar plantation. The buccaneers had their origins in those years when Barbados and St. Kitts were becoming a home for white smallholders. They were at the height of their power in the Caribbean in the years when Dutch traders and English planters were transforming Barbados and St. Kitts into sugar and slave plantations. In the period from 1650–1700 they exacted a terrible toll in cities ravaged, in human anguish, in the destruction of men, women, children. They used the islands as places of refuge but they had no home. They rejected loyalty. Violence was their method, plunder their purpose. Yet the powers of Europe made allies of these ruffians, gave legal authority to their lawlessness, added the royal name to the meanest theft, sanctioned robbery, rape, murder. The cost in the destruction of towns in human suffering and life was beyond computation. So was the toll that was to be taken by the system of production which we will now consider based on slavery and the sugar plantation.

CHAPTER 10

Black Labour for White,
Planter for Peasant

Black became the dominant colour in the Caribbean in the middle years of the 17th century, between 1654 and 1665. In that period also the pattern of West Indian society that was to endure for more than two centuries was set not only for the English-speaking Caribbean but for the whole archipelago. The dynamic moulding forces were slavery and the sugar plantation. These two institutions brought into being and supported a society made up of two distinct groups different in race, cultural background, religion, history. Both groups were immigrant in character, one under compulsion. Their way of life, their relationship with each other, the codes of law, the political and religious institutions were modified and changed by the twin systems of slavery and sugar monoculture, with the result that Caribbean society developed special characteristics of its own. Many of these characteristics remain a part of contemporary Caribbean society. When we turn our eyes to this seminal period we begin to see why it is that a Jamaica Census of twenty years ago shows that out of 66,000 landholdings in the island, only 16,000 were over ten acres in size and 6,000 were over twenty-five acres in size; why in St. Kitts the bulk of the land is in the hands of a small number of people; why West Indian agriculture is based on very large estates and very small holdings, with few middle sized farms; why in 1969 in St. Lucia the bulk of the bananas exported was produced by eleven growers out of a total of 15,765 growers; why Barbados and Antigua, Jamaica and Haiti and almost every other Caribbean island are black islands; why the archipelago is the only part of the new world in which black people make up the majority.

As we watch the unfolding of events it is well to bear in mind that we are looking at the beginnings of a new kind of society, our West Indian society. It was the slave-and-sugar plantation that transformed the islands into 'industrial' colonies devoted to the production of a single commodity, sugar. How did this come about? Why did the islands move from a diversified system of agriculture, with cotton, tobacco and indigo, to a one-crop system, for the production of sugar? How was it that within twenty years the population structure of Barbados changed from one with a white majority to one with an overwhelmingly large black population? And how did it happen that in the same period an island of small proprietors became one of large landholders?

The change began with a fall in the price of tobacco, the mainstay of Barbados and St. Kitts, though the Barbados tobacco was of poor quality. West Indians have often been taught how precariously placed they are, being small producers dependent on external markets over which they have no control. The first lesson was given in the late 1630's when Virginia tobacco, better in quality and greater in quantity, took the London market. In 1637 King Charles instructed the Carlisle trustees that they should forbid all trade with foreigners and that only the best quality tobacco was to be exported from the islands. We have seen how, Warner and de Poincy ordered that all tobacco cultivations in the island were to be destroyed and that there should be no new planting for a period of eighteen months. With production cut and trade with foreigners forbidden, the tobacco islands were in trouble.

The Dutch came to the rescue, the island trade being very much to their advantage. They suggested sugar. Aggressive traders, they were willing to give credit and they had the shipping. Colbert estimated in 1664 that out of a total European merchant shipping fleet of 20,000 tons the Dutch had 16,000 tons. The Dutch indeed were more than traders, as far as sugar was concerned. They, and Portuguese Jews from Brazil, were pioneers in introducing the technology of sugar production into the islands. Martinique was first. The French Company of the Isles of America made a contract in 1639 with a Dutch trader from Rouen, Trezel, to establish sugar cultivation there but the attempt failed. A few years later Charles Houel, a shareholder in the Company, started a sugar plantation and in 1647 he set up a sugar factory. Early in the 1660's sugar refineries were established with the help of Dutch refugees from Brazil, and the Dutch kept a close hold on the industry and the trade until Colbert came to power in France. He reorganised the colonies, using as his agent the Company of the West Indies which he established in 1664. To this Company he gave a monopoly of trade and navigaiton in the Caribbean, as well as the administration of all French possessions in America and West Africa.

Pieter Brower is credited with bringing the first canes from Brazil to be planted in Barbados. For several years the only use of the cane was to make cane-juice, our cane-liquor. Attempts at sugar manufacture in the island began in 1642, with the result that the slave-and-sugar plantation was established in the Eastern Caribbean. We are fortunate in having an eye witness account of what happened in Ligon's *History of Barbados*.

> At the time we landed on this island, which was in the beginning of September 1647, we were informed...that the great work of sugar-making was but newly practised by the inhabitants there. Some of the most industrious men, having gotten plants from Fernambock, a place in Brasill, and made tryall of them at the Barbados and finding them to grow they planted more and more...till they had such a considerable number as they were worth the while to set up a very small Ingenio, and so make tryall what sugar could be made upon that soyl. But, the secrets of the work not being well understood, the Sugars they made were very inconsiderable, and little worth for two or three years. But they finding their errors by their daily practise...and by new directions from Brasill, sometimes by strangers and now and then by their own people who...were content sometimes to make a voyage thither, to improve their knowledge in a thing they so much desired... And so returning with more

plants and better Knowledge, they went on upon fresh hopes, but still short of what they should be more skilful in; for at our arrival there, we found them ignorant in three main points that much conduced to the work, viz. The manner of Planting, the time of Gathering and the right placing of their coppers in their furnaces, as also, the true way of covering their rollers with plates or bars of iron... At the time of our arrival we found many Sugar-works set up, and at work; but yet the Sugars they made were but bare Muscovadoes, and few of them Merchantable commodities; so moist, and full of molasses and so ill-cured, as they were hardly worth the bringing home for England. But about the time I left the Island, which was in 1650, they were much bettered... Besides they were grown greater proficients, both in boyling and curing them and had learnt the knowledge of making them white, such as you call lump sugars here in England.

Oviedo had listed the imperatives of sugar and Ligon's listing which is similar, makes clear the considerable capital outlay required. Today the air traveller, flying down the archipelago, sees the same imperatives drawn out on the landscape, the extensive checker board of fields sea-green with cane or brown with stubble; the characteristic combination of factory and field, underlining the fact that sugar-cane is a crop but sugar is an industrial product that must be processed within forty-eight hours of reaping lest the juice begin to ferment in the stalk; ground provisions planted on marginal land; rolling stock and power lines. Ligon listed the essentials on Thomas Modyford's Barbados estate; 500 acres of land, dwelling house, factory buildings, stables, storehouses, smithy, houses for the ' Christians ', and shacks for the slaves, and with a system of land use that allowed 200 acres for sugar, 80 acres for pasture, 120 for woodland from which to feed the furnaces, 70 acres for growing corn, plantains, potatoes, cassava.

Ligon gives examples of those who, having money to invest, made a fortune. One of those was Colonel James Drax,

whose beginning upon that island was founded upon a stock not exceeding £333 sterling, has raised his fortune to such a height, as I have heard him say that he would not look towards England, with a purpose to remaine there the rest of his life till he were able to purchase an estate of tenne thousand pound land yearly; which he hoped in a few years to accomplish, with what he was then owner of; and all by this plant of Sugar. Colonell Thomas Modiford, has often told me, that he had taken a Resolution to himselffe not to set his face for England till he made his voyage and employment there worth him a hundred thousand pounds sterling; and all by this sugar plant.

With money to be made, the sugar fever spread. In St. Kitts the French governor was reported to have had set up six sugar mills, some of them in the neighbourhood of Cayon. There were complaints from the islands that not enough foodcrops were being planted because of the growing dominance of sugar. Where tobacco and cotton had been the currency, sugar became the new money, supplanting the others. Christopher Jeaffreson, writing from St. Kitts in 1676, noted that ' indigo of late has yielded small profit ' and ' I see everybody that is able, working upon sugar, which is certain gaine '.

As in Brazil, the introduction of the sugar industry was much more than the establishment of a new crop or of a new industry. The change over from tobacco cultivation to sugar production carried with it a change over from one system of land-ownership and land-use to another, from one kind of society to another. Nowhere is the contrast put more vividly than in a study of the tobacco and sugar industries in Cuba, *Cuban Counterpoint*, by Fernando Ortiz. Tobacco, he writes, requires constant care and intensive cultivation but it can be grown profitably in patches by smallholders without capital, since it can be processed without costly equipment. Sugar calls for cultivation in large units; intensive against extensive agriculture; steady work on the part of a few and intermittent jobs for the many; the immigration of whites on the one hand and the slave trade on the other; skilled against unskilled labour; hand versus arm; men versus machines; the cultivation of tobacco on smallholdings and sugar bringing with it the latifundia, the estates and huge land grants. Within a few years of the introduction of sugar into Barbados the supply of land for indentured servants ran out. In 1647 the Earl of Carlisle gave notice that there was no more land available in the island for those servants who had completed their term of indenture. Those with money bought out the smallholders, of whom there were nearly 12,000 in 1645. By 1665 the number of landholders had fallen to 750. Land ownership was concentrated in the hands of a relatively small group of owners, and thousands of white peasants emigrated to New England, Guadeloupe and Martinique, Jamaica and the Carolinas. A century later the Governor of the Leeward Islands reported that ' it is here as it is elsewhere, the larger fish swallow up the small. The estates of the poor cotton planter which were contiguous to sugar estates have been swallowed up by them.' The large fish were everywhere and the small had no chance, even when backed by a Governor. The year 1676, in which Jeaffreson made his report about St. Kitts turning to sugar, was the year of the Treaty of Breda by which the French ceded their part of St. Kitts to the English. The Governor saw the opportunity of building a community of white smallholders alongside the plantations, and he proposed that the land in the interior should be divided into estates of 200 acres each to be offered for sale to owners who would undertake to keep a certain number of white servants; and that lots of ten acres should be distributed free to white families that undertook each to supply a man for the militia. The second part of the proposal was scrapped.

The first radical change was the absorption of smallholdings into estates. It proceeded swiftly because these were the ' fat years '. By 1666 Barbados had increased its wealth sevenfold. But the land was of little value without a labour force. The estate drove out the small white smallholder. A swiftly expanding market was created for black labour. The money that could buy a white servant for ten years could buy an African for life. At first the white labourer was still used in work that required certain manual abilities or technical skills. But as soon as the slaves were trained in all the trades his only recourse was emigration. It was not a question of negro and white, of European and African, but of underpaid as opposed to expensive labour. The problem was not racial but social and economic. In 1643 there were 6,000 African slaves in Barbados. There were 20,000 in

1655, 40,000 in 1668, 64,000 in 1672. By 1698 there were some eighteen slaves to every white man in Barbados. In Antigua the same sort of change took place; in 1707 just under 3,000 whites to about 13,000 blacks, and in 1774 2,590 whites to 27,800 blacks, or one to fifteen. In 1707 English St. Kitts had approximately two blacks to one white, in 1774 (when St. Kitts was wholly British) twelve blacks to one white. Even the British Virgin Islands, lands not well suited to sugar cultivation, showed a similar change; one white to little more than one black in 1707 and eight blacks to one white in 1774.

Jamaica presented many contrasts to Barbados and St. Kitts. At the time of its capture from Spain in 1655 it had a small population of about 1,500 whites, some 550 negro slaves and 107 free negroes. The first task of the civil government was to attract settlers. Grants of land were offered; Governor Stokes of Nevis and 1,800 settlers had already moved into the island in 1656; but it is reported that of these not eighty remained in 1661. Thomas Modyford and some Barbados planters moved in; and two sets of colonists from Surinam. These were followed by some Jews who also migrated from Surinam. But at this period Jamaica was not a plantation island. Its life was trade and piracy, and some saw these as obstacles to the island's progress. Governor Lynch said that buccaneering encouraged servants to run away, another thought buccaneering ' the only enemy of planting '. By 1670 the island was on the way to a diversified system of agriculture, with some sugar, indigo, dyewood, pimento, and with cocoa walks, cattle and salt ponds. Cocoa was a suitable crop for small farmers. A report on Jamaica by Blome in 1678 described cocoa as ' the principal and most beneficial commodity of the island '. His account reminds us of Barbados in the tobacco years but the Jamaica holdings were much larger. Blome speaks of the cost of establishing cocoa walks of 500 or 600 acres. With six negroes, four white servants and an overseer and cattle he puts the cost at £275 as against that of a sugar estate of 1,000 acres, the figure in that case being of the order of £5,000; and the profit of about £1,000 would not start coming in until the fourth year. But the English were not as experienced in cocoa cultivation as the Spanish. The cocoa walks were wiped out by neglect and disease, so that when Hans Sloane wrote his famous *Natural History of Jamaica* at the end of the 1680's, he reported that there were few cocoa trees left. By that time efforts were being made to start a sugar industry. The pioneer was Thomas Modyford, who brought to Jamaica as Governor the experience he had gained in Barbados as a sugar planter. Modyford knew well that sugar meant large landholdings, and it is possible that he influenced the provisions contained in the Act of the Jamaican Assembly of 1672, by which the earliest settlers could take out patents for as much land as they could plant in five years. The land was virtually tax free, the ' quit rent ' due to the Crown being one penny an acre, and that only on land under cultivation, ' manured '. Even so, Governor Beeston complained ' that no people come '. The white population in 1658 was 4,500; in 1670 it was 8,000; it rose slowly to 9,000 in 1677. In that year the black population, which was 1,400 in 1658, was just over 9,000, about the same as the white. What with disease, a high death rate, the great earthquake of 1691 which destroyed Port Royal, and the devastating raids of du Casse who carried off 1,300 blacks, settlement languished. At the end of the century Jamaica, with 4,400 square miles, produced half as much sugar as did Barbados and the Leeward Islands. But sugar began to take hold. In 1707 John Styles commented on the destruction of the existing small settlements, many being forced to sell their plantations to their Lords and Masters for what they could get or else run from them and leave the island. The number of whites rose from 7,000 in 1694 to 10,000 in 1739; and the number of slaves increased also from 9,500 in 1673 to 99,000 in 1739.

The change in land ownership, in systems of agriculture and in population structure occurred wherever the plantation went. In 1701 Martinique had 6,900 whites, 23,000 blacks and mulattoes; in 1751 the numbers were 12,000 whites, 65,000 negro slaves and 1,413 free mulattoes. In 1726 St. Domingue had 30,000 whites and 100,000 slaves.

As the plantation system expanded the cry for black slaves intensified. In 1518 Judge Alonzo Zuazo had reported to Spain from Hispaniola that ' there is urgent need for negro slaves ' and his words had been echoed by another judge writing from the same island in 1550, that ' Negroes are essential in the Indies '.

The insistence was repeated a century later from the new plantation colonies. In 1647 a correspondent reported of the planters in Barbados that ' the more they buy the better able they are to buy, for in a year and a half they will earn (with God's blessing) as much as they cost '.

In consequence, the Atlantic Slave Trade grew to huge proportions.

CHAPTER 11

The Atlantic Slave Trade

Even at this distance of time the experience of slavery is so recent and so traumatic for people of the Caribbean that an immediate reaction is to shrink from any reference to it. On the other hand many of our writers such as the Cuban, Guillén, and the West Indian, Edward Brathwaite, see it as what it is, a central fact in our history. Seymour of Guyana pictures the time when:

> *the dark sweet crystal owned the land*
> *And if the chattel and the cattle died*
> *There always would be more to take their place;*

the Haitian Jean Briere recalls that:

> *Together we knew the horror of the slave ships*
> *and often like me you feel the cramps*
> *awaking after the murderous centuries*
> *and you feel the old wounds bleed in your flesh.*

Slavery, as an institution, is as old as mankind. It has existed in almost every part of the world and amongst most peoples. In this respect Toynbee has remarked that of the penalisations imposed by man the most obvious, most universal and most severe has been enslavement. The name 'Slav', borne today by so many of the peoples of Eastern Europe, reminds us that at one time they were reduced to slavery by conquest. Many of the great cities of Italy, such as Venice, Genoa and Florence dealt in slaves; Genoa for example, had a trading centre on the Black Sea where Christian slaves were sold. An Old-World trade in African slaves in the middle of the 15th century existed alongside other Mediterranean slave trades. In Africa and in Europe slavery was a fact of life and codes existed for the treatment of slaves. In Africa for example, prisoners of war were enslaved. This was more merciful and less wasteful than killing them. A slave, being the property of a chief or of the head of a family, might be sold. But generally slaves were treated as servants with limited rights, and it was possible for them to move upward into fuller or even complete liberty. In much the same way African slaves in Portugal and in Spain had some rights, however limited. An account published in 1451 says that the Portuguese, finding the blacks ready to become Christians, made no difference between them and their free servants,

> but those whom they saw fit for managing property, they set free and married to women who were natives of the land... Yes, and some widows of good family who bought some of these female slaves either adopted them or left them a portion of their estate...treating them as entirely free...

But there was slavery and slavery; the milder house slavery of Europe and Africa, the harsh punitive slavery of the galleys, and the industrial slavery of Rome in which masses of slaves were worked to death to supply such products as salt from the mines of Sicily. Slavery was not based on race or on colour. It was not limited to Africa. Davidson puts the point clearly;

> European traders sold their fellow countrymen to the overseas states of Egypt and North Africa. Pressurized by the need for European goods, the lords of Africa would sell their own folk to the mariners who came from Europe... Out of this common acceptance of bondage in a feudal situation there would flow, in post-mediaeval times, a common acceptance of the slave trade between the two continents. Thus the African notion that Europe altogether imposed the slave trade on Africa is without any foundation in history. This idea is as baseless as the comparable European notion that institutions of bondage were in any way peculiar to Africa.

Europe and Africa were jointly involved. Yet it is also true that Europe dominated the connection, vastly enlarged the slave trade, and continually turned it to European advantage and to African loss.

The Atlantic Slave Trade was economic in its origins. In a recent study of the Trade, Philip Curtin shows that the Old-World trade in African slaves was neither as small nor as unimportant as some have thought. He estimates that in the seventy-five years between 1450 and 1525, when the trade was limited to the old world, about 75,000 African slaves were involved. The New World trade began with the importation of African slaves into Spanish America and Brazil, and expanded with the development of the plantation system in the Caribbean and in the Deep South.

What numbers are we talking about? Some historians have estimated that 20 million Africans were imported into the new world between 1518 and 1870, when the trade came to an end. Curtin, after a careful study, puts the figure at about ten million. He emphasises that his figures are given ' only as the most probable figures at the present stage of knowledge '. Ten million is three times the population of the Commonwealth Caribbean of today. This trade, in which so many men and women were bought and sold, is central to the history of all the Atlantic peoples, African, European, American. It is not something that affects only Africa, only the Caribbean, only Britain. It affected West Africa by encouraging pillage and warfare among the tribes of that region, and by depopulating large areas, so that by 1850 one-third of the people of African descent lived outside of Africa. Further, it prepared the way for the European colonisation of Africa. As for America, as Curtin points out, ' both North and South Americans who came by way of the slave trade were the most numerous of Old World immigrants before the late 18th century. Today their descendants are the largest racial minority in many countries.'

North America benefitted from a lucrative twin trade in sugar, rum, molasses and in a wide range of plantation supplies, including flour, fish, horses and timber, obtaining from this West Indian trade cash with which to meet her trading debts in Europe.

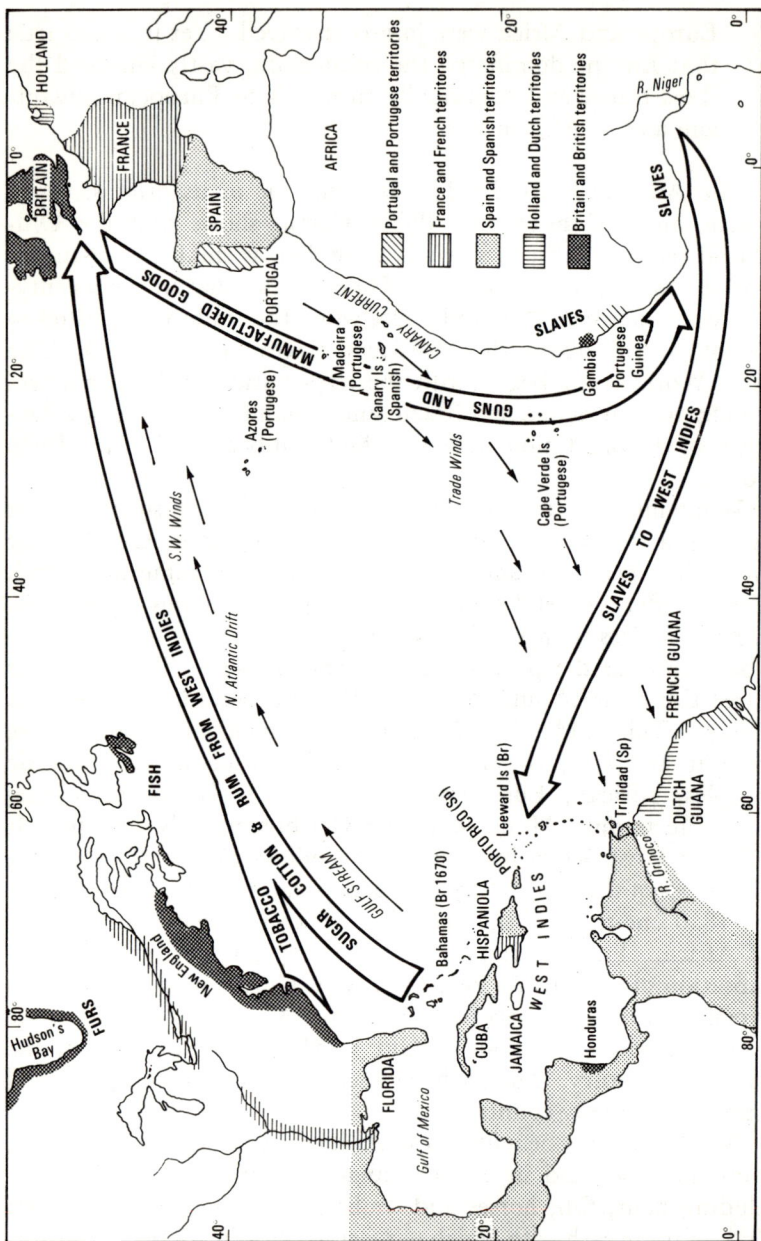

Triangular Trade

In the Caribbean the trade contributed to political fragmentation and island rivalry, and led to the establishment of colonial societies ruled by small white oligarchies committed to racial discrimination. As for Europe, the twin trades in black slaves and sugar provided capital for Europe's industrialisation. In his study *Trade and Politics in the Niger Delta*, the Nigerian historian Anwuka Dike observes:

> In the 18th century economists reckoned that the wealth of the Indies was one of the main supports of the contemporary British empire. This wealth was largely the product of African labour. It is now known that the triangular trade—that is the trade between Britain, West Africa and the West Indies—provided one of the many streams from whence emerged the capital that financed the industrial revolution.

The Atlantic Slave Trade, economic in its origins, was later justified and defended in racial terms. It generated trade, and it also generated ideas and value systems in which merit was ascribed on the basis of skin-colour. There was an important difference between the African and European systems of bondage and the Atlantic Slave Trade, which had no other purpose than that of profit. There was present in it no humane intent such as there may have been in those systems of slavery in which the life of a prisoner of war was preserved; nor was there any shred of morality to it, however flimsy, as in systems that enslaved a man guilty of crimes on the ground that he should pay the penalty for breaking the law. Its sole purpose was the supply and use of man as merchandise, a ' piece of the Indies ', a chattel to be used up and replaced because it was ' cheaper to buy than to breed '. It did not deprive man of half of his manhood but of all of it, for in law the slave was held to be a thing, a chattel; and the only way in which a slave could remain a man was by rejecting the system, whether through subtle forms of labour withheld and of sabotage or through outright rebellion.

The region of Africa that was linked most closely to us by the Trade has a coastline extending from the Senegal River to Benguela. It is inhabited by people of many cultures and languages, some bearing names known and remembered in the Caribbean,

Ashanti, Ibo, Fante, Yoruba, Egba, Efik. The region is usually divided into areas:

Senegambia; Sierra Leone and the Windward Coast; the Gold Coast, now known as Ghana; the Bight of Benin, including Whydah and the Niger delta; the Bight of Biafra, which includes Calabar; Central Africa.

We will consider some aspects of the history and way of life of some of the dominant nations of this region, which is the homeland of the New World black. Before European traders came to this part of Africa the people along the coast had no sea-trade. The great empires, the chief markets and cities lay inland; Timbuktu in the days of the greatness of Ghana when traders from the north exchanged textiles, leatherwork and metalwork with exporters of gold from the forest regions to the south; Jennah and Gao on the middle Niger; and to the east the Hausa City of Kano which exported dyed cloth to many parts of North and West Africa. Whatever the commodity, whether gold, slaves, ivory, salt or kola nuts, the trade routes and trading cities lay inland. Trade and contact stopped at the coast. As we consider the growth of the Atlantic Slave Trade we will find that the development of a sea-trade altered the economy of the region. New trade-routes developed. Trade which had moved inland and then north began to move to the coast and across the Atlantic. Up to 1450 West Africa had one intercontinental trading system based on inland centres. The sea-trade led to the growth of a second trading system in which, as Dike says, ' The coastland became the frontier of opportunity.'

By permission of the African chiefs, the Europeans established forts along the coast. The Dutch, for example, built forts at Cape Coast, Koromantin and Accra among other places; and the name Coromanti came to be applied to those Africans who were shipped from Koromantin. We will refer to Koromantin and the Coromanti when we consider the history of the Ashanti people. There were two chief reasons for the establishment of forts by the Europeans, who were on the coast to trade rather than to attempt conquest. One was the cut throat competition between the white nations, each intent on keeping the trade to itself. The Portuguese then the Dutch and finally the English became the chief traders. Another reason was that the forts

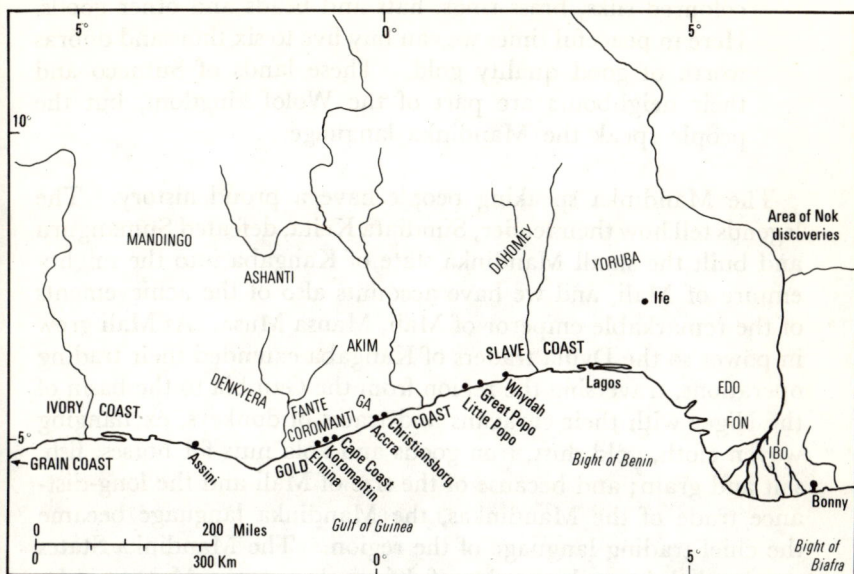

West Africa showing main shipping ports and main tribes shipped to West Indies as slaves

served as bases for buying and keeping slaves, as well as for conducting trade in gold, pepper and other commodities.

Senegambia early became an important source of slaves. Two of the chief people of this region were the Wolofs and the Mandinkas or Mandingoes. European traders soon realised that the Mandingoes were expert traders, and that they belonged to societies with well organised political and social systems. As early as 1506 a Portuguese, Duarte Pereira, reported that his people traded horses, cotton goods and other manufactured goods with the Wolofs in exchange for slaves and a little gold. He described the great markets along the Gambia River:

> At Sutucoo there is held a big market. Mandinka traders came there with many donkeys. And when times are peaceful, these traders visit our ships (in the river) as we sell them red, blue and green cloth of cheap manufacture, linen and

coloured silks, brass rings, hats and beads and other goods.
Here in peaceful times we can buy five to six thousand dobras
worth of good quality gold. These lands of Sutucco and
their neighbours are part of the Wolof kingdom, but the
people speak the Mandinka language...

The Mandinka speaking people have a proud history. The
legends tell how their leader, Sundiata Keita, defeated Sumanguru
and built the small Mandinka state of Kangaba into the mighty
empire of Mali, and we have accounts also of the achievements
of the remarkable emperor of Mali, Mansa Musa. As Mali grew
in power so the Dyula traders of Kangaba extended their trading
operations, traversing the region from the Gambia to the basin of
the Niger with their caravans and trains of donkeys, exchanging
woven cloth, gold dust, iron goods and kola nuts for horses, fish,
salt and grain; and because of the size of Mali and the long-dist-
ance trade of the Mandinkas, the Mandinka language became
the chief trading language of the region. The Mandinka States
were ruled by a hierarchy of Kings, known as Mansas, who
governed through nobles or village chiefs. With the spread of
Islam through this region these officials came to be called al-
cadis—the same term which Spain borrowed from Arabic, and
gave to the mayors of her towns. The al-cadi had power to distribute land, try minor offences and collect the Mansa's revenue.

European traders found that Senegambia was a region of
relative stability. There were wars between tribes from time to
time, as there were wars in Europe at the time. Trade was conducted with great skill. To the south of Senegambia lies a long
stretch of coast often referred to as the Windward Coast because
it was so exposed to the Atlantic. It includes Guinea, Sierra
Leone and Liberia.

The Windward coast has turbulent water and massive breakers.
At Cape Palmas the coast turns and runs east to the Bight of
Benin, Old Calabar and the Bight of Biafra. The largest number of forts and trading posts in this area were on the Gold Coast,
from Assini east to the Volta, for this section of the more sheltered
Leeward Coast offered safe anchorage for ships. The coastal
land is low-lying. Behind are the hills and mountains of the
rain-forest belt, and inland, beyond the rain-forest, the savannah

kingdoms of the Sudanese people. In the 11th and 12th centuries Akan-speaking people moved into this forest belt, mingled with the older inhabitants of the region, and established a number of states that traded in gold with the Savannah kingdoms. The coastal lands were inhabited by small clans and states that owed allegiance to the forest-states. When the Europeans arrived off the coast they traded with these smaller states and sometimes tried to push them around; but, said a report from Accra in the 1680's, the blacks were of a temper ' not to suffer anything to be imposed on them by Europeans '. The most powerful state in the early years of the trade was that of Akwamu, which was overcome by the Ashanti, who built up a strong empire.

Toward the end of the 17th century many units of the Akan people were subject to continual harassment by the Denkyera, who were working closely with the European traders, supplying them with slaves. The various groups of Ashanti could not meet the threat separately. Their only hope lay in organising themselves as a military power. Two great leaders found the answer, Osei Tutu, an outstanding soldier and military statesmen, and a priest, Okomfo Anokye. Ward, in his *History of Ghana*, describes how Osei Tutu led the Ashanti forces to victory over the Doma, and then over the Tafo. He had proved himself as a soldier and he had shown what the Ashanti could do when united. But was the alliance, its immediate objects being attained, to break up again? Ward says ' Okomfo Anokye determined that it must not. He set to work to unite the Ashanti people by providing a common stool, in order that the whole nation might be united in the same way as each section was united through its common stool. He began by taking three cuttings of the kumnini tree and planting one each at Kwaman, Juaben, and Kumawu. Those at Juaben and Kumawu died, the one at Kwaman lived; and this was taken as a sign that Osei Tutu was the leader chosen by the gods to be the permanent head of the nation. Henceforth Kwaman was known as Kumasi, ' under the kumnini tree.'

Having settled this point, Anokye set to work in earnest and the culmination of his efforts was the institution of the Golden Stool. One Friday a great gathering was held at Kumasi; and there Anokye brought down from the sky, with darkness and thunder, a wooden stool adorned with gold, which floated to earth and alighted gently on Osei Tutu's knees. This stool, Anokye announced, contained the spirit of the whole Ashanti nation, and all its strength and bravery depended on the safety of the stool... Whatever we may think of the heavenly origin of the stool the fact remains that somehow or other Anokye succeeded in impressing on the national consciousness that henceforth Ashanti was a nation, linked by a common mystical or religious bond, of which the Golden Stool was the visible symbol. This was the origin of the famous ' Sika Agua Kofi ' (Friday's Golden Stool) of Ashanti which survives today with its unifying power unimpaired.

The Ashanti now embarked on a policy of expansion in order to win a share of the rapidly expanding coastal trade. To the

Ibibio carving

north of them there were forest states that supplied the coast with gold and slaves. On the coast were Fante and Ga people, middlemen who bought from the inland traders and sold to the Europeans. The Fante were expert in playing off African neighbour against African neighbour, European trader against European trader, becoming rich and haughty in the process.

The Denkyera had been active in the trade up to the time when the Ashanti checked them; and in the booty that the Ashanti gained was the ' Note ' or agreement by which Elmina had been leased to the Dutch. This gave the Ashanti direct contact with the European traders. But they had other rivals for dominance in the slave trade. Between 1660 and 1680 the Akwamu, who ruled the region around Accra, controlled the trade. The Akim, who had been allies of the defeated Denkyera, then successfully challenged the Akwamu, and for a short time they even gained ascendancy over the Ashanti; but not for long. By 1775 the Ashanti had become the supreme military power on the Gold Coast. An inland people, they had been able to get European goods, only through middlemen who charged high prices. They needed European goods especially firearms, and they had to pay for these imports by exports; some gold, and slaves. Ward points out:

> The one export commodity that Ashanti could produce in large quantities was slaves. Ashanti thus deliberately became a slave dealing state. Many slaves were bought in the markets of the north, but many were obtained by raiding and warfare, and the great slave market at Hanso, near Cape Coast, was largely kept supplied from the proceeds of the Ashanti wars.

Many of the Africans imported into the Caribbean came from this region, and of all the African names that ring around the Caribbean none sounds more clearly than Ashanti and Coromanti a name given to Gold Coast blacks who were ' the most turbulent and desperate of any on the coast of Guinea '. These people, a West Indian planter reported, were accustomed to war from infancy, were energetic of mind, hard and robust, ' but bringing with them into slavery lofty ideas of independence, they are dangerous inmates of a West Indian plantation '. Codrington,

Governor of the Leeward Islands, spoke of the Coromanti as ' not only the best and more faithful of our slaves but are really all born heroes... There never was a rascal or coward of that nation '. But the Coromanti and Ashanti people wrote their own testimonials in the history of our region, in the Maroon wars and countless slave risings. We will consider these in the chapter on the African protest; and we will find that elements from the culture of all these Twi-speaking people survive and form a part of our heritage; the day names of children, like Cudjo and Quaco; the names of some of our foodcrops like yam and ackee; elements of the Ashanti religion and mythology in the worship of Obi and the stories of the Spider God Ananse.

East of the river Volta is Dahomey. There the Fon people, like the Ashanti, lived inland; there were slaves to be had, and in such numbers that this stretch of coast came to be called the Slave Coast. Along the coast there were small states like Jakin, Whydah, Grand Popo. These traded eagerly with the Europeans, who paid tribute and customs dues to the rulers. A trader, John Barbot, recorded how the King of Great Ardrah was given the value of fifty slaves in goods, and customs duties in respect of each ship. In addition, the King's son was paid the value of two slaves for the right to get water for the crew and the value of four slaves for the right to cut timber.

The Fon people on the inland savannahs were exposed to these slave raiders, and to Yoruba raiders from the Kingdom of Old Oyo. Just as the Ashanti came together to protect themselves against the slave-raiding Akim and Denkyera, so the Fon people came together, grouping themselves under a King and forming a state on military lines. A chief came to power because he was a good leader, successful in war, and not because he belonged to a certain family or clan. Women as well as men had to serve, and the women warriors of Dahomey gained a formidable reputation. In many West African nations the King was regarded as the Father of his people. He was likened to a strong pot, his people to the water in the pot. If the pot was not damaged the water was safe. The Fon people, however, pictured the King's power as the water in the pot. They saw their national life threatened from every side, by Great Ardrah and the coastal states and from Oyo. They thought of these dangers as making holes in the pot. The water, symbolising the power of the king, would be lost if every Fon did not cover a hole with his finger. Every citizen owed a duty to the King. The Fon came together, based their kingdom on the city of Abomey, and under the rule of an outstanding general, Agaja, took and sacked Great Ardrah, Whydah and Jakin. In this way they became a powerful slave trading nation, with direct access to the coastal trade. Some of the small coastal states, though under the overlordship of Dahomey, also continued trading with the Europeans. In his study of Haiti, *Life in a Haitan Valley*, Herskovits says he found practically no trace in the valley of Marbial of Gold Coast or Ivory Coast custom or belief, but that most of the African traits derived from the region of Dahomey, and he points out that even the famous word ' voodoo ' is Dahomean: it is the ' vodun ' of the Fon-speaking people— a word best translated as ' god '.

East of Dahomey, in the region of the Lower Niger, live nations and tribes whose names are remembered by us: Yorubas who inhabit the west part of the forested region of the Lower Niger, the Ibos of the eastern region, Ibibios and Efiks from the Delta of the Niger and the Calabar River. These, like the other people of West Africa, had no knowledge of the arts of writing, and they handed down their history by word of mouth from generation to generation. The Yoruba for example explain their origin in a legend telling how God created man at Ile Ife, the site of their most revered city, and how ages ago some of their ancestors dispersed throughout the earth. Yoruba civilisation was based on settlements and cities in the forest belt, but their oldest state, Oyo, lay to the north, on open grassland country bordering the Hausa states. This position gave Oyo an advantage over the forest states, which were in the Tsetse fly zone. Unlike these, Oyo was able to build up a force of horsemen; and its well-disciplined army enabled it to become a powerful state. By the time Portuguese traders arrived on the coast the Oyo empire was well established, its ruler, the Alafin, being lord of many lands and ' companion of the gods '. One of these Alafin, Sango, was deified as Shango, God of Thunder. The Alafin was not an absolute ruler, however, for he was advised by a Council of seven, called the Oyomesi; and it was in their power to advise any Alafin who behaved tyrannically to ' go to sleep ', that is, to commit suicide.

The Oyomesi were in turn advised by a number of freemen widely respected for their age and their wisdom, so that the administrative system provided for participation by many elements in the society. The other Yoruba states, bound together by ties of language, family and clan, were ruled in the same way as Oyo, power being delegated to princes and governors of provinces.

Old Oyo began to weaken in the second half of the 18th century. Internal division and civil war led to an increase in the number of Yoruba sold into slavery. Some of these people were imported into the Caribbean. In Trinidad for example, they are well represented. Many of those who used to participate in Shango ceremonies referred to themselves as ' Yoruba people ' and to their ceremonies as ' Yoruba work '. De Verteuil, in his *History of Trinidad*, described the ' Yarraba ' in the population as a fine race, tall and well-proportioned, the men working on estates and many of the women engaging in petty trading, or ' higgling ' in the Jamaican phrase.

Ife Terracotta found in 1957

One of the glories of Yoruba civilisation is its sculpture. The most distinguished work was done at Ife, where artists were encouraged to celebrate the work of the ruler, the Oni, and his kinsmen, and produced work that is world famous. Moving along the coast east of Lagos we come to Benin, where Edo people established a trading settlement that grew into a city important both for its military power and its culture. Its artists celebrated the power of its ruler, the Oba, in splendid sculpture, and its craftsmen produced cotton cloth in designs of great beauty. A Dutch trader's account, which dates back to the beginning of the 17th century, described Benin as a city with houses that ' stand in good order one close by and even with the other ', with galleries ' where a man may sit drie; which Gallerie every morning is made clean by their slaves, and in it there is a mat spread for men to sit on '; But as with Oyo, decline set in. Years later another visitor reported that the houses stood widely distant from each other. The tribal wars, the continual raiding for prisoners to supply the slave markets, left the country depopulated. The priests, seeking to check the decline, sacrificed human beings and as the power of the fetish priests grew Benin became a city of blood.

Very different is the history of the States which came into existence in the Delta of the Niger and Cross Rivers. The Ijaw were among the first to begin turning the river banks into settlements, the waterways into roads. Other people, including Ibos, moved in, trading with the Europeans who made their way up the channels, and settlements sprang up at the mouths of the rivers. Gradually as Anwuka Dike points out, a kind of social system developed that was

> neither Benin nor Efik, Ibo nor Ibibio a people apart, the product of the clashing cultures of the tribal hinterlands and of the Atlantic community to both of which they belonged. The tribal Ibos called them People of the Salt Water, and so long as the frontier of trade was confined to the Atlantic seaboard so long did they remain the economic masters of their territories...

In order to gain the strength they needed for the slave trade, and in order to trade as equals with the Europeans, these delta states, some of which were monarchies and others republics, developed a unique kind of social organisation. In order to keep their own identity and yet gain the strength that comes from co-operation, they developed a system of ' Houses '. Each ' house ' was both a co-operative trading unit, says Dike, and also a local government institution. Each was governed by one powerful trader. Each could have many ' houses '. Membership of a house included the ruling family, relations, servants, slaves. In Dike's words, ' Master and servant, the bond and free, all became members of one House, a veritable hierarchy, with numerous graduations, each rank with its duties and responsibilities, its privileges and rewards '. Divisions of language and tribal origin broke down. Houses might have anywhere from a few hundred members to many thousand. House government was oligarchic, and there were secret societies that settled disputes, exercised justice, and functioned as a secret police force. The power of some rulers can be seen in the account given of King Eyo of Calabar, who had many thousand slaves, 400 canoes, each with captain and crew, and who not only carried on an extensive trade but also employed his people reclaiming waste land, founding towns, planting farms. The ' House system ' was flexible enough to allow a slave to become a freeman by hard work. Dike comments that the wealth produced by a slave eventually set him free, ' for the master knew his slave intimately and the value of his work and rewarded him accordingly.'

This brief outline does little more than indicate how long and varied is the history of the peoples of West Africa; how they developed effective systems of social and political organisation; how they gave a place of importance to the artist; how they respected authority and valued justice. It indicates also how profoundly the Atlantic Slave Trade affected this vast region, drawing the West African people into the Atlantic community, changing the base of their economy, altering their social systems, encouraging war and pillaging amongst them. In a later chapter we will identify some of the important elements in the Caribbean way of life that link us to West Africa; but at this point it is appropriate to recall the words of a West Indian, Edward Blyden, who made West Africa his home and, nearly a century ago, wrote that ' Africa is no vast island, separated by an immense ocean from other parts of the globe, and cut off through the ages from the men who have made and influenced the destinies of mankind... Africa has been closely connected, both as source and nourisher, with some of the most potent influences which have affected for good the history of the world.'

CHAPTER 12

Man as Merchandise

The first object which saluted my eyes when I arrived on the coast was the sea, and a slave ship, which was then riding at anchor and waiting for its cargo. These filled me with astonishment which was soon converted into terror which I am yet at a loss to describe. I was immediately handled and tossed up to see if I were sound, by some of the crew, and I was now persuaded that I had got into a world of bad spirits and they were going to kill me. When I looked round the ship too and saw a large furnace of copper boiling, and a multitude of black people of every description chained together, every one of their countenances expressing dejection and sorrow, I no longer doubted of my fate. Quite overpowered with horror and anguish I fell motionless on the deck and fainted.

When I recovered a little I found some black people about me who I believe were some of those who brought me on board and had been receiving their pay. I asked them if we were not to be eaten by those white men with horrible looks, red faces and long hair. They told me I was not. . .

The African who wrote these words, known as Gustavus Vasa and also as Ouladiah Equiano, was born in Benin somewhere about the year 1745. His father, the elder of the village, had a number of slaves. One day, while Ouladiah was playing with his sister near their home, a man and woman dashed out of the jungle and carried off the children. They were sold to different traders. After journeying for some months, and being sold by one trader to another, Ouladiah was taken down river in a large canoe with other slaves and sold to a waiting ship in the way he described. He laboured as a slave in America, then served under an American naval officer, and later was resold as a slave in the West Indies. Slavery did not overcome Ouladiah. He learned to speak English fluently, became an expert barber and seaman, saved enough money to buy his freedom, and finally settled in England where he wrote his Journal. Ouladiah was only one of some ten million or more West Africans who were sold into slavery and transported across the Atlantic.

While we consider various aspects of the system of trade based on the sale of man as merchandise we recognise that we are concerned also with flesh and blood, with human dreams, sufferings, hopes, passions, with human greed, blindness, cruelty. The system of trade that developed grew out of a demand for labour. Negro slavery, as Williams emphasises was ' only a solution in certain historical circumstances, of the Caribbean labour problem. Slavery in no way implied, in any scientific sense, the inferiority of the Negro.' Moreover the Atlantic Slave Trade developed in an age when many aspects of European life were marked by savagery; in France by serfdom, in Britain by penal codes that provided the death penalty for more than one hundred offences, with barbarous punishments, the drawing and quartering of the body, torture, gibbets fouling the countryside with rotting bodies, debtors prisons, demented persons in Bedlam treated as a public spectacle, the raiding of villages by press-gangs to find sailors for the Royal Navy. Even so, the brutalities of the Atlantic Slave Trade and of plantation slavery make bitter reading, for we are concerned with a system in which a man was treated as a piece of merchandise. Thus, the Captain of the *Arthur* of Liverpool reported in 1677 that ' came on board the King of New Calabar with some others of his gentes and after a Long Discourse came to Agreem'tt for Current for Negro man 36 Copper bars; for Negro woman 30...' But though in law the slave was a chattel, a thing, a ' piece of India ', it remained true that he was also a man, able to think, to accept or reject, to feel, to rebel, to love and to hate. The Atlantic Slave Trade begins not with poor men driven by need, not with lawbreakers, but with royalty, the rich and the lawmakers. This applied to European and to African. The Spanish Crown farmed out the right to buy slaves in Africa and to sell them in Spanish America under a system of licences or *Asientos*. The first of the licences was for the supply of 4,000 slaves. That was in 1518. In 1592, the *Asiento* granted to Gomes Reynal was for 4,500 slaves annually for nine years.

To the Spanish Crown the *Asiento* was a valuable source of revenue. The Portuguese Crown, like the Spanish, claimed a monopoly of trade with its newly acquired territories. John II of Portugal, who in 1485 took the title of Lord of Guine, enforced the royal monopoly of the West African trade through licences, contracts and charters to private persons and in 1482 he established in Lisbon the House of the Mine of Guinea *Casa de Mina de Guine* to administer the royal trade and control the licences. In the same year he built the castle of Elmina on the Guinea Coast, making it a place of residence for the Portuguese official who had the task of defending the rights of the Crown and asserting its authority. By the middle years of the 15th century the Portuguese turned from haphazard slave trading to established procedures for the purchase of slaves from West African rulers, and they also opened up new sources of supply in Angola and the Congo. In the process a new trading language came into use, containing words that we know in the Caribbean; pickaninny from *pequenino* very small; *palaver* for talks or discussions; *fetish* from a Portuguese word for charm or sorcery; ' cash ' for a gift or bribe.

The Dutch, English and French developed their trade in African slaves by establishing corporations with special privileges in which private persons were able to take shares. The advantage of this method was that the cost of fitting out ships, employing crews, providing goods for the West African trade, setting up trading posts, purchasing slaves and transporting them to the West Indies was shared by a number of investors. Once it was established, however, private traders gained a substantial share of the trade, and by 1734 the Company's special trading privileges were abolished. The Dutch Company gradually lost its trading monopoly and came more and more to function as an administrative body which got its revenue from war and taxes as well as from commerce, and which in return preserved Dutch interests and provided a framework within which the private traders operated.

French interest in the trade sharpened with the acquisition of West Indian colonies and the development in them of sugar plantations. Colbert established one giant corporation in 1664, the Company of the West Indies, but few private persons put money into the Company. Most of the capital was provided by the Crown or came from public funds. The West Indies Company functioned more like a department of state than a private corporation. Within three years of its founding, from 1666 onwards, private traders were able to buy licences to trade; and in 1672 the Company of Senegal bought out the trading rights for North-West Africa. For a brief period the Senegal Company flourished, acquiring the Dutch trading bases at Goree and Arguim as a result of the French-Dutch war of 1672-8. Thereafter the story of the Company and its successor the Company of Guinea is one of failure. The French consolidated their hold on the Senegal region and both the Company and private traders supplied the Antilles with slaves. It is estimated that in the last quarter of the 17th century the French Antilles imported between 4,000 and 5,000 slaves annually; but the situation changed dramatically in the 18th century as the result of insistent demands from the plantations of Martinique and Guadeloupe and of St.Domingue. Throughout this century the chief French slaving port was Nantes which in some years supplied as much as one half of the slaves, La Rochelle, Rouen and Bordeaux supplying the rest.

Throughout the 18th century the ships of the West Indian Company and of private traders ferried Africans to the Antilles and in small numbers to French Guiana, Puerto Rico and Cuba. Curtin, in his census of the trade, estimates that in the decade of 1711-20 about 46,000 slaves were carried by French slavers. The number very nearly doubled in the following decade and it reached 27,000 in the peak period 1781-90 when St. Domingue became the world's largest sugar producer. Martinique and Guadeloupe took a diminishing number of slaves, St.Domingue an increasing number. At the same time Barbados and the Leeward Islands were taking fewer, and Jamaica with its expanding plantations was taking more. In the 19th century the cycle was to be repeated in Cuba and Puerto Rico, which imported large numbers of Africans when the two islands displaced Haiti and Jamaica as large sugar producers. Another point of similarity between Jamaica and St.Domingue is that since each required slaves urgently, each tended to be less selective, importing from a number of regions, but with the largest number of slaves coming from Benin, the Gold Coast and the Windward Coast.

The English also started by creating chartered Companies; first in 1618 a small Company of Adventurers of London, trading to Guinea and Benin, then a Company of Royal Adventurers in 1660; and finally in 1672 the Royal Africa Company with a monopoly of trade with West Africa. The Royal Africa Company established forts and trading posts on the African coast, transported about 100,000 Africans to the Caribbean, and was finally dissolved in 1725 after being under continual attack from the West India planters and from private traders who strongly opposed its special privileges, claiming that it could not meet the demand for slaves and that it sold at too high a figure.

The Chartered Companies therefore lost ground to private traders; but the words of an agent of the French Royal Company on the Guinea Coast, John Barbot, retained their force, that the Slave Trade was the business of kings, rich men and prime merchants. The words applied to West Africa as well as to Europe, and the African slave Cugoana put into words what many Africans must have thought. Seized as a boy and sold into slavery, he was transported to Grenada. Later, like Equiano, he wrote the story of his life, in which he said:

> I must own, to the shame of my own countrymen, that I was first kidnapped and betrayed by my own complexion, who were the first cause of my exile and slavery; but if there were no buyers there would be no sellers. So far as I can remember some of the Africans in my country kept slaves, which they take in war or for debt; but those which they keep are well, and good care taken of them... But I may safely say that all the poverty and misery that any of the inhabitants of Africa meet with among themselves is far

inferior to those inhospitable regions of misery which they meet with in the West Indies where their hard-hearted overseers have neither regard to the laws of God nor the life of their fellowmen.

On the coast the trade was under the authority of the chiefs and kings. They wanted European manufactured goods, and firearms. The cloth and metalware might be looked on as luxuries, but increasingly the chiefs regarded firearms and gunpowder as necessities; for with muskets one could establish superiority over another tribe and capture slaves, and slaves meant profits. In *Black Mother*, Davidson sums up the position in these words:

> Wherever the trade found strong chiefs and kings it prospered almost from the first; wherever it failed to find them it caused them to come into being. Whether in the accumulation of wealth by customs dues, gifts or trading profits; or in the political authority which slaving lent to those who organised it; or in the military superiority which derived from the buying of firearms, slaving built chiefly power where it did not exist before or else transformed that power where it was already present from a broadly representative character into an autocratic one.

An account of the voyage of the *Albion* to New Calabar River on the coast of Guinea in 1698 includes descriptions of the negotiations with the King of Bonny and of a mutiny among the slaves. The Journal runs:

> On the 26th we had a conference with the King and principal natives of the country about trade which lasted from three o'clock till night without any result, they insisting to have thirteen bars of iron for a male and ten for a female slave; objecting that they were now scarce, because of the many ships that had exported vast quantities of late... Four days later we had a new conference at which the King's brother made us a discourse ending by saying they would be content with thirteen bars for males and nine bars and two brass rings for females, and the next day the trade was concluded on these terms; and the King promised to come aboard and be paid his duties...

Two days afterwards the King sent aboard thirty slaves, men and women, out of which we picked nineteen and returned him the rest, and so from day to day...by degrees we had 648 slaves of all sexes and ages including the sixty-five we purchased at the Gold Coast, all very fresh and sound, very few exceeding forty years of age. The King supplied us with yams and bananas and plantains...

It has been observed that some slaves fancy they are being carried away to be eaten, which makes them desperate, and others are so on account of their captivity, so that if care be not taken they will mutiny and destroy the ship's crew, in hope to get away. One day about one in the afternoon, after dinner, according to custom we caused them, one by one, to go down between decks, to have each his pint of water. Most of them were yet above deck and many of them were provided with knives which we had indiscreetly given them two or three days before... It afterwards appeared that others had pieces of iron which they had torn off the forecastle door... They had also broken off shackles from the legs of several of their companions, which also served them. Thus armed they suddenly fell upon our men and stabbed one of the stoutest, who received fourteen or fifteen wounds from their knives so that he expired shortly. Next they assaulted our boatswain and cut one of his legs so round the bone that he could not move.

Others cut the cook's throat to the pipe and yet others wounded three of the sailors and threw one of them overboard...we stood in arms (on the quarter deck) firing on the revolted slaves, of whom we killed some and wounded many, which so terrified the rest that they gave way and dispersed themselves, some between the decks and some under the forecastle. Many of the most mutinous leaped overboard and drowned themselves with much resolution, shewing no manner of concern for life.

Thus we lost twenty eight slaves, and having mastered them, caused all to go betwixt decks, giving them good words. The next day however we had them all up again on deck and caused about thirty of the ringleaders to be severely whipped by all our men...

The *Albion* having crossed the Atlantic, we are told that

> As soon as a slave ship arrives at a port in the West
> Indies the planters and other inhabitants flock aboard to
> buy as many slaves as they have occasion for. The prices
> being agreed upon, they search every slave, limb by limb,
> to see whether they are sound and strong... This done every
> buyer carries away his slaves and provides them with nou-
> rishment, clothing and health. We sold off all our slaves
> briskly at about seven thousand pounds worth of brown sugar,
> a piece, the Indian pieces, as they term it there, and set
> sail on our return voyage deeply laden with sugar, cotton
> and other goods...

We will not recount here the hideous brutalities of the Middle
Passage, save to refer to the most terrible case of all, that of the
Zong, of Liverpool, of which the Master was Luke Collingwood.
The *Zong* left São Tomé on September 6, 1781 with 400 slaves
and seventeen seamen. Dysentery struck down many of the
crew and slaves. Sixty slaves died, and seven seamen. Many
other slaves were desperately ill. On November 29th having
sighted land in the West Indies, Collingwood told his officers
there was not enough water for all the slaves, that if they died of
thirst the loss would be borne by the owners of the ship, but if
they were thrown into the sea the loss would be covered by insurance, since it would be a legal jettison. The weakest of the
slaves, 133 in number, were picked out. Fifty four were thrown
overboard that day, forty two on the following day. Some days
later twenty six were handcuffed and thrown overboard. The
last ten leaped overboard of their own accord, refusing to let
the sailors come near them. On December 22nd the *Zong*
anchored in Kingston harbour, and Collingwood sold the remaining slaves then sailed to England. The owners of the *Zong*
claimed £30 of insurance money for each of the 132 slaves who
had been 'jettisoned'. The underwriters refused to pay, and
the case was taken to the courts. At the first trial the jury found
for the owners, on the ground that ' the case of the slaves was the
same as if horses had been thrown overboard'. The underwriters appealed to the Court of Exchequer, and Lord Mansfield
presided. He agreed that the law, as it stood, supported the

owners of the *Zong*, but distinguishing between legality and justice, he went on to affirm that ' a higher law applies to this very shocking case ' and gave judgment against the owners. His ruling was the first decision in an English Court that a slave could not be treated simply as merchandise.

Curtin reminds us that the cost of the trade in human lives was many times the number of slaves landed in the Americas.

> For every slave landed alive other people died in warfare, along the bush paths leading to the coast, awaiting shipment, or in the crowded and unsanitary conditions of the middle passage. Once in the New World still others died on entering a new disease environment.

It appears that many slaves died from dysentery and lung troubles, and that the crew, among whom the death rate was also high, were struck down also by malaria and yellow fever. On the average about one slave out of every eight died on the voyage, and about one seaman out of five. The South Atlantic System was a cruel and wasteful operation, most damaging for the slaves themselves, but deadly even for those who were free and voluntary participants.

What did this mean for Africa? Somehow West Africa appears to have borne the loss of these millions of people without irreparable damage save in Angola, where the Portuguese were especially active in promoting inter-tribal war in the interests of slave labour for Brazil. In this respect West Africa seems to have been more fortunate than East Africa, which showed the disastrous results of depopulation through the Slave Trade carried on by Arabs. Also, out of the contact with Brazil came the introduction into Africa of basic American foodcrops like cassava, maize and the sweet potato; and of other plants like the pawpaw, the peanut and guavas. Portugal itself contributed lemons and oranges. The addition of important foodcrops like cassava and maize must have led to an increase in population. We have seen already that the coastal region, through the contact with Europe, became the ' economic heartland ' of the region displacing the Savannah Kingdoms which had been on the southern and western ' coastline ' of that other ocean, the Sahara. Politically, the most important change

Group of Ibeji figures

that took place as a result of this shift was the emergence of African states like Benin, the Akan state of Akwamu, its more powerful successor the Kingdom of Ashanti, Dahomey and Oyo. The expansion southwards of Oyo led to the growth of Badagri and Lagos, while Dahomey made Whydah its chief outlet. In this way the political map of West Africa was transformed.

It remains a fact however that West Africa suffered grievously. Like Brazil and the Caribbean it became an area of excessive exploitation. It imported consumer goods from Europe, all of them expendable firearms, cloth, metalware, discouraged local industry and removed the incentive to improve or expand local production. In exchange West Africa exported men and women who were used to produce sugar in Brazil and the Caribbean, becoming units of production for the benefit of European owners. The effect of the trade was to stimulate production and encourage capital formation in Western Europe; but in West Africa the increased demand for slaves resulted in raiding and warfare. In time these local rivalries and struggles gave Europeans on the coast an opportunity for interfering in West African politics, and prepared the way for the European colonisation of the region in the 18th century.

Before considering in further detail the system of trade, let us follow the African in his forced migration from West Africa.

CHAPTER 13

The Cutting of the Birthcord

Arrived in the Caribbean, the African found himself in a world that was not markedly different from his homeland; but how utterly different was the society into which he was thrown, not as a man but as the instrument of those who purchased him. He knew that he was alone, for he had been forcibly deprived of family, tribe, country. Many of his shipmates were foreigners, who spoke other languages and belonged to other cultures. His solitary state was made obvious by the fact that he was now in a white world, one in which those who had authority over him spoke a strange language, lived by incomprehensible laws, had different values, worshipped a strange god. At the time of sale he found himself forced to undergo a minute physical examination in public at the hands of strangers, and thereafter he was compelled to follow the routine of the plantation under the constant threat of bodily punishment. So severe was the deprivation and the mental strain that many lost the wish to live, fell into a 'fixed melancholy', and died. The procedures of the sale drove some to suicide. Falconbridge, who made several voyages to the Caribbean as captain of a slave ship, told of being present at a number of sales by 'scramble'. The slaves were lined up on deck, the men and women separately, and at the firing of a gun the purchasers waiting ashore 'rushed through the barricado door with the ferocity of brutes' to secure such slaves as they needed. He described a 'scramble' in Kingston Harbour aboard the ship *Tyral*, when forty or fifty of the slaves jumped overboard, and he spoke of another 'scramble' at a slave market in Grenada when several of the female slaves escaped over the fence and ran about the streets of St. Georges in sheer panic, as if demented. After purchase there followed two or three critical years of acclimatisation on the plantation, getting accustomed to the routine of work and to being fed and housed inadequately, and falling a victim to new diseases against which they had no immunity. Measles, for example, proved almost as deadly as smallpox. An early historian of Jamaica, Edward Long, reported that one out of every three Africans died within the first three years of arrival. The records of Worthy Park estate in Jamaica show that the owner purchased 225 slaves in 1792–3 and that fifty six died during 1794. The estate was well run, and had a good doctor; even so, at the end of the three year period of seasoning one out of every four of the 225 slaves had died. The fact is that without the constant replenishing of the labour force the African would have perished.

It is generally true to say that plantation slavery was a death sentence, and it follows that emancipation was a reprieve. We have to bear in mind, however, that some slaves did reach old age, and that once the slave population became stabilised there were demographic changes. In the sugar colonies these changes, as Curtin points out, tended to fall into a regular pattern. At first, as the sugar and slave plantation system developed, the ratio of slave imports was high because the death rate in the slave population was higher than the rate of natural increase. When the country reached full production the total slave population levelled off. Slaves were imported but, to use Curtin's words, 'only enough to make up the deficit between births and deaths. Over time the proportion of American-born slaves increased, the deficit diminished and then disappeared. Barbados reached this point by about 1810, Jamaica by the 1840's. From this point on, even without further imports of slaves, the population began to grow slowly at first, and then more rapidly.' In contrast the United States and some Latin American countries had slave populations that increased naturally.

The record of the extraordinary resilience and endurance of the African in this struggle for survival bears out the judgment of one of Ghana's outstanding poets, Kofi Anwoonor, that ' The

African, even while seeking an equilibrium, as indeed he must, can accommodate change.' Anwoonor also described the African of today adapting to the contemporary world and at the same time seeking to keep his traditional customs and beliefs, and so asking ' Cannot we find where they buried our birthcord?'

In many West African societies the place where one's umbilical cord is buried has a mystical significance. That is where one's home is, the place where one is bound most closely to one's ancestors. The new-world African carried this memory with him, the mother guarding the navel-string carefully, burying it in the ground and planting over it a young tree which became the child's own ' navel string tree', the natal tree. Thus the birthcord becomes a source of rich imagery in the work of the poet Edward Brathwaite who returns to West Africa with its drums and deities, its ancient cities and ' seven kingdoms, Songhai, Mali, Chad, Ghana, Timbuctoo, Volta, and the bitter waste that was ' Benin ', and sets out on a search through Ashantiland, a stranger come back after three hundred years, knowing that ' somewhere under black gravel that black cord of birth is hidden.' Because ' my navel string screams ' he seeks desperately to find himself, and to discover what flaws existed in himself and in West African society that might account for his enslavement.

Other West Indians put Anwoonor's question in other forms, whether it be Walcott's ' How can I turn from Africa and live?' or the Ras Tafari reaching out for Ethiopia, or the Haitian Jacques Roumain remembering

> *Its the slow road to Guinea*
> *Where your fathers await you without impatience*

But for the African landing in the Americas the agony was the cutting of the birthcord.

In the preceding chapter we took note of the number of Africans who were brought to the new world as slaves. The number brought to the Caribbean during the first quarter century of English and French settlement, 1625–1650, was small, about 20,800, of whom Barbados took 18,000. Barbados was then embarking on sugar production. In contrast only 2,000 went to the Leeward Islands, which were still planting tobacco, indigo, cotton. So were the French colonies of Martinique and Guadeloupe which took 2,800.

Between 1650 and 1675 sugar production expanded in the Leewards and Barbados and the number of Africans imported rose steeply, reaching a total of 69,000. Barbados took 51,000, the Leewards about 10,000. Jamaica, still devoted to buccaneering and cacao, took 8,000. In 1675 the population was evenly balanced between black and white with 9,500 of the former and 8,000 of the latter. The French colonies imported 28,000. Martinique, rapidly becoming a sugar island, took 22,000 whereas Guadeloupe imported 3,000, and St. Domingue, still a frontier colony like Jamaica, received 3,000.

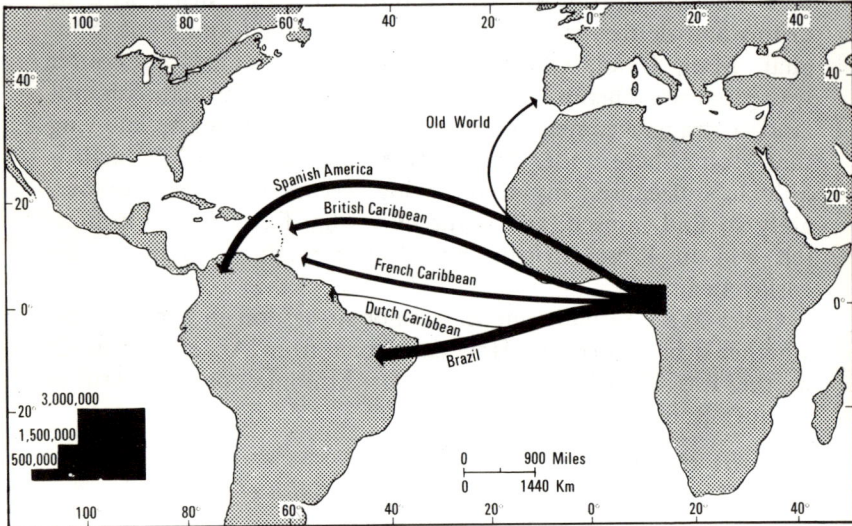

Destination of Atlantic Slave Trade 1601–1700

The estimate of imports of African labour for 1675–1700 show an even sharper increase. The total brought to the English colonies during those twenty five years was 173,000. Jamaica was rapidly becoming the premier sugar producer, bearing out the prediction made by the island's governor in 1673 that within six years the island would equal Barbados in its production. The number of slaves imported was 77,000. Barbados took 64,000 and the Leewards 32,000. The numbers for the French colonies show the same trend. St. Domingue took 71,000; Martinique 42,000; Guadeloupe 8,700; French Guiana 2,000.

The estimates show that during the second half of the 17th century about 400,000 Africans were brought to the French and English Caribbean. Whatever the status of the African may have been, these islands were rapidly becoming black in terms of numbers. In 1694 for example, Jamaica's population consisted of 40,000 blacks and 7,000 whites. In 1710 Barbados had 12,525 whites and 41,970 blacks. Antigua had at that time about four blacks to one white, and in Nevis the proportion was about three to one.

After 1700 the flow of Africans reached the proportions of a flood. Jamaica alone took 662,000 between 1701 and 1810; the Leewards 301,900; Barbados 252,000. The total of 1,376,000 for these is equal to the present day population of Trinidad,

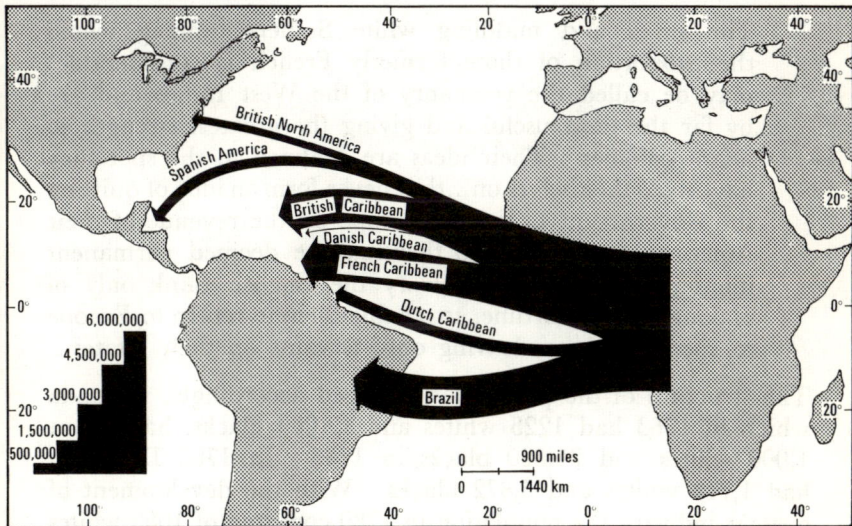

Destination of Atlantic Slave Trade 1701–1810

Tobago and Guyana. The French colonies took 995,000 over the same period. St. Domingue, Jamaica's rival, took three out of every four Africans imported.

The changes that took place in the 18th century in the make-up of the population in the islands, following on the introduction of sugar, illustrate the displacement of white by black. The sequence of events in the sugar-plantation islands began with settlements of white yeomen and peasant, their displacement by large numbers of black slaves, the substitution of plantation agriculture for smallholdings; lean years as a result of other islands becoming sugar-producers, and emancipation or revolution. Thus Nevis had about 1,400 white men and 1,739 blacks in 1672. The island turned to sugar, and in 1756 it had 1,118 whites, 8,380 blacks. Up to 1763 neither St. Vincent nor Dominica exported sugar; and Grenada though it had a sugar industry, was not wholly a sugar island, growing also cocoa, coffee, and cotton. After the three islands were ceded to Britain in 1763, sugar production expanded. The result in St. Vincent was described by Governor Morris in 1777, in words that can be applied to Barbados and the Leewards at an earlier date:

> The small and middling white Settlers (among whom the proportion of those formerly French is considerable) may be called the yeomanry of the West Indies and are by far the most useful and giving the greatest strength to infant colonies. Their ideas are confined to the spot they have fixed themselves on...they never form an idea of quitting the Government to live in Europe on the revenue of their American possessions and they may be deemed permanent inhabitants. On the contrary the English think only of making a rapid fortune, to enable them to return to Europe to spend it there, leaving only servants on their estates...

The structure of the population changed accordingly, Grenada which in 1763 had 1225 whites and 12,000 blacks, had about 1,000 whites and 24,620 blacks in 1783. In 1763 Dominica had 1,718 whites and 5,872 blacks. With the development of a sugar industry the population in 1780 consisted of 1066 whites and 12,713 blacks.

After the abolition of the Slave Trade by the British the flow

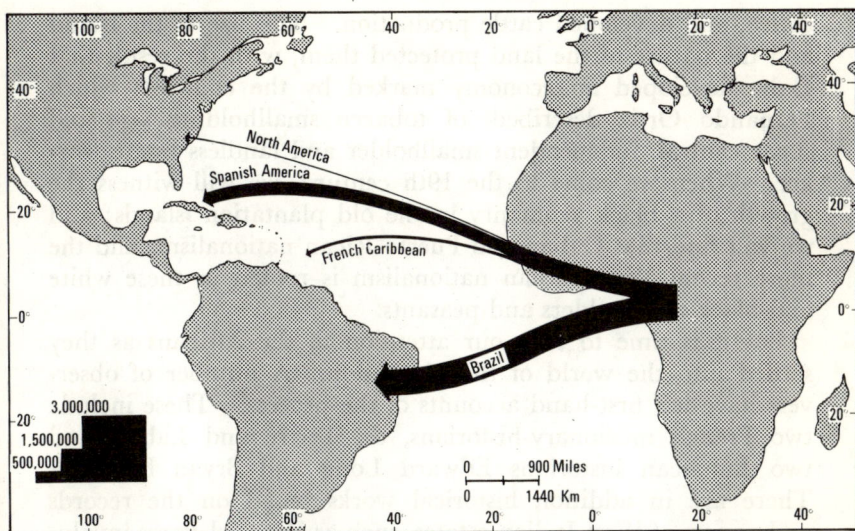

Destination of Atlantic Slave Trade 1811–70

of Africans into the Caribbean changed course. In the 19th century the French colonies continued to import Africans up to 1848 when France abolished slavery. After that date liberated slaves were imported as indentured labourers. The total number of Africans imported between 1810 and 1860 was 96,000. But there were two newcomers in the sugar-relay race, Cuba and Puerto Rico. Cuba was the giant, equal in size to all the other Caribbean islands, with ample reserves of flat fertile land, ideal for sugar production. Between 1811 and 1870 she took 550,000. Over the same period Puerto Rico took 55,100. In the older sugar islands the bringing in of the African had resulted in a population that was predominantly black. This did not happen in Puerto Rico, where a white peasantry had established themselves. The white peasant did not migrate, but he lost his land to the estates and was reduced to being a landless estate worker. Also, the number of whites was increased after 1815 by an inflow of Spanish settlers. Nor did it happen in Cuba, which also had a predominantly white yeomanry that, slowly and without over-much interference, had established cultivations of tobacco and coffee, and developed cattle production. The size of the island and the nature of the land protected them, with the result that Cuba developed an economy marked by the contrasts which Fernando Ortiz described, of tobacco smallholding *vega* and sugar central, independent smallholder and landless estate worker. When we come to the 19th century, we will witness the growth of a black yeomanry in the old plantation islands; and we will find that Cuban and Puerto Rican nationalism, and the more recent West Indian nationalism is rooted in these white and black smallholders and peasants.

But it is time to turn our attention to the Africans as they settled into the world of the plantation. A number of observers have left first-hand accounts of the process. These include two French missionary-historians, du Tertre and Labat; and two Jamaican historians Edward Long and Bryan Edwards. There are in addition historical works based on the records and papers of West Indian estates, such as Richard Pares invaluable *West India Fortune* and Craton and Walvin's *Jamaica Plantation*, which is a history of Worthy Park from 1670–1970. Father du Tertre, as Dr. Goveia points out 'never forgot that the slaves were also men, and he assumed in them the same sentiments of attachment to liberty and much the same motivations of behaviour which he assumed in the case of free men, even though he realised that their expression was limited by enslavement'. Du Tertre described the new society of the Caribbean with detachment, whereas many other writers, such as Edward Long, Attwood in his *History* of *Dominica,* and Bryan Edwards wrote from a white standpoint, and justified the condition of the black man by arguing or assuming that he was an inferior being.

Du Tertre described the way in which the African slaves set about building new relationships, establishing homes, families and circles of friends. He wrote about conditions in the French islands in the 1650's and 1660's, before the sugar plantation had taken firm hold, and he points out that the very fact that they were all slaves created a bond between the Africans. Marriage among the slaves was not only permitted but even encouraged, for practical reasons: ' Our French people take care to marry them as early as possible so as to get children from them '. The colonists tried to find for their male slaves wives who came from the same country of origin because they were much fonder of these than of other women. There were also masters who, not wishing to part with a valuable slave, forced him into marriage with a woman from another country so as to keep his services.

The quickest way to win a slave's affection, said du Tertre, was to take an interest in his children. The slaves could not bear to see their children punished, and they became uncontrollable when the interests of their children were threatened. The mothers carried their babies to the field, strapping them to their backs by strips of cloth. When the children reached the age of three or four they were left in the care of a six or seven year old girl or of the woman who had charge of the kitchen. The first thing the parents did when they returned in the evening from the field was to call their little ones. They would not eat until they found them.

Godparents had a special place in the circle of friends. Writing fifty years after du Tertre, Pere Labat says that when a slave asked another to be godfather for his child it was almost as if he gave up his own right to the child. The godchild and the children of the godfather called themselves brothers and sisters and often loved each other more tenderly than blood-relatives. Looking back from our twentieth century viewpoint we can understand this, for we know how strong is the bond between ' goddy ' and the godchild; and how important the role of the godparent remains, especially in rural communities. Both du Tertre and Labat speak of the slaves as being friendly to each other, and of sharing each others troubles, especially in times of sickness and death. Labat says that if a slave ran away, others would hide him in their huts, making hiding-holes so skilfully that it was difficult to find the runaway.

The hours of work were long. Du Tertre lists the things that made the long hours all the more difficult to bear; the heat of the sun, the bad temper of the overseers who directed the work and drove the slaves so harshly that many died at their tasks without the cause of their death being known and without their masters even knowing that they were ill.

Housing, food, and the conditions of service varied from estate to estate according to the character of the master. Du Tertre described the slave huts as being nine or ten feet long and six feet wide, roofed with reeds, with a door as the only opening. The bed was made of branches of trees, interwoven and resting on four posts. The domestic utensils consisted of some calabashes of different sizes for keeping food. The housing appears to have been less primitive fifty years later, for Labat wrote of larger huts roofed with palmleaves, of beds with wooden lathes, of a log of wood as a pillow, and of cooking pots, wooden benches and wooden utensils.

From the beginning food was a problem. Some food was supplied by the master, and slaves were required to grow the rest of what they needed. Du Tertre says the slaves were permitted to keep chickens and pigs, and that they were allowed to trade in these. He describes the slaves trading chickens with the captains of ships, exchanging them for cloth, brandy and other goods. They were given Saturday free, so as to cultivate pieces of land set aside by the owner for this purpose. They planted peas, sweet potatoes, cassava, yams, melons, cucumbers, pumpkins and kitchen herbs. The men took the produce to the shops for sale between the two Masses on Sundays and Feastdays. Without the chicken and pig-rearing and growing of vegetables and ' hard food ' the slaves would have suffered grievously, for the rations given to them were meagre; so much so that in Martinique the Governor had to order owners to supply the slaves every week with at least two pounds of meat per head in the off season, and three pounds when the ships arrived with supplies. The best food rations went to the sugar boilers. Their skill in making the sugar determined whether the estate made a profit or not; so the master spared neither food nor drink for them.

Du Tertre understood well that the slave was at the mercy of the owner and of those whom the master employed to supervise them, and he saw that the whole system of slavery depended on the absolute obedience of the slave. The whip was the sign of authority. Slaves who ran away were flogged brutally. Revolt, sedition and conspiracy were punished with public executions. Du Tertre emphasized that the slaves were happy or melancholy, diligent or idle depending on the treatment they received. He tells how they repaid kindness with loyalty. Labat testified to the courage of slaves who saved his own life, dragging him from the saddle of his horse when a party of Englishmen were about to fire at him, and throwing themselves between the attackers and himself. He adds that in the clashes between the English and French in St. Kitts, the French slaves fought as bravely as their masters.

Even though in exile, and in a strange land, the Africans danced and made music. On Sundays and Feastdays they danced to the music of drums made of skin stretched tight over part of the trunk of a tree that had been hollowed out; and to the rhythm of two dried calabashes filled with small stones and shaken. Their most popular dance was the Calenda of Guinea, and for this there were two drums, the Big Tambour and the Bamboule.

Conditions varied from island to island and from decade to decade. Labat, for example who made a visit to Barbados in 1700, said:

> The English do not look after their slaves well and feed them very badly. As a rule the slaves are free to work on Saturday to provide themselves with all their own and their families requirements. The overseers get every ounce of work out of them, beat them without mercy for the least fault, and appear to care far less for the life of a negro than for a horse.

There were important differences between the conditions that du Tertre described and those in the English colonies with respect to marriage and religion. A French code of laws issued in 1685, the Code Noir, ordered baptism and christian instruction for slaves. The sacraments of the church were to be open to them, and the right to burial in consecrated ground. Those who supervised their work were to be Catholics. Slaves could marry provided they had the consent of their master, but the master was not to enforce marriages. Two sets of clothing were to be provided, and a detailed list was given of the food to be supplied each week to the slaves. Slaves could appeal to officials against ill-treatment or neglect. The penalties for assault, theft, running away and other offences were harsh, including heavy physical punishment and death. Many of the regulations in the Code were disregarded in practise, but the right to marriage and to the sacraments were in themselves recognition that the slave was a person; there were no such provisions in the English colonies.

Other points of difference arose in the various islands because of the changes that were taking place in the Caribbean. The background to settlement in the second half of the 17th century was turbulent, buccaneers and pirates frequented the seas, and smugglers were everywhere. A report made by an investigating officer in 1687 said that most of the islands had so many bays and inlets that Customs officers were unable to check the shipments of sugar. Planters were ready to trade illegally with the Dutch, and ' being loaded the Dutch ships sail direct to Holland without paying the King a penny of duty'. Wars occurred every few years for Europe too had its tribal wars; the first Dutch War (1652–54); the Second Dutch War (1665–67); the third Dutch War (1672–74); the long War of the Grand Alliance, with England and Holland ranged against France (1688–1697); and the War of the Spanish Succession which began in 1702 and ended with the Treaty of Utrecht in 1713. In 1669 St. Kitts was ravaged by the French and ' the English plantations so ruined and destroyed, and without stock either of negroes or cattle, but bare lands...a new settlement may be made upon any other uninhabited island as easily as there'. In 1706 a French force burnt the boiling houses on Nevis, and the dwelling houses also, ' not leaving at their going away above twenty standing'. They stripped the island of its sugar mills and coppers, and carried off 3,000 slaves, some to serve in the fleet and some with French privateers. D'Iberville compelled the Council of Nevis to agree to send him 1,400 more Negroes within six months or pay a heavy fine.

Wars led to swift change. So did the expansion of the plantation system. The African who entered the Caribbean in 1750 moved into a society very different from that of 1650. He may not have found the friendship and spirit of mutual help that du Tertre described. There seems to have been more of this among slaves of the same tribal grouping than within the community as a whole. In St. Domingue, for example, the owners of Ibo slaves found it was in their interest to buy more Ibos, since the seasoned helped to look after the newcomers. Lewis, an absentee Jamaica proprietor, in his account of his visit to the island in 1816, remarked on the strength of tribal bonds between the Ibos. Edward Long noted that in Jamaica the Gold Coast slaves did not mix with the others. There are reports also of division between the newcomers and slaves who were born in the Caribbean, the Creoles. The new slave found a black community in which the creole black ridiculed him as a ' salt water negro ' and a ' Guinea-bird '. The newcomer also found a brown as well as a black community in which the mulatto prided himself on being superior to the black and at the same time suffered acutely because he saw himself inferior to the white. It was of the nature of the slave and sugar plantation that it divided society into tight circles, and that within each circle individuals and groups struggled to assert their superiority.

Differences and changes notwithstanding, the general pattern of African entry into the life of the Caribbean remained the same. There was also an ' inner ', more personal and intimate adjustment which each individual made, ranging from apathy and resignation, or an effort to make a fresh start within the limitations of the system, to a rejection of the system through ' go slows ', escape, rebellion. The newcomer retained some of his traditions, folk tales, religion, some of his customary ways of doing things; and he learned new techniques and adopted new attitudes in order to survive. Consequently the Atlantic Slave Trade meant not only the importation of large numbers of Africans into the Caribbean but also the establishment of two societies, two worlds, that were very often different; one European-centred, with European laws, institutions, languages and cultures; and the other a black world of displaced and dispossessed folk, who gradually developed their own folk-institutions, codes, ways of speech. The process was not the merging and shaping of a single society out of these two diverse communities, but rather the growth of two societies that like circles, intersected each other, but differed fundamentally from each other.

CHAPTER 14

The Slave and Sugar Plantation

The black and white circles intersected and overlapped on the sugar and slave plantation. The Caribbean plantation of the 17th and 18th centuries was designed for one purpose, the cultivation of sugar cane and the manufacture of sugar, rum and molasses for export. Brought into being by economic forces, the plantation was much more than a business or an industry. It gave rise to a form of society that endured for two centuries and that still influences our way of life and our attitudes today. Our very language bears witness to the dominance of sugar, in words and phrases like canepiece for canefield; junks of cane, for short pieces of sugar-cane; arrowing cane, for cane in flower; crop time for harvest time; dunder for the lees from the rum still. The landscape of the present testifies to it with fields of sugar-cane and sugar factories that still sustain the Caribbean economy. Buildings and fortifications speak of the power of sugar; the Great Houses of planters now dust, Farley Hill and Drax Hall in Barbados, Mt. Travers in St. Kitts, Rose Hall and Good Hope in Jamaica; circular stone windmills in the Leeward Islands and Barbados; the ruins of Bath Hotel in Nevis, once a fashionable centre of planter life; broken aqueducts and ruined estate buildings along the north coast of Jamaica; Pall Mall Square in Basseterre and Kings Square in Spanish Town; battlements and fortifications that ring the Eastern Caribbean from Brimstone Hill in St. Kitts to the broken walls of Fort St. George protecting the harbour of St. George's in Grenada. And deep in memory are the scars of past anguish and misery which speak through Caribbean writing, as in the Haitian Bernard:

> *And now only*
> *in the night and the silence of the St. Domingue*
> *mountains*
> *a timid throb of the drum still sometimes tries*
> *to raise*
> *up to the stars*
> *the profound nostalgia of the transplanted ones*
> *of Africa*

The West Indian experience of the sugar and slave plantation is a link not so much with Africa as with North-Eastern Brazil and the Deep South, the other new world plantation regions.

Old Plantation House at Drax Hall, St George Barbados

The dual character of the slave-and-sugar plantation leads us to consider it as a system of production; the way it functioned, the lay-out of the plantation, its land-use, its source of power, its food supply and its profitability. Following on this we will consider the social aspects; the two worlds of bond and free, black and white; and the kind of society in which they functioned, its characteristics, its value systems and the laws that regulated it.

Two of the most important systems of social and agricultural organisations in the contemporary Caribbean and Latin America are the commercial plantation and the *hacienda*. Their chief characteristics provide points of comparison and contrast with the West India plantations based on slavery or indentured labour. West Indians have experience of the modern commercial plantation on sugar estates in Cuba and banana plantations in Spanish Honduras and Costa Rica as well as in their homelands; and in Latin America they have seen the *hacienda* in operation. They find in the modern plantation a complex high-cost organisation which is often owned by a company because of the large capital investment required. It is developed for the production of one crop for a large external market, and often it employs imported labour and technicians. It operates on a cash basis and makes use of up-to-date scientific knowledge and technology because it aims at the maximum use of land, labour and equipment in order to get the largest possible returns. Its investors or managers tend to interfere in the political machinery of the host country in an effort to protect their investment.

The *hacienda* requires some capital investment, but far less than the plantation. It is owned by an individual or family, is land-hungry, keeps much of its land idle, produces for a limited internal market, draws on the peasants in the neighbourhood for labour and generally pays them in perquisites rather than in cash. Conservative, resistant to technology and innovation, it aims at being self-sufficient in all things, food, housing, materials, equipment, labour force.

The slave-and-sugar plantation, like the modern plantation, required a large capital investment. Ligon, in his account of the Barbados plantation of 1650, said that Modyford bought half a share in a 500 acre sugar plantation for £7,000. More than a century later Bryan Edwards, in his *History of the West Indies*, said that ' the business of sugar planting is a sort of adventure in which the man that engages must engage deeply...it requires a capital of no less than £30,000 sterling to embark on this employment with a fair prospect of advantage '. He wrote with reference to a plantation of 900 acres, of which one third of the land was under sugar. Ownership was in the hands of individuals or families. Like the modern plantation and the plantation based on indentured labour, the slave-and-sugar plantation imported its labour force, much of its food, most of its supplies. Unlike the *hacienda*, it was self-sufficient only to the extent that it provided its own medical and hospital services, grew some of its food, employed its own artisans and craftsmen. It produced for a large external market, and even though its labour force was not paid it had to lay out large sums of money for its purchase each year. It was developed for exportation. Its labour force, unlike that on the modern plantation, was tied to the estate, without prospect of reward or profit. On some plantations there developed a labour-owner relationship somewhat like that of the *hacienda*. The owner sought and exercised political power and a plantocracy came into existence in the West Indies that dominated the local assemblies and built up a powerful lobby in Britain.

Bryan Edwards described in detail that lay-out of a Jamaican plantation and the annual cost of labour and supplies. It consisted of three parts, land, building and stock. The general practice was to give up one-third of the land to planting sugar-cane, one third to foodcrops like plantains, cocoes, yams, cassava, corn and other vegetables and to raising livestock and poultry; one third to woodland, as a source of building material and firewood for the boiling and distilling houses. To reconstruct the lay-out is easy; for it was in many respects similar to that of the present; the Great House, the overseer's house, quarters for the book-keepers, and the works, the mill, boiler and distilling houses, stables for the mules and horses, shops for the cooper, carpenter, blacksmith; a ' hot ' house or hospital for the sick, with room for ' lying-in women ', and possibly with room also for ' disorderly persons '. At a discreet distance was the slave-village, the huts standing in lines or in clusters. The whole made up a compact unit which expressed in stone, timber and thatch the values and the structure of plantation society.

Observers have described the organisation and routine of the plantation. Writing of Antigua, John Luffman said:

> The negroes are turned out at sunrise, and employed in groups from twenty to sixty or upwards under the inspection of white overseers. . . subordinate to these overseers are drivers, commonly called dog-drivers, who are mostly black or mulatto fellows of the worst dispositions, and these men are furnished with whips which, while on duty, they are obliged, on pain of severe punishment, to have with them, and are authorised to flog wherever they see the least relaxation from labour. . . paying at the same time little or no regard to age or sex.

A passage from Bryan Edward's History sets out the practice in Jamaica:

> The negroes are divided into three sets or classes, usually called gangs: the first consisting of the most healthy and robust of the men and women, whose chief business it is out of crop-time, to clear a hole and plant the ground, and in crop-time, to cut the canes, feed the mills and attend the manufacture of the sugar. It is computed that, in the whole body of the negroes on a well-conditioned plantation, there are commonly found one-third of this description, exclusive of domestics, and negro tradesmen, viz: carpenters, coopers and masons. . . The second gang is composed of young boys and girls, women far gone with child, and convalescents who are chiefly employed in weeding the canes; and the third set consists of young children, attended by a careful old woman, who are employed in collecting green meat for the pigs and sheep; or in weeding the garden, or some such gentle exercise, merely to preserve them from habits of idleness.
>
> The first gang is summoned to the labours of the field either by a bell or the blowing of a conch-shell, just before sunrise. They bring with them, beside their hoes or bills, provisions for breakfast; and are attended by a white person and a black superintendent called a driver. The list being called over, and the names of all the absentees noted, they proceed with their work until eight or nine o'clock, when

they sit down in the shade to breakfast. . . of boiled yams, eddoes, ocra, calalue and plantain. . . seasoned with salt and cayenne pepper. . . At breakfast they are seldom indulged with more than half or three-quarters of an hour; and having resumed their work continue in the field until noon, when the bell calls them from labour. They are now allowed two hours for rest and refreshment. . . Their dinner is provided with the addition of salted or pickled fish, of which each negro receives a weekly allowance. . . At two o'clock they are again summoned to the field. . . At sunset, or very soon after, they are released for the night. . .

In the crop season, however, the system is different; for at that time such of the negroes as are employed in the mill and boiling-houses often work very late, frequently all night, but they are divided into watches which relieve each other. . .

The crop dictated the sequence of activities. It began with clearing about one-third of the cane-land, ' holing ' it, manuring the holes and planting the crop. ' Holing ' was heavy work, for it meant digging holes about four feet square, nine inches deep and nine inches square at the bottom. As for the collection and carrying of dung, an observer wrote of Barbados in the 1680's that it was ' a mighty labour ' and ' Our negroes work at it like ants or bees '. As Goveia says, ' The slave with his hoe and his basket of dung, symbolised the prosperity or ruin of sugar cultivation in these islands.'

The holing and planting having been completed, the slaves were directed to other tasks, the planting of crops, weeding, repairing buildings and the like. There was no slack season, for in the words of an observer, the discipline of a slave plantation was as exact as that of a regiment. The slaves were there all the time. They could not be paid off. They must be used; so there was no incentive to use labour-saving devices or improved equipment. Instead of a plough, slaves with hoes; instead of carts carrying manure, slaves with baskets; and instead of a plantation routine that speeded up production one that ensured that the slaves would be fully occupied throughout the year. The system carried within itself the seeds of its own decay, for, as the price of slaves rose and the reserves of new fertile land ran out the use of labour became wasteful and costly. One calculation was that the cost of hoeing was from two and a half to three times as great as the cost of ploughing.

There were a number of reasons for this resistance to change and innovation. One was that in the English colonies many of the planters were in debt. The merchants gave long term credit, charging at least five per cent on monies advanced and on credit. As time passed the debts grew and the sum paid in interest also grew. Owners would leave shares in their estates to relatives, and so added to the burden imposed on the estate. An increasingly large share of each year's profits went to pay creditors in Britain. It was reported in 1787 that most of the estates in Antigua were either in trust or mortgaged to merchants in London, Liverpool and Bristol. A St. Kitts planter estimated the profits from an estate of 320 acres of caneland, with 340 slaves, at ten per cent but reckoned that five per cent of this had to go in interest payments on the purchase money, before any allowance was made even for the repayment of the debt.

Besides, many owners lived in England. Antigua was fortunate in having a large number of resident proprietors. So was Barbados. St. Kitts on the other hand suffered grievously from absenteeism. The land was owned by a small number—there were only 120 of these large landholders in 1770—and the high yields for which the island was famous enabled these to live in England, abandoning their estates to overseers and managers. Many of the large landholders of Jamaica did the same. The managers and overseers were more intent on reaping their commissions by extracting all they could from the plantation than on following a long-term policy of spending money on improvements and on better methods of agriculture. The difference made by resident ownership can be judged by the work of John Martin in Antigua and Rose Price of Worthy Park in Jamaica. John Martin, after living for some time in England, returned to Antigua to put his run-down estate of Greencastle in order. Martin made changes in the practice of cultivation which reduced soil exhaustion and kept production at a satisfactory level. Another owner Rose Price ' at the age of twenty-three, set sail for Jamaica in 1781...for more than three years of residence at Worthy Park, during which he was said to have nearly doubled the value of the estate... Rose Price's overriding purpose was the increase of the profits from Worthy Park by improved efficiency, but his first concern was to increase production'. Owners like these were the exception. Generally the planter resisted change.

The rigidity and conservatism built into the system were reinforced by the system of slavery. The slave laws were repressive, their purpose being to keep the society as it was, to safeguard the authority and standing of the white owner, manager and official, and to keep the blacks, who were much more numerous, in a subordinate position. In these circumstances change and innovation might eat away the foundations of society and they were therefore to be resisted.

A review of the spread of the plantation and of the increase in sugar production will show, among other things, that there were many types of sugar-and-slave plantation within the general system. Variations of type were the result of differences in the size of country, in the nature of the land, the fertility of the soil, rainfall, and climate; in the availability of capital; differences in the cultural and social background of the colonists and also of the slaves; differences in religious and political institutions, and in the trading policies of the metropolitan power.

The first phase was that in which Dutch traders enabled Barbados to turn to sugar in the 1640's. The fertile soil, gentle rolling country, seaports within easy reach, trade winds to turn the windmills, and the availability of capital speeded up the transformation of Barbados into a one-crop island. A pattern was laid down that has remained virtually unchanged, most of the land being given up to the cultivation of sugar and most of the food being imported. By 1709 the island had 1300 plantations and 485 sugar works whose mills were powered by wind or cattle. Exports of sugar reached a total of 7,000 tons between 1700 and 1710. Production then fell, levelling off to between 5000 and 6000 tons a year. Since there were no reserves of land, sugar, as one planter said, was produced 'by dung and much labour'. Although the sugar plantation displaced many whites, sending them in search of a new start in St. Kitts, Jamaica, in Carolina or other mainland colonies, the ratio of white to black remained higher than in other English colonies, the proportion being one to four for most of the 18th century. Land ownership was concentrated in the hands of a small number of landholders but the island did not suffer from absenteeism to the extent that Jamaica and St. Kitts did. Perhaps this was because Barbados was first settled by people who meant to make their homes there and who developed a 'Bajan' sentiment during their struggle against the proprietary governors and against Cromwell; and this local patriotism was reinforced by a system of local government in which landholders exercised considerable power.

The second phase lasted from the 1660's to early in the 18th century. It saw St. Kitts, Nevis, Antigua, Martinique Guadeloupe and St. Domingue turning to sugar. The contrasts multiply; in Nevis, stony fields, in St. Kitts a green rim of coastal plain so fertile that Bryan Edwards, recording its annual average yield of one ton of sugar to four acres, doubted whether so prodigious a return was equalled by any other sugar country in any part of the globe; low-lying Antigua and the rugged terrain of Martinique whose mountains were a refuge for sullen hostile Caribs; diversified agriculture in the mountainous islands and a one-crop economy in the small islands where the chief threat to the economy was from the exhaustion of the soil.

Martinique and Guadeloupe turned to sugar more slowly than did Barbados. Martinique was settled in 1635 by French indentured servants, and by colonists, many of whom had only limited capital for investment. The mountains and valleys offered the opportunity for growing a variety of crops, but up to the 1650's settlers were in constant danger from Caribs in the hill country. In 1660 the population was no more than about 3,000. The chief crops were tobacco, which was proving unprofitable, cotton, indigo and ginger. In the 1650's when 300 refugees from Brazil arrived in the island with their slaves and equipment, a second start was made at developing a sugar industry. The first attempt by Trezel in the 1640's had failed. The Caribs and the stegomoya mosquito almost put a stop to the second attempt. Sugar languished, and after twenty years there were only twelve sugar plantations and fourteen mills on the island. A hundred years later the island had 286 sugar plantations, and the population included 12,450 whites, 1,814 coloured and 70,996 blacks; a ratio of very nearly one white to six blacks. In contrast to St. Kitts and Barbados, there were a number of small proprietors who grew foodcrops and minor staples. Cocoa also was cultivated until a blight destroyed the trees in 1727. Coffee, which was introduced in the 1720's became the second most important crop in the middle of the century. Agriculture was diversified, and this in turn meant that there were a number of small and ' middling ' proprietors. When Abbe Reynal described the island he spoke of 1,500 planters who employed 12,000 slaves cultivating cotton, coffee, cocoa and cassava, and he placed in three classes those who were engaged in sugar production: the very rich who owned about 100 estates; a second group which owned 150 estates with 9,000 slaves, and did not have enough capital to purchase the full number of slaves they needed to man their estates; and a third group of poorer planters with thirty plantations and 2,000 slaves.

At the close of the 17th century Barbados was the premier sugar producer of the Caribbean, its annual production being around 7,500 tons. To us the figure seems ridiculously small, accustomed as we now are to a production of more than 150,000 tons a year from Barbados, and more than 400,000 tons each year from Guyana and Jamaica. Jamaica exported little more than 4,000 tons in 1703, Martinique 5,700 tons in 1709. But what had been a luxury food in Europe was becoming a daily necessity. To meet the growing demand for sugar the plantations spread across the coastal plains of Jamaica, St. Domingue and Martinique. At the close of the 1730's Martinique's production was very nearly 15,000 tons; Jamaica's 16,000, St. Domingue's 39,000 tons. The middle years of the century saw the two large colonies outpacing the others by far. In 1773 Barbados produced 5,600 tons; Martinique over twice as much 11,500 tons. Jamaica by then had moved into the 'big league' of the 18th century. In 1774 it produced 50,000 tons; and at the same time St. Domingue moved forward to 60,000 tons.

Jamaica and St. Domingue present interesting points of contrast and likeness. The colonies in the Eastern Caribbean were settled by the English and French a century and a half after Spain settled Hispaniola and Jamaica. The two shared a family likeness of coastal plains and mountains that rise sharply from the sea, but St. Domingue, much larger, had more fertile land. Both had a tradition of ranching and both had known the prosperity that flowed from piracy and buccaneering. Jamaica had its Henry Morgan, St. Domingue its du Casse. Both turned reluctantly from buccaneering to sugar, but Jamaica made the earlier start benefitting from the arrival of Governor Thomas Modyford with 800 Barbadian settlers in 1664. Even after their coming the start was slow, for Governor Thomas Lynch wrote to London in 1772 saying that the weather had been seasonable, the success in planting miraculous, and that Major Bannister would be sending to the Secretary of State ' a pot of sugar, and writes you its story '. In the 18th century sugar dominated the economy in both colonies but neither was devoted to a single crop like Barbados and St. Kitts. On the contrary they resembled Martinique in having a diversified system of agriculture. They had coffee, which was introduced into the Caribbean islands in the 1730's and became a crop second in importance only to sugar. In addition they had cacao, cotton, indigo. Cattle were essential to the progress of each colony, being used for turning the sugar mills, supplying manure, and hauling wagons laden with sugar and molasses from the estates to the ports. In these circumstances the chance introduction of Guinea grass into Jamaica was of great importance. St. Domingue had an advantage in being able to obtain supplies of cattle and foodcrops from the eastern part of Hispaniola, which was still in Spanish hands. Also in the techniques of sugar production it appears to have been ahead of Jamaica. Bryan Edwards said that the planters of Jamaica received smaller returns from the labour of their slaves than did those of St. Domingue.

> The true cause arose, from the superior fertility of the soil, and the prodigious benefit which resulted to the French planters from the system of watering their sugar lands in the dry weather.

The Jamaica and St. Domingue plantations were larger than those in the smaller islands of the Caribbean; and in Jamaica cultivation was land-intensive, not labour intensive as in Barbados or St. Kitts. The availability of land for cultivation by the slaves as provision grounds gave a measure of security against famine, though the local food supply in Jamaica always had to be supplemented by importations of flour, cornmeal, salted beef, pork and fish from Britain and North America. In the smaller plantation islands, the problem of food was a perpetual nightmare. The larger colonies also had problems, like the cost of transporting sugar from an island estate to the seaport, or a reduction of the labour force because of slaves escaping to the mountains.

Two other areas turned to sugar in the 18th century; the Windward Islands and Tobago, and the mainland colonies of Surinam and Berbice. In 1763, under the terms of the Treaty of Paris, Britain returned Martinique and Guadeloupe to France, and she also renounced any claim to St. Lucia. She kept Dominica, St. Vincent, Grenada and the Grenadines and Tobago. These Ceded Islands, as they were called, were like smaller versions of St. Domingue and Jamaica, with mountains that rise sheer from the sea and valleys of dark green. In St. Vincent the mountains sheltered the last of the Caribs, and blacks who had either been shipwrecked or had escaped by boat from Barbados, which lies to the eastward. The most developed colony was Grenada which, like the others, produced cotton, cocoa and coffee; but in addition she exported some sugar. Because of their strategic value the British Government wished to people the islands with as many English settlers as possible rather than to have large estates. The land in the islands was declared to be the property of the Crown and regulations were passed providing that they should not be sold in large parcels; the limit set for Dominica was 300 acres, and for the other islands 500 acres. The West India planters bitterly opposed this policy of establishing settlements of white smallholders, because it encouraged the migration of whites of limited means to the Ceded Islands. Holdings of from ten to thirty acres were reserved for poor settlers. A century and a half earlier the prospect of cheap land had drawn people from Britain. Now the prospect of cheap land in St. Vincent encouraged whites of limited means to migrate from the other islands. Planter pressure led the Secretary of State to censure Governor Morris of St. Vincent for making free grants of land to a number of smallholders and the grants were declared invalid. Morris in a spirited defence insisted that the King's interests were better served by placing as many smallholders as possible in ' this wild and mountainous unsettled country, in so bad a neighbourhood ' than by allowing one individual to hold large tracts of land.

Between 1763 and 1775 the Ceded Islands increased their production of cocoa and coffee. Grenada trebled its sugar exports and St. Vincent lifted its small production to 20,000 tons in 1765. A period of turbulence set in after that time. France regained Grenada in 1779, and slave risings and rebellion brought the islands to the verge of ruin.

In the second half of the 18th century slave-and-sugar plantations were established on the shoulder of South America, by the French in their colony of Cayenne, and by the Dutch in Berbice, Essequibo and Demerara. A French attempt to settle 14,000 white colonists in Cayenne in 1763 ended disastrously, disease and famine killing 11,000 of the settlers within two years. After this Cayenne became a sugar-producing slave colony, with a small white population and 10,000 slaves.

The Dutch who had established themselves on the coast of Guyana in the 1620's in order to plant tobacco and other tropical staples, developed a profitable export trade in sugar during the 18th century. Using their long experience in controlling and harnessing water to their purposes, they transformed the low-lying coastal plans of Surinam into flourishing sugar fields, protecting them by dikes from the floodwaters of the rivers and from the sea, draining them by canals, and using the power of the wind and the tides to turn their mills. In 1775 Surinam had 430 estates manned by 60,000 blacks, and the exports of sugar and coffee to Holland were reckoned respectively at about £347,000 and £350,000. In the forested areas of the interior fugitive blacks established settlements of another kind, in which as free men they supported themselves by hunting and by growing food.

Dutch settlers on the river Berbice, after a flurry of prosperity in the middle of the 18th century, ran into difficulties that practically broke the colony; first a seven-year epidemic that was a combination of enteric fever and dysentery, then a slave revolt under Coffey, who for a brief period gained control of the colony.

Essequibo and Demerara became sugar producing colonies with the help of immigrant English planters from the Leeward Islands and Barbados, who left the islands because of the exhaustion of the soil on their former plantations and because of rising costs. On the coastlands of Essequibo and Demerara they found a system of cultivation very different from that which they had known, based on black mud which, when drained, yielded four successive crops of sugar-cane before replanting became necessary.

The system of plantation production was flexible enough to adapt to a variety of circumstances; to extensive coastlands where the black mud had only to be drained in order to grow a succession of crops from the same planting by ratooning, to arid coastlands where the secret of success was manuring, to coastal plains on the north coast where the trade winds turned the mills; to flat land on the leeward coast where cattle powered the mills; to small islands with labour-intensive cultivation; to large islands with land-intensive cultivation; to land-scarce islands where an estate of 300 acres was reckoned as large and to large countries where 1000 acres was the average size of an estate.

The types were many and diverse, but the basic characteristics remained; specialised production for a large external market by slave labour; the subordination of the human being and of the land to the market; a rigid hierarchic structure in which owners, subordinate employees and the enslaved labour force were kept separate from each other; and a colonial relationship in which the colony existed for the benefit of the metropolitan country.

In Hispaniola, in the first quarter of the 16th century the first sugar planters of the Caribbean, Gonzalo de Velosa and his fellows, had depended on African labour. In the middle years of that century the Portuguese made North-Eastern Brazil the chief supplier of sugar to Europe. As the plantations spread across the plains around Bahia, Portuguese ships sought their labour force along the coast and up the river highways of West Africa. A century later the traders of Europe, Dutch, English, French, Danes, Swedes, even the Brandenburgers, were at each other's throats competing fiercely for a share in the African slave trade. In the Caribbean, as island after island turned to sugar the slave-traders intensified their efforts to supply more African slaves. Through the archipelago and in the Guyanas every acre of new land cleared and planted with sugar had its counterpart in more slave-coffers driven toward Benin, Koromantin, Whydah, Bonny and

Angola; in African canoes searching for slaves in scattered settlements along the Gambia, through the Niger delta and up the Congo. These in turn had their counterpart in expanding shipyards in England, France, Holland; larger numbers of sailmakers and shipwrights, larger foundries to produce metalware, more looms for weaving cloth, more counting houses to handle cargoes of sugar and rum, more capital for new factories, larger fleets, larger armies, and with these more farms on the North American seaboard to supply the Caribbean with horses, beef and flour; more fishing vessels to carry cod, more mills to saw wood for puncheons and cart wheels, more cordwainers and candle-makers, more sloops for the Caribbean and African trade, more distilleries to make rum for the fur trade, more silver coins to pay trading debts in Britain.

We turn now to considering some of the most important commercial and political features of this dynamic trading system.

CHAPTER 15

'The First Happy Instruments'

The African on a West Indian plantation found himself in a world without horizons. He could not of his own free will move beyond its narrow limits without exposing himself to severe penalties. Newly arrived Africans linked him with the world to which he once belonged. The sugar he produced, the osnaburg he wore, the salted meat that he ate at week-ends linked him vaguely with a white world that he did not know. The European, looking at the growing system of international trade, at the profits made out of the forced movement of Africans to the Americas, at the new shipping routes and the inflow of capital, recognised that the generating force came from the slave trade and the plantation. The trading system was dynamic and international; but in a mercantile world each nation sought a monopoly of trade, monopoly being a prerequisite for power and commercial competition—a mild form of war. The contradictions inherent in the system become clear when we review the struggle for the *Asiento*, the sugar trade and the North American-Caribbean trade.

The Slave *Asiento* was a formal contract between the Spanish Crown and a contractor, by which Spain limited her own claims to a monopoly of trade with her colonies. Spain was never in any significant way a supplier of slaves. After she failed in her attempt to break the Portuguese monopoly of the West African trade, Portuguese traders, some under licence and some without, became her suppliers of slaves. Spain regularised the situation in 1595 when she farmed out the trade to a contractor who undertook to supply slaves to the Spanish colonies, and to maintain his own stations in Spain, West Africa and the Indies. The contractor in turn sold licences to sub-contractors and remitted the money to the Spanish Crown. From 1595 to 1640 Portugal supplied Spanish America with most of its slaves under contracts of this kind. The grant of *Asientos* to Portuguese traders came to an end in 1640, when Portugal successfully rebelled against Spain.

By then the Dutch had become Europe's chief slave traders. Their West India Company had broken the Portuguese monopoly of the West African trade, established trading bases on the West African coast, conquered a part of Brazil, crippled Spain in the Caribbean and was supplying slaves and goods to the Spanish American colonies and the infant plantations in Barbados. But Dutch free trade could not survive for long in the face of English and French hostility. England's Navigation Act of 1660 spelled out the principle:

> For the increase of shipping and encouragement of the navigation of this nation...no goods or commodities shall be imported into or exported out of any lands, islands, plantations or territories to His Majesty belonging...but in such ships or vessels as do truly and without fraud belong to the people of England...or are of the build of and belonging to any of the said lands...and whereof the master and three fourths of the mariners at least are English, under the penalty of the forfeiture and loss of all the goods...

The Council and Assembly of Nevis complained that ' whereas they formerly enjoyed freedom of trade with all nations, in amity with His Majesty, they are now debarred from the same ' and they pointed out that the tobacco planters, ' now that supplies come only from English ports where tobacco is no commodity, and not being able to produce sugar, are forced daily to desert the island '. In France also Colbert insisted that the West Indian colonies were ' nothing but commercial establishments ', that colonial trade belonged to the mother country, that it should be protected there, but that it should never be allowed to compete with home industries. For this reason the refining industry in Martinique, which had made a good beginning, was destroyed by two acts passed to protect the home refiners: an Act of 1682 that increased the duty on refined sugar to eight livres as against two on raw sugar, and an Act of 1698 that imposed the same duty on colonial refined sugar as on foreign sugar, twenty two livres, and reduced the duty on raw sugar to one livre. No other nation was to come between colony and metropolitan power, so if necessary the Dutch were to be driven from the seas. England and France became the suppliers of slaves and goods to their colonies in the Caribbean, each setting up a chartered company for the purpose. Charles II of England granted a charter to the Company of Royal Adventurers of England trading into Africa, in dyewoods, ivory, gold and slaves. Its successor, incorporated in 1672 was the Royal Africa Company, which was to supply the English sugar colonies with 3,000 slaves a year at an average price of £17, or one ton of sugar, per slave. At the time the purchase price in Africa was £3.

The Company soon ran into difficulty. Its commerce was seriously affected by the third Dutch war of 1672–4, in which it lost forts and ships. Other private traders took advantage of the arrangements made with the slave-dealing chiefs in West Africa, bought slaves and then undersold the Company in the West Indies. Also, the Company was cheated at times by its agents who bought slaves on their own account, transported them at the Company's expense and sold them privately in the West Indies.

In these circumstances it was to the Company's advantage to increase its profits by selling slaves in Spanish America at higher prices than it was permitted to charge in English colonies. Legally however, Spanish American ports were closed to English shipping. One solution was to allow Spanish ships to enter ports in Barbados and Jamaica, buy their slaves and take them away. This was contrary to the Navigation Act, but in the same way that Spain had infringed her own monopoly by the use of the *Asiento*, the English granted dispensations from their laws. West Indian planters bought slaves from interlopers whenever they could, attacked the Company constantly and were insistent that there should be a free trade in slaves, with the result that in 1698 Britain, by Act of Parliament, threw open the African slave trade to all British subjects, provision being made for the Royal Africa Company to receive a duty on imports into Africa and on certain exports, excluding slaves, in order to enable it to maintain its forts for the protection of all British traders.

Were the English slave traders simply to supply their own colonies with slaves or were they to sell in any market? And how were the Spanish colonies to obtain their slaves? There were two suppliers eager to deal with them, France and England. One solution appeared to be the granting of a separate contract, an *Asiento* for a supply of slaves to Spanish America. Spain knew that if the *Asiento* were revived at all it would go to a foreign company since she did not command sources of supply. A contract of this kind was regarded as being of the greatest value; so much so that its grant acquired all the characteristics of an international treaty. It represented a valuable source of revenue to Spain, and it seemed to offer rich profits to the country that gained it. Of the two rivals, circumstances favoured France, which dominated the Senegal region, had slave ships based on Nantes, La Rochelle, and Le Havre and enforced a monopoly operated by chartered companies that supplied slaves to French and Spanish colonies. Toward the end of the century there seemed to be every prospect of a union of the Spanish and French Crowns or at the very least, of a French prince succeeding to the Spanish throne, so it was to Spain's advantage to grant the *Asiento* to France. England and Holland united to wage war against France, having no wish to see Spain and the Netherlands pass under the control of Louis XIV. There is no doubt that in England a subsidiary motive was to prevent the French Guinea Company from keeping the *Asiento*.

The War of the Spanish Succession was fought chiefly in Europe. England sent out Benbow to the Caribbean to ward off any attack that might be launched by the French against the English islands. In the same year, 1702, the French part of St. Kitts was occupied. But English shipping and some English colonies suffered heavily. The Bahamas colony was wiped out in 1703. St. Kitts and Nevis were raided in 1706, Montserrat in 1712. Victories in Europe enabled Britain, by the Treaty of Utrecht in 1713, to obtain assurances that Spain and the Netherlands would not come under French domination, and they secured the transfer of the *Asiento* with certain other trading rights to the South Sea Company. Spain bitterly resented having to make this concession and France resented the fact that England had gained the *Asiento*. England and the South Sea Company must have known that the privileges they had gained were certain to be challenged. By the *Asiento*, the South Sea Company was to supply slaves to Spanish America over a thirty year period. The Company was granted land and facilities at Spanish ports for the ' refreshment ' of slaves. It was permitted also to send a shipload of general merchandise to Spanish America every year. The size of the annual ship was restricted, and the King of Spain was to have a quarter share in the cargo and five per cent of profit. The cargo was to be sold at the Porto Bello fair, and not before the arrival of the galleons. The Company undertook to refrain from illicit trade and to supply slaves of a certain quality.

Storm clouds soon gathered over the Company. Planters in the islands complained that it sold the best slaves to the Spanish colonies. Private traders saw that they were being superseded in a trade that was essential for the islands, which in this way obtained the bullion they needed for purchasing their plantation supplies and food from North America. Underprivileged traders considered that they were being sacrificed in the interests of the Company. The Spanish authorities hated the Company because it was the visible evidence of their country's defeat and of the infringement of a monopoly which, though it was by this time largely fictitious, remained a source of national pride. They were convinced also that the annual ship was a device for smuggling on a grand scale. Certainly the Company's slave sloops from Jamaica carried other goods besides slaves and the annual ship was often accompanied by provision ships which also carried contraband. The Spaniards charged that the annual ship, while discharging its cargo off Porto Bello, was sometimes reloaded at night from Jamaica, and they delayed interminably over the granting of permits and clearance papers. In fact only eight voyages of this kind took place during the whole period of the concession.

Spain, insistent on its monopoly, claimed the right to stop and search foreign ships anywhere in the Caribbean, which was then frequented by French and English ships trading lawfully with their colonies, Dutch traders who went armed and openly engaged in illicit trade, the South Seas Company's ships and sloops engaged in lawful or ostensibly lawful trade with Spanish America, North American traders and smugglers. The Spanish patrol ships that carried out the search were fitted out privately. The crew were unscrupulous hirelings with a keen eye for prize money and little regard for the law. Any Spanish colonial produce–indigo, logwood, cocoa, silver–found on a ship, was accepted by the *guarda costas* and the Spanish courts as evidence of unlawful trade. The process of appeal by a ship seized and charged with carrying contraband was long and usually fruitless.

But smuggling was part of the Caribbean tradition. Trade with Spanish America yielded silver and the aim of the traders, whether North American, European or West Indian, was in the words of one of the Yankees, ' to gitt money '.

During the 1720's indignation grew in England and the colonies over the frequent seizure of English ships and the losses suffered by traders. Tempers were further inflamed by disputes over the presence of English logwood cutters in the Bay of Honduras and a boundary quarrel between Florida and the English colony of Georgia. The trading part of the nation clamoured for war against Spain. English anger knew no bounds when in 1738 Captain Jenkins appeared in London and told how his vessel had been seized, how he had been manhandled and one of his ears cut off. In October 1739 the ' War of Captain Jenkins Ear ' broke out between England and Spain. It came to an end in 1748 with the signing of the Treaty of Aix La Chapelle. This was supplemented in 1750 by a commercial treaty that wound up the maritime quarrel between England and Spain but was as inconclusive as the Treaty itself, making no reference to the freedom of navigation, one of Britain's chief purposes in the war. It left unsettled also the problem of the Honduras logwood camps which had expanded during the war years. Under the Treaty, the South Sea Company, whose last annual ship had sailed in 1733, and whose slave trade had ended in 1739, received £100,000 for the surrender of all its claims under the *Asiento*. These agreements, however, though inconclusive in these respects, marked the abandonment by Britain of its long effort to persuade and force Spain to allow direct trade with her colonies. Spain, influenced by the example of her rivals, began to organise joint-stock companies to handle certain colonial trades. An example is the *Compania de Comercio de la Habana* which had the monopoly of the trade of Cuba between 1740 and 1760.

The series of *Asientos* ran from 1595 to 1773. We have referred to the extraordinary value placed on the contract, and we have looked also at Britain's experience with the *Asiento*. We have noted the antagonisms it produced between the various British interests as well as between Spain and England, and the illusory nature of the dream of rich profits from the sale of slaves in Spanish America. The number of Africans imported into Spanish America during the period of the *Asientos* is estimated by Curtin at 700,000, the annual average between 1641 and 1773 being of the order of 3,880. This total includes the slaves re-exported from Jamaica, which LePage, in his *Introduction to Jamaican Creole*, estimates at 84,000 during the years 1711–1740, and at 206,200 for 1701–1807. These numbers, though large, are surprisingly small when set against the immensity of Spanish America. In the Spanish colonies the *hacienda* served a local or regional market, and never developed an export trade based on one or two tropical products as did the plantation islands, where sugar production was land-intensive and where there was always a shortage of labour because deaths exceeded births. Between 1701 and 1801 the British Caribbean, smaller in area than the smallest country in South America, imported 1,401,000 slaves, twice as many as all Spanish America. The Spanish imports showed a marked increase when Cuba, in the closing decades of the 18th century, began to turn to sugar, and when Puerto Rico followed her example some decades later. These two, having embarked on sugar production, imported one and three quarter million slaves between 1800–1874.

In the light of these figures we can see that the *Asiento* gave an entry into a market that was relatively limited and that was further restricted because of Spain's insistence on quality. What added greatly to the value of *Asiento* was that it gave the contractor an opportunity to hide an illicit trade in goods other than slaves.

The War of Captain Jenkins Ear merged into the War of the Austrian Succession and in 1744 war broke out openly in the Caribbean between England and France. It was a direct result of bitter rivalry with the French sugar islands which, larger in area and with more virgin land, were producing cheaper sugar and were capturing some of the North American-West Indian trade.

The theme was repeated in the House of Commons: that the French were the greatest rivals England had in the sugar trade; that this happened because of their North American trade which gave them a ' vent ' for their rum and molasses and ' easy access to horses, lumber and other necessaries;' that as a result they were able to undersell the English colonies. Arguments like these led to the passing of the Molasses Act of 1733 which imposed high duties on foreign sugar molasses and rum imported into the British North American colonies. The Act proved difficult to enforce, and it irritated the North Americans. In order to help the West Indian planters, sugar was removed from the ' enumerated ' list in 1739 to permit direct trade with Europe but this did not remove the basic cause of the difficulty, high production costs. The war, however, offered the English an opportunity to attack the French sugar islands, set fire to the canes, wreck the factories and carry off the slaves, the most necessary and the most mobile part of the planter's capital.

In a region like the Caribbean, only a nation that had command of the sea could carry out this policy effectively. The events of 1744 – 48 showed that the French were at a disadvantage because they had no naval base in the Caribbean where their ships might be refitted. Sent out direct from French dockyards, the ships arrived in good condition but having no dockyard facilities in the islands they had to come out after the hurricane season and return just before the hurricane season of the following year. It was difficult to replenish supplies. Many of the sailors, unaccustomed to the climate and to the new disease environment, fell ill with malaria, yellow fever, dysentery. The only line to follow was to engage the enemy as soon as possible after arrival, or not at all. Often French fleets came out and sailed back to France without having accomplished anything.

The West India interest insisted on English warships being permanently stationed in the Caribbean. As a result the English system, which was developed in the 1740's was quite different from the French. Fleets were based in the Caribbean, where there were two naval dockyards, one at English Harbour in Antigua, the other at Port Royal in Jamaica. The dockyards made it possible to repair and refit ships and to keep stores of equipment and food. Seamen on a two or three-year period of service in the West Indies became seasoned to the new environment. The system was expensive. It tied up ships that might have been used elsewhere, and did not do away with the need for major expeditions because the squadrons were necessarily small; but it did provide shipping in the Caribbean, and the islands themselves, with protection, while at the same time serving as a constant threat to the French who, rather belatedly established a naval base at Martinique in 1784.

Profitable as were slaving and smuggling with Spanish America, the sugar trade with Europe was the heart of the business and Africa kept the heart beating. From Surinam and the Guianas to Jamaica and St. Domingue, on every sugar plantation and throughout each tedious year, Africans sweated and died producing more sugar for Europe.

By 1750 England was taking all the West Indian sugar and was demanding more. Her population was beginning to grow. In the first decades of the century cheap gin played its part in lifting the English death rate above the birth rate. An Act of 1751 that imposed a duty on spirits and put an end to the retailing of spirits by distillers and shopkeepers helped to change this. In 1700 the total population of England and Wales was about five and a half million. In 1750 it stood at nearly six and a half million, in 1801 at 8,892,536. The figures point to changes that were beginning to occur in Britain, and that were in time to destroy the slave and sugar plantation. But a West Indian planter of the 1750's, watching his sugar move from the wharf, must have found the world a pleasant place. He could recall that the Act of 1739 permitting the direct export of sugar to southern Europe had helped to save him from bankruptcy, sending up the price of muscovado sugar to an average price of 33/8. That was fifty per cent higher than in the decade before the war of 1739 to 1748. He knew that the profits from a well-run estate ranged between seven per cent and nineteen per cent. The presence of British warships at Port Royal and at English Harbour gave a comfortable feeling of security and were proof of the value

England put on the islands. The Maroons in Jamaica had kept the peace after the treaty of 1739. A disastrous hurricane of 1744 that had wrecked 100 ships in Kingston Harbour and ripped through the wharves and warehouses there and at Old Harbour was but a memory. In Barbados the depression of the 1730's belonged to the past. Sugar production in the island had increased from about 6,000 tons in the 1730's to just under 7,000 tons in the 1750's. The hated South Sea Company had ceased selling slaves. British traders had gained the leadership in the slave trade, and were able to supply the slaves that were needed, whereas the French Sugar Islands found difficulty in obtaining an adequate supply. Above all, the value of the West India trade was universally recognised, and the sugar planter took pride in the fact that he was held high in public esteem, that he was a symbol of indispensable power and wealth. True, the North Americans were continuing their trade with the French colonies, but the Molasses Act had shown where Britain's sympathy lay, and the West India interest commanded a political influence second to none at Westminster.

Even war was a benefit. Though it caused delays in shipping and the loss of ships and cargoes, it crippled the trade of the French islands, raised anti-French feeling in England, and diverted attention from awkward questions about the wisdom of British dependence on high cost British-grown sugar. War, or the constant possibility of war, in the middle 18th century was to the advantage of the British West Indies.

In 1756 the Seven Years War broke out, with England and France ranged against each other. Pitt aimed at safeguarding English North America by taking Canada. The Caribbean became one of the main theatres of war. Each side sent out powerful expeditions that sought to take the enemy's sugar colonies, for imperial policy had changed. The aim was not merely to cripple rival sugar producing colonies but to take them and use them as bargaining counters at the end of the war. The West India interest accepted the policy, realising that Barbados or Antigua would be safer if Martinique and Guadeloupe were also in English hands; and if it were decided to keep any of the islands the danger of their becoming competitors could be avoided by turning out the French colonists, settling the island with English colonists and prohibiting them from planting sugar. For a time in 1757 it looked as if the French would gain the upper hand. One of their squadrons off the coast of North Africa threatened English control of the slave trade, another in the Caribbean damaged English trade and threatened Jamaica, and a third operated ágainst the English in North America. Gradually the tide of battle turned, the English taking Louisburg in Canada, the French bases of Senegal and Goree in West Africa, and Guadeloupe. The West India interest was outraged at the terms of capitulation granted to the French planters. They were to be neutral while the war lasted, their goods were to be admitted to the English market, they were to retain French law under English military occupation, and they were fully protected in the possession of their property. Guadeloupe soon began to prosper. English and American merchants readily provided supplies, often on credit, for here was a welcome new market. The Guadeloupe planters also gained access to new markets in Europe and North America, to the envy of Martinique and the dismay of the West Indians. This was the kind of conquest that they most disliked, for it put another competitor in the market and their fears were justified. The flooding of the market with Guadeloupe sugar in 1760 caused a fall in sugar prices.

Spain entered the war on the side of France in 1762. She resented the support England had given to the Belize settlement on the mainland of Central America which now numbered some 500, and the activities of English agents on the Mosquito coast, who intrigued against them with the Indians. In addition, the Treaty of Commerce of 1750 had not led to a suppression of smuggling, as Spain had hoped. Privateers still infested the Caribbean. Spanish merchant shipping was frequently molested. The situation grew worse during the Seven Years War, when the French, desperately seeking to help their starving sugar colonies, threw open the trade to neutrals. This measure, under the ' rule of war of 1756 ' exposed to seizure any Spanish ship suspected of having touched at a French colonial port. Also Spain watched with apprehension the unfolding of Pitt's plan to seize all the French possessions in the Caribbean and North America. Spain realised that if England and France made peace she would have to negotiate with an England that was all powerful in the Caribbean. She was closely linked with France by dynastic ties. She took the final step toward war when, by the Family Compact of 1761 she undertook to declare war before May 1762 if peace had not been made between England and France by that date.

Peace was not made. In the month that Spain declared war Rodney took Martinique, a French naval force under Blenac arriving too late from Brest to intervene. Blenac made for St. Domingue and his nearness caused panic in Jamaica. Blenac's fleet was blockaded in Cap Français. Martinique was granted terms similar to those Guadeloupe had obtained, and this angered the West India interest. The other islands soon fell: Dominica, Tobago, St. Lucia, St. Vincent, Grenada. Only St. Domingue was left in French hands.

Spain had entered the war just in time to be stripped of some of her colonies. In August 1762, while Blenac, short of provisions and with half his men sick, remained bottled up at Cap Français, Pocock and Albermarle took Havana. In the Far East another English fleet captured Manila. Spain capitulated in October and discussions began leading to the Treaty of Paris in 1763.

It was clear that Britain would have to give up some of her many conquests; but which? It was to her advantage to keep some colonies from which an immediate revenue might be obtained, since the war had to be paid for. There was heated public debate about the desirability of keeping Guadeloupe in preference to Canada, even though the principal object of the war had been to safeguard British North America and this could be achieved most effectively by keeping a part or all of Canada. Many argued that Guadeloupe could be settled by Englishmen more easily than the vast spaces of Canada; that Englishmen who settled in the West Indies returned to England to spend their money whereas settlers in North America stayed at home and spent there what they had. The slave traders urged the retention of Guadeloupe, since this would give them a new market. Exporting merchants favoured the acquisition of more sugar land since the British islands were not producing enough sugar to allow for re-export to the continent. Even the West India interest recognised that colonies like Barbados were more secure with Martinique and Guadeloupe in English hands. In the

end Britain returned the French islands and the French slaving
stations in West Africa, but kept Grenada, all the neutral islands
except St. Lucia, all North America east of the Mississippi River,
and obtained the right to navigate the Mississippi itself. Spain
objected to having the English on the shores of the Gulf of Mexico,
where they could isolate Florida, run a smuggling trade under
the pretence of navigating the Mississippi, and intercept the
Spanish flotillas with greater ease than before; and France ceded
Louisiana to Spain in order to buy her consent. England gave
back Cuba to Spain and got Florida in exchange. Also Spain
accepted the presence of logwood cutters in Honduras and agreed
to respect their property, while England undertook not to fortify
the camps. The arrangements remained vague, however.
Boundaries were not defined nor were the rights of the logwood
cutters clearly stated. As a result the exact position of the English
in British Honduras remained in dispute to the end of the century.

Our West Indian planter of the 1760's still saw the world as it
had appeared to him in the 1750's; and he could find grounds for
optimism in the terms of the Treaty of Paris. But disturbing
things had been said during the peace talks about the West
Indies, that wherever sugar grew population decreased, and that
the sugar islands weakened and depopulated the mother-country.
During the decades of the 1760's and 1770's there were numerous
signs that the forces of change were gathering strength. An Atlantic Revolution was in the making, which revealed its hurricane
strength in the War of Independence, 1775–84; the French
Revolution which began in 1789; the Haitian Revolution of
1800–04; and the Latin-American Revolutions of 1800–30. As
we continue the story of the West Indian sugar trade we find
Britain and North America moving gradually into the 19th
century, their economic base changing and expanding, their
societies accommodating themselves, however painfully, to new
principles of commerce and of government; and on the other hand
we find the West Indian slave-holding planter class firmly fixed
in the beginning of the 18th century, the West Indian economy
weakening because it became increasingly non-competitive, and
West Indian society unable to change because it rested on an
institution that could not be reformed, freedom being the only
alternative to slavery.

The general background can be sketched briefly. Up to the middle of the 18th century England had been a country with a fairly simple social and economic structure. It prided itself on its yeomanry of whom there were about 180,000 at the start of the 18th century. Few of them were left by 1832. They were displaced by large farms as effectively as, a century earlier, the smallholders of Barbados and St. Kitts had been displaced by sugar estates. A new England was coming into existence, different from the old in population density, social structure and political organisation. We who are in the midst of a world revolution characterised by ideological conflicts, advances in science and a technology based on computers, electronics and instant communication can understand something of the sweep and force of the Atlantic Revolution of 1775–1830.

Of fundamental importance was the growth of population that took place in England and Wales in the second half of the century. Between 1700 and 1750 the death rate had often been higher than the birth rate, but the population grew by fifty per cent between 1750 and 1800. England, which had been a corn-exporting country up to 1760, was by 1800 unable to produce all the food she needed. She could not have sustained so high a rate of population growth had it not been for an agricultural revolution produced by the spread of large scale farming and by notable innovations in agriculture.

This was one aspect of the general transformation. It is in contrast with the West Indian rejection of the plough and of improved methods of cultivation. The discovery of a new source of power through the use of steam was in itself a revolution. Watt's steam engine, invented in 1768, and first used in cotton manufacture in 1785, made possible the expansion of the industry, and this in turn led to increased cotton production in Antigua and the Deep South. Iron smelting was improved by the invention of the reverberatory furnace and an effective blast from the use of water power. Canals were built to improve communications. Industry began to cluster round coal and iron mines.

The new technology had its parallel in new thinking, much of it centred on the discovery of the ' common man '. Wesley and Whitfield preached man's direct personal relationship and responsibilities to his Maker and to his fellow-man. Priestley

threw new light on man's relationship with the physical universe
Voltaire insisted on man's need for freedom, Rousseau insisted
that ' Man is born free but is everywhere in chains,' and Tom
Paine popularised the view that ' Society in every state is a blessing but Government, even in its best state, is but a necessary evil.'
John Howard directed attention to man's responsibility even for
those who transgress, Captain Coram established the first Found-
lings Hospital to save thousands of unwanted children who were
left to die in empty rooms and by the roadside, Thomas Clarkson
documented the barbarities of the Slave Trade, and Adam Smith
attacked the whole system of monopoly, and branded the ban on
colonial manufacture as ' impertinent badges of slavery '.

This is the setting against which to review events in the Caribbean. One effect of the Treaty of Paris was to widen the area of
the plantations, which included Portuguese Brazil, French Guiana;
Dutch Surinam, Essequibo and Demerara, French Martinique,
Guadeloupe and St. Domingue, English Barbados, St. Kitts and
Nevis, Antigua, Dominica, Grenada, St. Vincent, Tobago, Tortola and Jamaica, Danish St. Croix, St. Thomas and St. John,
and for the first time Spanish Cuba. The English occupation
of Cuba had led traders to introduce some 10,000 slaves into
the island and to encourage the development of sugar production, on the assumption that Britain would keep the island. The
importation of slaves continued after the return of Cuba to Spain
in 1763. At the same time Havana became less of a military
outpost because Spain abandoned the rigid convoy system and
developed a more flexible defence system based on the great forts
of San Cristobal and San Felipe del Morro in Puerto Rico. No
longer could the West Indian hope to restrict sugar production
to the English colonies.

Nor could the English colonies produce enough to meet English
demands. The years from 1760 to 1790 were the golden age of
the French sugar islands. In 1767 they exported 77,000 tons
and the British colonies, including the neutral islands, 72,000
tons. On the eve of the French Revolution the French islands
were producing 100,000 tons, the British from 85,000 to 90,000
tons. French sugar was more in quantity and was cheaper
because the planters could produce sugar more cheaply. They
still had access to virgin land, did not have to manure as heavily,

and paid lower export duties. In addition they were ready to sell their rum and molasses at low prices because France put a heavy duty on these two products in order to protect their brandy industry. As a result the North Americans continued trading with the French colonies, in defiance of the Molasses Act; and they found in these islands, as well as in the English colonies, ready markets for their provisions—candles, corn, lard, leather, onions, bricks, oak boards, pine boards, hogsheads, shingles, hoops, staves, rice, cattle, horses, hogs, sheep, bread, flour, beef, pork, dried fish, pickled fish, peas, beans and the like. The Yankee merchants tended more and more to sell in the English markets for cash or for bills on London and to buy sugar and molasses chiefly from the French.

In the British islands some planters were growing uneasy. The older settled islands carried still the burdensome export duty of four and a half per cent on their produce, which had never been levied in Jamaica and which the imperial government now failed to extract from the neutral islands. Their exhausted land required heavy and costly manuring, and this called in turn for a larger labour force at a time when the price of slaves was going higher and higher. The ceded islands attracted a number of poorer white settlers, and they were at the same time turning to sugar and demanding slaves for their new plantations. The expansion of sugar production in Jamaica and in the ceded islands kept the prices of sugar on the London market from rising to cover increased production costs. These islands and Jamaica had, through other export crops like coffee, cacao and cotton, some protection against disaster. Though this was so, Jamaica, like the older colonies, suffered from price fluctuations and high taxation in the years following the war.

The English colonies turned to the Government for relief. They sought lower duties on their sugar, cheaper slaves, an end to the North American trade with the French colonies and easier loans on West Indian security; but now the Government was less willing to legislate in favour of the West Indian interest. Grocers, refiners and distillers were pressing for cheaper sugar, whether British or foreign grown. English merchants and manufacturers were finding that the West Indies could not absorb English production and that there were expanding markets in North and

South America. Finding themselves in a world that was becoming hostile after the Seven Years War, the English West
Indian planters, factors and merchants came together for their
own. protection, organising a powerful parliamentary lobby.

The British Government passed a Free Ports Act in 1766
which aimed at finding legitimate outlets in the Caribbean
for British and North American goods. In each of those
countries production was expanding and there was a surplus,
for the West Indian market was too small to absorb the full
production. The Act opened four ports in Jamaica—Kingston,
Lucea, Montego Bay and Savanna-la-mar—and two in Dominica—Roseau and Prince Rupert's Bay—to foreign shipping.
Foreigners were permitted to buy and export slaves and any
British goods legally imported save naval stores and tobacco;
and they were allowed to pay in their own coin or in their own
produce, subject to certain exceptions. At the Jamaica ports
it was forbidden to import goods that Jamaica produced—
sugar, coffee, pimento, ginger, molasses, tobacco—and manufactured goods. In Dominica, where the object was trade with
the French islands, sugar, coffee and the rest were allowed
to be imported. This meant that foreign West Indian staples,
sugar for example, could enter through Roseau and Prince
Rupert's Bay, and could be used to increase British re-exports
of sugar to Europe. By providing French sugar with this market Britain was encouraging sugar production in the French
islands, and by permitting the sale and export of slaves to
non-British colonies like Cuba, she was enabling them to keep
down their sugar production costs. In these respects the policy
ran contrary to West Indian sugar-planting interests. The Free
Port Act put British and North American producers in a position
where they were able to find markets for their surplus goods outside their own colonial trading system.

The clouds on the horizon grew thick and menacing as
relationships between Britain and her North American colonies
deteriorated. War against France had often brought benefits
to the West Indies but war against the North American colonies would be disastrous. The West Indian interest held meetings, drew up petitions, sought by every possible means to
avert the conflict. The North Americans urged them to join

in the revolution, pointing out that they also had representative but not responsible government, that they had suffered from taxation without representation, from interference with their power to make laws, an adverse trade balance, and from many hardships and restrictions due to the Act of Trade. Some West Indians had rioted against the Stamp Act. Like the North Americans they were taxed to pay for their defence. Unlike the northern colonies, however, the West Indians knew that their islands were small and highly exposed, with small free populations, large numbers of resentful slaves, and with many of their leading landowners living in England. They needed the Royal navy. For all these reasons, as well as from loyalty, the islands refused to join the Americans.

Fighting broke out between England and her North American colonies in 1775. France entered the war against England in 1778, Spain in 1779. The islands, heavily taxed and short of supplies, suffered grievously. Between 1780 and 1781 Barbados was on the point of starvation, and her situation was made all the more desperate at this time by two hurricanes and a tidal wave. Her slave population fell from 68,500 in 1773 to 54,500 in 1783, largely as a result of malnutrition and physical hardship. Famine threatened Jamaica even though the island had its provision grounds and access also to supplies from Georgia and Carolina, which were under British control. Reports said that in 1778 Antigua lost more than 1,000 negroes, Montserrat near 1,200, Nevis three or four hundred, and St. Kitts as many from want of provisions. The merchants began to refuse the planters credit for the provisions they needed, and Antigua was forced to pass an Act in 1779 ' for enabling Persons therein named to borrow a sum not exceeding £20,000...on the Public Credit of the island ', in order to buy provisions for distribution among the planters. Sugar prices rose and the grocers and refiners in England demanded that when the price of sugar on the London market reached a certain figure importations of foreign sugar at a low rate of duty should be allowed. The West India interest managed to block this move but it could not prevent the British duty on sugar being doubled in the course of the war. During the Seven Years War they had watched with some satisfaction the economic strangulation of the French colonies. It was now their turn to experience this strangulation, and it was their turn also to watch the French gain naval supremacy in the Caribbean, the British fleets being tied down to supporting the armies in North America and defending the coasts of Britain. Dominica fell to the French in September 1778. Rodney countered by capturing St. Lucia and using that island as a base for watching the French in Martinique. In 1779 France took St. Vincent and Grenada. In the following year Holland declared war on Britain, and so offered Rodney the opportunity to take the ' Golden Rock ', St. Eustatius. He followed this up by capturing the three Dutch mainland colonies, Demerara, Berbice, Essequibo but the surrender of Cornwallis at Yorktown released a French fleet under de Grasse for operations in the Caribbean. The French retook St. Eustatius, the three Dutch mainland colonies and Tobago while Spain captured Pensacola, Florida and New Providence. St. Kitts capitulated in 1782 to a French force of 8,000 men under de Bouille. Nevis and Montserrat went down like dominoes. At this stage Rodney returned to the Caribbean, and resumed his watch on de Grasse who had gathered thirty five warships and 150 merchantmen carrying 5,000 troops for an attack on Jamaica. The two fleets went into action off The Saintes on April 12, 1782. Rodney on the *Formidable* broke the French line, Hood's squadron did the same, and after a day of heavy fighting de Grasse hauled down his flag. The war came to an end with the signing of the Treaty of Versailles in 1784. Britain regained Grenada, St. Vincent, St. Kitts, Nevis and Dominica. The right to cut logwood in Central America was restored in the same ambiguous terms as before. Florida was ceded to Spain, Tobago to France.

Hard times continued after the war. The United States, having gained its independence, was treated as a foreign power, notwithstanding strong West Indian pressure for a resumption of the West India-North American trade on the old terms. Parliament, in its Act of 1783, in subsequent Orders in Council, and an Act of 1788 laid down the policy—

> That no goods or commodities whatever shall be imported or brought from any of the territories belonging to the United States of America into any of His Majesty's West India islands under the penalty of the forfeiture thereof. . . except tobacco,

pitch, tar, turpentine, hemp, flax, masts, yards, bowsprits, staves, leading, boards, timber, shingles and lumber of any sort; horses, meet cattles, sheep, hogs, poultry... bread, biscuits, flour, peas, beans, potatoes, wheat, rice, oats, barley and grain... And that none of the goods herein excepted shall be imported... except by British subjects and in British-built ships owned by His Majesty's subjects and navigating according to law.

The West India interest urged that the British Free Port Act should be extended to allow American ships to ' trade ' the British West Indian ports on the same terms as French and Spanish ships. This also was refused.

Since supplies had to be obtained, the West Indies resorted to smuggling while the British navy played policeman. The price of supplies continued to rise. In 1874 the planter had to pay three or four times as much for white oak staves than before the war; double for rice; between a third and a half as much as formerly for meat and fish from Canada. Amid this shortage, hurricanes struck Jamaica in 1784, 1785, 1786. Fifteen thousand slaves died from famine. Problems multiplied when in order to meet the cost of war, Britain raised the duty on sugar to 12/4d per hundredweight in 1787 and to 15/- in 1791. The quantity and value of sugar was increasing steadily, but the West Indies got little benefit from the increase in sugar production and in the value of sugar because most of the profit went to the London factors. Hardship and distress, complaints about the burden of mortgages, reports of the sale of estates for debt drove home the lesson that it was unwise to depend overmuch on sugar as a cash crop for export and on imported grain and meat. The West India interest went searching for food. ' Every encouragement' resolved the Jamaica House of Assembly, ' is to be given to the cultivation of Yams, Cocoes, Maize, Plantain and the like, and such products as the Breadfruit, Nutmeg, Cloves and Cinnamon... and Coffee; it being believed that the cultivation of such exotics would, without doubt in the course of a few years lessen the dependence of the sugar islands on North America for food and necessaries '. Coconuts and coffee became valuable crops. Barbados and the Leeward Islands expanded their production of

cotton. Sugar however remained the chief crop. There was to
be one further burst of prosperity, following on the destruction
of the rival French sugar trade through revolution and war; and
after that the deluge.

CHAPTER 16

World of White Power

Sugar brought traders crowding into the Caribbean each year from the ports of Western Europe and North America. Sugar set the fleets and armies of Europe grappling with each other in the Caribbean for as much as a third of the 18th century. Sugar made the plantation islands of Barbados, and then Jamaica, the most valuable colonies in the British Empire, and put St. Domingue far ahead of all other French possessions. Sugar produced the wealth that dazzled Britain. Cumberland in his play, *The West Indian*, produced in London in 1771, presented the popular image of the West India planter, who had rum and sugar enough belonging to him to make all the water in the Thames into punch. Sugar revived the fortunes of Peter Beckford, who died in 1710 leaving ' the largest property real and personal of any subject in Europe '. William Beckford his grandson, became the most powerful of the West India absentees in Britain. Other powerful absentee owners included the Hibberts, among them George who helped to modernise the Port of London through the construction of the West India docks; the families of the Longs, Pennants, Gales, Dawkins, Ellis, Barrets, Scarlets, Mannings; the Tobins and Pinneys of Nevis; the Lascelles, Holders, Harrisons, Alleynes of Barbados; and a host of others. Sugar put into the House of Commons Lascelles, Paynes, Beckford, Bryan Edwards, John Gladstone, Dawkins, Pennant, Rose Price, Codrington, Charles Ellis, and others so that at one time, through its absentee proprietors, the West Indies held more than fifty seats in the house, providing the islands with strong direct representation in Westminster. The North American colonies had nothing to compare with this massive pressure group. In 1764 the colonial agent for Massachussetts wrote of the formidable number of votes possessed by the West Indian proprietors, and Benjamin Franklin confessed that the West Indians vastly outweighed those of the Northern colonies. Planter power forced the Molasses Act of 1733 through Parliament.

The West India interest was the manifestation in England of planter power, the dominant force in West Indian society from 1660 to 1833, a longer period than our 140 years of freedom. Nor did planter power and white minority rule come to an end at the date of emancipation. They continued well into the present century. The value systems established during that period, the basic social structure and the power base only began to change in the late 1920's. In considering the sources of white power, the methods by which it controlled the political system, the purposes of its laws, the procedures by which it enforced those laws, we are looking at forces and institutions that in many important respects made our society what it is today. Historically, for us of the Caribbean, the most important products of that long period were these; that race became a determinant of the standing and merit of individuals and of groups within the society; that slavery as an institution was protected and preserved in the interests of a minority; and that the colonial relationship was preserved because the minority were tied to the metropolitan power by protected markets, and the need for security against rebellion from within and attack from without. A long period of minority rule and a rigorous system of racial discrimination are part of the West Indian experience. White power rested primarily on control of the political system and the maintenance of plantation slavery and was protected and preserved by a special body of legislation and by an impassable white barrier around all the key points of power.

In the political system which was established first in the Eastern Caribbean, in Barbados and the Leeward Islands, the instrument of colonisation was the proprietary grant, but even in Carlisle's charter the principle of representative government was recognised, for though he was given the power to make laws it was to be with the ' consent, assent and approbation ' of the freeholders of the colony. Similarly when Lord Windsor was sent to Jamaica in 1661 to establish civil government he was instructed not only to set up a Council but also to arrange for the election of a House of Assembly, and to appoint justices and to pass laws that were for the good of the colony and were not repugnant to the laws of England. When Charles II set out to encourage Englishmen to migrate to Jamaica he declared that they and their children ' shall from their respective births be reputed to be free denizens of England; and shall have the same privileges. . . as our free born subjects of England '. In 1663 the Crown took over from the proprietors the government of the Caribee Islands, but kept the constitution, with governor, council and assembly. When the administration of the Leeward Islands was separated from that of Barbados, and the group put under one Governor General, each island was given its own Governor, council and assembly. Some years later, in 1675, the Crown declared its wish that a ' full and complete legislature ' should be established in Dominica and instructed that writs should be issued for the election of representatives to serve in the House of Assembly in that island. West Indians looked on this system of government as being essentially the same as that of England. But the popular base of the system was changed by the Sugar Revolution in the middle of the 17th century. It put black slaves in the place of white bondservants and it put large landholders and slave-owners in the place of white smallholders tending their ten acres of indigo, cotton and tobacco and electing regularly their assemblymen and vestry-men. It transformed a large white majority into a small white minority, so that representative government became representative not of the people but of a class. The system as it existed in England represented a stage in national development, by which representative government was gradually widened and the king's power diminished until full power finally passed into the hands of the House of Commons. In the Caribbean the system became an instrument in the hands of a white oligarchy, a means for preserving and protecting their property, including their property in slaves, and for enforcing their control. In the early years of settlement the central question in West Indian society had been ' Are you a freeholder?' In the society which developed after the

1660's it became ' Are you bond or free?' This in turn meant ' Are you black or white?' In every English colony of the Caribbean the political system was used to preserve white supremacy and a social structure based on racial discrimination.

The island legislatures, like those on the North American mainland, became centres of constant conflict between the assemblies and governors, with the assemblies insisting on control over appropriations. In the West Indies skilful measures taken under the later Stuarts went some way toward curbing the power of the Assemblies. Barbados and the Leewards were obliged in 1663 to accept the imposition of a permanent $4\frac{1}{2}\%$ export duty tax in return for the resumption by the Crown of the Carlisle grant. From the period of the Restoration the English government insisted that colonial laws should be sent to England for confirmation and from time to time it used its powers of disallowance. It was by commission under the Royal Seal that governors were appointed. Senior officials were appointed from England by letters patent. But since the Governor had no choice other than to choose members of his Council from among the men on the spot, and since patent officers were served by deputies, and in effect therefore by local people, the administration rested largely in West Indian hands. Every Governor's report reflected an unceasing struggle with the Assemblies which retained considerable power and constantly sought to enlarge it, as one enraged governor after another reported. In 1712 the Governor of Barbados stated that the Council and Assembly had disputed heatedly about the Excise Bill; ' I did all I could to accommodate the matter but some here aim at nothing less than to make themselves an independent people...' His lament was echoed by the Governor of Jamaica in 1716. The Assemblies found ways of evading a review of their laws by the King's Council, and they challenged the English Parliament itself when it made laws that were to be applied to the West Indies. In Jamaica the constitution had been designed so that the Assembly should play a minor role, and its powers were limited in the Governor's instructions. In 1752, however, Governor Knollys reported that it had become the predominant element in the government. It maintained its position of strength by keeping a strangle-hold on supplies. The Governor had the power to dissolve the House but the House put a limit to the exercise of his power by voting supplies for short periods only, not more than six or twelve months at a time. Another device was to tack on a measure it wanted to a money bill, ' marrying ' the two in such a way that if the Governor wanted the supplies he had to take the measure also.

The system of government was very different in the French colonies. In these there were no traditional obstacles to centralised rule. When the Company of the West Indies went bankrupt in 1674, the French Crown assumed direct control. Supreme command in the area was entrusted to a Governor General, under whom were military governors, one for each colony. The authority of the governor was balanced by that of an intendant or civil administrator, responsible mainly for justice, economic regulation and finance. Each Governor was assisted by a Council that advised him on policy and served as a Court of Appeal. The intendants were the presidents of these Councils, and the members were nominated by the Governor. Being made up of local people, the Council had a good deal of influence, but it had no power, for it could neither vote money nor pass laws. Legislation and taxation were by royal decree. The Governor had the responsibility and the power to govern, whereas in the English colonies the Governor had the responsibility and the Assembly had the power.

Representative government was firmly established but it was government representative of a small class, the whites, and because the blacks were increasing in number through the heavy importation of Africans strenuous efforts were made to increase the number of whites also. Writing in the 1780's, Bryan Edwards estimated the population of the West Indies at about 520,000. Of these 65,305 were white and 455,664 black, a proportion of one to seven. There were, he thought, about 20,000 free people of colour. Edwards himself stressed the difficulty in calculating the population accurately because of the inadequacy of the records but his estimates may be taken as presenting a fair picture. The figures demonstrate how the African slave trade determined the growth and ethnic composition of the population. They show also why the English and West Indian governments were worried about the growing preponderance of blacks in the population. Jamaica was very concerned because she found it difficult to attract white settlers in any number. The contrast stands out when we remember that Barbados, twenty years after settlement, had a population of about 40,000 white persons, whereas twenty years after its conquest Jamaica had only 9,000 whites. The whites in Jamaica and the other colonies saw and felt themselves threatened by the inflow of blacks, and as a result the legislatures passed Deficiency Laws requiring planters to keep a certain number of white servants, one to every twenty or thirty blacks. The Jamaica Act of 1702 did little to improve the situation. A more effective Deficiency Law was passed in 1720, and similar laws were passed annually thereafter, but by 1750 the system of white indentured labour had broken down and the Deficiency Acts had become sources of revenue rather than means to settlement. When this became obvious Jamaica did what the smaller colonies had done in their early years and offered free grants of land. Laws were passed ordering planters who had grabbed more land than they could use to surrender a part. Free grants of one hundred acres, free transportation and a year's supply of provisions were offered to immigrants. The Governor of the Leeward Islands complained in 1733 about the ' temptations thrown out of Jamaica ', but on the whole the results appear to have been disappointing. The position toward the close of the century is summarised by Cratton and Walvin in *A Jamaica Plantation*:

> The white personnel on Worthy Park changed with astonishing speed. Most whites stayed in their jobs only for a matter of months... Throughout the two last decades of the 18th century a group of slaves, never smaller than 300 and at times more than 500 strong, was kept at work and in check by a rapidly changing handful of whites in times of great internal and external stress...

The whites were the governing class. There was an elite of large planters and rich merchants, the *grands blancs* of the French colonies. From this close knit group came the members of the Council and House of Assembly, the officers of the militia, the judges and justices. Next in order came managers and attorneys, professional men, lesser government officials; and on the lowest rung were the overseer and the poor whites. As the plantations spread and developed many of the elite returned to live in England.

From Grenada through the islands to Jamaica the governors complained that ' There are so many Absentees elected, that it is with great difficulty they can make a House.' It became necessary to widen the circle of power by recruiting into the public service the ' middling men ', and even those whom St. Kitts called ' adventurous merchants ' and ' self-educated physicians'. The shift was from property to whiteness. Professor Goveia, in her analysis of *Slave Society in the Leeward Islands* at the end of the 18th century points out that ' instead of their being bound together by their solidarity as men of wealth, the leaders of the ruling class at that time were chiefly unified by their solidarity as whites and slave owners.'

Reference was made earlier to the difference between the systems of government in the British and French colonies. By the middle of the 18th century all these islands, different in language, religious faith and government, had developed societies that were similar because they had their roots in the sugar-and-slave plantation. In each, oligarchies controlled the political system and reinforced their control by a system of racial discrimination. The situation was different in Puerto Rico and Cuba, where there were a large number of poor and ' middling ' whites. In the French and English colonies there were, in contrast, minority groups of whites who controlled the political system and used their law-making and law-enforcing powers to maintain control of the black and brown majority. Professor Goveia's description of society in the Leeward Islands at the end of the 18th century holds true for all of them: ' racial inequality and subordination had become the fundamental principles of economic, political and social organisation. The slave society of the islands was integrated on the basis of a hierarchy of racial groupings linked to differences of civil and political status and of economic and social opportunity. A heavy emphasis on racial particularism characterised the social order.'

The society accepted slavery as an institution, and one that continued in perpetuity, since a slave mother automatically passed on to her children the condition of being slaves. In the West Indies it was a crime for a slave to reject slavery. The basic concept was that in law the slave was property, a thing. The Jamaica Act of 1674 laid it down that ' All negroes lawfully bought as bondslaves shall here continue to be so and further be held and taken to be goods and chattels...' A century later, after examining the slave laws, a law clerk to a House of Commons Committee pointed out that the leading idea in the slave-laws was ' that negroes were property, and a species of property that needed a rigorous and vigilant regulation... To secure the rights of owners and maintain the subordination of negroes seem to have most occupied the attention and excited the solicitude of the different legislatures; what regarded the interests of the negroes themselves appears not to have sufficiently attracted their notice.'

But slavery was a peculiar institution because, though the law said the slave was property, it could not be denied that the slave was also a person, with the power to think, act, obey or rebel, run away or attack and perform a wide variety of tasks. The owners recognised this and passed laws regulating the conduct of slaves. By law he had to obey his master. To run away was an offence punishable by whipping and on occasion even by death. The law empowered justices and officers of the militia to form armed groups and hunt down runaways, and if the runaway was killed in the process then compensation was paid to the owner for his loss of property. To strike a white person was punishable by flogging and to wound him was punishable by dismemberment or death. It was an offence for slaves to communicate with each other by beating a drum or blowing a horn. The power of the master was almost absolute, and sickening cruelties were inflicted on slaves who had no means of redress. In 1788 Beckford, writing on the situation of the Negroes in Jamaica, admitted that he knew of nothing in the West Indies so shocking to humanity and so disgusting to individuals as the savage and indecent manner in which the trial of slaves was conducted; and Beckford was pro-slavery. As for the trial of masters, the case of Edward Huggins shows how difficult it was for slave owners to condemn one of their own, and how ineffective were laws that sought to protect the slaves. In 1810 some years after measures for the amelioration of slavery had been passed, Edward Huggins of Nevis marched twenty of his slaves into the market place in Charlestown. Among them were men and women. They were, said Huggins, troublemakers. They were charged with having run away from the plantation in order to avoid carrying dung into the fields at night. Huggins, who was known to be a cruel master, had with him his two sons and two expert whippers. The twenty blacks were flogged in the market place, the beatings being so severe that some were made invalids and one woman subsequently died. Five magistrates saw what happened and took no action. When the Assembly met a week later it held the floggings to have been barbarous and against the law. Huggins was thereupon brought to trial. Among the jurors was his son-in-law. Another juror was in charge of the estate owned by his son-in-law. The evidence of guilt was clear. Huggins was acquitted and was feasted by his friends.

Not long after this, Hodge a planter of Tortola, was charged with murdering some of his slaves. Even after he had been found guilty the jury recommended mercy. Had it not been for the firmness of the Governor, Hodge would have escaped execution. Some whites were shocked by what Hodge had done, but more were shocked at the hanging of a white planter for the murder of slaves. In a slave society words like amelioration had little effect because both the political system and the power of making and enforcing of laws were in the hands of slave owners.

There were in the white world opportunities for bettering oneself, and for moving from one class to another. Small whites, hucksters and victuallers could acquire property and become eligible to serve as jurors, to vote in elections and even as John Luffman of Antigua remarked, to purchase estates and return to England to live ' in awkward splendour.' Overseers who survived the hardships and the degradation of their occupation, the fevers and drinking, could buy a few slaves, make some money by hiring them out and gradually become persons of some consequence. Those settlers who had little capital began their climb upward on the shoulders of fifteen or twenty blacks, who cleared land, built shacks, planted ground provisions, then put in some cotton, indigo or other crops that could be raised by a few hands. The opportunity for movement upwards and the solidarity of whiteness in the midst of a majority of blacks resulted in the ' independent spirit ' which Bryan Edwards described:

The poorest white person seems to consider himself nearly

on a level with the richest, and emboldened by this idea approached his employer with extended hand and a freedom which in the countries of Europe is seldom displayed by men in the lower orders of life toward their superiors. It is not difficult to trace the origin of this principle. It arises without doubt from the pre-eminence and distinction which are necessarily attached even to the complexion of a white man, in a country where the complexion, generally speaking, distinguishes freedom from slavery.

In the brown world no amount of property could propel one over the barrier into the white world. Edwards said that the lowest white person considered himself superior to the best educated freeman of colour, ' treating him as the Egyptians treated the Israelites, with whom they held it an abomination to eat bread.' John Waller, in *A Voyage to the West Indies*, published in 1820, found that in Barbados the free people of colour were far indeed from being in a comfortable condition. Many had learned some useful trade, saved and acquired ' a comfortable independence '; ' but no property, however considerable, can ever raise a man of colour, not even when combined with education, to the proper rank of a human being, in the estimation of English or Dutch Creoles. They are always kept at a respectful distance; and it would be looked upon as a kind of sacrilege for a man of colour to sit down in the house of a Barbadian.' The situation was the same in the French colonies even though the Code Noir of 1685 had provided that a white and a slave who had children might marry and that through marriage she and her children became free. Bryan Edwards said that a significant result of discrimination against the people of colour was ' that it tends to degrade them in their own eyes and in the eyes of the community to which they belong. This is carried so far as to make them at once wretched in themselves and useless to the public...these unhappy people are a burden and a reproach to society...' Edwards went on to point out that this treatment of the browns did not arouse in them any sympathy for the blacks; ' To the Negroes they were objects of envy and hatred, for the same or a greater degree of superiority which the Whites assume over them, the free Mulattoes lay claim to over the blacks. These again abhor the idea of being slaves to the descendants of slaves'. There is an illuminating reference by Professor Goveia to the enquiry into the planning of a slave revolt in St. Kitts in 1778, when the rebels regarded the free coloured of the district not as potential allies but as probable enemies, one conspirator asking 'Don't they stand like Buckra already?'

Racism grew and flourished in the society because it was a way of justifying slavery. The Atlantic Slave Trade developed because, as Eric Williams has demonstrated, 'As compared with Indian and white labour, negro slavery was eminently superior'. The African became the 'sinews of the plantation'. However, after slavery had become the foundation of West Indian society, ways had to be found of justifying it, and the rationalisation that most easily dulled the conscience and eased the pocketing of profits from the Slave Trade and the Slave plantations was that the Negro was an inferior being. It was claimed that African society was barbarous, and that to enslave the black was to confer a benefit on him.

Among the slaves there were divisions also. Reference has already been made to the division between the newcomer from Africa and the creole slave. Another division was that between mulatto slaves and black slaves. Often the mulatto slave was assigned to work in the Great House, not in the fields where the blacks laboured.

The words and sayings of the folk mirrored this world of contempt and hate, and captured its corrosive quality. *Backra* or *buckra* was 'white man' and the white man who could not afford a horse or who worked in the fields was a *walking backra* or *cha-cha* or *red leg*. Those who moved in the highest class were 'pure pure buckra'; and the word became an adjective meaning 'of the best quality' in terms like *buckra* yam, *buckra* calalu, *buckra* pine. On the other hand, as Cassidy points out in *Jamaica Talk*, the creole black referred to newcomers from Africa not only as 'Guinea Birds' but also with contempt as *nayga* with the meaning 'good for nothing'. In white and brown creole society honourable African day-names like *Quashie* for Sunday, *Quaco* for Wednesday, *Cuffee* for Friday were applied derisively to blacks. *Cuffee* meant a stupid person. So did the words *Congo* and *Bongo*. The word mulatto was

taken over from the Spanish to designate, at first, the cross between black and white, and then as time passed, any person of
mixed blood. The definition of race was complex to the point of
lunacy; white and black produced mulatto, mulatto and white a
mustee or mustefino, and so on. Sambo was a cross between
black and brown. The distrust and dislike between black and
brown is reflected in the folk terms ' white-a-middle ' and ' red
Eboe '.

The works of historians like Edward Long, Bryan Edwards
and Charlevoix present a record of West Indian society that is
critical and at the same time full of pride in the West Indies; and
one learns from their work that many of the weaknesses of our
contemporary society and economy have their origin in the peculiarities and in the structure of planter society of the 17th and 18th
centuries. They picture a society that had to its credit certain
substantial achievements, some of which survive as memorials;
Drax Hall and Farley Hill in Barbados; Pall Mall Square in
Basseterre; Kings Square in Spanish Town; charming late 18th
century buildings of brick and stone, with tiled roofs, on the water-
front in St. George's; fortifications like Brimstone Hill, Shirley
Heights, Fort Charlotte overlooking Kingstown, the elaborate
works on Richmond Hill above St. Georges; and there was eleg-
ance in the stone work of houses, windmills and aqueducts, and
in mahogany furniture in the style of Chippendale and Sheraton.
But there was a curiously brittle quality to this society. It was
never wholly secure. At no time was a general prosperity shared
by all. Barbados reached its peak first, in the second half of the
17th century; then a little later, Martinique, Guadeloupe, St.
Kitts, Antigua and Nevis. Jamaica was next in the middle of the
18th century and St. Domingue, a little later, in the last three
decades before the French Revolution. And even in the periods
of prosperity everything appeared to be vulnerable. The whites
were small islands of homesick and often quarrelsome exiles sur-
rounded by black slaves, often deceptively calm, for the currents
of suspicion and hatred flowed deep and strong. Today a man
seemed well, and tomorrow he was struck down by yellow fever,
dysentery, malaria, typhoid, tuberculosis. In some islands there
was always the fear of earthquake, like that of 1691 which
destroyed Port Royal. Every summer hurricanes threatened.

Two or three years of drought might parch and burn the provision grounds. In times of war there was the danger of destructive raids like those of the French against St. Kitts and Nevis, or the English attacks on Martinique and Guadeloupe. Yields fell off as the soil became exhausted. In Europe the prices for sugar, coffee and cacao and other tropical products fluctuated from one year to another. Today's fortune became tomorrow's debt. It was an essentially unstable society.

The chief features stand out clearly. One was absentee ownership. Absenteeism led to the inefficient management of estates, hindered the growth of a West-Indian based white society, encouraged the schooling of children in Britain and so lessened pressure for the growth of educational institutions in the West Indies, and increased the total indebtedness of the West Indian sugar industry through bequests that became a charge or encumberance on the estate. On the other hand, through the absentee proprietors the West Indies gained political power far greater than anything they could have achieved by other means. For many years they pressed the home government with much success to take measures that were of benefit to planter society in the islands. Through the seats that a number of absentees held in Parliament the West Indies gained direct representation in Parliament. Planter society may well have gained more than it lost through the system. In any case, though absenteeism was a distinguishing feature of the society it was not central to it.

Monoculture was another feature, but here again the term is sometimes used in too sweeping a sense. Certainly the West Indies relied heavily on one crop, but while Barbados, a flat fertile island, and St. Kitts, were in the fullest sense 'sugar islands' more mountainous and larger islands grew a variety of crops. Monoculture denoted an excessive reliance on one crop, but certainly sugar was a crop that suited the West Indies and that found a profitable market in Europe. This in turn resulted in dependence on the metropolitan power for markets, capital and protection. These two features, dependence on one crop and dependence on the outside world were features of West Indian society not only during the period of planter power but throughout the whole period of colonial rule. They originated in a trading system in which the colony was complementary to, and existed for, the benefit of the metropolitan power; and in which the final political authority rested with the metropolitan power.

These were significant peculiarities. But the nature, the character of the society, was determined by a political system in which a white minority exercised almost absolute rule, by a legal system which protected that rule by enforcing racial discrimination, and by the maintenance and preservation of slavery as an institution. This is what made West Indian society vicious. In the last resort it depended on force. This is what explains the constant fear of rebellion. Bryan Edwards analysed the position frankly and with understanding:

> In countries where slavery is established the leading principle on which the government is supported is fear; or a sense of that exclusive coercive necessity which, leaving no choice of action, supersedes all question of right.

CHAPTER 17

The Roots Strike Down

Power of a different kind resided in the black majority; the power to adapt to change, to retain old traditions and customs, to create new forms to meet new needs, the power to combine pliability with toughness, pliability expressing itself through adjustment and toughness through the rejection of slavery.

This resilience was not something new. It was part of the West African heritage developed through centuries of adjustment to conquest and defeat, to changes in tribal groupings and to shifts of power. It had its origins in societies that could take over the gods of another conquering tribe while retaining their own; in enduring family and kinship relationships; in systems of religion in which ancestral spirits were protectors; and in close links with the tribal past through an oral tradition which has been described by a West African, Bernard Dadie, in these terms:

> We have stories and legends by which our forefathers transmitted their knowledge. These stories and legends are our museums, monuments and street names—our only books in fact. This is why they have such an important part in our daily lives. Every evening we leaf through them and despite the whirl of our present-day life we cling to our past. This gives us strength...

Yet not all the resilience and toughness could have saved the African on the new world plantations with their high mortality rates had it not been for the unceasing flow from Africa. These newcomers constantly fed African strength and African wisdom into the Creole communities spread from Brazil to the Caribbean and the United States. They came from a large, culturally complex region, but one in which underlying similarities quickly enabled them to understand each other.

The way in which the African adjusted to the slave plantation was influenced by the new environment, the nature of the land, the climate, differences in occupation, in plantation regime and in the size of the particular work force to which he belonged. The African's way of life in Barbados differed from that of his countryman on the Potomac who had a winter to face. The condition of a slave on a large Caribbean plantation differed from that of a slave working with his owner in a logwood camp in Yucatan or by the banks of the Belize River. In Antigua there was no path to freedom save by a sloop or a canoe, no hope of escape like that offered by the jungles of Surinam or the mountains of Jamaica. These variations notwithstanding, African new world cultures do not differ fundamentally from each other. Whether in Brazil, the Caribbean or the Deep South common elements are recognisable. In the Caribbean the political institutions of Europe and the use of different European languages have been divisive forces. The African experience forms a common bond.

Slowly a folk-culture came into existence, in which the home-traditions and experiences of Africa were blended with elements from Europe and with other elements born of the new environment. This period from 1650 to 1800 is of the greatest importance for us today, because it was then that an African new world culture emerged in which there were three distinctive types, Afro-Brazilian culture, Afro-Caribbean culture and Afro-American culture. Three or four examples will show how, in finding new ways to meet such universal human needs as food, language, family life, religion and artistic expression, the African gave to our West Indian culture some of its most vital and valuable characteristics.

First then, the need for food in which both planter and slave were involved. Feeding the growing army of slaves became one of the major problems of the West Indian economy. Bryan Edwards emphasised that it was true economy for the planter to export sugar and import food since the product of a single acre of his cane fields would buy more Indian corn than could be raised on five times that area of land, and pay the freight as well. Whites and blacks depended on imported food; beef, cheese, and supplies of madeira and porter for the whites, herrings, salt fish of the poorest quality, corn and flour for the blacks. Craton and Walvin in their study of the Worthy Park papers describe the situation on that well-managed estate in the 1790's. It relied to a large extent on cattle for the heavy work of cartage and ploughing and for manure, but no attempt was made to provide the estate with home grown beef. For fresh meat it relied on local butchers. In 1793 the owner ordered that each white man on the estate should get two pounds of fresh beef each day; 'and since in the last three months of 1793 meat for the tiny band of white men alone cost over £55 it was economically unthinkable that Price should order similar allowance for the hundreds of slaves. Only on one occasion, at Christmas, did the slaves ever savour the nourishment of fresh meat, when 357 slaves shared a caw and a steer.'

To depend so heavily on distant sources of food two thousand miles away was to stand naked to disaster. War and hurricane brought famine. When supplies of food were cut off during the War of American Independence, slaves died. We have already noted how heavy was the toll that famine took among the slaves in the Leeward Islands in this period. The two islands of Barbados and Jamaica suffered even more severely, for in 1781 they were hit by a savage hurricane, which added its blow to those already inflicted by the American war and many slaves died from hunger. Calamities drove the British government and the West Indian governments to pass legislation requiring estates to allocate more land for provision grounds.

An obvious way of improving the food supply was to import food-plants. At the time when Ligon wrote, in the middle of the 17th century, the chief breadstuff was cassava, a foodplant that grows where little else will, is not much affected by hurricanes, and is a valuable stand-by in hard times. To this day in Jamaica in dry districts ' cassava without salt, coffee without sugar ' is proverbial diet for the hard years. Ligon mentioned also sweet potatoes, maize, beans and plantains; and there was a dreary seaman's gruel made from corn, called Lob Lolly, which the slaves disliked so much that at the sight of it they shouted ' Oh, no Lob-lolly, no Lob-lolly '. In the years that followed there were valuable importations of foodplants, including varieties of yam. Coco was another importation, brought in from West Africa by the Portuguese. The ackee was brought to Jamaica in 1778, to be married by the folk to codfish, with the result that codfish and ackee became one of the delicacies of the Jamaica kitchen. An even more important newcomer was the mango, an Asiatic tree which now grows throughout the tropical world. It had a long association with the slave trade, and to this day in some parts of Central and East Africa lines of mango trees planted by Arab slavers mark the routes down which the slave caravans were driven to the coast. Many new improved varieties have been introduced since then into the Caribbean, but from the time of its first planting the mango became a valuable supplement to the Caribbean food supply.

The bread-fruit was imported in the 1790's from the Pacific Islands by Captain Bligh, but for fifty years the slaves would have nothing to do with it. It was fed to pigs. Only after emancipation did it begin to win favour from the peasant, who began to speak with appreciation of the ' yellow heart ' and the fine textured St. Kitts Sukey.

The search for food plants links the provision grounds with experimental botanical gardens that were established in the West Indies in the last decades of the 18th century. One of the most famous and now almost forgotten of these gardens was created by Hinton East, West Indian-born Receiver General of Jamaica. Through sheer persistance he brought together hundreds of varieties of plants from other parts of the world.

Another method of increasing the food supply was to grow food on the estate and to provide the slaves with plots of land for cultivation. Practice varied according to the size of the territory and the nature of the land. Barbados for example, could not afford to give up much land for growing food, whereas Jamaica could. In St. Kitts it was at one time the custom for estate owners to put a field of good land under yams and to leave one or two cane-fields fallow each year and divide these up for use by the slaves as provision grounds, but when the pressure on sugar land increased the provision grounds were squeezed out on to ' gutside ' and steeper mountain slopes.   In Nevis the land allotted to the slave was often alongside the slave cottage, whereas in Jamaica the slave's provision ground was usually well away from the negro village, on marginal land.   In Bryan Edwards' account of the provision ground, we find not only a picture of the Sunday market but also, even in the work of this cultivated man, the characteristic planter attitude of racial superiority, which regarded improvidence as a characteristic of the black, whereas the extravagance and improvidence of the West Indian planter had by then become proverbial:

> The practice which exists in Jamaica of giving the Negroes land to cultivate, from the produce of which they are able to maintain themselves (except in times of scarcity, arising from hurricanes and droughts, when assistance is never denied them), is universally allowed to be judicious and beneficial, producing a happy coalition of interests between the master and the slave, who has acquired by his own labour a property in his master's land, has much to lose, and is therefore less inclined to desert his work.   He earns a little money by which he is enabled to indulge himself in fine clothes on holidays and gratify his palate with salted meats and other provisions that otherwise he could not obtain, and the proprietor is eased, in a great measure, from the expense of feeding him.   In some of the Windward Islands they have not land enough for the purpose...   In fact if the owners territory is sufficiently extensive the Negroes make it a practice to enlarge their own grounds or exchange them for fresh land each year.   ...The misfortune is they trust more to plantain-groves, corn and other vegetables, that are liable to be destroyed by storms, than to what are called ground-provisions; such as yams, eddoes, potatoes, cassava and other esculant roots, all of which are out of reach of hurricanes; but prudence is a term that has no place in the negro vocabulary.   To obviate the mischiefs which fatal experience has proved to flow from this gross inattention, the Slave Act of Jamaica obliges, under a penalty, every proprietor to keep, properly cultivated in ground-provi-

sions, one acre for every ten Negroes, exclusive of the Negro grounds...

In Jamaica the Negroes are allowed one day in a fortnight except in time of crop, besides Sundays and holidays, for cultivating their grounds and carrying their provisions to market. Some of them find time on these days, besides raising provisions, to make a few coarse manufactures, such as mats for beds, bark ropes of strong and durable texture, wicker chairs and baskets, earthen jars, pans etc. for all of which they find a ready sale... The most industrious of the Negroes do not, I believe, employ more than sixteen hours in a month in the cultivation of their own provision gardens... and in favourable seasons this is sufficient. Sunday is their day of market, and it is wonderful what numbers are then seen, hastening from all parts of the country towards the towns and shipping places, laden with fruits and vegetables, pigs, goats and poultry, their own property. In Jamaica it is supposed that upwards of 10,000 assemble every Sunday morning in the market of Kingston where they barter their provisions etc., for salted beef and pork or for linen and ornaments for their wives and children. I do not believe that an instance can be produced of a master's interfering with his Negroes in their peculium thus acquired. They are permitted also to dispose at their deaths of what little property they possess; and even to bequeath their grounds or gardens to such of their fellow slaves as they think proper...

The provision ground, however small, gave the slave a bread-basket of sorts. It also enabled him to practise his skills in subsistence agriculture and to learn the secrets of the new environment, the effects of the seasons, the times for planting different crops, and the like. From the sale of his produce the slave obtained some cash, so the provision ground was in many cases the only means the slave had of bettering himself and getting a little money, so much so that Sir William Young, commenting on the difference between the slave in Antigua, ' fed by allowance from his master ' and his counter-part in St. Vincent ' supported by provision grounds of their own ' remarked that ' a negro without stock and the means to purchase tobacco and other little conveniences and some finery for his wife, is miserable '. He could have written ' man ' instead of ' Negro '. The market also was more than a trading centre. Important in most countries, markets formed an essential part of West African life and amongst the Ibo people they had a special significance as a means of keeping the assortment of tribes together. The French in Haiti early recognised the importance of the market and in the 18th century the Government of St. Domingue passed legislation permitting slaves to meet at certain rural cross-roads to sell their produce. Trade routes sprang up, and an internal marketing system came into existence based on the markets, like the one at Rendezvouz, just north of the mountain township of Kenscoff, overlooking Port au Prince.

The provision ground and the market were the training grounds where unwittingly the slave-owner enabled the slave to prepare himself for freedom. The economy was dominated by the large plantation. The days were to come when black peasants would establish their small holdings away from the estates, supporting themselves and their families by subsistence farming, selling their produce in the local markets, raising a pig to pay the taxes and some chickens to buy clothes at Christmas time; creating a peasant economy which, in the 1950's in Jamaica, provided almost one-half of the total agricultural output. It is little wonder that an American historian, Mintz, noting the way in which the planter compelled the slave to begin, in effect, an internal marketing system should have reminded his readers of the statement by Karl Marx that ' there is something in human history like retribution that its instrument be forged not by the offended but by the offender himself '.

From the field to the kitchen. By the end of the 18th century West Indian food habits were generally fixed. The chief addition in the following century was rice, its wider use being a result of the importation of East Indian indentured labourers, though some rice seems to have been grown in Trinidad after the Napoleonic wars by disbanded negro soldiers who were recruited in those wars from among escaped slaves from Charleston and other parts of the American south. By then the combination of provision ground and slave kitchen had provided us with some of our typical dishes: cuckoo and its Jamaican counterpart of turned cornmeal, each liberally sprinkled with hot pepper; fungee, in its present form a porridge of green bananas or corn; meatkind, the general term for any kind of meat, a parallel form to bread-kind; and salted meatkind, salted or pickled meat or fish.   Salt did the work of a refrigerator, to the extent that it preserved; and Cassidy, in his rich treasury of West Indian history, *Jamaica Talk*, reminds us of its extraordinary value.   Slaves had to be supplied with an allowance of salt meat or fish, and the general term ' salt things ' or ' saal t'ings ' included salt fish, pickled herring, mackerel, shad, corn pork.   A man well-stocked with these was described as being ' in his salt ', so ' in his salt ' came to mean ' having a good time '.   Also that kind of herring which was long and straight came to be known as ' long saal '.   Other delicacies that moved from the slave kitchen to our tables were pepperpot, casareep being used in the best kind; crab and calalu, with dasheen leaves and crabs as the chief ingredients; ' cook up ' which is very much like *san cocho*, a soup containing every possible piece of vegetable and meat, popular throughout the Spanish-speaking mainland countries as well as the islands; *bammy* or some other form of cassava bread; fritters of salt fish and flour, varying from the heavy Jamaican stamp-and-go to the lighter Trinidadian *akra*, a delicacy that takes its name from the Yoruba *akara*, a cake or dish made of beans and palm oil; escoveitched fish, known to our Latin neighbours as *escabeche*; *Jerk pork*, strips of the flesh of wild hogs salted and dried; varieties of *pone* and a variety of drinks like *mawby*, mostly made of wet sugar and fruits easily available.

Another immediate problem which faced the African on arrival was that of communication with his fellows and with the whites who exercised authority over him.   Our Creole languages had their origins in his response to this challenge.   The Papiamento of Curaçao and Aruba, the Taki Taki of Surinam, the Creole French and English of the Caribbean are not infantile forms of expression used by illiterate people attempting to speak the language of the metropolitan power and failing to do so, but languages in their own right.   Because this has not been generally understood there has been almost as much snobbery about the Creole languages as about skin-colour and race.

The process of adaptation and blending can be illustrated from the French Creole of Haiti which has a basic vocabulary drawn chiefly from French, Indian, African. The French elements in the Creole contain words from Normandy, Picardy, Brittany and other provinces. The Indian words describe the indigenous Caribbean fruits, flowers and animals. The African words often have to do with religious beliefs and customs, with foods, cooking, and folk tales. As in so many African languages, repetition is frequently used for emphasis, and words also that convey the sound of the action described. Like all living languages, Haitian Creole keeps growing through the addition of new words, including Spanish words and phrases from the neighbouring Dominican Republic and borrowings from United States English.

The formation of the Creole language of the English speaking islands parallels this. It has its own syntax, phrasing and vowel sounds. It contains, like French Creole, Indian words: *iguana, coney,* or *aguti, cashew, casareep, guinep, guango, calabash, avocado, cassava, yuca, annatto,* and many others. In Trinidad especially, there are numerous place names taken over from the Indians, such as Piarco, Arima, Naparima, Curepe. Spanish and Portuguese supplied other words, like *pickanninny, ratoon, dunder, pimento, escabeche, palisado, savannah, chaklata* meaning chocolate from the Aztec word *chocolat* and scores of others. There is less of French in Jamaica and Barbados and the older Leeward Islands than in Trinidad, but even in those islands that were settled first by the English there are French plant names, like *Bourbon* cane, *Gros Michel* bananas, *immortelle, coratoe, dasheen.* Africa supplied Jamaica Creole with about 400 words, including *ackee, yam, afu yam, nyam, eddo, gungu* (pigeon peas), *sorasy, susumba, akra* (cakes), *duckonoo, toto, anansy, gingy fly, abeng, calembe, obeah, shango, cotta* or *cota, cocobay* and *pra-pra.*

In recent years scholars have begun to give to these Creole languages the attention they deserve. For long they were neglected and despised as 'Quashie talk'. English or French were thought of as the language of the elite, patois or Creole as corrupt forms of the 'master-tongue', spoken by illiterate people who could do no better. The languages shaped by generations of plantation blacks remains the only medium in which it is possible to communicate with the whole community, containing as they do nuances and imagery beyond the reach of English or French; and much of the sparkle, vivid phrasing and picture language of present-day Caribbean writers derive from the folk-language. That the black had fashioned an effective and vivid medium of speech was noted by Clement Caines, a member of the St. Kitts General Assembly in 1798, in his history of that body.

The harshness of the penalization imposed on the African by slavery comes home to us when we turn our eyes from the West Indian plantation to West Africa. When we do this we perceive the consequences of the loss of an accustomed family structure and of a system of religion that was the basis of life. Since many of the people of the West Indies have their origins in Ghana we will refer especially to the Akan people, bearing in mind the fact that the societies of West Africa have many basic similarities. Among the Akan the unit of society is the family; and ' family ' denotes a large group of kinsmen bound together by ties of blood and by the worship of common ancestral spirits. Land is owned by a tribe and apportioned to the various families, which in turn apportion the ' family land ' to individual members of the family. A village is a collection of people belonging to one or more families governed by a Council of Elders made up of heads of households or families in the village. The Council elects a Headman who exercises authority over the village, but his power is limited by the fact that he has to behave reasonably and in accordance with tradition. The village is a corporate body in whose affairs all the blood-relations have a voice. Or, to put it in another way, a Headman is like one who administers an estate in which every one of his kinsmen has a share.

One of the Akan people, transported to a slave plantation, found himself in a society in which the power of the owner was personal and arbitrary, and could be exercised without any appeal to reason. There was no family in the sense that he understood it. There were no social sanctions regulating the relationship between man and woman. In the English colonies, unlike the French, slaves were not permitted to marry. As for the whites, a sugar planter in Jamaica in the middle of the18th century remarked that it was the greatest disgrace for a white man not to cohabit with some woman or other. One reason for this was that there were relatively few white women in the colonies.

A West Indian Governor and sugar planter, Sir William Young, writing at the end of the 18th century said that compared with any country of England, there were few aged white persons, women or children, in any Windward or Leeward Islands, Barbados perhaps excepted; many of the proprietors lived in England; those who were in trade or service on the plantations and who lived to be fifty or so, went back at that age to England and Scotland with any fortune they might have made; there were scarcely any white women of the menial and lowest condition and few of the middling class. Concubinage prevailed among whites and blacks. But the trouble went even deeper. Slavery transferred to the slave owner many of the functions natural to a father: it was he who exercised authority, provided food and clothing, decided on the nature of the work to be done, inflicted punishment, determined the future of the slave children.

Even so, the blacks developed another form of family structure which had no legal status, was marked by no ceremonies, was regulated by few social sanctions, a ' common law marriage ' or non-legal union which gave as much stability to the union as could be achieved within the plantation framework. Also, the concept of an extended family remained, and of respect to one's elders. The word ' family ' included those who were ' aunt ', ' cousin ' or *tata* by name and not necessarily by blood. Visitors to the West Indies remarked, as Caines did, that ' whenever the negro addresses a person older than himself he gives him the title of daddy or uncle; if a female, of mammy or aunty; while those who are nearly of his own age, he styles ' buddy ' or ' sissy '. ' Family ' means ' related or akin:' so we say ' me and him is family '. Cassidy gives an amusing instance of this usage: ' Flying ants are family to duck ants '. To say that someone is ' fe we ' means that he is kin with us. The belief in ancestral spirits did not perish utterly but lived on in customs like that in which someone, throwing out water at night, warns the family spirits, calling to them ' Mind yourselves, me family ', or ' good people, anybody fe we move '.

The reference to a spirit world leads us to religion; to the West African view of the world, of man's origin and of the mysteries of life and death. The attitude of modern scholarship to African religions is expressed by a Catholic priest who served as a missionary in the Congo for many years. Discussing the philosophy of the Bantu and thinking of European educators working amongst the Bantu, he wrote:

> We have thought ourselves beginning with a bare sheet from which we had only to erase valueless vanities in order to start afresh... We have thought we were educating children, 'big children' and this seemed an easy task. But now suddenly we see that we are dealing with a humanity that is adult, conscious of its own wisdom...

The subject of African religion is a vast one, and the only points to be made here are that the African imported into the new world came from people who had highly developed systems of religion, which were polytheistic, involving the worship of many gods, that religion was interwoven into the political system and that it formed a natural part of everyday life. Our newcomer from the Akan people brought with him memories of the house in his village or township in which the blackened stools of dead chiefs were

Golden Stool of Ashanti

kept, to be visited on special days, with sacrifices and prayers to the spirits that inhabited them; of the Golden Stool of Ashanti, in which lived the ancestral spirits of the nation; of the annual festival of the Odwira, when the Akan people thanked the gods for the new harvest and honoured the spirits of the nation's dead. The newcomer from Dahomey brought memories of his gods, chief among them the god Vodun; the Yoruba brought memories of many gods, among them the god of thunder, Shango.

Before turning to the plantation, two observations of Herskovits should be mentioned. Speaking of the Dahomey and Yoruba systems of religion, in which the world is thought of as being ruled by fate, the destiny of each man being worked out according to a plan already made, he points out that there were ways of escape from an evil destiny by seeking the aid of a particular god; and this concept ' gives insight into deep rooted patterns of thought in which a man refuses to accept any situation as inescapable...' The other observation bears on the fact that the African was prepared to add the gods of other people to his own, provided there was good ground for accepting the new god. If, for example, one tribe was conquered by another, it followed that the gods of the conquering tribe were more powerful, and it therefore was wise to add them to the less powerful gods. The concept was one of relationship between the power of a tribe's gods and the power of the tribe itself. Transferred to the new world, this could mean a readiness to add the God of the Christians, the people who had been so powerful as to enslave them, to the tribal gods they remembered. ' That this was actually the case is to be seen in those parts of the new world where opportunities have presented themselves to retain African gods despite contact with Europeans...'

The African newcomers to the plantation in the French colonies had an opportunity of learning something of the religion of their owners. Ramsay, in his account of slavery in the Leeward Islands at the end of the 18th century, said that within eight days of the purchase of a slave, the French slave owner had to report on the matter to·the French authorities so that a missionary might be assigned to instruct the African. ' All the fasts and festivals of the Romish Church, which it is well known are very numerous, are commanded to be strictly observed, during which the slave is forbidden to labour, that he may have leisure to attend mass.' This introduction to Christianity and the intermingling of Christian and African elements in the folk cult can be illustrated from the history of Haiti, which became independent in 1804 and where the French colonists were Roman Catholics. Recent studies show that Haitian peasants have retained many elements of the religions of their ancestors, of the Fon, Ewe, Yoruba, Congo and other tribal groups; that they have combined these with elements of the Catholic doctrine; that they have added magical beliefs imported from provinces of France; and that they have added elements of their own; and that under the conditions that have existed in Haiti for more than a century and a half the vodun complex had, and still has, meaning for the mass of the people.

CHAPTER 18

Black Resistance

Adjustment to the conditions of the slave plantation did not mean acceptance of servitude by the African. His struggle for freedom began on the day of his enslavement. The African rulers who sold the slaves and the European slavers who bought them knew this. Along the West African coast every barracoon had its fort, every slave-market its whipping block to check rebellious spirits. At sea the captain of a slave ship knew he had trouble on his hands. One of them, James Barbot, part owner of the *Albion*, gives an account of a slave mutiny, ' they suddenly fell upon our men and stabbed one of the stoutest... Many of the most mutinous leaped overboard and drowned themselves with much resolution, showing no manner of concern for life.' Having told of the three mutinies in which he was involved Henry Snellgrove, in a *New Account of Guinea and the Slave Trade* (1754) writes that he had heard of several others that turned out tragically like that on the *Ferres Galley* when Captain Messervy was killed, and he recalls his warning to the captain, that ' he might depend upon it they always aim at the Chief person in the ship '. Slave mutinies became so much a feature of these voyages that some captains sought insurance against loss caused by them; and on some slave ships the decks were heightened to make it difficult for slaves to jump overboard.

The struggle against enslavement continued in the new world. It took many forms; go-slows, theft, poisoning and outright rebellion. Like a chain of Andean volcanoes, black resistance erupted in blood and flame from the far south of Brazil through the Caribbean to the United States. The first eruption took place in Hispaniola in 1522, the last in Jamaica in 1865, a time-span of almost three and a half centuries. Between 1522 and 1600 there were slave risings in Hispaniola, Mexico, Peru and Central America. During the 17th century there were insurrections in Jamaica, Barbados, Haiti and Brazil. In the period from 1700 to 1834 there were slave insurrections in Barbados, Haiti, St. Vincent, Surinam, Guyana, St. Lucia, and Jamaica. In the Caribbean black resistance achieved the independence of the Maroons and of Haiti; but to focus attention only on black resistance in the Caribbean is to miss the significance of one of the most notable resistance movements in recorded history in two continents. It was not an organised movement, and for this reason it is all the more remarkable, for it represents the spontaneous reaction of black people widely separated from each other: blacks in North Eastern Brazil who established the Palmares Republic and maintained their independence from 1650–1696; blacks in Berbice who under Coffey gained control of the colony for a brief period in 1763; blacks who gained recognition of their right to a separate existence as free people in Jamaica; blacks who under Toussaint and Dessalines made Haiti independent; blacks who established free communities in the Surinam bush; blacks who wrote the name of Daaga into the history of Trinidad and the names of Gabriel Prosser, Denmark Vesey and Nat Turner into the history of the United States.

The Africans of the Caribbean played a notable part in this resistance movement. The slaves who rebelled in San Domingo in 1522 were the pioneers. They were followed by the Maroons of Jamaica. At the time when the English took Jamaica the blacks who had been slaves of the Spaniards numbered about 1500. For five years they helped the Spanish leader Cristobael de Ysassi in his guerilla campaign against the English forces. In 1660 one of their leaders, Juan Lubolo, and about 150 men surrendered on condition that they would be pardoned. Another group, smaller in number, made a refuge for themselves in the north-eastern part of the island.

There were frequent slave escapes and slave risings after 1670, when the English colonists began to establish their plantations.

The Governor of Jamaica in August 1690 gave an account of one of these risings. It took place on an estate in the middle of the island. More than 500 slaves forced the dwelling house, killed the caretaker and overseer, seized arms and ammunition. The alarm was given. Fifty horse and foot attacked them. After a skirmish the blacks went into the canes where some were killed, others wounded. They were pursued into the forest and about twelve more were killed. ' Sixty men and women have since come in who report that many have died of wounds and that they have few good arms. Fresh parties are after them, but I am afraid that so many will be left as to be a very great danger to the mountain plantations.' The Governor's fears were justified. A few years later Peter Beckford warned that the rebels had mightily increased in numbers and if serious steps were not taken against them the plantations in the north-east would have to be abandoned.

The ' serious steps ' that Beckford advocated were taken during the period 1725 to 1739 when the First Maroon War was fought. It resulted in the formal recognition of the independence of the Maroons. They were free men, free to choose their own rulers, to manage their own affairs, to till their own land. For the first time in the history of the Americas a metropolitan power was forced to recognise the right of their subjects to independence. This happened half a century before the North Americans gained their independence, and seventy years ahead of the blacks of Haiti. This, in essence is the meaning of the Treaty of 1739 which brought to an end the first Maroon War. The Maroons fought for freedom and the right to manage their own affairs and they won against great odds.

The war lasted from 1725 to 1739. Two groups of Maroons were involved. The most aggressive group consisted of the Windward Maroons, under a skilful guerrilla leader, Quaco. His force of more than 1,000 men operated from bases in the heartland of Jamaica, geologically the oldest and most rugged part of the island, the John Crow Mountains and the upper valleys of the Blue Mountains. A second group led by Cudjoe operated in the mountains behind Trelawny and St. James, in the ' Land of Look Behind', of ' You-no-call, me no come'. During the war a third group emerged in Hanover. Two regiments of British

Trelawney Town the chief residence of the Maroons

soldiers were brought in to crush the rebels. The planter Assembly met and voted supplies. But in 1732, seven years after the war started, Governor Hunter was forced to report to London that every attempt against the Maroons had either failed or achieved little. In 1739 a treaty of peace was signed with Cudjoe and in the following year with Quaco. Looking back at the struggle, Bryan Edwards summed up the matter in terms of losses: for forty years the Maroons had distressed Jamaica, and during that time the Assembly had passed forty four Acts and expended a quarter of a million pounds for their suppression. We count the results in terms of gain save in one respect. The Maroons agreed to hand over slaves who escaped to them. This particular agreement split the blacks in two, isolated the Maroons from their fellows, and made them allies of the whites in denying freedom to the plantation blacks. But the plantation slave did not give up. Each year the will to strive for freedom was reinforced by Africans brought in to keep the labour force up to strength. These, having been born free, rejected slavery more readily than did the Creole slaves.

The risings were much more frequent in Jamaica than in the English colonies in the Eastern Caribbean for several reasons. There were more blacks in proportion to whites than in the other islands; the whites were not able to supervise the slaves on large widely dispersed plantations as effectively as on smaller islands with plantations limited in size, set in open country, with few natural places of refuge. When the Coromanti slaves in St. Mary rose in rebellion under Tacky in 1760 they numbered 1,000 or more. Sixty whites were killed and terror gripped the planter world. Tacky was killed. More than 300 of his men were killed or committed suicide rather than be taken. After the rebellion 900 blacks were executed or deported. This did not put an end to the risings. In 1765 Gold Coast Negroes on seventeen estates rose. They were put down and thirteen of them were executed; but the very next year Coromanti slaves in Westmoreland rose. In 1776 slaves in St. James and Hanover rose. Thirty were executed. In the following year another insurrection was discovered. In 1795 the Second Maroon War broke out. After this there was a mutiny of Chamba and Coromanti blacks who had been recruited into the West India Regiment. In 1815 there was a conspiracy of Ibo slaves; and three other conspiracies were reported between 1823 and 1824. There followed the great slave rising of 1831, the last and largest of the slave risings, involving 20,000 slaves. Daddy Sharp and more than 500 slaves were executed, but news of the rebellion put new force into the efforts of the abolitionists in England.

The names ' Coromanti ' and ' Gold Coast ' occur frequently in the foregoing paragraphs, and Orlando Patterson in his *Sociology of Slavery*, points out that almost every one of the serious rebellions in the 17th and 18th centuries was instigated and carried out by Akan slaves who came from a highly developed militaristic regime, skilled in jungle warfare.

Surinam, the most advanced of the Dutch colonies, shipped large quantities of sugar, cacao, coffee and cotton to Holland. African slaves and Dutch technology had transformed the coastal region into very productive agricultural country by draining canals, building dikes and supplying power from windmills and tidemills. There were more than 400 large plantations with 60,000 slaves. From time to time numbers of the slaves escaped to the jungle where they founded villages and followed as best they could African custom and practice; and in order to maintain security and retain their own culture they refused to admit Creole slaves to their number. Like the Maroons of Jamaica, they raided the coastal plantations, their attacks becoming so damaging that the Dutch sent an expedition against them; but few of its members survived. Finally, in 1825 the Dutch made a treaty with the Bush Negroes guaranteeing their freedom. In return the Bush Negroes undertook to stop raiding the plantations and to return any slaves that escaped to them. Unlike the Maroons, who have been absorbed into the life of Jamaica, the Bush Negroes have kept themselves apart, establishing a way of life in which are to be found many elements of African religion, the African clan-system, African words and names and African art.

Slave risings were frequent also in Demerara, Berbice and Essequibo. Essequibo, oldest of the three, had ninety plantations and about 4,000 slaves in 1770, after a hundred years of settlement. Demerara, organised as a colony in 1746 had just over 200 plantations and 6,000 slaves in the 1770's. We noted in an earlier chapter that English planters from the Eastern Caribbean islands contributed to the development of both these colonies, which by 1750 had become part of the sugar-and-slave plantation system of the Caribbean.

The most serious of the slave risings in the Guianas was the Berbice rebellion of February 1763, led by Coffey, now the national hero of Guyana. About two thirds of the white population of 350 were killed, and for a brief period almost the whole colony was under Coffey's control. In March 1763 the rebels surrendered to a combined force of Dutch and English soldiers.

Bush settlements were established in Demerara, but they did not survive. At the end of the 18th century there were eight of them, laid out in the manner described by Pinckard, a ship's surgeon who served in the Caribbean at that period: a circular piece of ground was cleared, huts built in the centre, and oranges, yams, eddoes and other foodcrops were planted around the houses. Round the settlement there was a wide deep ditch. This, being filled with water, and stuck at the sides and bottom with sharp pointed stakes, formed a formidable barrier of defence. The path across the ditch was placed two or three feet below the surface and was kept hidden by the mud-brown ditch water. But by 1800 all these settlements had been destroyed by a force of Negroes and Amerindians organised by the Dutch. The story is part of history's lesson of the extent to which human nature is debased by greed and hate. The members of the expedition got 300 guilders for every right hand brought in. On one occasion they brought in seventy six hands and some prisoners who were tortured before being killed.

Moving north to the islands, we find a combination of Carib and African resistance in the island of St. Vincent, which, along with Dominica, Grenada and Tobago had been declared a neutral island in 1748, and which, with them, was ceded to Britain in 1763. We have already referred to the establishment of English colonists in these islands in the years after they came under British rule. In St. Vincent the Black Caribs disputed the British right to occupation of the island. They were the descendants of African slaves who had been shipwrecked on the island and had intermingled with the Caribs. They insisted that they were there before the English, and were independent owners of the land. They raided and plundered the white settlements. An expedition was sent against them. After having been subdued they were granted land for their exclusive use in the northern part of the island.

Toward the end of the century these Black Caribs and the surviving Caribs in the Eastern islands were caught up in the turmoil and conflict that followed the French revolution. Reference will be made to this when we deal with the Haitian revolution. In St. Vincent, where the French and Black Caribs combined, the British regained control of the situation, hunted down the rebels, executed a number of them and transported 5,000 of them to the Bay Islands in the Gulf of Honduras.

The climax was reached in St. Domingue where fifteen years of bloody agony led finally to the independence of Haiti. C.L.R. James tells the story in considerable detail in his book *Black Jacobins*.

Bryan Edwards who visited the colony in 1791, said there were 30,000 whites, 24,000 free people of colour, and 480,000 slaves. As these figures show, there were many more mulattoes in the population than in any other West Indian colony, and they bitterly resented living in a no-man's-land, in which they were free but without the privileges of freedom. Pigmentation was all-important; the condition of the free mulattoes was even more degrading and wretched than that of slaves in the West Indies. Though free they were regarded as public property and were compelled to serve in the militia and in labour gangs organised for the upkeep of the highways. They were forbidden to hold public office; 'neither did the distinction of colour terminate, as in the British West Indies with the third generation. There was no law nor custom that allowed the privileges of a white person to any descendant from an African, no matter however remote the origin... But the circumstances which contributed most to afford the coloured people of St. Domingue protection, was the privilege they possessed of acquiring and holding property to any amount. Several of them were the owners of considerable estates...' And, since slaves were property, they owned slaves. The whites and free coloured were divided from each other by a great gulf but they had this in common, that both had an interest in maintaining slavery. The whites aimed at preserving their power and property; the free coloureds at gaining equality and a share in political power. The blacks, who were neither much better off nor much worse off than their fellow slaves in the other plantation colonies, notwithstanding the Code Noir of 1685, had only one commitment—to freedom.

The economy of the colony rested mainly, but not wholly, on sugar. By 1775 it had moved well ahead of Jamaica and became the most valuable plantation colony in the world. Sugar made up sixty three per cent of its exports in 1775, cotton, coffee and indigo making up the rest. In contrast, Jamaica's sugar constituted eighty nine per cent of its exports. In Barbados and St. Kitts sugar was virtually the only export. But this was common to all, that the economy rested on the backs of African slaves. The more sugar, the more slaves. Curtin estimates that in the French slave trade 955,000 Africans were exported from West Africa between 1711 and 1800, the peak period being the decade 1781–90, when the annual figure may have been as high as 30,000. St. Domingue took three out of every four of the slaves imported into the Caribbean by France in the second half of the 18th century. The reason for the heavy importation however, was not simply that sugar production was expanding. Slaves did not live long. France pointed with pride to the splendid engineering works that brought 100,000 acres of the Cul de Sac plain under irrigation, the reservoirs, dams, sugar works and reckoned that though the cost was in millions of livres, the profits were assured. The blacks reckoned the cost in lives. Heavy work under relentless pressure, underfeeding and disease made the death rate extraordinarily high; twice or three times that of any country on earth, said a planter of St. Domingue, Victor Maluet, in 1773. Studies of plantation records show that the slave labour force had to be constantly renewed. Among the slaves who made up the labour force in the colony in the last quarter of the century were Macandal; a Jamaican, Boukman; a negro from St. Kitts, Christophe who was working in a hotel at Cap Français; Toussaint, who by reason of his ability had been put in charge of all the livestock on his owner's plantation; and Jean Francois Dessalines.

There was a larger setting. The words Liberty, Fraternity, Equality were coming into use, and capturing the minds of men. France stood on the verge of revolution. On 14th July, 1789 the

Bastille fell to the mobs of Paris. The cry was liberty, and the cry echoed through the plantation islands, but most clearly and loudly in St. Domingue. The planters of St. Domingue had sent delegates to the Assembly meeting of the States General in Paris. They joined in the demand for liberty; but they meant liberty to run St. Domingue in the way they wished; autonomy rather than liberty. With autonomy they would be able to act with even greater harshness against the mulattoes and the slaves, even though in France slavery was coming under attack. Autonomy was attractive to them for many reasons; for it meant that they would be able to repudiate their massive debts to France and also that they would be able to trade more easily with the United States. The newly founded society, Friends of the Blacks, demanded the grant of civil rights to the mulattoes. Moreau de Saint Mery warned that if once the slaves suspected that there was a power greater than that of their masters, if once they saw that the free coloured had successfully appealed to this power, France should give up all hope of holding her colonies.

There had been an earlier warning. Eight years earlier there were in Paris delegates from the free coloured of St. Domingue, whose demand for equality was supported by the Friends of the Blacks against strong opposition from the whites. They won their case when on 15th May 1791 the National Assembly granted to the free coloured the right to vote for local and provincial assemblies. In St. Domingue the whites refused to obey the decrees. The Governor refused to enforce it. The free coloured were already in arms. One of their leaders, the Paris-educated Ogé, had with another mulatto leader, Chavanne, staged a premature rising against the whites and both had been broken on the wheel and left to die, their faces turned to the sun. Ogé's execution strongly influenced French opinion against the colonists. In Haiti whites and browns confronted each other when suddenly in August 1791 the slaves of the north rose, set the countryside ablaze and killed the white inhabitants. Watching the desolation, Edwards described the whole fertile plain, with the exception of one plantation near the town of Le Cap, everywhere on fire, 2,000 whites dead, 180 sugar plantations and 900 coffee and indigo plantations destroyed, 10,000 slaves killed. Only Cap Français and a string of fortified camps remained in the hands of the whites. In the West the slaves were quiet but whites and mulattoes were at war. In the South the whites had armed their slaves against the mulattoes.

In Paris the Jacobins blocked the effort of the French government to send troops to restore order. After they gained control of the National Assembly in September 1792 they despatched a revolutionary army under the orders of Commissioners who were to enforce the rule of liberty, equality and fraternity. Their leader, Sonthonax, faced with royalist resistance, associated himself with the rebel slaves who, at his instigation, entered and sacked Cap Français. In August he proclaimed a conditional emancipation of the slaves. The surviving whites realised that their cause was lost. Many fled to the United States, Cuba, Jamaica, Puerto Rico and Trinidad.

The declaration of a conditional emancipation was evidence that the central question was no longer brown equality but black freedom. Events confirmed Revolutionary France as emancipator and Britain and Spain as leaders of a counter-revolution, in which the chief objectives were to maintain order and the establishment throughout the English colonies and to weaken France by conquering St. Domingue, thereby gaining a monopoly of sugar, coffee and cotton. Pitt's advisers urged also that it was difficult to defend the dispersed English colonies. St. Domingue would constitute a formidable central bastion in a West Indian defence system. Its acquisition would enable Britain to exclude France and the United States from the Caribbean. Pitt and Dundas found the arguments overwhelmingly strong; and the moment was propitious. In 1791, wrote Bryan Edwards, many French colonists had applied to the English King's Ministers, requesting that an armament be sent to take possession of the colony and receive the allegiance of the inhabitants. When, in 1793, England and Spain went to war with France, plans were made for sending an English expeditionary force to St. Domingue and a first detachment of 900 men from Jamaica landed at Jeremie on the south coast, where they were greeted by the whites as deliverers. In the Eastern Caribbean a force of 9,000 men sailed from Barbados and took Martinique, Guadeloupe and St. Lucia. In St. Domingue the English soon gained control of the seaboard of the Gulf of Port Au Prince. The counter revolution was underway and appeared assured of success.

The question for the leaders of the Haitian blacks was: ' Where does freedom lie?' The situation was confused. There were in the country royalist whites, independent mulattoes, a French revolutionary force under Jacobin Commissioners, an English expeditionary force that would certainly support the royalists, and a Spanish force that was allied with the English. The only anti-slavery declaration came from the French Jacobins. In August 1793 Sonthonax decreed a conditional emancipation. In February 1794 the Assembly in Paris declared that all men domiciled in the colonies were French citizens, regardless of distinction of colour. All, and not only the ' aristocracy of skin ', were to enjoy all the rights assured under the constitution. The Declaration applied to Guadeloupe and Martinique, where slavery still existed. It applied also to Haiti, where the slaves had already freed themselves, and there it was of value as a legislative confirmation by the metropolitan government of the end of slavery. A mulatto, Victor Hugues, was sent into the Caribbean with a small force of 1500 men. Hugues was the kind of revolutionary to whom nothing is impossible, and under his leadership the blacks in Martinique and Guadeloupe, whose interests now coincided with those of France, drove out the British. Fédon rose in Grenada. The Black Caribs rose in St. Vincent. In Jamaica the Second Maroon War broke out in 1795, provoked by the action of a magistrate in sentencing two Maroons to be flogged; but some thought it was inspired also by the example of the French agents. Alarmed, the Government of Jamaica prevented any more reinforcements being sent to St. Domingue, where Sonthonax was in peril of defeat. Toussaint, Biassou and other black leaders had joined the Spanish forces and had won most of the north. The English had taken Port au Prince. But the decree of the Assembly won over the blacks. Toussaint joined the French Revolutionary force under Leveaux, and in a brilliant campaign recaptured the line of fortified camps in the north that he had earlier gained for Spain. When he joined the French he had 4,000 disciplined troops under his command. First he routed the other black leaders, like Biassou, who had remained with the Spanish forces. Then, turning on the English who were led by General Maitland, he drove them from the points they had gained on the right bank of the Artibonite River, and threatened their stronghold of St. Marc. The struggle against the English, which lasted till 1798, was a major campaign. C.L.R. James has summed up the situation:

> By the end of 1796, after three years of war, the British had lost in the West Indies 80,000 soldiers, including 40,000 actually dead, the latter number exceeding the total losses of Wellington's army from death, discharges, desertion and all causes from the beginning to the end of the Peninsular War... Early in 1797 the British Government decided to withdraw and maintain control only of Mole St. Nicolas and the island of Tortuga...

But not even that foothold was allowed them by Toussaint. Yellow fever played its part in the defeat of Maitland. So did climate. But the architect of victory was Toussaint; and the force that carried his army to victory was the commitment to freedom made by the blacks and confirmed by France. In the words of James,

> The fever killed many more men than the blacks and mulattoes did but we have seen with what poor resources and against what internal intrigues Toussaint fought. Santo Domingo was not the first place where European invaders had met fever. It was the decree of abolition, the bravery of the blacks and the ability of their leaders that had done it. The great gesture of the French working people towards the black slaves, against their own white ruling class, had helped to save their revolution from reactionary Europe. Helped by Toussaint and his raw levies, singing the *Marseillaise* and the *Ca Ira*, Britain, the most powerful country in Europe, could not attack the revolution in France.

After expelling the English Toussaint attacked the mulatto faction of the west and south, defeated the competent and brave Rigaud, and sacked his headquarters at Les Cayes. About 10,000 mulattoes were killed in the vendetta that followed. Disaster piled upon disaster, for in that tragic autumn of 1800 the heavens opened, and the irrigation dams of the Artibonite and Cul de Sac, weakened by ten years of neglect, gave way. Irrigation had made the West and South prosperous. The dams were never repaired. The area swiftly degenerated into an eroded wilderness. After 1800 Toussaint put a stop to the massacres that were taking place, set himself and his people to the task of rebuilding their agriculture, induced some of the whites to return to their estates, and by 1802 there were signs that the economy was beginning to gain strength. He drew up a constitution in which St. Domingue was declared part of France, but one with its own special laws; and he declared himself Govenor-General for life. The decree was submitted to France for confirmation but was promulgated in anticipation of that confirmation.

Toussaint L'Ouverture

France, which had come under the rule of Napoleon, now became the chief enemy. The process was gradual. Napoleon's plans called for an alliance with Spain. But in 1801 Toussaint, in defiance of Napoleon's instructions, had brought Spanish Santo Domingo under his rule and showed no disposition to give up his conquest. Napoleon was determined to bring Toussaint under his command, and to revive the prosperity of the colony by restoring slavery. With St. Domingue under his control he would be able to rebuild the French colonial system in the Americas. Spain had already yielded Louisiana to him. In order to crush Toussaint, Napoleon sent out a large expeditionary force under his brother-in-law General Le Clerc. In a series of compaigns Le Clerc put Toussaint and his generals on the defensive. Toussaint was devoted to Republican France and did not fully realise that the France of Danton had become the France of Napoleon. He wished to come to terms with Le Clerc, and he permitted Christophe to negotiate with the French general. Christophe, accepting Le Clerc's assurances of good faith and his promise to maintain him and his officers in their command, went over to the French. Le Clerc then agreed that if Toussaint submitted himself to the order of the Republic, liberty for all in St. Domingue would be maintained without question, that all native officers would be maintained in their grades and functions, and that Toussaint would keep his staff and be free to retire to any place he wished in St. Domingue. Toussaint and his generals submitted. Following on this Toussaint accepted an invitation to the headquarters of the French general Brunet. There he was bound, taken aboard a frigate in the harbour and shipped off to France, where he was confined to prison in the French Alps. His last words as he stepped aboard the French ship were: ' In overthrowing me you have cut down in St. Domingue only the trunk of the tree of liberty. It will spring up again by the roots, for they are numerous and deep.'

But Le Clerc was also in trouble. Campaigning against the blacks in the mountains and forests was very different from campaigning in Europe. He wrote in despair from his sick bed that yellow fever decimated his troops. Bands of blacks in the mountains harrassed his forces without pause, for though the generals had gone over to the French the masses continued the revolution. Le Clerc wrote: ' We have in Europe a false idea of the country in which we fight and the men we fight against '. Then the news spread that General Richepanse, who had been sent out by Napoleon, had reached Guadeloupe and had re-imposed slavery. Pétion, a mulatto who had emerged as an outstanding soldier, Clairveaux, Dessalines and Christophe broke with France. General Rochambeau succeeded Le Clerc who had died from yellow fever, and he attempted to break the spirit of the rebels by a campaign of utter savagery. Dessalines matched horror with horror. Without question the most formidable now of Haiti's leaders, Dessalines dramatised the fact that the Haitian Revolution had became a war of independence by calling mulattoes and blacks together at Arcahaye. There he took the red, white and blue tricolour of France, tore out the strip of white, and replaced the letters R.F. that stood for *Republique Francaise* with the words ' Liberty or Death '. In April 1803 Toussaint died. On the last day of December in that year the officers of the army of Haiti, mulattoes like Clairveaux and Pétion in concert with the blacks, Dessalines, Christophe and their companions in arms, formally declared the independence of their country, and re-turned to it the old Indian name Haiti, mountainous land, in place of St. Domingue.

In 1804 Dessalines proclaimed himself Emperor of Haiti. He ruled up to the year of his death, 1806, and was succeeded by Christophe who held the country together even though he lacked the administrative machinery for the everyday tasks of government. He sought to repair the ruined economy of the country by the use of forced labour. Toussaint and Christophe both saw the plantation as the road to prosperity but Petion who became President in 1820 yielded to popular demand and broke up the plantations into smallholdings. The result was a rapid breakdown of the export trade. ' Yet ', as James says, ' subsistence agriculture...has preserved the national independence and out of this has come something new which has captured a conti-nent and holds its place in the institutions of the world.'

Though there were set-backs in some places the counter-revolution triumphed in the Eastern Caribbean. In the early days of the revolution Martinique and Guadeloupe appeared set on the same course as Haiti. They had, however, been settled as sugar and slave plantation colonies at an earlier date than St. Domingue. They had a larger number of resident planters and there was probably less hatred between white planter and black slave than in St. Domingue. Also, there were tensions within the white world itself, for the two islands were important commercial centres and the interests of the merchants of Saint Pierre and Basseterre frequently conflicted with those of the planters who were often in their debt. Since there was no prejudice against whites cohabiting with blacks, there was a growing class of free coloured. There was no colour bar to entry into the crafts or trade or to becoming land owners, so that many of the mulattoes prospered. Social distinctions were preserved, however, for as de St. Mery observed, ' For the sake of order the humiliation attaching to the coloured people, in whatever degree it may exist, must not be lessened.' Further, brown was set against black by a deliberate policy of dividing the non-white world. As a result, though the browns resented their inferior status, their first desire was that which is characteristic of all colonised people; they sought to emulate and become equal to the coloniser, in this instance the French Whites. Therefore, though the browns formed a third element in the conflict, they tended to follow the white planters; and, left to themselves, the planter assemblies of Martinique and Guadeloupe, with mulatto support, might possibly have controlled the situation. But, as we have noted already, in 1792 Jacobin Commissioners arrived from France, rallied commercial and poor-white support, and compelled the governors to submit. As in St. Domingue, the planters turned to the English for help.

After war broke out between France and England in 1793 both sides sent fleets to the West Indies. The French had the advantage of a revolutionary battle cry that won over the slaves, and the English had the advantage of superior naval power and of help from the white planters. In 1793 the English took Tobago. They conquered St. Lucia, Martinique and Guadeloupe in 1794. In Martinique their alliance with the royalists proved effective. Slavery was maintained, and since both the captured French colonies had access to the English sugar market, they prospered. As we have seen, Victor Hugues changed the situation. He proclaimed immediate emancipation, organised slave risings, retook Guadeloupe and St. Lucia, and stirred up the Black Caribs in

St. Vincent and possibly the Maroons in Jamaica. Abercromby retook St. Lucia in 1795. When the Netherlands and Spain were included in the French system, the English seized Demerara and Essequibo in 1796 and Trinidad in 1797. By 1801 England controlled the Caribbean, save for Hispaniola, which was held by Toussaint, Guadeloupe, which was under the French, and Cuba and Puerto Rico which were in Spanish hands. Under the terms of the Treaty of Amiens, in 1801, France regained all her colonies in the Eastern Caribbean, save Trinidad. Napoleon used the breathing space to try and re-establish French power in Haiti with disastrous results, but he was successful in Guadeloupe, where General Richepanse overthrew the browns who had seized power after the departure of Hugues, and re-imposed the sugar-and-slave plantation system and colonial rule. After Le Clerc's failure in Haiti, Napoleon gave up his attempt in the West Indies, and when war broke out again in 1803 the British re-occupied all they had held before the Treaty of Amiens. In 1805 Nelson's victory at Trafalgar put an end to any fear of French power in the Caribbean. The final settlement of 1815 added St. Lucia, Tobago, Trinidad, and (by purchase) Demerara, Essequibo and Berbice to the British Empire. Martinique and Guadeloupe were restored to France.

In terms of trade the English colonies appear to have benefitted from the war. With St. Domingue in revolt, the price of muscovado sugar and coffee increased, coffee doubling its price between 1792 and 1796, and sugar reaching a record of 100s a hundredweight in 1815. But there were sharp fluctuations in sugar prices which slumped steeply in 1799 and after, especially in 1805–17. Also an increase in production costs and in duties on colonial produce cut into profits.

Cotton production also increased. For most of the 18th century Britain bought the bulk of her cotton from the East, but the East could not meet the increasing demand of the factories in Lancashire and Lanarkshire. By 1790 the West Indies were supplying over seventy per cent of British needs. Up to 1810 West Indian cotton remained a profitable crop; then green seed cotton from the southern United States, cleaned by Whitney's patent gin, took the market from the more expensive hand cleaned cotton of the West Indies.

Money also flowed in from increased trade with Latin America during these years. The Anglo-American war and the British blockage of American ports cut down the American trade with Latin America, and as a result both Jamaica and Trinidad bencfitted.

This war-time prosperity could not last with peace. Sugar prices fell, but duties remained high because the war had to be paid for. The East India interest was actively attacking the West Indian monopoly. It was certain that West Indian sugar would lose the European market to beet sugar, newly developed in France, and to cane sugar from newer and larger plantation colonies. St. Domingue was no longer a competitor, but Cuba had taken its place. Also the attack on slavery as an institution would be resumed by the humanitarians, the churches, by new economic interests and by economists who were vigorously criticising slavery on the grounds of wastefulness and inefficiency.

CHAPTER 19

New Directions

At first glance, our history in the 19th century seems confused, with contrary forces at work. In the first quarter of the century a number of nations declared the slave trade illegal, yet the trade flourished up to 1870. While in the British colonies the ' new frees ' were celebrating the end of slavery in the 1830's, newly enslaved blacks on the plantations of the Deep South and in Cuba were lamenting their fate. Bankrupt West Indian sugar planters watched with dismay the collapse of an economic system they had thought everlasting, while their counterparts in Cuba and Puerto Rico made fortunes, and in Trinidad and Guiana sugar plantation economy based on East Indian indentured labour burgeoned with life. In Latin America revolutionary leaders, Simon Bolivar foremost among them, freed their countries from Spanish colonial rule and established independent republics while in the remaining island-fragments of her American empire Spain instituted a harsher colonial regime. In the same period Britain, having extended the franchise at home, jettisoned the principle of representative government in most of her West Indian colonies, and brought them under absolute Crown Colony rule.

But there is an underlying unity, for the same forces of change were at work throughout the region, manifesting themselves in different countries at different times. For example, the movement against colonialism, which achieved its first triumph in the Caribbean with Dessalines' declaration of Haitian independence, was carried further by Bolivar in the two following decades, and in the second half of the century by José Marti, who died on a Cuban battlefield in 1874, fighting against Spanish colonial rule. The black struggle for freedom which found its first victory in Toussaint's emancipation of the blacks of Haiti was continued by blacks in Guiana, Barbados and Jamaica in the following three decades, and by blacks in Martinique up to the date of the abolition of slavery in all French colonies in 1848. The mulattoes who gathered round Edward Jordan in Kingston in the 1820's were influenced by the same ideas about knowledge and the rights of man that led Pétion of Haiti to offer refuge to Bolivar, and that found their most passionate expression in North America in the writings of Thomas Paine.

Alongside this unity there is the diversity that springs from different metropolitan connections, as well as from differences in the nature of the land, and in the time at which ' development ' began. Puerto Rico, for example, became a sugar-and-slave plantation colony a century after Jamaica, and its expanding estates were squeezing smallholders and peasants off the land and transforming them into landless labourers in the period when the collapse of the plantation system in Jamaica made possible the emergence of a peasantry. Our lands have a common history but that common history is only a part of the history of each country.

In the West Indian colonies the abolition of slavery, the collapse of the white oligarchies and the breakdown of the West Indian monopoly prepared the way for the emergence of a new society, a slow process because the old barriers based on race and colour remained and were in many respects reinforced by Crown Colony rule. In considering the chief themes in our history during the 19th century we will find that we are dealing with two societies differentiated by colour and we will find the first indications of a narrowing of the gap between the two. We will find also the first tentative April-signs of a new society, neither European nor African nor East Indian, with its own special character and creativity and we will note that though many of the institutions were European, the strength and vitality and in many respects the uniqueness came from the mass of the people, the blacks.

The themes that we will consider here and in the two following chapters are the abolition of the slave trade and of slavery, the destruction of the West India monopoly and of the old representative system, Crown Colony rule, the development of an administrative system and of social services, the search for labour, the coming of the East Indian, the rise of a black peasantry with its own folk-institutions and the social structure of the West Indies at the close of the 19th century.

The slave trade was abolished by Denmark in 1803. She was followed by Britain, whose Act declaring the trade illegal was passed by Parliament in 1807 on a motion by Wilberforce. His name deserves its high place in our history along with that of his successor, Buxton. Some British slave traders turned to slave-smuggling. To check this, the British Parliament passed acts that made slave-trading a felony (1811) and later a form of piracy punishable by death (1827). Between 1808 and 1820 the United States, France, Holland and Sweden declared the trade illegal, but passing laws was the thing, enforcing them another. The British navy patrolled the seas seeking to suppress the traffic, but the United States, France, Spain, Portugal and Brazil, which became independent in 1822, were half-hearted in their attempt to put an end to the trade. Portugal and Brazil had the benefit of agreements with Britain by which slave traders of the two nations were safe from British warships south of the equator, up to 1839 in the case of Portugal and 1843 in that of Brazil. The three chief centres of demand were Brazil and Cuba, where sugar had taken hold, and the Deep South where slave labour, coupled with Eli Whitney's invention of the saw-gin that cleaned short-fibred cotton cheaply and well, enabled the United States to become the world's greatest supplier of cotton. Up to the end of the 16th century the West Indian colonies, which produced fine long-fibred sea-island cotton, had supplied Britain with seventy per cent of her cotton. Between 1816 and 1820 the West Indian percentage fell to seventy-one, whereas the United States proportion rose to forty-seven per cent. The profits that flowed from these slave plantations convinced many Americans that slavery was not so wicked an institution after all.

The black protest against slavery continued. In the United States, *Walker's Appeal*, written by a free-born black, Daniel Walker, and published in 1828, passionately attacked slavery.

Earlier, in 1800, Gabriel Prosser led a force of 1,100 blacks against Richmond, Virginia. Denmark Vesey, who had studied the Haitian Revolution, organised a rising in 1822, but was betrayed. In 1831 Nat Turner and a small band of slaves rose in Southampton County insurrection. In the year 1865 Lincoln issued his Proclamation of Emancipation. Two years earlier an even vaster army of white slaves, the fifteen million serfs of Russia, were freed by Alexander the Second's Edict of Emancipation. Referring to these two events, Karl Marx wrote ' In my opinion the biggest things that are happening in the world today are on the one hand the movement of the slaves in America started by the death of John Brown, and on the other the movement of the serfs in Russia.'

In the West Indies emancipation came thirty years earlier, as a result of the black rejection of slavery, the attack on slavery by white liberals and missionaries, the liberal political forces that brought about the reform of Parliament in 1832 and weakened the power of the landed gentry, and pressures from the new school of economists led by Adam Smith, who advocated Free Trade and attacked slavery as a wasteful and inefficient means of production.

Referring to the black protest in the first quarter of the 19th century in his study, *Creole Society in Jamaica* Edward Brathwaite points out that there was considerable slave reaction in Jamaica against the regime, and that this was especially noticeable after the Maroon War of 1795. Because of this war, and its association with the Haitian and French revolutions, these slave conspiracies, riots and risings took on, for white Jamaicans, ' an added threat of danger '. Brathwaite lists some of the risings; a rebellion of runaway slaves in Trelawny in 1798, a mutiny of Chamba and Coromantin recruits at Fort Augusta, and many others. Nor was the protest limited to Jamaica. There were risings in the 1820's in Guiana and Barbados and a mutiny under Daaga in Trinidad.

The largest of these ' rebellions ' took place in Jamaica in 1831. Like many similar risings, it expressed the religious and political interests of the blacks, and it is therefore appropriate to consider at this point the work of the missionaries and the black preachers in the years before emancipation.

In Europe the white anti-slavery protest was led by evangelists, humanitarians and radicals, but in the West Indies, missionaries sent out from England formed the only white group which expressed the new ideas about freedom and the brotherhood of man. As in England before the evangelical revival, the Church of England had become materialistic in outlook, and in the West Indies its clergy, firm supporters of the Establishment, were hostile to the missionaries. The local Assemblies, factious and quarrelsome, were united in their intolerance of dissenters and nonconformists and they legislated against Catholics, Jews and against the Methodists, Baptists and other Protestant groups that came to the West Indies toward the end of the 18th century. In this respect they behaved as the French planters and officials had done in the French Antilles, where they had frustrated the efforts of priests seeking to convert the slaves, and had brought to nothing the provisions of the Code Noir for the religious instruction of the slaves. Those in power in the slave colonies, whether British or French, knew that to preach the brotherhood of man was to throw sticks of dynamite around.

The first missionaries to reach the West Indies were Moravians. They established themselves in St. Kitts and St. Thomas in 1756, in Antigua in 1784. Another group of Moravian Missionaries started work in Jamaica at the invitation of two absentee proprietors, William Foster and Joseph Foster Barham, who gave them 300 acres of land at Bogue in the parish of St. Elizabeth. There malaria, yellow fever and dysentery struck down many of the missionaries and their children with them, as the tombstones at Old Salem testify. Their work, though limited in its impact, was significant, for here were white men who called the slaves ' brother ' and came with a book, not a whip.

The Methodists began missionary work in the West Indies on the advice of Dr. Thomas Coke, who visited the islands in 1789. His preaching led to the conversion of an Antigua planter, Nathanial Gilbert and the founding of a Methodist Mission in that island. Other groups of Methodists worked in Barbados, British Guiana and Jamaica.

The missionaries faced many difficulties. Their fellow-whites detested them. Those in authority regarded them as troublemakers, even though Dr. Thomas Coke and others argued that

Christianity would make the bondsmen more contented. The planter point of view about them was expressed by a friend of Simon Taylor, a rich Jamaican proprietor, that notwithstanding what their outward pretensions were, they stood for the abolition of slavery, and so their presence was certain to cause harm to the colony. The missionaries often went in fear of their lives. The newly formed reactionary Colonial Church Union burned the chapels of the missionaries on the theory that ' to get rid of the rooks you must destroy their nests '. Laws were passed restricting the activities of the missionaries, and in some places those wishing to preach had to get permits or licences. The evidence is that the missionaries, far from inciting the slaves, urged them to be patient and to obey those set in authority over them. But those in authority knew quite well that the missionaries represented ideas and values that threatened their position; that a claim to brotherhood was bound to lead to a claim to freedom; that groups brought together to learn to read or for religious instruction might begin to express political views and that a sharing of religious experience by white and black weakened the privileged position which the whites maintained by means of racial discrimination.

The Establishment assessed the position accurately for while the missionaries preached conformity the slaves remained steadfast in the commitment to freedom. Their religious and political interests found fullest expression in groups of black Baptists, for in many respects the leaders of these were nearest to the people. The Baptist Church in Jamaica was founded by two black preachers, Moses Baker and George Lisle, who came to the island from the United States. Lisle's preaching attracted large numbers of people, and the Establishment, sensing danger, prosecuted him for uttering dangerous and seditious words. The charge failed, but he was thrown into prison on a trumped-up charge of debt. Moses Baker, and Lisle after his release, continued their preaching, and some of their followers formed sects of their own. Where the missionaries emphasised the reading of the Bible, the black preachers witnessed to the power of the Spirit which spoke to them through dreams and visions. In her study of missionary activity in Jamaica before emancipation, Mary Reckord found that the slaves expressed their religious interests in groups which developed outside the mission churches, that they mingled Christianity with traditional African forms to produce a style of worship that satisfied their emotional needs more fully than did the services in the mission churches, and that since these religious groups were the only form of organised activity among them, the slaves spoke at their meetings of other matters, and especially of freedom, their chief and constant concern.

Whites, browns and blacks watched with intense interest events in Britain. British official policy at this period aimed at the amelioration of slavery. Britain put pressure on the Assemblies to improve the condition of the slaves by permitting them to receive religious instruction, allowing slaves to marry, prohibiting the flogging of women, and making it easier for a slave to be set free or to buy his freedom. The British Parliament was in a position to enforce its will in Trinidad because the island had not been granted representative government, but the Assemblies in the other islands and the Court of Policy in Demerara and Berbice resisted Parliament. The Barbados Assembly, for example, declared that the bill which Parliament passed in 1816, requiring the Registration of Slaves, was an infringement on the rights of colonial Assemblies and the Jamaica Houses of Assembly objected to ' the degradation of having our internal interests regulated by the Commons of Great Britain '. Under pressure, Berbice and Demerara accepted reforms, including a regulation that a record of punishments should be kept on all estates, the admission of the evidence of slaves in civil suits affecting their owner and in capital charges against whites and the prohibition of the flogging of women. After some hesitation St. Lucia fell into line, and indeed went further than the other colonies by giving the slave one day a week for his own work out of crop time, and a half a day in crop time. This enabled slaves to earn cash to buy their freedom. Tobago, St. Vincent, St. Kitts and Grenada made limited concessions, but the Assemblies in Jamaica and Barbados were resolute in their opposition. By 1826 it was clear that the policy of amelioration had failed. This was confirmed when the Colonial Assemblies rejected, or did not even reply to, an Order of Council sent to them from London in 1831 containing further regulations for protecting the slaves from cruelty and overwork. The Assemblies echoed the view taken by Tobago, that this was a species of dictation formerly unheard of. In Jamaica there was wild talk of secession. Events showed how deeply divided was West Indian society. Slave owners, through the institutions they controlled, notably the Assemblies, affirmed the absolute right that they had over their slaves as their property. The free mulattoes demanded the removal of the civil disabilities from which they suffered. The blacks were insistent on freedom.

The answer came in a major explosion at Le Resouvenir in Demerara in 1823, when the slaves, joined by others from the neighbouring estate of Success, demanded immediate emancipation. The movement spread. What took place was more of a general strike than a rebellion. About 13,000 slaves were involved. They behaved with restraint. There was little violence. Two overseers who resisted them were killed. There was no looting, no burning. The rising was put down with little difficulty. In punishment many slaves were flogged mercilessly and forty seven slaves were executed.

The ferment continued. The growing strength of the anti-slavery agitation in England, the obvious failure of the policy of ' gradualness ', revolutionary talk among the whites, the granting in Jamaica of civil rights to the free coloured in 1831, and discussions about freedom in the black religious groups strengthened the expectation of early emancipation. The Protector of Slaves in Guiana reported in 1832 that ' There is no protection for the slave population and they will very shortly take the matter into their own hands and destroy the property'. In Jamaica, reports spread among the slaves that their ' free paper ' had come but was being withheld. Samuel Sharp, through religious groups in St. James, organised a general strike. Many slaves swore that they would not return to work after the Christmas holidays in 1831. Knibb got word of what was happening and tried to restrain the slaves. So did the Methodist missionary Bleby, who told them it was futile to try to resist the authorities. On 27 December violence broke out, but by January 1 the British commander was able to restore order. The ' Baptist War ' or ' black family war ' involved 50,000 slaves. They did extensive damage to property and killed fifteen whites. As in Demerara, the punishment inflicted was savage. More than 1,000 slaves were flogged, and about 100 were shot or hung, Daddy Sharp among them. The black religious groups lived on, as we will see when we come to consider the Morant Bay rising, and Daddy Sharp was to have his counterpart in Paul Bogle.

Le Resouvenir and St. James showed that the blacks wanted freedom now, not a milder form of bondage. The masters and their agents showed that they wanted slavery, and not a milder form of servitude which left in doubt their absolute ownership of the slaves as property. In England the anti-slavery groups pressed for emancipation. The Whigs, who defeated the Tories in 1831, were committed to reform. The new Parliament contained industrialists and manufacturers, new men fully committed to the view expressed to Parliament in 1820 by London merchants that the best policy for the nation was that of buying in the cheapest market and selling in the dearest. This foreshadowed the destruction of the West India monopoly, which dealt in high cost sugar. Knibb campaigned through England for freedom, public opinion hardened against slavery, Buxton pressed Parliament, and in 1833 a Bill of Emancipation was passed, setting free every slave in the British Empire on 1 August 1834.

But not full freedom. There was to be a period of apprenticeship, during which the ' new frees ', except children under six years of age, were to work forty hours a week for their former masters without wages and were to be paid for the remaining thirteen hours of their work week. They could buy their full freedom from their masters out of the money saved. Specially appointed Stipendary Magistrates were to supervise the system and see that the slaves were not exploited. Apprenticeship was a continuation of the policy of ' gradualness ', a concept that prevailed in Britain as well, where as David Thompson comments in his work *Europe since Napoleon*, ' The Whigs were at one with the Tories in resisting democracy and in crushing popular movements.' And the English working class also had its Peterloo massacre and its agonies. Trevelyan records: ' in the winter of 1830, a few months before the introduction of the Great Reform Bill, the starving field labourers of the counties south of Thames marched about in a riotous manner demanding a wage of half-a-crown a day. The revenge taken by the Judges was terrible;

Commemorating Emancipation: 1838 Government House

three of the rioters were unjustly hanged and four hundred and twenty were torn from their families and transported to Australia, as convicts. Such panic cruelty showed how wide a gap of social misunderstanding divided the upper class from the poor...' How much greater was the gap where there were differences of race and colour as well.

The system of apprenticeship failed. The blacks saw it as a denial of freedom, for why should they be compelled to work for anyone, if free; freedom meant that they were free to withhold their labour, to work or not to work. To be compelled to work without pay was simply to continue slavery. The masters saw apprenticeship as a form of compensation to them for the loss of their slaves, an opportunity for exacting the utmost from the slave before he gained his freedom. Antigua was realistic about the whole business. She declared full and immediate freedom. There were some disputes over pay but nothing serious, and when the Baptist missionary Sturge visited the island in 1837 he reported that the experiment had succeeded beyond the expectations of its most sanguine advocate. Elsewhere there was trouble. Blacks in Trinidad and Tobago denounced the system as a trick, and the Governor as an ' old rogue '. Martial law had to be proclaimed in St. Kitts and some ex-slaves punished before the ' apprentices ' would work. In Guiana and Jamaica there were serious disputes, usually about wages and rights to the use of land for growing food. The system was terminated in 1838, two years earlier than had been intended.

The French colonies moved more slowly toward freedom. Blacks rioted in Martinique, at Cabet in 1822, at Grand Anse in 1833. Like Britain, but more slowly, France followed a policy of amelioration. She removed the tax on the manumission of slaves, simplified the procedures for manumission, prohibited the branding and mutilation of slaves, but all was done with deliberate speed. There was one man, Victor Schoelcher who, like Wilberforce in Britain, never relaxed the pressure for freedom. He finally triumphed in 1848 when slavery was abolished in all French colonies. He insisted that abolition should be absolute, pointing out that British experience showed the futility of a transitional system. Schoelcher went on to affirm that the Republic rejected distinctions in the human family and that, on emancipation, the slaves gained France as their fatherland and enjoyed all the rights of French citizens. These were the hopes of a brave man but neither in the West Indies nor in the French Antilles did emancipation remove the traditional barriers of colour.

In the black plantation islands of the central sector, the Haitian rebellion had roused apprehension and sharpened fears among the whites, but the Cuban sugar interests saw that they were in a completely different situation. Their island was large, and the whites were in the majority. Between 1774 and 1791, indeed, the proportion of free people to slaves had increased, and there were three free Cubans to each slave. In 1792 the island had a population of just over 172,000 including 96,400 whites, over 30,000 free blacks and coloured, and 44,000 slaves. In contrast, Haiti had almost half a million slaves and 38,000 whites and Jamaica in 1787 had 210,894 slaves and 25,000 whites. As in the early days in Hispaniola the demand rose, ' bring in Africans '. Between 1764 and 1790, 33,400 blacks were imported. In little more than half that time, between 1791 and 1810, the number trebled, slave importations rising to over 91,000. In another 14 years 1806 to 1820, it shot up to 131,000. Curtin estimates that between 1811 and 1870 some 606,000 African slaves were imported into Cuba and Puerto Rico, and in the same period some 96,000 into the French Caribbean, making a total of about 700,000 Africans.

The changes that took place in Cuba as a result of the development of the sugar and slave plantation have been described vividly by two Cuban scholars, Fernando Ortiz in *Cuban Counterpoint* and Guerra y Sanchez in *Sugar and Society*. Both have written of the growth of large estates, the displacement of smallholders by large proprietors, the concentration of power in the hands of a few, the degradation of the workers, the growing influence of overseas investors on the economy and politics of Cuba, the subordination of the interests of the Cuban people to the interests of a class, and the increase of black and brown in what had been a ' white ' island. Ortiz has shown how, by reason of the size of the island and the tough individualism of the smallholder, the tobacco smallholdings survived, the vega existing in the same country as the central, the free white peasant in the same country as the slave. Pointing to the contrast, José Martí dwelt lovingly on the tobacco planter, the veguero, tending his smallholding in the famous tobacco districts of Cuba, the Vuelta Abajo, the Vuelta Arriba, and the area around Santiago, caring for the individual plant with ' his protecting hands '.

Sugar, however, gained the dominance. When in the middle of the century it appeared as if British pressure on Madrid would result in the abolition of the slave trade, the Cuban planters, like their West Indian counterparts, went in search of cheap indentured labour, importing Yucatecans and Chinese, these being subject to the whip and irons as the slaves were. They sought to encourage white immigration also, but everyone knew that Cuban prosperity rested on the shoulders of the black slave and the spread of the sugar and slave plantations transformed Cuba from a predominantly white into a mestizo society. In 1792, as we have seen, there was one slave to every three free persons. By 1817 the population had risen to just over 600,000, with 224,268 black slaves and 115,691 free blacks, and for the first time the blacks were in the majority. In 1792 sugar production stood at about 15,000 tons. A century later black labour, and steam power which enabled estates to build steam mills, introduce the vacuum pan and lay down railways that greatly extended the radius of their operations, boosted production to over 600,000 tons. Indeed, before the close of the 19th century sugar-production twice rose above a million tons. Cuba gained the United States market and in turn became an economic dependency of the United States, in which the foreign investor influenced local politics, the foreign dealer dictated to the local producer, foreign capital replaced local capital and absentee control replaced local ownership.

The blacks protested against the life imposed on them, the conditions of which were described so vividly by Nicholas Guillén —' The Negro tied to the sugar plantation, the Yanqui on the sugar plantation '; the slave's life was one of the ' whip and sweat ' whereas American investment made Cuba ' sweet from outside and very bitter from inside ' a country where the black man was ' yesterday the slave of white overseers armed with angry whips '. The blacks registered their protest in 1840–43, when they spread terror in Matanzas by conspiracies and risings. In the same period national feeling was growing among the white Creoles who were bitter at Spanish absolutism. The gap between these and the peninsular Spaniards widened under the harsh competence of Tacon, Captain General from 1834–38. At a time when the West Indian blacks had been emancipated and the independence movement had triumphed on the mainland, Tacon was having no nonsense about civil liberties in Spain's last important stronghold in the New World. In 1838 the Cubans lost their one remaining constitutional right of representation in the Spanish Cortes, and in consequence Criollo resistance increased, but the Criollos found themselves in a difficult position, for how could they demand civil liberties and not black liberty? The liberal José Antonio Saco, author of the *History of Slavery*, driven into exile by Tacon, advocated the abolition of the slave trade and the emancipation of the slaves, but very gradually, since if there was black humanity in Cuba there was also white humanity— remember Haiti! Saco did not refer to the peaceful emancipation of the slaves in the French Antilles. Not until 1868 was the cry of freedom raised. In that year the ' glorious revolution ' in Spain overthrew the Bourbon monarchy and, in Cuba, Cespedes and a group of Criollo proprietors in the cattle-raising province of Oriente rose against Spanish rule with the demand *Independencia y Cuba libre*. Cespedes recognised the vital connection between Cuban independence and black liberty in his declaration at Bayamo at the close of 1868, when he declared that a ' free Cuba was incompatible with a slave Cuba'. The Ten Years War came to an end in 1878, with the surrender of the rebels; and the Spanish Government, in a series of concessions, abolished slavery in 1880. But so gradual was the process of emancipation that it was not concluded until 1886.

There followed the Second Cuban War of Independence in which the flaming spirit of white Martí and the military skill of coloured Maceo symbolised the mestizo society that Cuba had become, a society of which Guillén sings in his *Ballad of My Two Grandfathers*:

> *Lance with head of bone,*
> *Drum of leather and wood,*
> *My black grandfather*

Ruff round his broad throat,
Grey warrior's armour,
My white grandfather

They both
raise their proud heads
under the high stars
both of the same stature
Black anguish and white anguish...

Social distinctions remained, but the break with Spain and the struggle for independence had strengthened the commitment of Cubans to their country and to a common citizenship. But Cuban independence did not mean that the hope of the Cuban patriot Felix Varela had been fulfilled and that Cuba, already an island geographically, had become also an island politically.

Let us return to the English-speaking colonies, where up to the time of emancipation the established order was based on slavery, which provided a captive labour force that had to be fed and clothed but did not have to be paid; control of the local legislatures; and a monopoly of the sugar market in Britain, where West Indian sugar enjoyed a preferential duty that shielded it from foreign competition. Emancipation removed one column by giving the slave mobility and the right to sell his labour. It put the labour force on a wage basis, the planter having to find cash to pay his workers. A second supporting column was removed when the British Parliament succeeded in imposing Crown Colony rule in most of the colonies.

In 1763 when Dominica, Grenada and St. Vincent were ceded by France to Britain, the Board of Trade, mindful of the difficulties it constantly had with the Assemblies of Barbados, the Leeward Islands and Jamaica, tried to limit the powers of the new Assemblies. For nearly five years after the first Assembly met all the laws passed in these islands were disallowed by the Privy Council but in the end the attempt at imposing restraints failed, and in 1772 the Governor was authorised to sign any Bills based on the precedent of legislation in the Leeward Islands.

In 1815 Trinidad, St. Lucia, Berbice and Demerara became British colonies. In each of these the laws and the institutions to which the peope were accustomed were kept, but in Trinidad and St. Lucia, and in the two former Dutch colonies as far as was possible, the Crown kept legislative power firmly in its hands. Trinidad and St. Lucia were ruled by Governors, each with a nominated Council that had only advisory powers. The white residents in Trinidad had petitioned at an earlier date for an Assembly with legislative powers, and Lord Liverpool set out fully the reasons for rejecting the request: that in a new colony where the rights of the Crown and of Parliament were entire it was not advisable to surrender those rights in whole or in part, and establish a system of government like that in the older colonies.

For the first half of the 19th century there were two fundamentally different systems of government in the British colonies, that of the older colonies where Assemblies had legislative power and that in the newly acquired colonies which were under Crown Colony rule. Trinidad from time to time sought some measure of representative government. But gradualism won. A deep-rooted distrust in the capacity of subject peoples prevailed. Representation in the legislature would be granted whenever the spread of education and 'the advancement in civilisation of the inhabitants justified it'. Trinidad had to wait until 1924 for any form of constitutional reform.

The power of the purse was used by Britain to gain some control over the Jamaica House of Assembly, which received a loan of half-a-million pounds in 1856 on condition that it would give up its traditional practice of permitting individual members to move motions for government spending, and agree that this should be done by the Governor assisted by a special Executive Committee made up of two members from the Assembly and one from the Council. This made it impossible for the Assemblies to spend more money than the government had, and it enabled the Governor to exercise much greater initiative in financial matters. This step was taken also between 1855–60 in Tobago, Grenada, St. Kitts, St. Vincent, Nevis and Antigua.

Following the rebellion in Jamaica in 1865, the Jamaica House of Assembly surrendered its power to the Crown and left it to the Colonial Office to decide how the island should be governed. Crown Colony government was introduced on the same lines as in Trinidad, with a Governor who ruled, and a nominated council which advised. A modest step toward representative government was taken in 1884. By 1870 Barbados and British Guiana alone retained its Assembly and Council, with their traditional powers. Slowly the political power-base of the old plantation system was destroyed, and in the process West Indians were stripped of the right to participate in the government of the countries to which they belonged.

What was wrong with the old representative system was not the principle of participation by the community in government through a process of election, but the narrowness of the franchise, which was limited to a small group of proprietors and merchants with vested interests in the continuance of those institutions on which the slave and sugar plantation rested. Their chief concern was the protection of that interest, and they blocked any action that was not directly to their benefit. Under Crown Colony rule the Governor was freed from these deadlocks and was able to get ahead with the tasks of government as he and the Colonial Office saw them. Governors like Lord Harris in Trinidad and Sir John Peter Grant in Jamaica showed what could be done by energetic and intelligent men. Public works were undertaken, primary education expanded, the administration of justice improved, medical services introduced and a start made in developing an efficient civil service. The governing principle was that of trusteeship, ' the direct protection by the Crown of the unrepresented classes, which takes the place of representation '. But from the beginning there were West Indians who opposed the system because it was paternal and exclusive. It had no roots in public support. A Baptist minister, writing from Jamaica in 1876, spoke of Crown Colony government as ' killing our very manhood '. In Guiana in 1889 the *Daily Chronicle* complained that 'we have not even the semblance of Representative Government '. In Trinidad Dr. Louis De Verteuil and his associates campaigned for constitutional reform so that the people of Trinidad might have a part in the government of their country and in Barbados a coloured lawyer successfully resisted Britain's attempt to change the constitution because this would have meant a loss of representative government.

The conflict that developed between Barbados and Britain

arose out of a Colonial Office attempt to tidy up the administration of the islands of the Eastern Caribbean, and lesson the administrative costs of government. Sir Benjamin Pine was sent out as Governor of Leeward Islands in 1869, with the task of bringing together Antigua, Dominica, Montserrat, St. Kitts, Nevis and the Virgin Islands under one government, with one Council, one Superior Court and one Police Force. Opposition in the islands, especially in Nevis, led the Colonial Office to give up its insistence on a Common Treasury. By a Leeward Islands Act of 1871 a Federal Government was established with authority over the administration of justice, education, a police force, the prisons, posts, currency and weights and measures: a system caustically described by Eric Williams as a ' federation of policemen and paupers, convicts and lunatics '. Had the measure preserved the principle of representative government and given to the people of the islands the opportunity of sharing together in political decisions that affected them all, progress might have been made in overcoming the traditional West Indian separatism. Instead, the pressure of each island against colonial office rule, as represented by the Governor and the federal institutions, reinforced old suspicions and rivalries.

The Colonial Office then turned its attention to bringing Grenada, St. Vincent, St. Lucia and Tobago and Barbados under one government. Pope Hennessy, who was sent out as Governor of Barbados in 1875 in order to establish the Federation, soon got into trouble with the Barbadian planters, who formed a Barbados Defence Association sworn to protect their independence and their system of representative government. The planters had no wish to be included in the new Federation for several reasons. They had control of the political system because the franchise was limited, and was based on property or income qualifications. They controlled wages because land was limited and estate work was the only available form of employment for the mass of people. Besides, they knew that their industry was threatened by the growth of the beet sugar industry in Europe and they feared that Federation with less prosperous islands would put their own future in jeopardy. On the other hand the workers favoured the new proposals, which opened up a larger labour market for them. They saw a prospect of higher wages and possibly of becoming landowners. Rioting broke out, eight persons were killed and troops had to be brought in from Jamaica and British Guiana to restore order. The planters charged Pope Hennessy with inciting the blacks to rebel and with seeking to destroy the Barbadian system of representative government. Their most powerful advocate was a coloured lawyer, Conrad Reeves, who by sheer ability had climbed the long ladder from poverty to being an elected member of the House of Assembly and then Solicitor General. He put the central issue clearly in a speech in the Barbados House of Assembly in May 1876: ' The question of Confederation had been laid before us and has been respectfully considered by us. We have declined Confederation because, in the form in which it takes in the case of the West India colonies it means, and can only mean, the surrender by us, in the long run, of our representative form of government which we have enjoyed for 250 years...' Pope Hennessy was recalled. Barbados preserved its old system of representative government with one modification, the addition of an Executive Committee to make financial proposals and influence the Assembly's expenditure of revenue. And Barbadian folk-speech preserves the memory of this turbulent time in its use of the word ' confederation ' to mean a commotion or disturbance.

Notwithstanding its defects, the Barbados system worked, and it was of importance that other West Indian colonies could point to one colony in which the principle of representation was preserved and was functioning. In Jamaica a modest advance toward popular representation was made in 1884 when a Legislative Council was established consisting of the Governor and an equal number of official and unofficial members. The unofficial members were elected on a restricted franchise, and they were in a provisional majority as not all the official members were appointed to the council. If they were unanimous the elected members could only be outvoted if the governor appointed the full number of officials and declared the matter of paramount public importance. Changes were made in Guiana in 1891, where the unofficial members of the Court of Policy (the legislature in other than in financial affairs) were to be chosen by direct election. But during the 19th century Crown Colony Government in the West Indies was challenged only by a few leaders of public opinion, and remained without drastic modification until the 1920's.

The third column on which planter-power rested was the preference given to West Indian sugar by Britain. This was removed in 1846 when Parliament passed a Sugar Duties Act although duties were not actually equalised until 1854. The sugar industry had long been in trouble. Prices were low in the 1820's. In the 1830's, during the period of apprenticeship, labour difficulties were common. With the abolition of slavery, planters, who traditionally had been financed by agents in Britain who received their sugar and rum and sent their supplies, had to find cash to pay their labour bills. Most of the £20 million that Britain had paid to slave owners in compensation went into the pockets of creditors to pay off debts and mortgages and there was little left for capital development or for working the estates. To shortage of labour and shortage of cash there was added in 1847 the opening of a formerly protected market to foreign sugar-producers who sold at lower prices. Piled on top of this was a commercial crisis in Britain which sent thirteen West India houses bankrupt within twelve months. The figures for production in Jamaica show the ruin that overtook the island. Sugar production fell from 71,000 tons in 1832 to 25,000 tons in 1852. Many sugar and coffee plantations were abandoned. The price of properties fell. Owners sold out. Some estates went into chancery because, by law, the purchaser of an estate that was subject to charge for debt had to take over these charges, or ' encumbrances ' as well. St. Lucia was the first colony to change this. It set up a mortgage office in 1829 and in 1833 passed a law that permitted the seizure and sale of real estate property without its encumbrances. In the 1850's St. Vincent and Jamaica, seeing the success of these measures, passed similar laws. As a result many estates were sold out or broken up for sale to smallholders.

We have taken note of the chief social and political changes that took place in the West Indies at this period (1830–60). Emancipation set three quarters of a million people free without providing for their participation in the affairs of the country as citizens. It also rendered the oligarchic rule of the planter assemblies more of an anachronism than ever. The Colonial Office, adopting a policy of ' trusteeship ', replaced the old representative system in many of the islands by Crown Colony rule. And when the British Parliament passed an act in 1846 that provided for the progressive equalisation of duties on British and foreign sugar, it removed the monopoly which had done so much to preserve the old plantation system.

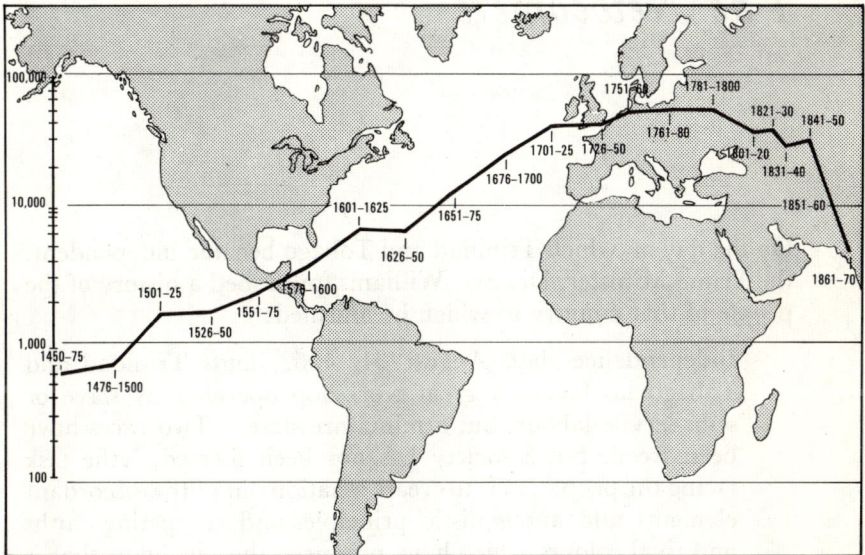

Major trend of Atlantic Slave Trade in annual average number of slaves imported

The Atlantic slave-trade furnished the Caribbean with the great bulk of its labour force for very nearly three centuries. By a massive importation of Africans it transformed the Caribbean region. The abolition of the Slave Trade and emancipation led to an intensive search for labour, and to a second large-scale importation of people which radically changed the structure and ethnic pattern of many Caribbean countries.

CHAPTER 20

The Newcomers

On the day on which Trinidad and Tobago became independent, the Prime Minister, Dr. Eric Williams, published a history of the people of that country in which he affirmed:

> Independence day, August 31, 1962, finds Trinidad and Tobago no longer a great workshop operated by slave or semi-servile labour, but a miniature state. Two races have been freed, but a society has not been formed...the task facing the people... is to create a nation out of the discordant elements and antagonistic principles and competing faiths and rival colours which have produced the amalgam that is today the approximately 875,000 people of Trinidad and Tobago.

Competing faiths and rival colours were characteristic of Trinidad in the last quarter of the eighteenth century, when white and coloured French settlers with their slaves moved in to the island, then a sparsely settled Spanish colony. An estimate of the island's free population in 1803, six years after its capture by the British, showed that there were just over 4,000 French, 2,200 Spanish and 1,200 British, and that there were about 5,000 free coloured out of a total free population of 7,500. In the course of the nineteenth century immigration added further to the complex of races and cultures, and contributed greatly to the growth of the country's population and of its economy. Similar changes took place in Guiana and Surinam. Before considering these let us look at a sample of the ethnic groupings in the West Indies today, as shown by percentages:

	Antigua	Barbados	Dominica
Black	85	77	25
East Indian	—	·07	·011
Chinese	·01	·02	—
Mixed	13	17	74
White	1·6	5	·03

	Guyana	Jamaica	Trinidad
Black	38	78	47
East Indian	44	2	35
Chinese	0·94	1	1·01
Mixed	10	17	14·12
White	3	1	2·74

The figures show that the older plantation islands are predominantly black in contrast with Trinidad, where about one-third of the population is East Indian. In Guyana roughly one-half of the population is East Indian. Guyana's neighbour, Surinam, has large numbers of East Indians and of Javanese, the term used generally for all Indonesians because the Javanese form the largest group among them.

This movement of people into the Caribbean took place during a century (1840–1940) that witnessed an astonishing outpouring of Europeans into every other continent, the largest population movement in history, involving between fifty and sixty million people. Railroads and steamships made it possible for them to traverse continents and cross oceans. A rising tide of liberalism in Europe resulted in the removal of laws and prohibitions that hindered freedom of movement; old laws, industrialisation, the pressure of a rapidly growing population and the growth of large cities were among the forces that caused people to migrate. Some immigrants were propelled from their homes by an outbreak of political or religious persecution, many by an urge to better themselves in lands where the horizons were expanding, where individual liberty seemed to be secure where silver and gold might be found and land bought cheap. One of the most remarkable facts about this long-sustained immigration of people, in which more than thirty million Europeans moved to the United States, is that it was undertaken by individuals on their own initiative. Individuals and families decided to migrate and found ways of meeting the cost.

How different was the movement of people into the Caribbean. It did not develop as a result of individual initiative. It was essentially a movement of desperately needy people, recruited by the agents of planters and Governments in the Caribbean who were in search of hands, not of free men. The planters realised that emancipation would reduce their labour force. They wanted a system of tied labour, like the apprenticeship system of the West Indies in the years 1834–8 or like the system of State supervision in Surinam in the ten years after the slaves there had been set free (1863–73); a system with guaranteed hours of labour and with control of the labourers by means of punishments and penalties. In every sugar-producing country from Surinam to Cuba the question of urgency was 'Where are the labourers to come from?'. In 1834, immediately after emancipation, the planters in Jamaica, Trinidad and Guiana and the governments of those countries gave priority to immigration policies designed to supply estate labour. Thirty years later an observer in Surinam in the year of emancipation remarked that very soon there would be felt generally the paralysing influence of the lack of labourers on the plantations. In the same period sugar planters in Martinique contended that the importation of labour was an economic necessity. A prominent Cuban planter, Aldama, put the matter bluntly: ' Today there exists a large number of landowners who are bent on bringing in labourers and we must bring them in from somewhere, even if it be from Siberia.' The plantations had long arms. The extent of the search of labour and its significance become clear when we consider the experience of countries across the Caribbean, like Surinam, Guyana, Trinidad, Jamaica and Cuba. Although the great majority of the newcomers were East Indians we will include in our review the Javanese, free Africans and Chinese. We will bear in mind, also, that at the start of the 19th century the most developed part of our archipelago, in plantation terms, was the central segment, extending from St. Domingue to Barbados. In the northern sector Cuba and Puerto Rico were inhabited largely by whites, many of them smallholders, with a high proportion of free people to slaves. In the southern sector Trinidad was virtually empty. At the time of the British conquest in 1797 it had a small labour force of 10,000 African slaves and a total population of 17,716. Only one twenty-fifth of the island was cultivated. Guiana was a plantation colony with ample resources of land, a majority of black slaves and a small group of white owners. The overall demographic picture was that of a crowded black central segment, a sparsely populated southern sector with blacks making up the largest ethnic group, and a northern sector that had a small population made up chiefly of whites.

Professor Goslinga, a Dutch historian who has devoted himself to the history of the Caribbean, in a study of immigration into Surinam, refers to the crisis in the colony's sugar industry in the period after the slaves there were emancipated (1863). The opening of the Suez Canal in 1869 shortened the distance between the sugar plantations of Indonesia and Europe, and put Surinam at a disadvantage since its sugar cost more to produce. The Emancipation Bill had stated that the free colonisation of Surinam would be encouraged. The Government undertook to supervise the supply of foreign labourers and encouraged their recruitment. Attempts were made to import Chinese labourers but the cost was high and the Chinese government was not in favour. In 1870 a treaty between Britain and the Netherlands regulated the importation of contract labourers from India into Surinam. A Department of Immigration was established, with an Agent General, soon termed a ' coolie papa ', who was to supervise the immigrants. Though there were crises of different kinds and though on occasion the importation of East Indians was suspended, 34,000 East Indians were imported between 1873 and 1916, when all Indian immigration was stopped. About one-third returned to India at the end of their contract term.

Indonesian contract labourers were also imported. At first they were brought in to work on the estates, but at a later period plans were made for establishing them as small farmers. About 32,000 Javanese were imported between 1890 and 1938, and about one-fourth returned home at the end of their five-year contract term. In 1964 in Surinam, out of a total population of

very nearly 300,000, about forty per cent was Creole, thirty eight
per cent East Indian and sixteen per cent Javanese. Goslinga
summarises the effects of East Indian and Javanese immigration
in these words: ' During these years the population climbed from
62,000 to 200,000. It became not only a very heterogeneous or
plural society but also a very segmented one. Plantation agriculture was not saved; the Indians and to a lesser extent the
Indonesians followed patterns of small scale farming initiated
by the Creoles. Like the Creoles the majority of the immigrants,
after contract expiration, wanted to be their own bosses '. Plantation agriculture declined in importance, because of a chronic
labour shortage and high production costs; and small farming, in
which the Asians greatly outnumbered the Creoles, expanded
rapidly. The change in the traditional system of agriculture is
indicated by Goslinga's figures showing the percentage of the
total agrarian production contributed by plantations and small
farms:

Year	Plantations %	Small Farms %
1900	90	10
1920	29	71
1940	17	83
1950	10	90

The small farmers produced vegetables, maize, citrus, some
cattle and poultry, but rice was their major crop. Through their
work Surinam, which was a rice-importer early in this century,
became a rice-exporter by 1930.

Guiana, like Surinam, is a large country with a relatively small
population. During the second half of the eighteenth century it
attracted sugar-planters from Barbados and the Leeward Islands,
and imported African slaves. The mortality rate among the
slaves was high. The West Indian demographer, George Roberts,
has shown that for the period 1820–32 the average length of life
for men and women slaves was only 22·8 years. Nearly one-half
of the children died before they were ten years old. Figures like
these meant that rearing a slave was an expensive business,
representing an outlay of about £87 each whereas it cost £45
to import a slave from Cuba. Even as late as the 1890's there was

little improvement, the average length of life for males being twenty two years, and twenty six for females. 'The enormous mortality throughout the nineteenth century,' writes Roberts, 'tended to make it economically advantageous for the sugar industry to depend on imported labour.' Also, from 1838 on, the blacks, who earned some money by growing produce for sale in Georgetown and New Amsterdam, and by working beyond the prescribed seven and a half hours a day, bought derelict estates and became smallholders. The shortage of labour through the high death rate and the flight of the blacks from the estates spurred the Government and the plantation owners to recruit contract labourers, and the inflow of immigrants boosted the country's population.

Attempts were made to recruit labour in Madeira, the Canary Islands, China and India. Between 1859–66 Guiana imported about 12,000 Chinese, but after 1866 Chinese immigration petered out, largely because the Chinese Government was opposed to emigration and China was in no mood to cooperate with European powers with whom she had recently been at war. Also, those Chinese who emigrated of their own will preferred to go to California and South-East Asia rather than to the remote West Indies; and shippers could make more money by carrying goods instead of emigrants to the West Indies. The cost of transporting a Chinese immigrant to the West Indies in the 1850's was high when compared with the cost of transporting an East Indian, £25 each as against £15.

The first attempts to encourage East Indian immigration failed. John Gladstone obtained permission to take East Indian workers to Guiana on a five year contract, but ill-treatment and sickness caused many deaths among them and in 1840 the ban on Indian immigration by the Indian Government was confirmed by Act of Parliament. Under pressure from the West Indies the Colonial Office lifted its embargo but a second attempt, made in 1845–6, also failed.

Trinidad and Guiana persevered, in spite of these failures. Between 1841 and 1847 British Guiana alone spent over £360,000 on immigration and obtained over 12,000 workers from India, about the same number from other West Indian colonies, 8,000 from Africa and about 16,000 from Madeira. The Africans tended to move away from the estates and set up as peasant squatters. A large number of the Madeirans died. The East Indians worked steadily on the estates, but the mortality rate among them was high, and they were then too small a group to save the sugar industry, which was in so critical a position after the passing of the Sugar Duties Act that the British Government had to lend the colony £250,000 to help the industry. Three-fourths of this money was to be spent on immigration.

Many of the East Indian indentured workers fell ill and died because of the conditions under which they were transported or under which they lived on the estates, without proper housing or health services, and with inadequate food. A local commission appointed to spend the money loaned to Guiana affirmed that the East Indian indentured labourer was the only person who could save the industry, and they made arrangements to improve the conditions under which the immigrants were transported and in which they lived. Housing and medical care were provided. Between 1884 and 1914 more than a quarter of a million East Indians were brought into British Guiana under indenture and only about one in every four was repatriated. The figures for sugar production indicate the change that took place in the industry. Production had fallen from 60,000 tons in 1830 to 23,000 tons in 1846. Though hard hit by the equalisation of duties it rose to 38,000 tons in 1851, to 62,000 tons in 1861, and to 92,000 tons in 1871.

The East Indians, like the free blacks, aimed at becoming landholders and farmers on their own. Like the blacks, they entered the Caribbean under heavy disadvantages. In the early years of the contract system they were recruited by dubious methods, so much so that the recruiting agents in India were nicknamed ' coolie-catchers .' On the estates to which they were assigned in the West Indies they endured conditions approaching those of slavery. They could not leave the estate without a permit, with the result that the blacks, who looked on them almost as strike-breakers, jeeringly asked, ' Slave, where is your paper?' They were subject to fines and imprisonment for absence from work or for not obeying instructions. They were herded into insanitary barracks, were despised by those who depended on their labour, and described as ' barbaric ' and ' half savages.' They were often stricken with fever and disease. Death visited the barracks frequently. The conditions are set out in some detail by Eric Williams in his *History of the People of Trinidad and Tobago*. Those East Indians who survived responded to the penalisation in two ways, by claiming the return passage due to them at the end of their contract term, or by establishing holdings of their own.

In Guiana by 1869 the Government's total liability for free passages was in excess of £250,000 and the number of East Indians able to claim return passages numbered over 30,000. Guiana could not afford to pay the passages nor could the planters afford to lose their workers. Land was offered to the landless in place of the return passage, and East Indian village settlements came into existence, but with some difficulty, since the land first offered on the Demerara Coast was unsuitable and the East Indians refused to take up the offer. Success came in 1880 when several hundred East Indians took up the offer of land on the Essequibo Coast. Trinidad followed a similar course. Thus, in Surinam, Guiana and Trinidad the East Indians turned to small farming, and in so doing radically changed the traditional system of agriculture. Eric Williams puts his finger on this vital point in describing the contribution of the Indian to Trinidad society and the economy of Trinidad:

> In the age-old battle which the planter had fought against the small farmer, the sugar planter who had prevented the emancipated negro slave from becoming a small farmer, that same sugar planter had to compromise with the Indian indentured immigrant, and in the social sense the outstanding result of indentured Indian immigration was the emergence, for the first time in the history of Trinidad, of a class of small farmers.

In this connection we will give our attention to the emergence of a black peasantry in the chapter that follows.

Very nearly half a million East Indians came to the Caribbean as indentured labourers between 1845 and 1917. The distribution of those who worked in the West Indies is shown here:

British Guiana	238,900 (55·3%)
Trinidad	143,900 (33·3%)

Jamaica	36,400 (8·4%)
Grenada	5,900 (1·4%)
St. Lucia	4,400 (1%)
St. Vincent	2,500 (0·6%)
St. Kitts	300 (0·1%)

The Cuban experience with Chinese indentured labour between 1847–74 provides us with interesting points of comparison. The island entered the sugar race late. At the end of the eighteenth century its population stood at 200,000, including about 40,000 slaves, and the chief occupations were ranching and tobacco farming. By 1828 however Cuba, with a greatly enlarged slave population, was producing more sugar than the whole of the West Indies. When the slave trade was abolished slaves were imported illegally; and their number was increased by the sale of Africans who had been liberated by the British navy and landed in Havana. Under pressure from Britain, Spain put an end to this. A few years later, in 1845, she passed a new abolition law with heavy penalties for Spanish citizens caught trading in slaves. Besides, the slaves themselves had grown restive, as the Matanzas rising of 1843 demonstrated. The planters tried to cut production costs by building railways, using steam engines instead of oxen, introducing mills with iron rollers, introducing vacuum pans which boiled the liquid sugar at a low temperature and could be heated by the same force that drove the steam engine. In the 1850's centrifugal machines were brought in. Mechanisation of this kind was costly, and a large number of factories were not able to afford it. Those that did had the benefit of higher production. In 1860 only four per cent of all Cuban factories were mechanised but they produced twenty per cent of Cuba's sugar. Mechanisation reduced the number of workers required; but it also required a tractable labour force that could be trained to handle machinery. To meet the demand, a number of workers were recruited from the Canary Islands and from Spain but the planters found Chinese contract labourers the most satisfactory and between 1853 and 1874 the Chinese were the chief support of the Cuban sugar industry. They were recruited for a term of years, had to work for twelve hours a day, were paid four pesos a month, and were given two changes of clothing a year and food. They could be punished like the slaves by beating and confinement in the stocks. In her account of this immigration Mary Reckord comments that ' to buy a Chino on these terms was clearly economical...eight years labour could be bought for 720 pesos. This compared favourably with the cost of a slave bought for 600 pesos.' About 124,000 Chinese were imported into Cuba between 1848 and 1874, almost all of them being men. The business of transporting the Chinese was Cuban financed and Cuban managed, in contrast with the illegal trade in slaves which was American financed and managed and which was carried on under the protection of the American flag.

Like the trade in East Indian contract workers, the trade in Chinese labour was marked by cruelty. In the words of a Cuban scholar, Perez de la Riva, only the chains were missing on the long voyage from China, called by the sailors ' death voyages ' because of the high death rates. Nevertheless the trade prospered and the proportion of Chinese workers in relation to slaves grew from about one to every ten slaves in 1862 to one to six in 1877.

In 1870, in the course of the Ten Years War (1868–78) Spain, yielding to criticism from many nations, abolished the slave trade. A year later she abolished the system of contract labour. Thus, in Cuba, the bondage of the blacks and the Chinese came to an end at the same time. Mary Reckord's judgment on the effect of Chinese contract labour on the Cuban economy is significant:

> The Chinese were conformable to plantation slavery and enabled the planters to deal with the crisis of the 1840's within this framework and in terms of labour supply... But in the 1880's the Cubans faced a new crisis in world market conditions. Competition with beet sugar pressed hard... Deprived of slaves and contract labour the Cubans met the demand for cheaper sugar by reorganising production. Economies of scale, technology and numbers of labourers led to the development of the ' centrales ', sugar factories fed by railways linking plantations employing seasonal labour... solutions all considered in the 1840's but postponed...

Free Africans were also brought to the Caribbean as contract workers. The total number was of the order of 36,000 in the period 1840–62. About 14,000 of these went to Guiana, 10,000 to Jamaica, and 8,000 to Trinidad. The remaining 3,500 were shared by St. Kitts, St. Vincent, St. Lucia and Grenada. Practically all of these immigrants were slaves liberated by the British navy in its campaign against the slave trade and taken to Sierra Leone. There was little interest among other African states in contract labour in the West Indies.

In 1840 the *Hector* brought 266 free Africans to Jamaica to work as contract labourers. This was done with the consent of the British government which, however, was chary of encouraging a large scale importation of Africans for fear of being charged with continuing the slave trade under another form. At the time the Brazilian slave trade was reaching large proportions, and consequently the number of liberated slaves increased. In turn, the number imported into the West Indies also increased. When the Brazilian slave trade came to an end in 1852 the supplies of liberated slaves fell off. When the Cuban trade, which was in fact largely an American trade, increased toward the end of the 1850's a larger supply of liberated slaves again became available, but supplies from this source ceased after 1862 when Britain and the United States, by the Treaty of Washington, agreed to suppress the Atlantic Slave Trade.

The immigration of free Africans, therefore, involved liberated slaves rather than Africans who desired to leave their homeland for the Caribbean. The total number was not large enough to have much impact on the West Indies, and the period of immigration was relatively brief. The trade, though relatively small, was marked by deception and fraud, like the trades in Chinese and in East Indian contract workers. Advertisements issued in Sierra Leone promised ' you can catch plenty of coppers...at Trinidad you can catch silver money... A man catches for a day's work 2 cut monies, half pound of salt fish and he will have a house and farm and will catch a little rum every day '... Recruiting agents went into the schools in search of children, but even there they had little success, for word had got around that some Africans had been refused their return passage, and there was a general impression of broken promises and conditions.

Yet, though the total number of free African immigrants was small, they added elements of African culture to the lands in which they settled. Studies of African survivals in Jamaica, for example, point out that a number of the free Africans worked on estates in St. Thomas, where their religious beliefs are reflected in the Kumina cult. The free Africans founded villages of their own like that at Waterfall near Rhine Estate. In the 1860's numbers of the free Africans in St. Thomas were overtaken by disaster. No evidence has been found to show that they gave support to Paul Bogle; but the Maroons and the Government troops treated them as rebels. They were brutally treated and some were executed.

The newcomers contributed in many ways to Caribbean development and to the growth of a Caribbean community representative of and enriched by diverse cultures and races. In many instances they enabled the estates to maintain and expand production. They played their part in establishing small farms and widening the range of export crops. The East Indians, for example, were largely responsible for increasing the consumption and the production of rice, which, with their arrival, soon became an important crop. They brought to West Indian agriculture their traditional skill in irrigation and in the intensive cultivation of vegetables. Our history has often suffered from those who have seized on the spectacular and colourful, or of those who, falling captive to the magic of the Antilles, romanticise even the sordid. Our history has deeper tougher roots. The positive response of the blacks and the East Indians to the penalization of slavery or of servitude, their patient unceasing struggle to stand on their own feet and make their own way in the world, the sheer endurance of harsh physical conditions, the painfully gained victory over deprivation, over the badge of inferiority and even of self-contempt, these are the West Indian triumphs. In these achievements the newcomers have their full share. But in the 1850's and the 1860's the East Indian farms and homesteads were far in the future. The immediate realities were the miseries of a system of contract labour and of plantation life against which liberal opinion protested.

CHAPTER 21

A 'Ground' of My Own

The struggle of the blacks for land, 'my own piece of ground', was part of his struggle for freedom. Land meant ownership, moving out of a position of being owned into one of possessing property, of controlling and managing it for one's own benefit. The effort did not begin when he was set free. It began long before that, with Maroons tilling clearings in the mountains of of Jamaica, Bush Negroes establishing villages and cultivations in Surinam and the Guianas, and free blacks laying out homesteads in Trinidad. Where land space was limited, as in St. Kitts, Barbados and Antigua, and ownership and political power were in the hands of whites, it was almost impossible for the free black to become either a landholder or a wholly free labourer. His condition was described by William Sewell, an American visitor to the West Indies in 1861. He said that Barbados, where labour was abundant and cheap, 'and where most of the land was under cultivation looked like a garden, and this was owing in a greater degree to an adequate labouring population than to the special benefits of abolition'. But no credit was due to the Barbadian plantocracy for retaining that adequate labouring population in its employ. ' To the latter it was the option of work at low wages, and on most illiberal terms, or starvation'. In Grenada only 6,000 out of about 14,000 Creoles lived on the estates. ' The remainder, preferring a greater independence than would be there allowed them, have rented cottages...and may be seen travelling along the roads every morning to their daily work.'

In Trinidad the planters ' adopted most stringent measures to prevent the increase of small proprietors, and keep up, by such unnatural means, a sufficient labouring force for the estates. They imposed heavy taxes on all lands and buildings except those devoted to sugar manufacture. But their measures were futile.' In Jamaica and in Guiana the landholders adopted similar measures in order to bind the free worker to the estate. In his *Memoir of William Knibb*, Hinton pointed to two acts passed by the House of Assembly in Jamaica for the express purpose of compelling the labourer to work for whatever wages they chose to give and to do such work as they required; the Ejection Act, under which labourers could be ejected at a week's notice from the homes where they had been born on the estate; and the Trespass Act by which the police were given the power to imprison any worker found in his home after the ejection notice had run out. Planter reaction was expressed at a meeting of freeholders in the Parish of Trelawny in 1838, that ' the people will never be brought to a state of continuous labour while they are allowed to possess the large tracts of land now cultivated by them for provisions, which renders them perfectly independent of their employers.' This was the general view throughout the West Indies. In Guiana, where there were large areas of unoccupied land, laws were passed making an apprentice found five miles from his plantation subject to arrest. Squatting was punishable with three months imprisonment with hard labour. The repressive measures failed. The free people were often aided by missionaries and in some cases by wise landholders who decided that, by giving the free apprentice land near to the estate, they had a better chance of retaining his services. This view proved correct, for, by the end of 1839, 268 cottages had been built on plots of land adjacent to one plantation on which the villagers continued doing piece work. In other cases groups of labourers combined to buy an estate and share it between them. In Guiana Perseverance was bought by 109 persons for $2,000 and Golden Grove by fourteen persons for $1716. So eager were the free blacks for land that some of the eighty-three labourers who combined to buy Northbrook on the east coast of Demerara for $10,000, were seen pushing wheelbarrows through Georgetown laden with the first instalment of $6,000. Soon after emancipation a visitor to the country declared that freedom did in three years what slavery had not been able to do in three centuries...it laid the foundation of a large number of villages wholly independent of the plantations. In Berbice in 1838 there were 15,000 ' new frees '. None of them were at that time landholders. Four years later 1223 families of emancipated people owned 7,000 acres, which had cost more than $100,000, on which they had built 1184 cottages. Up to 1848 more than 446 Guiana estates had been acquired by the free blacks, and parcelled out. On these holdings 10,000 houses had been built, and these were homes for 44,000 persons. A report published in 1852 pointed to the singular spectacle of a people just emerged from slavery enjoying property and land for which they had paid no less than a million of money.

Jamaica witnessed a similar change. The Governor, reporting to the Secretary of State in 1840, said that there had been a large increase in the number of proprietors of small freeholds, the increase consisting almost entirely of emancipated Negroes. The number of these freeholders had risen from 2,014 in 1838 to just under 8,000 in 1840. William Knibb described the process. He referred to the recent census returns which showed there were 19,000 persons, formerly slaves, who had purchased land on which they were erecting their own cottages. Fifty-eight free villages had been established in various parts of Jamaica containing 5,000 houses. By 1844 as many as 16,000 families had established themselves on their own lands in 116 communities, generally with the help of nonconformist missionaries. When Sewell visited Jamaica in 1839 he estimated that there were about 50,000 coloured freeholders in the island. The society was beginning to recover from slavery. As happens so often in our history, this change was taking place at a time when the reverse was happening in another part of the Caribbean, in Puerto Rico especially. There the number of slaves was increasing with the expansion of the sugar economy, and squatter farmers were being driven off crown land and set to work on the plantations in conditions of near-slavery. The census reports of recent years show the results. In 1940 in Puerto Rico, out of a labour force of 229,000 there were 54,200 who were farmers who owned or rented their land. In Jamaica at the same time out of a labour force of approximately the same size there were 49,000 farmers working holdings of ten acres or less; an additional 17,000 operators had larger holdings and a large proportion of the agricultural labour force listed as wage earners was also cultivating owned land in plots of less than one acre. As Sidney Mintz writes, ' Jamaica is still substantially a country of the peasantry, Puerto Rico is not '. Throughout the West Indies, where land was available the free black and the East Indian transformed the economy. Up to emancipation the plantation dominated West Indian agriculture. Since then thousands of small farms have been established. In Jamaica for example, farms of under twenty-five acres occupy about thirty-eight per cent of the cultivable land and provide almost one half of the agricultural output.

The first taste of freedom was often bitter. The emancipated people were starting to establish their homes and villages and to lay out their grounds in countries where the governments were not convinced that they were responsible for providing social services like education and medical care. Modern medicine was in its infancy. Environmental diseases like typhus, cholera, tuberculosis and malaria had not yet been brought under control. In England itself, the State did not fully take responsibility for public health until the Public Health Act was passed in 1848 and this first step was followed by the work of a Sanitary Commission of 1869 which insisted on the improvement of water supplies and precautions in the handling of food and with regard to epidemics. In the West Indies the estates, in the period before emancipation, ran their own health services, but in the early period of freedom the mass of the West Indian population was without health services. After the 1860's the position began to improve with the establishment of government medical services, improvement of water supplies, introduction of quarantine regulations.

Before emancipation, education was provided by charitable persons, and was limited to free people, for the most part whites. Those planters who could afford to do so sent their children to school in England, with the result that Edward Long noted: ' all the real interests of such students centred in England, which became home to them as it had been to their elders... Therein lies the lamentable lack of local pride and feeling...' The names of some benefactors are remembered, among them Codrington who left two estates and slaves for the founding of a College to teach medicine and theology; a Kingston jeweller, John Wolmer who in 1728 left money to found a free school; Harrison who left a benefaction for a school to teach twenty four poor white boys.

After emancipation the first steps in providing public education were taken by the British Government and the Churches. The concept of education as a national responsibility was new. Britain made its first grant for primary education in that country in 1831, and two years later it gave £25,000 for education in the West Indies. Further grants were made up to 1846. The Churches were chosen as the agents for spending this money and they established many schools, throughout the West Indies, but since the British Government retained some of its old distrust of Catholics, islands like St. Lucia, Trinidad and Grenada, which were largely Catholic, were at a disadvantage because the Catholic Church was reluctant to take Government money. Barbados, in contrast, benefitted from the fact that the Church of England was able to add some of its funds to the British Government grant, and so provide more schools. Money for training teachers came from the Mico Trust. Mico Training Colleges were founded in Demerara, Trinidad and Jamaica and Mico Schools, which were Christian but not denominational, were opened in St. Lucia and Trinidad. By 1850 the early enthusiasm had waned and money was short. The West Indian countries were hard hit by the Sugar Duties Act. The fall in public expenditure on education can be seen from the figures. An extreme example is Jamaica. In 1861 the island, which had a population of nearly half a million, provided £3,700 of public money for education. The result was that in 1883 only 22,000 blacks out of 250,000 were able to write. Improvement came in the last forty years of the century, when throughout the West Indies the number of children in school increased three or four times. The general improvement in the public services and in the expansion of the primary school system was due almost entirely to the Churches and the Colonial Office.

West Indian society before 1833 can be represented by a pyramid with a small apex consisting of whites, a narrow middle of free people of colour, and a broad base of black and coloured slaves. Each tier had its social gradings. The whites reached down from planter and official to overseers, book keepers and poor whites. The distinguishing feature in this group was possession of property or official position. In the second tier of free people the gradings were generally according to colour and property, the near whites being at the top and those with dark skins at the bottom. At the base, the slaves had their gradings also, based on colour and occupation, whether field work, domestic work, or the skilled work of carpenter, mason, wheelwright, sugar striker or driver. People in each tier had relationships with those in the other tiers, but it was impossible for persons to move upward save by the miracle of becoming white or an occasional act of manumission.

Emancipation removed the legal barrier between free and slave, and in the breakdown of the plantation economy in the mid-19th century enabled coloured men with money to become large landholders or merchants. Throughout the century however, the society remained essentially three-tiered, with a white apex of officials, propertied whites and a few coloured professional or landed people; a larger middle tier of coloured with a few black, and a large base, consisting of seventy-five per cent or more of the total population, mostly smallholders and landless labourers who were of African or East Indian descent. But though the society remained hierarchic there was no legal barrier to upward movement. Requirements for this were education and ownership of property—though colour remained a formidable obstacle. It was to be expected that those in the middle class would thrust upward into the upper class, and would take on the attitudes of that class.

The system of education reinforced the class cleavages. Lord Grey, then Secretary of State for the Colonies, wrote to the Governor of Trinidad, Lord Harris, in 1838 setting out the objectives: the people who had been freed should look to labour on the estates as their main dependence, and schools were to be set up with a curriculum that was largely industrial and would encourage a ' love of employment '. Lord Harris had other thoughts. He proposed the training of teachers, free schools paid for out of local rates and free secondary education for those who could pass the necessary tests. The last would have helped to increase social mobility and make education an integrating force. He was a century ahead of his time. The general view was that education should keep people in ' the stations to which God had called them '. The upward path for the pupils of elementary schools was through the few teacher training colleges, through Codrington College, Calabar, which the Baptists established for training a native ministry. The results of the traditional policy of the three R's for the masses and secondary education for the privileged few are indicated by the census of 1944. This showed that the percentage of illiteracy throughout the West Indies was highest among the blacks, lower among the coloured, lowest among the white. The same was true of occupational groupings. The unskilled, by far the largest group (sixty per cent of the labour force in St. Kitts, Montserrat and St. Vincent) was made up almost wholly of blacks. Skilled workers were predominantly coloured and owners and managers were almost wholly white.

From time to time however, exceptional men emerged in the middle tier, who saw the needs and requirements of the mass of the people and championed their cause. In so doing they bridged the wide gap characteristic of West Indian society, between the African and East Indian masses and the middle and upper classes.

Herein lies the significance of men like Henry Alcazar, Louis deVerteuil, Richard Hill and Edward George Gordon. These and a few others relate to the more numerous group of Criollos in Cuba, but their number was not to grow in size until a national movement developed in the 1930's.

Within this social setting, beneath this overlay of institutions, ' they ' made smaller worlds of their own, the East Indian and the African each in his own way. Rejected by the society that brought him to the Caribbean, the East Indian clung to his heritage. He retained his language, termed by some of his employers a ' barbarous tongue '. With the help of his pandits he built his temples and held to the beliefs of his fathers. He carried out his religious rites, celebrated Hosein and Diwalli, preserved his close-knit family structure, was married and buried according to Hindu rites. In consequence, his children were for long registered as illegitimate. For long they remained without schooling. In Trinidad many young East Indians owed their advancement originally to the Presbyterian Church of Canada which concerned itself with the welfare of the East Indian community long before the Government did. The separatism that still characterises many East Indian communities in the West Indies derives in part from the traditional conservatism of Hindu society but it is due also to the way in which, in the first period of East Indian immigration, all other sections of West Indian Society separated themselves from the immigrants.

With the blacks the task was not one of preserving a culture but of creating institutions that met their need. They had responded to the penalisation of slavery by protest and by creative adaptation. They met the challenge of freedom in the same spirit, continuing the adaption and continuing the protest against oppression and injustice. The religious group to which Paul Bogle ministered was in the tradition of the Black Baptists and Daddy Sharp. The attitudes of Custos Kettelhodt and Governor Eyre were in the tradition of the pre-emancipation Assemblies. The savage repression was similar to the repressions that followed slave risings in earlier days. Gordon on the other hand foreshadowed the identification of the Creole educated with the Creole underprivileged which marked the 1930's. Jamaica in 1864 had a population of just under half a million. The number of voters on the register was 1903. The people who actually voted numbered 1457. The peasantry were not concerned with votes but with their yams and sweet potatoes and three years burning drought that had brought them to the verge of starvation. Flour and saltfish were in short supply because the American civil war had interrupted the flow of North American supplies to the island. The magistrates were of the planter class, and they regarded it as their duty to reform an idle and immoral people. Gordon knew the grievances of the people. He knew the attitude of the Assembly. He told Eyre of the need of the people for medical attention, of overcrowded insanitary cells in which prisoners were kept waiting for trial, of the poor for whom there was no almshouse, of a pauper who had died in the lock-up in Morant Bay because there was nowhere else to send him. Angry at the letter Gordon wrote to him, Eyre withdrew Gordon's commission as a Justice of the Peace and so there began a bitter controversy between the two.

In St. Thomas, a friend of Gordon's, a black preacher Paul

Bogle and his group of followers, were bitter at the miseries they endured and at the injustice to which they were subject. They were not alone. Edward Underhill, a Baptist missionary who visited Jamaica in 1859, read the hurricane signals: an increase in larceny because the crops were poor; an increase in requests for poor relief; low and irregular wages; high prices due in part to the high import duties and in part to the American Civil War; indifference on the part of the Government. Underhill sent his letter to Eyre, who called a series of meetings of officials to discuss it. Finally the Colonial Office, on the advice of Eyre informed Underhill that the Jamaican people were not suffering from any troubles that could not be relieved ' at once by settled industry '. The stereotype of the lazy black was dear to authority.

In 1865 the people of St. Ann petitioned the Queen for help. They were in distress and it was to the Queen, under whom they had gained full freedom, that they appealed. The reply, sent through Eyre was curt and moralistic. It was to their own industry and prudence that the people were to look for an improvement in their conditions. The ' Queen's Advice ' was read in all Anglican churches. The nonconformist ministers refused to pass it on.

These things being commonly known, Bogle and his people decided that they would put their grievances direct to the Parish Vestry. He and his people had already that October sent a petition to the Governor. Now it was time to march to Morant Bay where the Parish Vestry was meeting. A confrontation took place between white authority and black protest. Rioting followed: for this was not a rebellion but an eruption of anger, frustration and misery. Twenty-one white and coloured persons and seven black rioters were killed. Eyre, suspecting without proof that Gordon was linked with the rioting, had him arrested, taken to Morant Bay, tried by court martial and hung. In the ' war ' that Eyre waged against the people, 580 blacks were killed, 600 flogged and 1,000 houses destroyed.

Chided by those in authority for idleness and immorality, neglected because in the West Indies and in Britain the long-established sugar industry was accepted as the only base for West Indian prosperity, the peasant nevertheless transformed West Indian society in the 19th century. Having little, he nevertheless saved money to buy land in the way we have described. He supplied his need for labour by group work, ' day for day ', ' morning work ', and 'gayap'. In order to accumulate capital he formed ' partnerships ' or ' su-su '. Lacking adequate credit and marketing facilities he developed an internal marketing system in every part of the West Indies, based on local markets and women traders ' higgler women ' and itinerant male vendors. ' Balm yards ' and folk medicine were his substitute for medical care; and through formal religion as well as through shango, obeah, myalism or pecomania, he found ways of meeting his deep emotional needs and sometimes of attempting to control the future by means of magic. In common with blacks throughout the new world, he created a family system in which the woman held an important place, and the mother-child bond and ties of kinship were strong. His proverbs, folk tales, riddles and song added laughter to his days. These various aspects of peasant life all had their function and today they are a part of the West Indian heritage.

The peasant brought about far-reaching changes in the economy. By 1860 Jamaica had more than 50,000 holdings of under fifty acres each. In that year St. Lucia, St. Vincent, Grenada and Tobago had more than 10,000 freeholders. In Grenada and St. Vincent the number of residents of villages built in the period after emancipation was of the order of 20,000. This expansion continued up to the end of the century. It is estimated that the number of holdings of under fifty acres doubled in Jamaica between 1860 and 1900, the total being over 130,000. In Grenada the number of smallholders grew from 3,600 in 1860 to more than 8,000 in 1910. Studies show that there was an increase in the number of holdings in the five to fifty acre range and they show a shift also from provision grounds to mixed farming, combining the cultivation of ground provisions with the cultivation of export crops like ginger, oranges, bananas, coconuts, logwood. In 1850 the agricultural output of the Jamaican peasantry was eighty-three per cent of ground provisions and eleven per cent of exports; in 1890 it was seventy-four per cent of ground provisions and twenty-three per cent of exports. In 1850 the peasant produced about fifty per cent of the total agricultural output; by 1890 his share had risen to about seventy-five per cent. In Grenada, from 1850 onwards, cocoa and spices were peasant crops, in St. Vincent so were arrowroot and cotton. In Trinidad small farming had been encouraged by the sale of Crown Lands in the 1860's. The Jamaica banana industry was started by peasants who supplied Edward Dow Baker, an American sea captain, with his first cargoes. The significance of these changes was recognised in 1897 by a Royal Commission which visited Jamaica. It gave official encouragement to the policy of land settlement and the encouragement of peasant agriculture. The peasantry, it said, were a source of economic and political strength. It recommended land settlement and the diversification of agriculture. This was radical talk in the ears of most officials and planters who claimed that if the blacks were not kept dependent on the estates they would lapse into barbarism. In his study of *Peasant Development in the West Indies*, W. K. Marshall emphasises that peasant activity modified the character of the original pure plantation economy and society: ' The peasants were the innovators in the economic life of the community... They diversified the traditional basically mono-cultural pattern. The peasants initiated the conversion of these plantation territories into modern societies. In a variety of ways they attempted to build local self-generating communities ...their increasing numbers and their economic importance made a cogent case for the adoption of broader based institutions. In this respect peasant development was emancipation in action.'

CHAPTER 22

For the Time to Come

A few perceptive observers understood what the black and East Indian smallholders were doing. One of these, having accompanied Phillippo in 1861 to a village of peasants near Spanish Town, mentioned especially Henry Lunan, an ex-slave a founder of the village, in order ' to mark with special emphasis the commencement of a new era not only of liberty but of an independent peasantry.' Sewell came to the conclusion in 1861, in his *Ordeal of Free Labour in the West Indies*, that freedom had opened new sources of industry and prosperity that under slavery would have remained closed for ever. But he warned also that a generation born in the night of slavery had not yet passed away and ' men who were taught to believe in that idol and its creations still control the destinies of these distant colonies.' How was it that so many of the upper and middle classes in the West Indies understood so little? Why was it that so many in Europe, America and the Caribbean held the view expressed by Trollope, that ' the black was a servile race fitted by nature for the hardest physical work, and apparently at present fitted for little else'.

Concepts and attitudes determine events, and so form an essential part of history. The image or stereotype leads to the judgment, without reference to the reality. In many societies the stereotype of the peasant was that of a loutish stupid person. Victorian literature abounds in examples of the church-going rich who regarded poverty and distress as evidence of laziness and wastefulness. In the West Indies and in the United States the classes differed not only in position and in possession but also in colour and race, and the basic assumption in the white world was that the black was an inferior being. West Indian society was so fixed in its attitude because it was racist, making its judgments on the basis of race.

Generic terms are often signposts to attitudes. Some words in common use during the period point to the basic attitudes in the society: *backra, coolie, quashie*—the equivalent to 'sambo' of the Southern States. The word *bakra* is from a West African word, *mbakara*, white man, one who surrounds or governs. It came into general use in the Caribbean and is found also in the Gullah dialect in the Carolinas. At first it was applied only to whites, but later to those browns and blacks who by reason of their money and education moved with whites. These became *pure pure backra*. The word was used also as an adjective to denote exceptionally fine quality, excellence, something fit for the white world, like *bakra* callalu, *backra* cabbage, *backra* house. In contrast, the word *coolie* was downgraded. Originally it was neutral, a Tamil word for a porter or labourer, a *Kuli*. In the Caribbean, white and black used it in a derogatory sense, every East Indian becoming a *coolie* man, or *coolie* woman and East Indian culture was despised as *coolie* culture. A coarse kind of spinach became *coolie* spinach and the cheap muscovado sugar that was swept up from the floor where East Indians had been bagging the sugar became *coolie* foot sugar. In one respect only did the West Indian ascribe power to the East Indian, and that was after death, for a *coolie* duppy was the most effective of all the spirits at an obeahman's command. But the word *quashie* was even more derogatory than *coolie* for it denoted an insignificant person, one of no account. *Quashie* is the Akan-Ashanti name for Sunday, the first day of the week, *Quasidi*. According to Ashanti custom, every male child is given a day-name as well as the family name. The bakra world drained the name of its meaning and loaded it with the implications of stupidity and inferiority. A half-fit breadfruit became a *quashie* breadfruit a peasant wedding a *quashie* wedding, a black government, a *quashie* government.

The mischief went deeper, for traits which were assumed to be permanent characteristics of blacks were built into the *quashie*

and sambo concept: deceitfulness, an 'inherent sense of false-
hood', laziness, stupidity, cunning, childishness, ingratitude.
This value judgment, which disregards the historical record of
black protest and black leaderships, follows from the basic assumption of white superiority, and explains the passionate protest
of contemporary black Americans like James Baldwin who, in
The Fire Next Time, writes:

> Negroes in this country...are taught really to despise them-
> selves from the moment their eyes open to the world. This
> world is white and they are black. White people hold the
> power, which means that they are superior to blacks (in-
> trinsically that is: God made them so) and the world has in-
> numerable ways of making the difference known and felt
> and feared...and in fact the truth about the black man as a
> historical entity and as a human being has been hidden
> from him deliberately and cruelly...

In the West Indies the prejudices and the divisions based on
colour and race prevailed, but they were not enshrined in legislation. In this respect the emancipated black of the Caribbean
had an advantage over the American black. In 1862, at a time
when in our smaller region and on our more limited stage Gordon
and Bogle were protesting at injustice, Frederick Douglass called
his fellow-blacks in the United States to arms in words that form
a part of our history, because they make clear the underlying
unity of the black struggle for freedom in the new world:

> The counsel I give comes of close observation of the great
> struggle now in progress, and of the deep conviction that
> this is your hour and mine. In good earnest, and after the
> best deliberation, I now for the first time during this war
> feel at liberty to call and counsel you to arms.
>   By every consideration which binds you to your enslaved
> fellow-countrymen, and the peace and welfare of your
> country, by every aspiration which you cherish for the free-
> dom and equality of yourselves and your children. By all
> the ties of blood and identity which makes us one with the
> black men now fighting in Louisiana and in South Carolina
> I urge you to fly to arms, and smite with death the power that

would bury the government and your liberty in the same hopeless grave...

Remember Denmark Vesey of Charleston; remember Nathanial Turner of Southampton; Shields, Green and Copeland who followed noble John Brown and fell as glorious martyrs for the cause of the slave...

More than 200,000 blacks answered the call. Black protest became part of the struggle for American unity. The war resulted in their liberation and blacks then played an important part in the reconstruction of the south. But within twenty years they were disfranchised, subjected to the notorious Jim Crow laws, harried and persecuted by the courts, the police and the Klu Klux Klan, discriminated against, hated, lynched.

In this survey we have followed the method adopted in earlier chapters, of relating our history to that of other countries in which the plantation system and slavery were dominant, and we have seen how the black movement for freedom affected the history of Africa, Europe and the Americas. We have seen also that, as Dubois insisted, the black struggle for liberty heralded the 20th century movement against colonialism, and formed a part also of the workers movement against exploitation. We have referred to the position in the United States where the black, having been liberated and made a citizen, was disfranchised twenty years later, largely as a result of two disatsrous decisions of the courts. One was the Dred Scott judgment that the descendants of Africans imported into the United States and sold as slaves were not intended to be included under the word citizens in the Constitution. The other was the Supreme Court decision in the case of *Plessy versus Ferguson,* in favour of separate but equal rule, apartheid in other words, One white voice, Justice Harlan, dissented from the judgment, giving an opinion that deserves to be remembered by us all. He stated that the statute of Louisiana was inconsistent with the personal liberty of citizens, white or black and in his statement he reminded the Court that personal liberty consisted in the power of locomotion, of changing situation, or removing one's body to whatever place one's own inclination may direct, without imprisonment or restraint, unless by due course of law, and he referred to the fifteenth amendment to the Constitution of the United States which declared that ' the right of citizens of the United States shall not be denied or abridged by the United States or by any state on account of race, colour, or previous servitude.' He added that in the United States, in terms of the Constitution there was no caste and that the Constitution was colour-blind.

This is what the Civil Rights movement in the United States is about. There the black struggle is not for national independence. That question was settled in 1784. The black protest is a movement for civil liberties, a struggle begun and continued by black leadership with the assistance of black and white citizens, a movement that has become one of the major historical developments of this century. We have referred to this at some length because, as we have seen in other chapters, the black freedom movement has an underlying unity. The Palmares Republic, the Haitian war of Independence, the Maroon wars, the flight of the bush Negroes of Surinam into the forested interior, the slave risings, the Morant Bay rioting, the call to arms by Frederick Douglass, the slaying of Metzgers and the murder of Martin Luther King all are part of a black movement for freedom that is as old as the Atlantic Slave Trade and new world plantation slavery. Herein lie the roots of the American black power movement.

The United States is an independent nation with a ruling white majority, a Constitution that commits the nation to the principles of equality and freedom for all Americans, and a large black minority committed to securing its constitutional rights. The West Indies were separate colonies without the cohesive force of nationhood, with populations predominantly non-white under the rule of whites. West Indians suffered from no legal disabilities but non-whites, subject to grievous social distinctions, were assigned the lowest status in the society, and were put at a disadvantage by inequalities in educational opportunity and in employment. The majority had no vote, and were unable to participate in any meaningful way in the government of their countries. While in the United States, a black minority, part of an independent nation, campaigned for civil rights, a black majority in West Indian society began a campaign for nationhood. In these circumstances there were two pre-requisites for progress. The first was the destruction of the *quashi-backra* concept, its removal from the minds of whites and from the minds of those blacks who had lost confidence in themselves and accepted their lower place in the scheme of things. Looking forward from the 1830's, the decade of freedom, to the 1930's, the decade of the emergence of West Indian nationalism, we recognise, first, the significance of Marcus Garvey. He destroyed the *quashi-backra* concept and undertook the work of building black confidence, black self-respect, a knowledge of black history

Marcus Garvey

and a regard for Africa's place in human history. He was, in a special sense, the liberator not only of West Indian blacks but of new world blacks. The second pre-requisite was a national movement which would lead to a campaign against colonialism and which, through its unifying dynamic force, would bring together our deeply segmented societies. Herein lies the significance of the national movement, in which the pioneers included the intellectual, C.L.R. James, and the labour leader Andre Cipriani: a movement which gathered strength in the 1930's through the combination of West Indian intellectuals like Adams, Manley, and later Eric Williams, with leaders who emerged from the great body of the people, Alexander Bustamante, Vere Bird, Robert Bradshaw, Eric Gairy, each with his special quality of charisma and of leadership.

Let us turn now to some of the events which prepared the way for the movers and shakers of the 1920's and 1930's. One of the most significant was the growth of the West Indian population. Up to 1807, when the British abolished their slave trade, the black population had been kept to strength by the regular importation of new slaves. Purchases made up for deaths. Between 1807 and 1834, when the Act of Emancipation was passed, it was virtually impossible to import slaves, and the black population declined in number because more blacks died than were born. The first West Indian census was taken in 1844. The records show that after emancipation the number of blacks increased, because more lived than died.

Population growth is affected by health, immigration and by emigration, which reduces the number of inhabitants. With the assistance of George Roberts, author of the *Population of Jamaica*, let us see how these influenced population growth in our countries. In order to do this we will take three pairs of countries that provide contrasts with each other: Barbados and Guiana, Trinidad and the Windward Islands, Jamaica and British Honduras.

Early in its history Barbados became an exporter of people. White smallholders, displaced by the plantation, left the island for other West Indian colonies and North America in the 1650's. In the second half of the 18th century planters from Barbados and Antigua emigrated to Guiana to develop sugar plantations there. Others moved to Trinidad during the 19th century. The island always densely populated, relieved the pressure on its limited land area by emigration, not only to Trinidad and Guiana but also to Curaçao and Aruba, after they established their oil refineries; to Panama, to work on the Canal; to the United States to work in the industrial cities of the north. In the 1950's the pattern shifted, emigrants going to the United Kingdom.

In contrast, Guiana imported people. It attracted emigrants from the older Caribbean colonies, and imported labourers from Madeira, the Canary Islands, Sierra Leone and, in large numbers, from India. As far as population density is concerned, it is misleading to take the vast area of Guiana into account, since nine out of every ten Guianese live on a 2,000 mile strip of coast, with an area of about 2,000 square miles.

Like Barbados, the Windward Islands became exporters of people, but they suffered less from population density, partly because they were settled at a later date, and because the mountainous nature of the islands limited the growth of plantations. In Barbados and St. Kitts the estate squeezed the labourers on to small worthless areas of land, and this in turn prevented the development of smallholdings. This was not the case in the Windward Islands where, as we have already seen, communities of smallholders came into existence after the 1850's, planting arrowroot, cotton, spices and cocoa. The number of peasant holdings increased throughout the period but, even so, employment opportunities were limited and people migrated to Trinidad, Aruba, Curaçao, Panama, and the United States. Trinidad, on the other hand, went in search of people when its sugar plantations began to expand.

Jamaica and British Honduras present an interesting contrast. Jamaica is one half the area of British Honduras. In 1844 it had a population of 377,400 more than three times the population of British Honduras at the present time. By 1860 its rate of population growth began to rise, and it appears as if the peasant holdings were nearing saturation point early in the present century. When the French started work on the Panama canal in the 1880's, Jamaicans emigrated to Panama; and the flow of emigrants started again when the United States took over the work of buildings the canal in 1904. Thousands of West Indians went to Panama, to find jobs, and after the canal had been completed many moved to the expanding banana plantations in Spanish Honduras and in Costa Rica. During the period 1912 to 1920 Jamaica suffered heavily from a series of hurricanes that destroyed the banana plantations and from a severe epidemic of Spanish influenza. As a result there was general hardship and lack of employment and thousands of people migrated to Cuba to work on the sugar fields, and to the United States.

Enough has been said to indicate the population increase which has brought almost every West Indian island to the point of over-population. We have indicated also how West Indians sought to solve the problem of too many people on too little land by emigration. This had important consequences. The outflow of emigrants was followed by an inflow of money for the support of families, the purchase of land and homes, the education of children. 'Panama money' helped many relatives who stayed at home in Jamaica and Barbados to survive. It is said that during the 'Panama period' Barbadians alone sent home over £500,0000. Similarly, the flow of 'greenbacks' from relatives in the United States made life easier for relatives who remained at home, and the various governments gained in revenue because savings increased and there was also more money to spend. But emigrants had their eyes opened to new and higher standards of living than those to which they had been accustomed. They compared the daily wage of 1/6d which a West Indian field labourer earned in the early 1930's with the hourly rate in the United States, and their dissatisfaction with West Indian conditions increased. The general pressure of people on the land, a depressed economy and this festering discontent contributed to the disturbances of the 1930's.

The economic base of the West Indian countries was broadened, as we have seen, by the establishment of smallholdings and the production by peasants of new export crops. Major economic developments were the establishment of a banana industry in Jamaica and the expansion of Guiana's rice industry, the start of an oil industry in Trinidad and the discovery of bauxite deposits in Guiana.

After Captain Lorenzo Baker took his first cargo of bananas from Port Antonio to the United States in 1870 the trade grew to the point where, fifteen years later, the Boston Fruit Company was formed to export bananas from Jamaica, Cuba and the Dominican Republic to the United States. During this period another American, Minor Keith, built railways and established banana plantations in Costa Rica. The Boston Company and Minor Keith's Company were merged to form the United Fruit Company which controlled Jamaica's banana industry for thirty years, through their monopoly of shipping, markets and of much of the production. The stranglehold was broken in 1929, when the Jamaica Banana Producers Association was formed with Government help to carry and sell bananas in the United States and Europe. Banana prices improved and the new marketing company made good progress but at almost the same time Panama disease began to wipe out the crop.

The last years of the 19th century were dismal ones for the West Indies, largely because they were so dependent on one crop and on one market. Small producers using out-of-date methods, they could not compete with Cuba whose large centrals, well equipped and served by railways, produced larger quantities at lower cost. The pressure on the West Indies from this quarter was eased by the first Cuban War of Independence (1868–70) but little comfort came from this, since European beet sugar was underselling West Indian sugar in Britain. The European powers encouraged and protected the industry because they wished to make themselves as self-sufficient as possible in sugar. There were other benefits. The crop fitted well into a system of agriculture based on rotation, and the industry provided employment. Since it was her policy to buy in the cheapest market, Britain imported beet sugar in preference to West Indian sugar. Jamaica was hard hit, for sugar in 1896 represented eighteen per cent of the total value of her exports but she had other crops, some cocoa, ginger, honey, and above all bananas and her central position in the Caribbean made it easier for her to export bananas to her new market in the United States as well as to export people to Central America. But what was a hardship for Jamaica was a disaster for the West Indian sugar-producers of the Eastern Caribbean, where sugar represented seventy-five per cent of the total value of their exports. The West Indies had supplied Britain with sixty-one per cent of her colonial sugar in 1861. In 1902 Britain took 2·5 per cent.

A Royal Commission, under Sir Henry Norman in 1897, found —in its cautious phrasing—that a ' very serious condition of things was approaching '. The Commission prescribed a more scientific approach to agriculture, more frequent steamship services to North America and Britain, credit facilities for small farmers, and more education. It endorsed the peasant revolution, and urged the settlement of the peasant population on small plots of land as peasant proprietors, the establishment of minor agricultural industries and improvements in the system of agriculture, especially in the case of the small proprietors. The Commission underlined the fact that a class of small proprietors among the population was a source of both economic and political strength, and it spoke bluntly about the monopolistic nature of the sugar industry, and its concern for its own interests to the exclusion of all else.

Several factors enabled the industry to survive. Efforts were made to modernise equipment and to lower production costs by building large central factories, like that at Usine Ste. Madeleine in Trinidad in 1871, or by centralising production as in St. Kitts. Through the work of a Scientific Research Station in Barbados, where sugar-cane was successfully grown from seed in 1888, improved varieties of sugar-cane were introduced in place of the transparent white and the Bourbon. When mosaic disease threatened to wipe out the industry, a resistant variety, the Uba, was introduced from South Africa. Competition from beet-sugar was lessened when, in 1903, European beet-sugar producers agreed, in the Brussels Convention, to stop giving subsidies or bounties by which ' the production or exportation of sugar may profit.' The critical question of markets remained, however. At the end of the Cuban-Spanish American War the United States established close trading relationships with Cuba, Puerto Rico and the Phillipines, granting their sugar high preferences and setting up a tariff wall against West Indian sugar. Fortunately, there remained the Canadian market. In 1897 Canada had given British West Indian sugar a special preference of twenty-five per cent, and in a trade agreement made in 1912 she gave further concessions to West Indian products. The boom years in sugar came with the outbreak of the First World War. The price of sugar, despite controls, rose nearly five times above its 1914 level.

After the bleak 1880's and 1890's the new century seemed to promise a brighter day. Sugar planters were optimistic as a result of the Brussels Convention but there was also a more general mood of optimism. Roads and railways had been built, and these were bringing the cultivator closer to his market. Improved and more frequent steamship services put the islands within a week of New York, within a fortnight of London. Agriculture showed signs of strength. Alternatives to sugar were being developed, and the pragmatism and energy of Joseph Chamberlain, who became Secretary of State for the Colonies, made popular the idea of colonial development through science and technology. Some governments had recognised the need for this at an earlier date. Anthony Musgrave, a far sighted Governor of Jamaica, had reorganised the island's Department of Agriculture in 1879, and Barbados, British Guiana, and Jamaica had appointed Government botanists. The vigorous new broom in London stirred up greater activity. An Imperial Department of Agriculture was established in Barbados to guide farmers to more scientific methods of cultivation and to encourage the development of export crops other than sugar. The new Department reached out to farmers through local Botanical Gardens which were subsidised to distribute better varieties of seed and demonstrate new methods of cultivation. Cocoa production in Trinidad and Grenada increased. In British Guiana, where blacks had first grown rice, steps were taken to develop the industry. As a result the country which imported practically all its rice up to the end of the 19th century, became a rice-exporter by 1912. Jamaica had a profitable banana industry. Sea-island cotton was introduced into Montserrat and St. Vincent. Limes became an important export crop in Dominica. Arrowroot production expanded in St. Vincent. In Barbados and St. Kitts sugar remained the only crop, but in the other countries of the West Indies more eggs were in more baskets.

Trinidad and Guiana gained also from the development of their mineral resources. Though oil had been found at Aripero in Trinidad in 1866, commercial production did not begin before 1905 and another five years passed before the first large shipment was made to the United States. By the 1920's oil and asphalt had become two of the island's most valuable exports. While these developments were taking place in Trinidad, oil refineries were being established in Aruba and Curaçao to process Venezuelan oil, and these attracted labour from the Windwards and Leewards. Guiana also gained a bauxite industry after deposits which had been noted by government geologists in 1868, were analysed in 1910 and found to be rich in bauxite. An American Scot in his seventies, George McKenzie, bought up large areas of the land that was found to be rich in bauxite and laid the foundations for the establishment of the Demerara Bauxite Company which began exporting crude ore in 1917. In addition the country also gained some benefit from the discovery of gold in alluvial deposits in the northern region.

The First World War (1914–1918) sent the prices of sugar, cotton and copra soaring. As we have seen sugar prices rose to a level nearly five times above that of 1914. Prices for cocoa, cotton and copra nearly doubled. At the close of the two decades a West Indian, reviewing events, could find solid ground for optimism. There had been disasters: the terrifying eruption of Mr. Pelé in Martinique in 1902, which overwhelmed St. Pierre with its 32,000 inhabitants; an earthquake that destroyed most of Kingston in January 1907; hurricanes like the three that flattened the banana plantations of Jamaica in three successive years, 1915–18; and an epidemic of Spanish influenza which resulted in a heavy loss of life throughout the region. Taking these reverses and disasters into account, there still remained good reason for hopes of a renewed and lasting economic prosperity.

Not that life was easy. In the period 1889–93 the death rate in Jamaica was 23·3 per thousand, in Trinidad 26, in British Guiana 25·4. The figures had changed little forty years later. For the period 1909–13 they were 23·3 per 1,000 for Jamaica, 27·7 for Barbados, 24·8 for Trinidad, 29·7 for Guiana. The rate of infant mortality was high. Medical services were inadequate and were not easily available to the poor. In 1922 an Under-Secretary of State for the Colonies, Major Wood, reported that the general conditions of health and sanitation in the West Indies were not yet satisfactory; yellow fever had been banished by quarantine regulations but there remained malaria, dysentery, typhoid, hookworm, yaws, tuberculosis and venereal diseases; the rate of infant mortality was high; Baby Saving Leagues were doing good work, but their task was rendered difficult by the high percentage of illegitimate births, ' the primitive character of social standards, and unhealthy housing conditions.'

Because there were more secondary schools and more primary

schools, poor and middle class West Indians had more opportunity for education, but since there were also more children to be schooled, the provision of education remained inadequate and its content, based on outmoded metropolitan models, was generally irrelevant. The system was based on class. In 1891 the Barbados House of Assembly defended its position in devoting one-third of the vote for educational purposes to providing for ' the intellectual wants of 500–600 students who attend the higher grade schools, while the remaining two-thirds are spent on the schools in which instruction is afforded to upwards of 23,000 children of the people ', the argument being that it was possible for ' children of the people ' to pass by progressive stages from elementary through secondary schools and even to one of the English universities at the expense of the colony. We see the other face of the coin in a report made in the same year, deploring the use of children as part-time estate labourers. ' How can we speak of enlightenment when we use saplings for fuel and cut the green corn for fodder? Or take pride in our industries when able bodied men are indolently roaming the country, and children of tender age are toiling in factory, workshop and field.' The pickney gang was still busy on estates and plantations. There was widespread public criticism of the educational system on the grounds of its inadequacy and irrelevance. Some, like Major Wood, wrote that education was rapidly spreading and was tending to produce a coloured and black intelligentsia, while others, like the Commissioner of Education in British Guiana in 1925, declared that primary school education had not changed in any significant way in the preceeding thirty years: buildings, furniture, books, and the slates all suggested the eighties or nineties of the last century. The changes that had been made in the curriculum were too few and feeble ' to dissipate the general atmosphere of late Victorianism ': sanitary conditions were bad, classes were too large, schools were overcrowded, there was no effective attempt to relate education to the society, and teachers were badly paid. The Report of the Royal Commission of 1938 showed that the long-sustained public criticism of the West Indian educational system was abundantly justified. The deficiencies did not come into existence suddenly in the 1930's. Of long standing, they had their origins in the *backra-quashie* attitude, planters and others of the upper class taking the view that to educate the mass of the people in more than reading and writing was to ruin the country. Child labour was defended on the ground that it taught children to be industrious. There is a comprehensive indictment of the system in Eric Williams' history *From Columbus to Castro*. As he emphasises, these inadequacies and this contempt for the people was common to other parts of the colonial Caribbean. West Indian colonial society accepted and approved of the system, and opposed any reform that appeared to threaten its position of privilege.

Norman Manley

The inadequacies were distressing since for the great mass of the people the only road to a future lay through the classroom. In the fragment of autobiography that he left at the time of his death Norman Manley shows what this meant:

> My father was the illegitimate son of a woman of the people. His father came from Yorkshire and he himself was

a bright boy who worked his way up to be one of the leading produce dealers in Jamaica...

I was born at Roxburgh in 1893, a small Manchester property about four miles from Porus—and there I grew up with a brother and two sisters, remaining for two years after my father died in 1899, when my mother went to the U.S.A. and got a job in Washington in the postal service... but returned to Jamaica as she could not support four children, all very young, on her U.S.A. earnings. Father left nothing but Roxburgh and a half share in a St.Catherine property... He, Father, was almost penniless when he died, having wasted his substance in litigious living.

Mother had one great fixed determination in life—to see that her children, two boys and two girls, got a good education. Belmont was a hard place to manage. It was quite undeveloped and, like so many of the old derelict places in Jamaica, it carried on as best it could with a little of everything: logwood sold after being cut into lengths of heart wood with the bark and sap chipped off; a few cattle; a few tenants, a little cocoa... Single handed she managed all these things and even found time to persuade the authorities to allow her to open a post office at Belmont itself which she took charge of. She made all our clothes, made jellies when guavas were in, kept a small chicken farm and ran things with firm efficiency. When night came she disappeared...and wrote letters to her few remaining friends, nearly all of whom deserted her when she married a near black man...

Mother could only afford to send me to the elementary school at Guanaboa Vale... Then after one year I went to Beckford and Smiths in Spanish Town... Finally I got a half scholarship at Jamaica College. It was 1906 and there I stayed till 1913 when I left after a final year as pupil teacher.

It is all there: lack of money, emigration, colour, the narrow gate that led to a secondary education, and behind it all a mother's indomitable will. There were many other instances of greater poverty and as strong a determination. Out of this drive for betterment through education came teachers from the Mico

College and other Teacher Training Colleges, teachers and clergy
from Codrington College, black and brown professional men from
the secondary schools, many of whom went on to work their way
through American and Canadian universities. Many were
preoccupied with preserving their hard won security in the white
world into which their professions took them. But there were
others who attacked colonialism and demanded participation
in the government. Some organised professional associations
like Teachers Unions. Others organised Friendly and Benevolent Societies and Burial Scheme Societies. They protested
against the low wages paid to labourers and the deplorable
conditions of the West Indian working man. At the end of the
19th century a Working Men's Association was formed in Trinidad. In 1906 a stevedore, Herbert Critchlow, organised a
strike of port workers in Georgetown. In 1907 a Jamaica Trades
and Labour Union was formed. In 1918 Bain Alves formed
the Jamaica Longshoresmen's Union and in the following year
Critchlow founded the British Guiana Labour Union.

These associations were created by a combination of grass roots
and lower middle class leadership. Generally, the thrust came
from the great body of the people, as it had done in the period of
the black protest against slavery and later in the establishment
of free villages and the development of mixed farming on smallholdings for subsistence and export. Out of the people's need
for credit facilities and security came the Friendly and Benevolent
Societies and the Burial Scheme Societies. Out of the elementary
school teachers concern about the child and the teacher came
Teachers Associations. Out of the workers' discontent at low
wages and intolerable conditions of labour came the early Unions
and Associations of Working Men.

In the years following 1912 Marcus Garvey began his mission
of making ' race pride and love ' a basis for an association of
blacks. Garvey was born in St. Ann's Bay, Jamaica in 1887.
After working in a Kingston printery, he went in search of better
things to Central America. There he was angered by the indigni-
ties and insults to which blacks were subjected. Later, in England ' my doom—if I may so call it—of being a race leader
dawned upon me.' Returning to Jamaica after the War of 1914–
18 he formed the Universal Negro Improvement Association

to improve the general condition of Negroes everywhere, and to establish a Government of Negroes in Africa. Finding little support in his homeland, he migrated to the United States. There Garvey's organisation grew and spread, attracting world notice and provoking bitter hostility in the white world. He was imprisoned in the United States, then deported to Jamaica, where he was rejected, and persecuted. Finally he went to England where he died in 1940, a disappointed man. Yet we have seen many of Garvey's dreams come true. There are now more than a score of African kingdoms that in his time were colonies. They have black airlines and steamship lines and their armies. But, as Gordon Lewis says in his book *The Growth of the Modern West Indies,*

> Garvey's greatness lay in the massive psychological warfare that he deployed to wipe out the inherited inferiority complex and the facelessness of the Negro in a white world. . . The intellectual push of the movement was felt more deeply overseas. Nkrumah has acknowledged his debt to Garvey's books just as, earlier, the great Latin American liberator Bolivar claimed to have learned much from the Maroon leader Cudjoe's guerilla strategy against the British regimental troops while he was resident briefly in Jamaica.

Forbes Burnham

CHAPTER 23

To Stand on Our Own Feet

Taking our stand at the year 1920, we see the West Indian economy more diverse than it had ever been, with markets in Canada and the United Kingdom for a variety of crops upon whose profitable sale West Indian society depended; an economy, moreover, that had been strengthened by remittances from West Indians overseas and by high wartime prices. We see also a population expanding faster than the economy under normal conditions could sustain; a rigid system of colonial government with a minimum of popular participation; an entrenched white society of colonial officials and local upper and middle class people that retained the attitudes of the plantation period and was committed to the preservation of the social structure; and in general a press committed to those objectives. Below, dynamic forces were at work. Bad labouring conditions, an unsatisfactory system of education and exclusion from any meaningful participation in the government agitated many. Garvey's message of race pride appealed to some. The black lower classes and the East Indians were dissatisfied at being shut out from a better and more secure way of life. The social tensions generated by this pressure from ' below ', the ferment that was beginning to stir the masses, could be contained only as long as the economy continued to expand and authority was sensitive to the needs of the mass of the people. The events of the 1920's and early 1930's increased discontent in the gradual build-up of tension, each event contributing to the final climax. Consider, first, the series of disasters caused by disease that overtook West Indian agriculture in the 1920's and 1930's. Disease and competition from other primary producers eroded the economic base of West Indian society. It was like an exercise in the inevitable. Cocoa producers in Trinidad and the Windward Islands, Grenada especially, had to face increasing competition from West Africa while they watched their cocoa trees being destroyed by witchbroom disease. The market for sea-island cotton almost disappeared because of changes in women's fashions, and the pink boll worm played havoc with the crop in St. Vincent and the Leewards. In Dominica and St. Lucia lime production fell because of a disease which caused the tips of the roots of the trees to wither. At the same time synthetic citric acid captured a large share of the market. Guiana rice had to compete on the export market with large rice-producers from the East, notably Burma and Thailand. West Indian oranges and grapefruit lost part of the United Kingdom market to South Africa and Palestine. In Jamaica banana production had risen despite a serious threat from Panama Disease, but the industry based on the Gros Michel banana was doomed when Leaf Spot disease began to ravage the banana plantations in 1934. Sugar prices remained high up to March 1920. In that month Cuban sugar sold at 22½ cents per lb. in New York. But Cuba and Java had stockpiled sugar, thinking that it would be long before European beet-sugar producers recovered from the effects of the war. They recovered much more rapidly than had been expected, the world had too much sugar, and by September 1930 the price of sugar in New York had dropped to one cent.

The world depression of the late 1920's and early 1930's piled disaster upon disaster. The demand for aluminium fell, and consequently Guiana produced less bauxite between 1930 and 1935. The overseas demand for West Indian labour disappeared almost overnight. With the fall in sugar prices, Cuba had no need for them and thousands of West Indians returned home. Because of the depression and the lengthening of breadlines in the United States thousands returned from the distress in the industrial cities of the north to poverty at home.

The closing of the exits caused widespread concern. In September 1924 a Guiana newspaper pointed to the fact that more than 1,000 persons had migrated annually from Barbados to the United States: that Trinidad claimed an exodus of 3,000 in one year, and Jamaica at least 1,500 annually, as well as a seasonal migration of many thousands to Cuba to cut sugar-cane. The drain from the Leewards and Windwards was also appreciable: ' and with the sudden damming up of this flow a serious outlook has to be contemplated.' Marryshow's paper, *The West Indian* took the same line: that the West Indies faced a serious problem, the door of the United States being barred and emigration to Cuba being threatened with prohibition. Maracaibo offered no good opportunity, there might be no quarter to turn for help in the future. ' Unless well-considered development works are started, there is likely to be great social ferment in these islands.' The position was even more serious than was realised. As Roberts makes clear, the restrictions on immigration into the United States and other areas not only put a stop to an outflow of people that had been going on for forty years, but reversed the process, each country receiving rather than exporting, and this at a time when there was a marked decline in the death rate. The West Indian countries, after a long period of high and stationary mortality were moving into an era of a declining death rate. So, more people came than went, fewer babies died, more people lived longer: and sea island cotton had no market, bauxite production fell, sugar prices were at rock bottom, banana trees were dying from Leaf spot and Panama disease and lime trees from roottip disease.

Besides, the indications were that by the 1920's there were too many people on the land. The fundamental reforms recommended by the Royal Commission of 1897 had never really got under way. Marshall, in his account of *Peasant Development in Jamaica* make this point:

> The potential of peasant development was never fully realised because government had tended most of the time to ignore the existence of the class... This neglect can be explained by the dominance of the estate sugar based industry over influential opinion both at home and in the metropolis... The sugar interests convinced official opinion in England that both the prosperity and civilisation of the West Indies were dependent on the survival of the estate-based industry...

Government attitude was modified only when discontent and restlessness among peasants and labourers combined with prolonged depression in the sugar industry during the 1890's and again in the 1930's to create a situation of crisis. The wisdom of the traditional policy was then questioned by those who had initiated it... The Report of the Royal West India Commission in 1897 seemed to point in a new direction... It recommended land settlement and a diversification of agriculture, ' no other reform affording so good a prospect for the permanent welfare in the future of the West Indies as the settlement of the labouring population on the land as small peasant proprietors.

We have shown that there was some diversification of agriculture, and that this strengthened the West Indian economy until disease and trading difficulties diminished the benefit. Both the Sugar Commission Recommendations of 1929 and the Moyne Commission's recommendation of 1939 were essentially palliatives. The saturation point had been reached. Efficient agriculture meant fewer people on the land, not more. The events of the 1920's and 1930's showed that it was anachronistic to think that the West Indian problem of unemployment could be solved by a return to the land.

While the economic supports were giving, internal pressures were intensifying. The great body of the people grew restive about their poor living conditions and low wages. A smaller group, including some of the middle class, wanted constitutional reform and participation in the government. Both groups became more insistent with the return of West Indians from overseas. Away, they had sent home money; returning, they brought home aspirations and ideas. Those who returned from North America knew the levels at which American labour lived. They had seen how trade unions functioned. They had suffered from racial discrimination in the United States and many were influenced by Garvey's message. Another group was made up of soldiers returning from the First World War. Having shared in the fight to save democracy, having witnessed the acceptance of the principle of self-determination, they saw no reason why democratic principles should not apply in their homelands. Their service overseas had strengthened their sense of community, of having an identity of their own. A third group consisted of professional men returning from their studies in Britain. There some had met Indian and West African nationalists, had watched Gandhi's anti-imperialist campaign and found common ground with Nkrumah and other West Africans in their rejection of colonialism. They had seen the influence exercised by two West Indian nationalists, George Padmore, who devoted himself to the West African cause, and C.L.R. James, who set out an intellectual framework for West Indian nationalism and also, in his *Black Jacobins*, illuminated the distortions of ethnic-centered history and carried further the theme of duBois that ' The abolition of slavery itself while due in part to direct moral appeal and political sagacity, was largely the result of the failure of the large farming slave system.'

The search for better labour conditions and higher wages led to the formation in the urban areas of the West Indies, of trade unions like Critchlow's British Guiana Labour Union (1919) and Bain Alves Jamaica Longshoremen's Union No. 1, to which we have already referred. Alfred Thorne a middle class teacher, became one of the labour leaders in British Guiana. O'Neale, a doctor, worked with Clennel Wickham in Barbados to form the Barbados Democratic League. In Trinidad Andre Cipriani breathed new life into the Trade Union movement and became an eloquent advocate of constitutional reform. Of French and Corsican origin, he went to St. Mary's School in Trinidad, served in the 1914–1918 War, and in 1922 entered politics. He became a member of the Port of Spain City Council and an elected member of the Legislative Council of Trinidad and Tobago. Ceaselessly he pressed home three demands, protection for the working man through a strong trade union movement, a claim to self-government based on the capacity of West Indians to run their own affairs, and racial harmony.

The pressure for constitutional change had results, but time showed that they were symbolic rather than meaningful. After Wood's visit to the West Indies in 1921, and his meetings with West Indians, the demand for an elected element in the Government, which had been granted to Jamaica in 1884 and denied to Trinidad and Tobago for more than a century and a quarter, was granted. In 1924 St. Lucia, St. Vincent and Dominica were allowed three elected members each. Planters and merchants blocked any change of this kind in Antigua, Montserrat and St. Kitts. In 1924 Trinidad was allowed seven elected members. But the Governor ruled. Only in British Guiana did elected members have any control—and then only in a limited way—over the country's revenue and expenditure. This power was taken from them in 1928, when British Guiana was given a new constitution. The right to elect fourteen members to the Legislative Council was retained but the elected members were stripped of the power to control revenue and expenditure. Throughout the West Indies the elected members of the Legislature were chosen by a small minority of the population, the franchise being restricted; so the mass of the people were not involved. Since elected members could criticise but had no power to change anything and since the Governor, who had power, had no money, the obvious course was to campaign for self-government. This was the line taken at a West Indian Unofficial Conference held in Dominica in 1932 which discussed West Indian self-government within a federation.

In these various ways frustration and discontent spread through the masses of the people and the middle class. The combination of mass poverty, growing race pride, and middle class impatience with what Cipriani called ' the humbug and platitudes of the past many years ' was explosive. Every West Indian country was a powder keg. The first to go off was Trinidad, where in 1934 there were a number of strikes on sugar estates. In 1935 sugar workers in St. Kitts struck for higher wages. Disorders broke out, and strikers were killed. In that year sugar workers in British Guiana rioted and set fire to canefields. Tension grew in St. Vincent where a Working Men's Association was formed to press for land settlement and a new constitution. In St. Lucia coal carriers went on strike.

Uriah Buzz Butler, a Grenadan who had migrated to Trinidad to work in the oilfields, became the leader of the oilfield workers. He had been a member of Cipriani's Labour Party and had led a hunger march of unemployed into Port of Spain in 1935. Expelled from the party, he formed his own militant Worker's Home Rule Party and called a strike in the oil fields in 1937. Two oil wells were set ablaze. The police attempted to arrest Butler. His followers turned against the police, killing two of them. The strikes and riots were brought under control after British warships landed troops in Port of Spain.

Clement Payne, a follower of Butler, had in the meantime moved to Barbados where he attracted large crowds by his attacks on the Establishment. He urged the formation of trade unions. The Governor ordered him to be deported. Payne was taken before the court, and found guilty of entering the island on a false declaration. A young West Indian lawyer, Grantley Adams, defended Payne and won an appeal against the verdict. Nevertheless Payne was deported. Thereupon rioting broke out in Bridgetown. Fourteen people were killed and fifty-nine wounded.

Sir Alexander Bustamante

In 1935 Bustamante and Coombs formed the Jamaica Workers and Tradesmen Union, and started holding mass meetings protesting against low wages and working class poverty. On several occasions in 1937 the police broke up noisy crowds of unemployed, who gathered in the streets of Kingston demanding work. The government followed the traditional pattern of concentrating on control rather than on the creation of opportunity and as a result there were occasional riots in Kingston in the first months of 1938. Crowds of unemployed people gathered at Frome in West-moreland that May, seeking work at the sugar estate. Disorder followed, some overseers were attacked, and the police killed four of the workers. In Kingston strikers paraded the streets, forcing shops and offices to close. Eight people were killed, about 170 wounded, and more than 700 arrested before order was restored.

These eruptions of misery and poverty marked the end of Crown Colony government. The riots did not take place because the labouring folk wanted self-government but because they wanted better living conditions and higher wages. They took place, however, in a period when blacks were beginning to listen to Garvey's message, and when middle class leadership was beginning to demand self-government. The leaders of the West Indian labour movement, who met in Georgetown in 1938, were quick to recognise the close link between labour and politics, as their demands show: trade union immunities and also a legislature wholly composed of members elected on a basis of universal adult suffrage: social legislation with old age pensions and national health insurance and also a limitation of plantations to a maximum size of fifty acres and free compulsory elementary education. The mass rejection of poverty and the middle class rejection of colonial rule came together, the demand for bread putting urgency into the demand for self-government which can be made only by people who have a sense of ' self ', of having a country, of belonging to a people. As Nettleford points out in his introduction to *Manley and the New Jamaica*, ' the social upheavals brought into focus the need for transferring power and responsibility to the majority of the people '. The 1830's had been the decade of emancipation and a demand for land ' of my own ' by people who ' did not care to hire themselves out again.' The 1930's was the decade of liberation and an insistence on the right to govern ' my own country ' by people determined ' to stand on our own feet and make our own way forward.'

The mass movement against low wages and unemployment was given purpose and a programme by West Indian leaders from the masses and the middle class. Alexander Bustamante for example gave a central place to the interests and welfare of the worker. A few went beyond this. Nettleford, analysing political change in Jamaica between 1938 and 1968 and the effects of Manley's leadership, underlines this in words that apply generally to the leaders who emerged in other West Indian countries in the 1930's and 1940's:

> For Manley that interest shared the centre of the political cosmos along with the greater need for man to master his own destiny. Manley's orientation was in the final analysis ' nationalistic ' (and universal) rather than ' labouristic ' (and narrowly interest-centred). Manley saw the Trade Union organisation as a bridge between the middle class movement for self government and the working class movement which implied social and economic reconstruction.

In our survey of the post-emancipation period we noted the debilitating effect of the plantation system and oligarchic rule on the upper class, whose chief concerns were law, order and the preservation of their own interests and we found, in contrast, a release of creative energy among the emancipated blacks who established themselves as independent smallholders and peasants. In the 1930's nothing shows more vividly the debilitating effect of Crown Colony rule, than the release of creative energy brought about by nationalism. Almost over-night, this creative power found a voice through groups of artists from every section of the community, who spoke in West Indian terms in wood and stone, canvas, music, folk songs, drama and the dance, drawing their inspiration from that which hitherto had been neglected and deemed of little merit, the Caribbean landscape, the West Indian people, their history and their dreams. The moods varied, the media were different, but there was one persistent theme, an assertion of West Indian identity, of a new concept of one's self, whether in the power of Edna Manley's carving ' Negro Aroused ' or in the passionate protest of H. A. Vaughan at those

> *who only prate of Greece and Rome*
> *and such like things but keep tight lips*
> *For burnished beauty nearer home.*

Of the sombre intensity of Mittelholtzer's or Lamming's peasant village on the fringe of encroaching sugar fields, with a boy taking shelter in the castle of his skin against encroaching whiteness. There had been instances of creative work before the 1930's but this decade witnessed the entry of the West Indian artist into the national life.

Every area of West Indian life revealed this creative capacity: the founding and organising of powerful trade unions, associations of primary producers, political parties, the planning and implementation of programmes for economic and social development and educational reform, the setting of national goals and the structuring of new institutions to support independence. The dynamism of this period gave a new quality to West Indian life, like the 'sudden startling season' of the flowering of the pimento or poui tree. The search was for autonomy and a viable economy.

The condition of the West Indian countries was described in detail in a Report made by the West Indian Royal Commission which the British Government appointed in 1938 under the chairmanship of Lord Moyne, for the purpose of investigating social and economic conditions and related matters in the area and submitting recommendations. The Commission took a positive line as far as social welfare and development were concerned. It recommended the establishment of a West Indian Welfare Fund to be financed by an annual grant of one million pounds from the British Government, to be administered by a special organisation independent of the various governments. This organisation was created without undue delay. Known at first as the Colonial Development and Welfare Organisation, it provided funds for services that the Moyne Commission had recommended, such as education, public health, housing and social welfare facilities. The growth of trade unions was encouraged. The provision of money and of advice from a team of experienced and competent officials enabled the West Indian governments to move forward in the directions indicated in the Report, and encouraged them also to plan ahead, an exercise that fed new life into the public services. The Commission was coy and hesitant on the subject of self-government and negative on industrialisation. It was impressed by the fact that:

> a substantial body of opinion in the West Indies is convinced that far-reaching measures of social reconstruction depend, both for their initiation and their effective administration, upon greater participation of the people in the business of government. . . the claim so often put before us that the people should have a larger voice in the management of their affairs represents a growing political consciousness which is sufficiently widespread to make it doubtful whether any schemes of social reform, however wisely conceived and efficiently conducted, would be completely successful unless they were accompanied by the largest measure of constitutional development which is thought to be judicious. . .

But the Commission did not recommend any fundamental changes; rather, the legislatures were to be ' more fully representative of all important sections of the community.' The West Indian demand for adult suffrage was an assertion of the fact that all sections of the community were important and had the right to representation and responsibility. It says much for the British Government that although beset by a powerful enemy, and beleaguered, it accepted the West Indian claim.

As far as constitutional change is concerned the period can be divided into three: 1944–58, when universal adult suffrage was introduced, and systems of ministerial responsibility developed; 1958–62, the years of the federal experiment; 1962–70, a decade of independence or of Associated Statehood. The pace of change varied from country to country. The general process got under way with the introduction of a new constitution in Jamaica, by which the country was granted an elected House of Representatives and a nominated Legislative Council. This, in form, was what Barbados already had. The radical change was the introduction of adult suffrage. Of the Jamaican leaders, Norman Manley in particular saw constitutional change as a first step toward wider and more fundamental political change. He recognised that elections on a franchise limited by property and income were no more than a pretence at democratic behaviour; that only through universal adult suffrage could the people be brought into the democratic process; and that in the long run only in this way could West Indian society be healed and modernised. Statistics show how urgent was the need to extend the franchise. In Trinidad in 1934 only 25,000 had the right to vote out of a population of 400,000. There were in Barbados in 1937 only 5,000 with the right to vote, out of a population of 200,000. In contrast, in 1944, in the Jamaica general elections, seventy-two out of every 100 adults exercised their right to vote, a far higher proportion than in any previous election. The other important change had to do with the transfer of power from the governor, as the Crown, to the elected representatives of the people by means of a system of ministerial responsibility. Hitherto the Governor had been advised by an Executive Council over which he presided and on which there were members nominated by him. Gradually, and at first hesitantly the number of elected members on the Executive Council was increased, and they were given greater powers, until the stage was reached where the council gave way to a cabinet composed entirely of elected members and presided over by the Premier. Under Crown Colony rule the Governor had the power to reject the advice of his Executive Council. With the transfer of power to the elected representatives of the people, the Governor could act only according to the advice of the Cabinet. By 1958 a number of our countries had achieved full internal self-government, with the Premier presiding over his cabinet of ministers. The slowness of pace indicated how sensitive the Imperial government was in respect of this change, and this was further demonstrated by events in British Guiana where, in 1953, the Peoples Progressive Party, led by Dr. Cheddi Jagan, won the general election. That December the Imperial Government charged the Jagan government with attempting to establish a communist state, suspended the constitution and moved in troops. The country was then governed for a time by nominees of the Governor. In the elections that followed Dr. Jagan's party was again returned to power, but under a constitution that gave the government less power than it had in 1952.

The second phase was that of the federal experiment. The

idea of a West Indian Federation was not new; and unfortunately in the Leewards, Windwards and Barbados history had loaded the word with mistrust and frustration. As late as 1936 a United Kingdom Commission found little support for a proposal for closer union between Trinidad and the Leeward and Windward Islands. The climate of opinion changed somewhat in the 1930's, with the realisation of common economic problems and the growth of West Indian national feeling. In 1938 a Labour Congress which met in Georgetown advocated federation, and Marryshow of Grenada made this his constant theme: ' Federate or Disintegrate.'

The United Kingdom, through its Development and Welfare Organisation, encouraged planning on a regional basis, and the Colonial Office, eager to create a self-reliant state that would take over all British West Indian responsibilities, supported proposals for a West Indian federation, with the proviso that it could be successfully created only by the West Indian governments themselves. At a Conference held in Montego Bay in 1947 a majority of the governments represented accepted the principle of a political federation and set up a Standing Closer Association Committee to study the feasibility of federation and draft a federal constitution. The Committee's recommendations were accepted, with some modifications, at a Conference in London in 1953. A major reverse was the decision of British Guiana and British Honduras not to join the proposed Federation. The decision to establish a Federation of the West Indies was taken at a Conference in London in 1956, the way being left open for the two mainland countries to join later, if they wished. In negotiation that followed, Trinidad was selected as the site for the federal capital. In elections that were held throughout the island the newly formed Federal Labour Party, led by Adams, Manley and Williams, secured a small majority. Jamaica remained lukewarm. Heavily dependent on customs duties for its revenue, it refused to consider a customs union. Trinidad, anxious about the growth of unemployment, strongly opposed any proposal for freedom of movement. Overpopulated Barbados regarded freedom of movement as essential in any federation. In these circumstances only a strong federal government with ample funds stood a chance of survival. Neither the Prime Minister,

Sir Grantley Adams, nor the Governor General, Lord Hailes, were in positions of strength. The federal government was extremely weak. It did not have the power to raise taxes. Its revenue of two million pounds a year came from ' unit contributions '. It had few areas of government under its control and in ' concurrent ' subjects it had neither the money nor the power to take the initiative. Foreign affairs, while awaiting independence, had to be conducted through London. Apart from struggling to keep itself alive, its principal activities were the distribution of grants under the Colonial Development and Welfare Acts, the administration of the West Indian Regiment and the support of the University College of the West Indies, as it then was. After four years the Federation collapsed. The immediate cause was the decision of Jamaica to withdraw, following on a referendum in which the majority vote went against remaining in the Federation. Thereupon Trinidad withdrew.

The causes of the collapse went deep. They sprang out of the colonial particularism that characterised the Caribbean for three and a half centuries. We noted earlier that the archipelago has no centre of gravity, and that politically, the centres of gravity for various groups of islands were in London, Madrid, Washington and the Hague. Within the Federation itself the disproportion between two of the units, Jamaica and Trinidad, and the other eight, was extreme. They had eighty-three per cent of the total land area, seventy-seven per cent of the total population, about seventy-five per cent of the wealth. In both these countries the Opposition party in the Federal Parliament won majorities so that most of the cabinet seats went to the smaller countries. The imbalance was made greater by the fact that the two larger islands had made remarkable progress in their economic development and had widened the gap between themselves, the ' haves ' and the others, the ' have nots '. The two were determined to press the pace, and were sensitive about any attempt to lessen their power to do this or to add to their already formidable problems by migration from other units. Neither of the political leaders of the two countries went to the centre, knowing full well where political power lay, so there was no chance of resolving these and other difficulties within the federal cabinet. Misgivings grew also about the intentions of the United Kingdom and these, in the eyes of many West Indians, seemed justified when the Imperial parliament passed a Commonwealth Immigrants Act to control immigration into Britain from Commonwealth countries. Britain's declared interest in membership in the European Economic Community roused further apprehension, for West Indians knew that their banana and sugar industries could not survive without Commonwealth Preference Agreements. Were these vital matters to be left in the hands of an ineffective federal government? The two larger countries decided to press forward to independence, and the smaller countries were left to make what arrangements they could with Britain.

After May 1962, the countries of the Commonwealth Caribbean entered into a period of statehood and independence. Jamaica under Bustamante's leadership became a sovereign state on 6 August 1962, Trinidad and Tobago on 31 August of the same year. Negotiations between Barbados and the Seven over establishing a Federation were abandoned in 1965. Barbados became independent in November 1966. The Seven had a proposal for unitary statehood from Trinidad and Tobago, but they preferred to negotiate with the United Kingdom for constitutional arrangements that would give them maximum autonomy yet leave them free to accept grants in aid. In 1966 it was agreed that Antigua with Barbuda and Redonda, St. Kitts, Nevis-Anguilla, Dominica, Grenada, St. Lucia and St. Vincent should each enter into a free and voluntary association with Britain as an Associated State, each fully self-governing in all its internal affairs but with Britain retaining responsibility for defence and foreign affairs. The Constitution provided for a parliament on the Westminster model composed of the Sovereign, represented by a Governor, a Senate and an elected House of Representatives; for a Premier and cabinet, collectively responsible to parliament; and for Public Service and Police Service Commissions. The Seven shared one Supreme Court. Self-government on a more limited scale was granted to Montserrat and the British Virgin Islands. In British Honduras full internal self-government came into effect on 1 January 1964. Under the leadership of Mr. George Price, founder and head of the People's United Party, the country moved steadily toward economic viability and independence as a republic.

The decade was a troubled one for British Guiana. In the 1961 general elections, held after the grant of internal self-government, Dr. Cheddi Jagan's People's Progressive Party defeated Mr. Forbes Burnham's People's National Congress and Mr. Peter d'Aguiar's United Force. Racial rivalry intensified. Economic difficulties increased, and the government's proposals for an austerity budget and for unaccustomed tax measures roused strong opposition. On 6 February 1962, while Georgetown was crowded with people protesting against the proposals, buildings were set alight and the centre of the city destroyed. In the following year the government's proposal to introduce controversial labour legislation led to an eighty-day general strike. Violence broke out, a state of emergency was declared, British troops moved in, and for several months rural and urban areas suffered from outbursts of racial hatred which cost 159 lives. While these things were taking place, the three parties, having failed to reach agreement in discussions in London about a new constitution, requested the British Government to put forward proposals. That which was accepted was for election by proportional representation, the idea being to discourage the development of parties on racial lines by treating the whole country as a single constituency. Calm returned to the country in the second half of the year. More than ninety per cent of the electorate voted in general elections held in December. Dr. Jagan's party gained twenty-four seats, Mr. Forbes Burnham's party twenty, Mr. d'Aguair's seven. Mr. Burnham and Mr. d'Aguair joined forces in a coalition government which set independence as its first objective. This was achieved in May 1966, when Guyana became a sovereign state. The Burnham-d'Aguair coalition soon came to an end. In general elections held at the end of 1968 Mr. Burnham's party gained power, winning thirty of the fifty-three seats in the Assembly.

The constitutional changes we have outlined were an essential and supremely important part—but a part nevertheless—of a larger all-embracing movement of social change that transformed the faceless masses of the West Indies into citizens, the colonies in which they lived into their countries. The process was much more than decolonisation. That word might appropriately be applied to peoples and nations with an earlier identity as tribe

Eric Williams

or nation, who are engaged in ridding themselves of the institutions and values that characterised their relatively brief colonial experience. The West Indian experience was, up to the middle of this century, wholly colonial. In their many different ways Bustamante, Williams, Manley, Adams and many other leaders of the '30's set the goal but formidable difficulties stood in the way. As Norman Manley once observed, ' it unfortunately happens to be the case that the awakening of the spirit of a people often coincides with all sorts of practical difficulties that make it hard to find a way of using the new spirit aright.'

In the economic sphere the major task was to provide employment; in the social sphere it was to unify people divided by race, colour, property, education. The record of the past twenty-five or thirty years in our history is that of attempts to meet the problem of employment by improving agriculture, establishing new industries, promoting tourism, setting up regional organisations for trade and for financing development, creating national institutions to give greater control of fiscal policy, adopting employment policies based on work permits in order to safeguard employment opportunities for citizens, expanding and diversifying the educational system, and drawing on international institutions and organisations for grants, loans, and advice. The list is not all-inclusive. It serves to indicate the change from the laissez-faire philosophy and methods of the period up to 1940, and how indispensable independence was for any effective attempt by the state to transform an economy traditionally characterised by sugar-monoculture, foreign ownership, the export of raw materials and importation of food and manufactured goods, and a system of production based on imperial preferences.

Restructuring the economy was part of the process of restructuring the society, which for long had seen itself through other eyes: To quote Lloyd Best:

> The newspapers, the books, the comics the cinema all showed us ourselves as second-class people. All the evidence said we were nothing... We tried in every way to save ourselves by denying ourselves. We denied our music while we loved it. We suppressed our art. We became Afro-Saxons, black skins, white masks...

Naipaul satirizes the denying of ourselves in his novel, *Mystic Masseur*, where a Trinidadian East Indian, Pandit Ganesh Ramsumair, on a visit to England, now elevated to being a Member of the British Empire, describes himself as G. Ramsay Muir. Social inequalities were institutionalised in the system of education, in employment opportunities and in the system of land ownership. It was significant that advance in political responsibility was accompanied by an expansion of the educational system and the establishment of more technical and vocational schools in order to supply the manpower needs of the country, to break class barriers and overcome social distinctions.

In order to see why these attempts at economic development and social transformation were so urgent and essential let us look at two areas that are vital to West Indian development: education and agriculture. In each case we will refer to the position in 1944 and indicate changes that have taken place since then. Following on this we will consider the problem of population, probably the most urgent and difficult of all.

Many of the basic facts about West Indian society are contained in the census reports of the 1940's. These gave much more detailed information than had been available previously. In looking at the figures we need to bear in mind that our region is so diverse that no general statement is wholly accurate for any one country. References to illiteracy, for example, do not apply to Barbados, which has a comprehensive system of education and one of the highest literacy rates in the world. References to population pressure apply with less force to Guyana, even though nine out of ten Guyanese live on a coastal strip of about 2,000 square miles. They do not apply to Belize, which has a population of 100,000 and 8,000 square miles of land. Bearing this in mind, it remains true that the figures for education show the effects of a system in which educational opportunity at the secondary and higher level was closely linked with means, and this in a society in which ownership and means were largely in the hands of a small minority group of white and brown with a scattering of blacks. Secondary and higher education were open to those with money, the only exceptions being a few talented ones who won grants or scholarships. In turn, only the well educated got well-paid jobs. The result is described by George Cumper in his analysis of the *Social Structure of the Caribbean, and of Jamaica*, based on the Census Reports of 1943 and 1946:

> The increase in social standing as one moves along the scale from black through coloured to white is clearly reflected in the occupations followed by the three groups. The three most distinctively unskilled occupations—agriculture, general labour and personal service—are commonest at the black end.
>
> In most of the islands this difference is emphasised by colour, or caste, or even language in the French speaking colonies. There is no point in arguing whether the economic or social causes of division are more important... the economic factor alone would be enough to cause a deep disunity; for no society can feel itself to be truly one in which a minority maintain the economic and moral standards of a European or American middle class, while a majority live at or near a level of bare subsistence.

That, in fact, was how the majority had lived for three hundred years or more.

Agriculture showed similar inequities. Barbados and the Leeward Islands were, by and large, plantation islands. As in the early days of the sugar-tobacco conflict, the plantation gained the victory. There were few peasant holdings. In British Honduras the economy rested on forestry and timber products, and the plantation had never dominated the economy. But in Guyana, Trinidad, the Windward Islands and Jamaica there were two systems, that of the plantation and that of the small-holding or peasant farm. The plantation held the best land; small farmers worked less fertile and marginal land.

At this point population pressure and land reform are closely linked. Let us look, then, at the population problem of the West Indies, making reference in so doing to an important study of *The Post War Development of Jamaica* by Dr. Owen Jefferson, a West Indian economist on the staff of the University of the West Indies. In considering population we will think of population increase, migration, employment and urbanisation; and since at the present time the most complete studies are those for Jamaica we will refer to these. They hold good, in general terms, for the West Indian countries, except Belize.

In 1943 Jamaica had a population of 1·2 million persons. By 1960 it had increased by 378,000, about thirty per cent, reaching a total of 1·6 million. The growth was not equal for all parts of the island. The Kingston metropolitan area grew in population from 203,000 in 1943 to 376,000 in 1961, an increase of 173,000 or eighty five per cent. As in Puerto Rico, and in many other countries, metropolitan areas draw people toward them, in search of jobs, better public services, better schooling. In most West Indian countries this internal migration indicates that the land available to the largest section of the population cannot support a steadily increasing number of persons. Neither can the cities whose factories and service industries cannot absorb all the migrants. As a result urban unemployment increased and slum areas grow in size.

E. W. Barrow

Another result of the pressure of numbers was a renewed search for exits. Most new world countries had closed their doors, but West Indians who had served in Britain during the second world war, in the armed forces and in the factories, brought back reports of job opportunities in Britain. In the 1950's West Indians began to move to Britain. Transport was made easier and cheaper for many when some European steamship lines that were engaged in carrying European migrants to Latin America started calling at West Indian ports on their return voyages. Travel services multiplied and offered easy-credit facilities. Census figures show how rapidly the number of West Indian migrants to Britain grew between 1950 and 1962, when Britain passed a Commonwealth Immigrants Act that greatly reduced the flow of people. The pattern changed after 1965 when entry to the United States and to Canada was made somewhat easier. Many of those who now migrate to Britain are dependents or children, non-workers, whereas a very large proportion of those who migrate to the United States and Canada are professional people, like nurses, teachers and doctors, technicians and skilled workers.

The difficulties, already acute, were sharpened by the fact that so large a proportion of the population was under fifteen. In St. Vincent, for example, the proportion was of the order of forty-five per cent. In most of our countries it ranged between forty per cent and forty-five per cent. This meant an increase in the number of those who were dependent. To sum up, we find a growing population that could not be supported by the land, a growth of urban areas and an increasing number of unemployed in these areas, a drain of skilled and highly trained talent to countries with higher wage and salary rates, a growing disproportion between skilled labour and unskilled, and an increase in the number of persons dependent on the labour force for food, shelter and clothing. Jefferson's remarks about Jamaica hold good for most if not all of the Commonwealth Caribbean:

> Unemployment is undoubtedly Jamaica's gravest problem. Unlike developed countries Jamaica makes no provision for unemployment insurance and the unemployed are forced to rely on the charity of relatives or friends. Concern with employment should not be allowed, however, to obscure other problems that are just as real. The figures for employment conceal almost as much as they reveal. The problems of ' under-employment ' and ' disguised unemployment ' are also serious. In addition to the seventeen per cent unemployment rate reported in the Labour Force Survey of 1957, it was brought to light that sixteen per cent of the employed labour force worked for three days or less in the survey week... Apart from open unemployment of the order of twenty per cent, seasonal patterns of employment account for under-utilisation of the potential labour force by another twenty per cent. This does not include the large number of persons who, because of no alternative, crowd into the service industries (such as petty trading) and who may be classified as being employed for all or the greater part of the year but whose productivity (and income) are low.

A point is reached when the meaning of these figures is written in fire and blood. In October 1966 the Government of Jamaica had to declare a state of emergency in order to check disorder and violence in West Kingston, where the largest number of urban unemployed exist. In October 1968 rioting broke out in Kingston as a result of the rise in the cost of living that followed on the devaluation of the British Pound, increasing unemployment, deterioration of the public utilities, two years of drought that crippled farmers, and the agitation of Black Power militants. The spark that set off the explosion was an orderly but illegal march by University students protesting at a government exclusion order against a member of the University staff, a Black Power militant. Three people were killed in the rioting in the city and heavy damage was done to property. In 1969 rioting broke out in Curaçao, up to then apparently a model of stability. We have already referred to the causes of this outbreak, the most important of which was unemployment. In the spring of 1970 disorders broke out in Trinidad, one of the most prosperous countries in the Commonwealth Caribbean. The unemployed staged marches and demonstrations, Black Power leaders attacked the Government on the grounds that political independence was meaningless if the black and East Indian masses remained poor while foreign investors made the crucial financial decisions, and a part of the army mutinied. With the help of the loyal section of the army, the police and the fire brigades the government restored order. But the hurricane warnings were out. Unemployment, and linked with this, race, would be the central issues of the 1970's.

CHAPTER 24

Search for a Future

Other colonial people in the Caribbean, the Netherlands Antilles, the French Antilles and Puerto Rico were engaged in a search for economic security and autonomy at the same time as ourselves. Their history, like ours, was moulded by colonialism, a plantation system based on black slave labour, and limited land space. Like the countries of the Commonwealth Caribbean, they had felt the impact of two world wars and the influence of ideas about democratic systems of government. Their economic difficulties were increased by rapid population growth. Let us review the solutions that they adopted.

There are 250,000 people in the Netherlands Antilles, two-thirds of them living in Curaçao and Aruba, which between them have an area of 120 square miles. The remainder live in Bonaire and in three northerly or ' Windward Islands ', St. Martins, Saba and St. Eustatius, which lie north-east of Puerto Rico. The population is predominantly black. The history of the plantation period is not etched out as clearly in the landscape as it is in Nevis or Antigua, but it can still be traced in old Dutch colonial style houses and decaying slave quarters with walls of beaten earth in the arid north-western districts of Curaçao. The few whites are in positions of authority. Sephardic Jews are powerful in commerce. More recently East Indians and Lebanese have established themselves as merchants. After 1915 oil refining became the chief industry, the refineries providing employment for Antilleans and also for some thousands of West Indians. The educational system was closely integrated with that of Holland and numbers of Antilleans went to Dutch universities for their professional training.

In 1945 Holland, stripped of her far-eastern empire, and facing the task of national reconstruction after four years of occupation by the German armies, entered into new constitution arrangements with the Antilles and Surinam, the governing principle being that of partnership. A tripartite Kingdom of the Netherlands was created, in which Holland, Surinam and the Antilles are partners, each being autonomous and internally self governing. Provision was made for Surinam and the Antilles to share with Holland responsibility for external affairs and defence. As members of the Kingdom of the Netherlands both Surinam and the Antilles benefit from membership in the European Economic Community. They also have access to Dutch capital, both public and private, and they receive direct contributions by Holland to their revenue. Exploiting their proximity to the South American mainland, their reputation for stability, their beaches and the beauty of Dutch-colonial architecture, they achieved a level of national income per capita second only to that of Puerto Rico and the American Virgin Islands. The figure was $950 in 1965.

In 1955 the refineries decided to introduce automation and phase out labour. By 1960 most of the immigrant workers had been displaced by machines. Antillean labour then began to feel the effect, and unemployment increased. Toward the end of the decade the refineries began to contract out services they had previously undertaken, like cleaning and construction; and there developed a differential in wages, the contractor offering lower rates than those the refinery had paid for the same work. Discontent increased when workers found their wages cut in this way; and the situation deteriorated because the government, which had been in power since 1954, had lost touch with the mass of the people. Pent-up anger at unemployment and lower wages erupted on 30 May 1969, when rioters looted and burnt shops in the centre of Curacao. The troubles were largely economic, but they had racial undertones, for expatriate officials and merchants were obviously much better off. They also made the important decisions. General elections were held, a black Prime

Minister came to power, and a black Governor General assumed office. The Antillean solution is that of membership in a tripartite Kingdom in which the strong partner is Holland. This arrangement provided autonomy and a considerable measure of security. It was acceptable to the Antilleans by reason of their long and close linkage with Holland, and their relative isolation in cultural and commercial terms from the West Indies.

The French Antilles chose assimilation with France. Representation in the French Parliament had been restored to them in 1871, and in form they had a government that was representative on a wide franchise but in fact the Governor was in control. Paris made the policy, gave economic help, provided a protected market for the chief products of the colonies, sugar and rum. The period between 1871 and 1920 was one of stagnation, broken by occasional riots or natural disasters, the most destructive of these being the eruption of Mt. Pelé which destroyed the town of St. Pierre, the chief centre of European wealth and culture in Martinique.

During the years following the second world war the French empire was in trouble. The struggle of the third world against European colonisation was beginning. In Indo-China war was being waged against the French. At the same time France was under pressure from nationalist groups in Tunisia, Morocco and in Algeria where nationalists organised their own Movement for the Triumph of Democratic Liberties. An *Organisation Special* (O.S.) came into existence, and by 1954 various groups of nationalists, convinced that war was the only possible course toward independence, organised the Front of National Liberation. Her Caribbean colonies presented no threat to France. On the contrary, in March 1946 the General Councils of Martinique, Guadeloupe and French Guiana, all elected bodies, voted unanimously in favour of becoming Overseas Departments of France. The Governor gave way to a Prefect, who, as in the metropolitan departments, was the agent of a highly centralised authority. Because of distance and economic difficulties in the islands, the Prefect was given special powers, including control of the armed forces and the power to declare martial law without first obtaining permission from France. In consequence, the Prefect looked very much like the vanished governor. The General Council was limited, in principle, to dealing only with administrative matters and was forbidden to express any political desires. It raised its voice, nevertheless, when this seemed necessary, as in 1959 when a riot broke out in Fort de France, arising out of an incident between a white man and a black man. The Council then protested against the brutality of the Republican Security Forces, as well as against the prevailing high rate of unemployment, high taxes and low wages. Responding to the protest, France in 1960 enlarged the powers of the General Councils and of the Prefects.

Those parties that favour the present political status, ' departmentalists ', are opposed by those who press for autonomy, ' autonomists '. In this latter group are the communist parties of Martinique and Guadeloupe which, in 1970, commanded about forty-five per cent of the vote. They urge that the people of the Caribbean Departments should administer their own affairs and they advocate agrarian reform, the nationalisation of the big sugar and banana concerns, diversification of agriculture and industrial development.

Assimilation brought financial benefits to the French Antilles. There has been substantial public expenditure on roads, schools, health services and the like. They have access to the European Economic Community, and receive from it funds for strengthening the infrastructure for development. On the other hand the highly centralised system of government provoked resentment and the general elections of 1967 showed some gains by the autonomists. The dilemma in which many of these find themselves was expressed by Aimé Césaire, leader of the communist Parti *Progressiste de la Martinique*, in his welcome speech to De Gaulle in 1966:

> We can no longer avoid facing a problem that obsesses our youth; the problem of the necessary remodelling of our institutions (I refer to our local institutions) so that they will be better suited to our Antillean conditions... so that we may no longer have the feeling, the most depressing feeling that a group of poor but proud men can experience, the feeling that they helplessly look upon the unfolding of their own history, the feeling that they submit to history instead of

making it; in short the feeling of being frustrated about their own future...

This feeling, however, has not expressed itself in any strong demand for independence, as it did in the British colonies. This is so because, as a Martiniquan, Victor Sable, said in 1955: ' The Antilles cannot and do not want to be anything other than French. They are French in spirit, in heart, in blood'. This does not imply that French Antillean society is either united or one in heart and blood. In Martinique there are 2,300 resident whites in a population of 320,000. They are divided into about 500 small whites who make up a white peasantry like the Barbados redlegs, and big whites, *grands blancs*. There is an exclusive middle class, which breaks into big mulattoes, *grand mulâtres*, light-skinned *backra* folk who move with the big whites, and a dark skinned lower middle class, between the lowest of whom, and the black and brown masses there is a great gulf fixed. Writing of his visit to Martinique in his book *Middle Passage*, Naipaul remarked tnat Martiniquans may all be Frenchmen but in the island they were black Frenchmen or brown Frenchmen or white Frenchmen. That all these should still be French ' in heart, in blood ' indicates a sense of cultural identity, not of national identity. It also throws light on the difficulties that confront those who have been colonised for a long period of time. They seek to become like the coloniser, ' to resemble him to the point of disappearing in him.'

During this period (1930–1970) two black Martiniquans, a poet-politician Aimé Césaire, and a revolutionary, Frantz Fanon raised their voices against assimilation—and in Fanon's case, against colonialism. Césaire made popular the theme of negritude. In his best known poem, *Statement of a Return to the Country of my Birth*, published in Paris in 1939, Césaire wrote of the misery of the black masses in Martinique and the exclusiveness and subservience of the middle classes, and of his journey to Paris where he found that as a West Indian he had no national identity, and he turned to the land of his ancestors, Africa. He rejected the doctrine that one race is superior to another, not on racist grounds:

you know that it is not from hatred
of other races
that I seek to be cultivator of this
unique race...

but because the black man has a unique and essential contribution to make to mankind's wellbeing:

for it is not true that the work of man
is finished... and no race possesses the monopoly of beauty,
of intelligence, of force, and there
is a place for all at the rendezvous
of victory...

Negritude became a literary fashion, an assertion also of an irrational black vision of the universe, a manufacturing, in Fanon's words, of ' a Negro consciousness.' The headquarters was Paris, and the Haitian Stenio Vincent acidly remarked: ' What I do know is that they preferred the Boulevard des Italiens to the swamps of Bahr-el-Gazel or the mountains of Kilmanjaro.' In this first period, Césaire was nevertheless, setting about the same kind of task that Garvey had undertaken, insisting that the whites had no ground for assuming that they were superior people, rejecting the notion that they had the right to impose their way of life, and their values on anyone. It does not diminish Césaire to say that Haitian and Cuban writers and musicians had already begun to do this. In his illuminating study, *Race and Colour in the Caribbean*, Coulthard has shown that ' negritude ' grew out of the work of Haitians like Antenor Fermin in his *Rehabilitation of the Black Race by the Haitian People* (1885), Hannibal Price's *Equality of the Human Race* (1900) and Jean Price Mars *Thus Spoke Uncle*, a collection of Haitian folk tales (1928). The roots of negritude are found in their emphasis on the value of African culture and their attack on the doctrine that the black is an inferior kind of human being. It is not surprising that Césaire countered the stifling effects of assimilation by developing this theme in his own creative way: but by the 1950's ' negritude ' was being criticised as a negative cult, a reaction to the white man's original view of Africa, the antithesis of the colonial view of black life. A younger black Martiniquan, Frantz Fanon, attacked not only assimilation but colonialism in general, advocating with volcanic eloquence a black and third world revolution. Fanon was born of a lower middle class black family in Martinique in 1925. The assimilative power of the French colonial system, and especially of the system of education, is revealed by Fanon's reaction, as a young man in Paris, to talk of a Negro nationality: ' What is all this talk of a black people, of a Negro nationality? I am a Frenchman,... I am personally interested in the future of France, in French values, in the French nation.' His experiences in France helped him to liberate himself. In *Black Skin, White Mask* he described the shock on a black Martiniquan of French racism, and in the conclusion he declared that appeals to reason and to respect for human dignity could not alter reality: ' For the Negro who works on a sugar plantation in Le Robert, Martinique, there is only one solution, to fight.' From Paris Fanon went to Algiers, served as a psychiatrist, came face to face with the hideous cruelties of repressive colonial government, and became one of the leaders of the third world revolt against colonialism. In the last and most powerful of his four books, *The Wretched of the Earth*, Fanon analysed the difficulties that face a nation that has just freed itself from colonialism, especially the danger that comes from those nationalists who simply stepped into the shoes of European colonisers, who ' have come to power in the name of a narrow nationalism and representing a race: they will prove themselves incapable of triumphantly putting into effect a programme with even a minimum of humanist intent '... He urged action, insisted that violence was essential, and advocated the education of man ' to be actional, preserving in all his relations his respect for the basic values that constitute the human world...' Fanon's work did much to transform non-violent black protest in the United States into a militant action-oriented movement spearheaded by the Black Panthers. Fanon died early in December 1961.

How different from the Netherlands Antilles and the French Antilles was the island of Puerto Rico, which, like Trinidad, had been for long a Spanish colony, but not as neglected as Trinidad was because San Juan formed a vital link in the Spanish American defence system. It remained a Spanish colony up to 1898 when

Spain ceded the island to the United States. The first phase of its history ran counter to that of the English and French plantation islands, for though sugar-cane was introduced into Puerto Rico in 1515 a large scale sugar industry did not develop, those Spanish colonists who had capital being attracted to the mainland. Up to the end of the 18th century the population was made up of a large group of free whites and browns and a minority of black slaves. The economy was based on subsistence farming, and in the second half of the century on coffee. Legitimate trade increased after 1815, when Spain removed the prohibition against the island trading with any other country. Sugar also became important. The plantations were greedy for land and labour. Planters with capital bought up smallholdings and imported slaves. Curtin estimates that between 1811 and 1870 Puerto Rico purchased about 55,000 slaves, a tenth of Cuban slave imports over the same period. In order to provide the plantations with labour, laws were passed that compelled the landless freemen to work on the estates. As Mintz observes, Puerto Rico in this period presented the curious picture of a Caribbean colony where slaves were treated little worse than landless freemen.

In the second half of the century sugar production fell. Puerto Rico's sugar, like Jamaica's, could not face competition from overseas producers. Coffee production, on the other hand, expanded. There were serious defects in the system of cultivation. Clean weeding speeded up soil erosion. The peasants who tended the crop were paid low wages and were badly housed. On the other hand, ninety out of every hundred coffee planters resided in the island. The farms were small-scale, the number of coffee plantations in the 1890's being about 40,000. At that time about forty per cent of the arable land was covered with coffee. The rest produced sugar and tobacco. Smallholders eked out a living on marginal land and on eroded mountain slopes. The coffee planters received their death sentence in 1898, when the Spanish-American war came to an end and Puerto Rico was ceded to the United States, whose tariff was constructed to protect crops and goods produced or made in the country. Puerto Rico's sugar industry benefitted, because sugar was produced in the continental United States but coffee which was not a United States product had to compete with large foreign producers like Brazil. By 1939 coffee, once the chief crop, made up about one half per cent of the island's exports, whereas sugar made up forty per cent. The sugar plantation ate up the land of the small coffee planter and of the small cane farmer, the *colono*. Between 1910 and 1935 the acreage of farms of twenty to ninety nine acres declined eleven per cent and the acreage of farms of 100 to 499 acres nearly twenty two per cent. Puerto Rico had become a plantation island in which, by 1930, seventy-eight per cent of all capital invested in manufacturing was invested in sugar. It exhibited all the characteristics of a plantation colony, its economy being based on one crop and being orientated to export and most of its plantations being foreign owned. As in Cuba and the Dominican Republic, American capital and American technology boosted sugar production and earned large profits. A Puerto Rican economist, Esteban Bird, estimated that during 1928 the average return was as high as thirty-one per cent. Sugar was everything, and everything was sugar.

Politically, the island was very much like a Crown Colony. Congress, by its first Organic Act of 1900, put power in the hands of a Governor and senior officials appointed in Washington. Provision was made for a bicameral legislature, a nominated upper house and an elected lower house. The island's Supreme Court was appointed in Washington. Puerto Ricans had hoped for more autonomy and greater responsibility. Excluded from meaningful participation in the government, they saw four or five American corporations acquiring control of more than half of the land suitable for growing cane. They saw the *colonos*, who owned most of the remaining sugar land, becoming utterly dependent on American owned mills for the sale of their canes and many of the benefits of economic union with the mainland being drained away from their country.

Puerto Rican pressure for constitutional change produced some cautious concessions in 1917, when amendments to the Organic Act deprived the governor's Executive Council of its law-making power. An elected senate was created, and Puerto Ricans were declared to be United States citizens though they could not exercise their full rights as American citizens unless they resided in the United States. These concessions did not satisfy the Puerto Ricans, but there was no further constitutional change for thirty years. In the meantime misery grew amongst the people in the country and the poor in the ghettos in San Juan, and the great depression of the late 1920's widened the circle of poverty and frustration.

In 1932, in the United States, the Democratic Party came to power and Franklin Roosevelt set his New Deal in motion. In the preceding year Luis Muñoz Marin, who had been in voluntary exile in New York for some years, returned to his country, determined to solve Puerto Rico's problems ' not with doles but with social justice, operating within an economy that shall be as far as possible planned and autonomous.' In his work *Puerto Rico, Preedom and Power in the Caribbean*, Gordon Lewis examines in detail the purposes and programme of Muñoz, and tells how he was supported by a new Creole group of rising intellectuals and how he benefitted from ' the new growth of a real professional ethic in the island middle classes ' who, in consequence, helped ' to counteract the socially debilitating habit of leaving political expression exclusively in the hands of the professional politicians.' The change in mood was not unlike that which was making itself felt in the West Indies, and which was bringing together the ill-fed peon, poverty-stricken and apathetic, with middle class intellectuals and professional people. Agencies were created by the Federal Government to implement relief and development programmes, the most notable being the Puerto Rico Reconstruction Administration, which aimed at a diversification of agriculture and improving the working conditions and wages of the peon or jibaro. Yet, concludes Thomas Mathews in his analysis of *Puerto Rico and the New Deal*, with possibly one exception, none of its projects had ever really managed to become an enduring or important part of the Puerto Rican scene.

Luis Muñoz Marin brought all Puerto Ricans, including the peasant and the San Juan slum dweller into the full stream of Puerto Rican politics in 1940, with his message of Bread, Land, Country. His Popular Democratic Party set itself three objectives: first, social reform through the purchase of land for smallholdings and the protection of trade unions; second, the improvement and expansion of public services and facilities like electricity, transport, water supply, sewerage, and the comprehensive improvement of the educational system at all levels;

third, direct promotion of industrial development through a specially-founded Industrial Development Company and a Development Bank to provide long-term credit.

White Puerto Ricans were throwing themselves into the task of making the island's economy viable and lifting working class living standards, they were also seeking ways of changing the political status from a wholly colonial relationship to one that gave greater autonomy. The result was the establishment, in 1952, of the Commonwealth of Puerto Rico. By the terms of the compact, the Commonwealth relationship can be changed by mutual consent. Puerto Rico elects its own Governor, and is governed by its own bicameral legislature. The Legislative Assembly approves the Commonwealth budget, controls the system of education at all levels, and legislates for the full range of Commonwealth affairs. A Federal Relations Act defines the responsibilities of the Federal Government which include defence and foreign affairs. The Commonwealth is part of the United States internal market, and all United States tariffs apply. Puerto Ricans do not pay federal income tax, and although they are United States citizens they refrain from voting in United States federal elections.

Spectacular results flowed from these arrangements and from the energy and initiative of Puerto Rican leadership, Recent World Bank reports classified Puerto Rico as a rich nation, the only one in the Caribbean, with a per capita income of just over $1,000, and this despite a high rate of population growth.

Migration to the continental United States eased population pressure to a very substantial degree. In 1967 about one third of all Puerto Ricans resided on the mainland. Encouraged by the Economic Development Administration, more than 1,000 new manufacturing plants entered the island between 1952 and 1967. Tourism became a major industry. The speed and scale of the transformation of a poor rural island community into a literate wage earning industrialised community was possible only because the island was closely linked with the United States. A student of Puerto Rican affairs, Ben Stephansky, points to this issue which is a central one for all our West Indian countries:

> The small state, for its growth and development, finds it imperative to seek vital linkages with external sources of

growth. Unlike the larger under-developed state, which can look toward a future, however distant, of self-sustained growth, the small state requires vital external linkages of a permanent nature, for its continued growth can only be externally supported rather than self-sustained.

In the 1960's there was evidence that a large number of Puerto Ricans wished to change the Commonwealth relationship, some to Statehood, a smaller number to independence. Young Puerto Ricans who had not known the rigours of life in Puerto Rico in the 1940's were dissatisfied with the materialism of their island society, with an ambiguous political relationship which they termed colonialism in disguise and with a party that had been in power for twenty five years. In the general election of 1968 Luis Ferre's New Progressive Party defeated the Popular Democratic Party, which had been weakened by a split in its leadership. This raised many questions. Were Puerto Ricans unhappy about the ambiguity of Commonwealth status? Had the issues narrowed to a choice between statehood and independence? Had they concluded simply that the time had come for a change? In November 1972 they gave their answer, the *Populares* gaining a landslide victory under the young successor to Muñoz Marin, Hernández Colon.

In comparing the development of Puerto Rico with that of the British West Indies, we need to remember that in the 1940's external circumstances were very favourable to that island. The high level of economic activity in the United States in the post-war years was a crucial factor. A strong continental demand kept up the level of Puerto Rican agricultural products. American manufacturers, facing high taxes and high wage bills at home, found it attractive to set up factories in the island, within the same tariff walls, but with lower production costs. In their turn Puerto Ricans, only three jet hours away from the United States, migrated in large numbers to earn higher wages on the mainland. The island was a part of the United States market. In these and other respects therefore, Puerto Rico's position was very different but Puerto Rican experience has served us well. We have learned much from her experiments in the use of legislation and credit-financing to attract industry; and we have been able to study the process of development by examining the social changes that result from rapid modernisation, the growth of entreprenuership, the shift of the labour force into non-agricultural activities, the decline of handicrafts and growth of factory work, the ways in which regional economic development draws people from less developed regions in the country, leading to a redistribution of the population, and especially of persons within the younger age range, with the attendant problems of urban growth such as the urgent need for low income housing, schooling, health services and the like.

Our West Indian community of four million people is about one-fifth the size of the total Caribbean community. Thus far we have looked at the experience of smaller communities, all of them engaged like ourselves in the tasks of achieving autonomy and strengthening and stabilising their economies. But what of the larger Caribbean nations that became independent long before we did? The magnitude of the task we have undertaken comes home to us when we look at the record of the Dominican Republic, Haiti and Cuba.

The Dominican Republic was a Spanish colony for three centuries, up to 1795. Then in rapid succession it was taken over by the French, reverted to Spain, declared itself independent in 1821, passed under Haitian rule from 1821 to 1844, when it drove out the Haitians and became an independent republic, ruled by a succession of dictators of whom, in the last century the most tyrannical was Ulises Heureaux (1882–1899). We have noted the sensitivity of the United States which found expression in Roosevelt's Corollary to the Munro doctrine of 1904. Chaotic conditions in the Republic added to the concern of the United States that one or more European powers might intervene in any Caribbean country not under American or European tutelage where there was the possibility of a major default on foreign debt or disorder involving damage to foreign property, and as a result Roosevelt proclaimed his famous corollary to the Munro doctrine, which implied the intention, where necessary, to exercise a degree of supervision over the internal affairs of independent states. From 1905 to 1940 the United States supervised the finances of the country and administered its customs; and its marines kept order from 1916 to 1924.

Trujillo ruled the Republic from 1930 to 1961 when he was assassinated. Brutal, ruthless and efficient, he curtailed individual freedom, crushed opposition, strengthened the economy by attracting foreign capital, chiefly American, into an expanding sugar industry. He built up an efficient army, ran a spy-system based on secret police and informers, enriched himself and his family, massacred about 10,000 Haitian peasants who had squatted on Dominican territory and created a formidable pyramid of power that had all the appearance of being permanent. On his death it disintegrated and fell apart. A brief period of instability followed, in the course of which the United States intervened, provoking outspoken criticism throughout Latin America. In an attempt to remedy the situation, the United States force of about 20,000 was incorporated into a force sponsored by the Organisation of American States to which Brazil, Paraguay, Costa Rica and Honduras contributed. In June 1966 Joaquin Balaguer defeated Juan Bosch in the general elections and became President. The American peace-keeping force was withdrawn, an austerity programme introduced, and the economy began to improve.

Since Balaguer became President in 1966 economic development has proceeded apace. Well-constructed blocks of apartments for low-income workers have replaced shacks and hovels on the banks of the Ozama River on the limits of Santo Domingo. New roads have been built, areas in the arid south-west have been transformed into green fertile land by irrigation, hydro-electric projects are supplying power for the industrial expansion that is taking place, dams are being built at Tavera and are being designed for parts of the upper Nizao River, and agricultural production has been increased. There is a general feeling of freedom. The general elections of 1970 were open and well-conducted. In 1971 the Inter American Press noted that there were fewer restrictions on the Press than in most other Latin American countries. The new liberalism is expressed also in a policy of friendship and cooperation with Puerto Rico, Haiti and Jamaica. It is true that the Republic has considerable potential, with good agricultural land and a low population density of about 170 to the square mile. The odds are in favour of a government that is devoted to economic development. Even so, the record of the years since 1966 constitutes a remarkable achievement, especially against a background of traditional tyranny, boss-rule, obedience at the point of a gun.

But the attitudes and institutions of democracy have yet to be created. The government of President Balaguer is reformist, not revolutionary, and it has found difficulty in attracting to itself the radical youth of the country. There is no civil service in the sense that we understand it, with a permanent staff of men whose talents and experience are at the service of the country, whatever political changes might occur. In his recent study, *The Caribbean Community*, Robert Crassweller quotes a revealing comment by a Dominican on the lack of institutional stability in the country: ' in the United States you have institutional stability, your institutions remain. The policy people change. Here we have the reverse. Our institutions change, but the people remain the same kind, whether it be Trujillo or what...' A related aspect of this is the habit of thinking of the whole political process in terms of a person, a strong man on whom rests the business of running the country, who personifies policy, takes the decisions, expresses in himself the ultimate authority and power of the State.

In Santo Domingo the chief memorials are to Christopher Columbus, in Haiti they are to Toussaint L'Ouverture, Christophe, Dessalines, the three leaders whose courage and triumphs made Haiti the first independent nation in Latin America. But Haiti was odd-man out. It had no links of language, institutions and religion with surrounding countries, as had the republics of Latin America. It was a French-speaking black republic, neglected and isolated; a nation with a small brown elite in the capital city, who had power and such riches as there were, and a large rural population of black peasants who lived by hand to mouth agriculture, parcelled out their fragments of land into ever smaller portions with each generation, spoke their own Creole language, practised their own folk-medicine, were wholly illiterate, and were cut off to an extraordinary degree from the twentieth century. In 1915, when widespread disorders broke out following on the assassination of President Guillaume, the United States intervened, marines were sent in, and the affairs of the country were supervised for nineteen years. But

American officials failed to win the effective co-operation of the Haitian leaders and they encroached more and more on the powers of the Haitian administration. They built roads, provided health services, improved sanitation, but they did not understand the society in which they were working. In an effort to hasten road building and relieve widespread unemployment they made the mistake, in 1916, of reviving the old *corvée*, which was still lawful but which had not been enforced within living memory. The manner of its enforcement led to an uprising under Charlemagne Péralte, which lasted into 1920, and cost the lives of about 2,000 Haitians, a few United States marines and a score or so of gendarmes.

In 1956 Haiti entered upon yet another period of strong man rule, but this time more ruthless and destructive than anything the country had known. The strongman was Dr. Francois Duvalier, who succeeded Magloire as President in 1956 and who in 1963 succeeded himself without troubling about the formality of an election. In the following year he declared himself President for life. Symbolising the triumph of the black peasantry over the privileged mulatto caste, he brought the republic under his control by atomising its institutions and splitting up every possible nucleus of strength. Thus, while destroying the officer corps in the regular army he created his own private army, the Tonton Macoute. He destroyed whatever elements existed of a civil service, replacing administrators with his own followers. The cabinet ceased to meet. A unicameral legislature was created in place of the traditional bicameral legislature, but its only function was to give unanimous approval to bills. Making shrewd use of voodooism, Papa Doc controlled attitudes as well as conduct in his police state. It remains to be seen to what extent his son Claude, and the ruling group around him, can strengthen the country's tottering economy, and give to Haiti some ease and time for healing.

Haiti, by reason of its history, its contribution to Caribbean literature, music, painting and sculpture, and its respect for Africa, holds a special place in the esteem and affection of the predominantly black Caribbean. So does Cuba, whose land area is equal to that of the rest of the archipelago and whose sugar industry drew thousands of West Indians to that country in the 1920's.

The Cuban-American war against Spain was brought to an end by the Treaty of Paris, December 10, 1898, when Cuba became an independent nation. The military government which the United States established in the island was withdrawn, but only after Cuba agreed to terms set out in the Platt Amendment, which stipulated that Cuba should never enter into any agreement with any foreign power that impaired its own independence, nor grant to them military bases; that the United States would have the right to intervene in order to preserve Cuban independence or to ensure that Cuba fulfilled the obligations imposed on it by the Treaty of Paris; and that Cuba would lease or sell to the United States land for use as coaling or naval stations. As a result of this last agreement the United States established bases at Guantanamo and Bahia. In 1912 it gave up Bahia in return for more land at Guantanamo.

We have already referred to a second basic statement of United States foreign policy, the Roosevelt Corollary. Behind the Platt Amendment and the Roosevelt Corollary there were three considerations: the strategic importance of the archipelago and of the Panama Canal on which work was started in 1902 and completed in 1912; the need for military bases in the archipelago as a defence against hostile attack; anxiety over the cession of any of the islands to another power, and over intervention by any other power in order to protect its citizens or its property in cases of disorder or revolution.

In this period Cuban sugar production grew through the investment of American capital, and Cuban-American relations were governed by the state of the sugar industry. During the First World War Cuba was forced to accept a price for its sugar fixed with reference to the price at which the leading American beet-producers agreed to sell. In 1918 the United States, through a recently appointed Sugar Equalisation Board, contracted to buy the Cuban sugar crop of four million tons, about one-fourth of the world's supply. Two months later the war ended. Sugar prices rose. The Equalisation Board sold the Cuban crop, making a profit of $42 million. This evoked angry protests from Cuban producers and started a series of investigations in Washington. The 1919–20 crop was thrown on the world market free of controls. There followed what journalists called the Dance of the Millions, a wild scramble for sugar estates, sugar mills, sugar in any form. Up to this time, although the growth of the Cuban sugar industry had depended on American capital, the actual production of sugar had remained largely in Cuban hands. Cubans owned the estates and mills. Through the *colono* system, small sugar farmers shared in the profits. Now, seeking to protect their supplies of sugar, United States refiners, distillers, confectioners and others rushed to buy mills and estates in Cuba, offering unheard of prices. Some fifty large factories changed hands. Thousands of *colonos* sold out. But the boom did not last. By 1920 sugar was down to seven cents a pound and still falling. In February 1921 the United States through an Emergency Tariff Bill increased the duty on Cuban sugar by about sixty per cent, the blow falling on Cuban producers at a time when they were already in trouble. The Havana banks, which had made large advances on the sugar crop, on mills and standing cane, were also in difficulty. Many of them failed early in 1921. The Government Treasury was empty. To make matters worse, there occurred at this time a political crisis as a result of an election in which Zayas was elected President. The Liberal Opposition charged that Zayas' predecessor Menocal had rigged the polls. Under pressure from the protesting Cuban liberals and from United States financiers, the United States sent an envoy, General Crowder, to confer with President Menocal on the political and financial condition of Cuba. His arrival heralded what was in fact, though not in name, an intervention. A loan was negotiated with an American company of financiers, the political confusion was sorted out, and when in 1923 the price of sugar improved the economic health of Cuba also improved. Politics returned to normal. The end result was that the economic control of Cuba passed into the hands of a relatively small group of United States financiers, both through the increased importance of sugar to the Cuban economy and also through the increased part played by foreign capital in the Cuban sugar industry. Of the 1926–27 crop of 4·4 million tons, sixty two per cent was made by American-owned mills, another eight per cent by mills jointly owned by Americans and Cubans, and four per cent by Canadian-owned mills. Wages rose, but the unbalanced condition of the economy and an increasing demand for food, clothing and the like increased the cost of living greatly. Further, the economic freedom of the peasant was destroyed. The smallholder who owned a vega in one of the favoured tobacco areas was able to survive, but the many who did not were caught up in the impersonal vast business of an industry that was largely foreign owned.

Many Cubans resented the vassalage of their country to the United States, and this accounts in part for the support they gave to Machado, the brutal successor to Zayas. Many Americans also were unhappy about political interference in Cuba, and after 1923 open political intervention ceased. But in fact Cuba was under American control, and Machado was left to run his course. In 1933 Fulgencio Batista, a sergeant in the Cuban army, led a successful mutiny against the dictator. The Cuban people had had enough of his brutal repression, his cruelty. The Sergeants' Revolt of 1933 was followed by a return to elected government and for a time by more efficient, more honest administration. Batista had a flair for picking and supporting respectable Presidents before he sought that office himself. In 1952 he stood constitutionally for election as president and when the election seemed likely to go against him he resorted to a military coup and made himself dictator of Cuba. The army, which supported him, became utterly corrupt. The civilians who supported him enriched themselves. Once again Cuba was betrayed by its leadership. In Havana a resistance movement grew in strength. Fidel Castro, who had failed in his first attempt to overthrow Batista, made a second attempt, gained a foothold in the Sierra Maestra mountains, and for over two years carried on a campaign against Batista while in Havana an urban underground movement ate away at Batista's strength. Suddenly the structure crumbled and Batista fled. Castro immediately proclaimed himself Commander in Chief, made an eight day victory march through Cuba, and took charge of the country. He became Prime Minister in 1959. In 1960 he established close ties with the Soviet Union and other nations in the communist bloc, and his position was greatly strengthened when, in April 1961, he defeated, at the Bay of Pigs, a group of exiles armed and supported by the United States.

In October 1962 the world was brought to the brink of nuclear war. Photographs taken by the United States airforce showed that missile sites were being erected in Cuba. At the same time President Kennedy learnt that Soviet ships were on the way to Cuba with offensive weapons. He immediately imposed a quarantine on all offensive military equipment under shipment to Cuba and declared that missiles launched from Cuba against the United States would be regarded as an attack by the Soviet Union, calling for immediate retaliation by the United States. On 28 October Kruschev came to terms with the United States, to the disappointment of Castro, who soon found in China a valuable counterpoise to Russia. But Russia remained the major trading partner, accounting for nearly one-half of Cuba's foreign trade in the period 1960–65. In 1966 and 1968 Cuba signed further trading agreements with Russia.

In the face of many difficulties, Castro consolidated the Cuban revolution by sheer force of personality. In the eyes of the masses of the Cuban people he was the embodiment of the revolution.

The Revolution has achieved notable results in some areas of Cuban life; in education, for example, with the conquest of illiteracy, the provision of nursery schools and of free education up to university level and the founding of technical and scientific institutes; in agriculture with important developments in the cattle industry; the establishment of agricultural settlements in rural areas; and the development of fishing industry. Beyond this, it has generated enthusiasm for and dedication to an integrated Cuban society. In Crasweller's words ' a modern integrated state has been created—a national entity rather than a collection of regions and classes.' But at a price, and that price was raised by inefficient administration and sudden shifts of policy. The country did not gain economic independence. Instead, it is now closely tied to, and dependent on, Russia and the Eastern European Communist nations. Thus, in 1970 it is estimated that Soviet aid to Cuba was of the order of $600 million and that the Cuban debt to Russia on capital account was $3 billion. Attempts made in the 1960's to broaden the economic base of the country by establishing heavy industry failed, and as a result the traditional reliance on sugar was renewed and the resources of the nation mobilised to reach a target figure of ten million tons in 1970. Production was high, over eight million tons, but Castro declared that the country's failure in her ' great leap forward ' was a ' moral defeat '. He declared also that the many problems and difficulties of the country would not be solved till toward the end of the present decade.

It is a tribute to Castro's volcanic energy and political skill that he has retained widespread popular support, but participation in the government of the country is denied to the people. There are no free institutions. There is no free press. There are no democratic procedures. New directions have been charted but Castro has failed to create an administrative and political organisation that can take Cuba to her goals.

This review of the solutions that have been adopted by other Caribbean nations points to certain general conclusions. Obviously, independence of itself is no safeguard of freedom. It is obvious also that our new nations have an indispensable and priceless asset in institutions and established procedures that we too easily take for granted: a free press, popular participation in general elections through universal adult suffrage and a secret ballot, a two party system which provides an alternative government, a capacity to tolerate dissent, a trained civil service under an independent Public Service Commission, an independent Judiciary, a vigorous trade union movement, a number of independent professional and civic groups accustomed to presenting and pressing their views, religious bodies that represent a variety of doctrines and beliefs, and an educational system that is not the expression or instrument of an ideology. Where these are maintained independence can be preserved; where any of these are weakened by political personalism, the whole structure of national freedom is put in jeopardy.

CHAPTER 25

To Make Our Own Way

Were the complete record no more than this listing of rising difficulties and increasing constraints our journey would have taken us from the boglands of the slave plantation into a cockpit country of unscalable limestone pinnacles and dead-end valleys dark even at noonday. But the West Indian response was positive. We found this when we surveyed the pressure for constitutional change that took our countries from Crown Colony status in 1940 to statehood or independence in the 1960's. In order to gauge the full measure of the response let us review the period 1940 to 1970. The questions we will ask are these: Was there evidence that the various segments in the society were coming together to form a more united community: or, in other words, was the split society of the plantation days showing signs of integration? In the area of politics, was there evidence of a capacity to organise parties and to transfer political power by an orderly process from one party to another? These questions have to do with social ' wholeness ' and political organisation. Next, we will consider the economy. Here we will ask whether there is evidence that our societies are becoming ' modern '. We will ask if there is proof that the West Indian countries have broken through the apathy of the Crown Colony period and taken the initiative in bringing about economic development? Have both government and private enterprise joined together to do this? Have our West Indian countries moved from a ' rural life style ' based on two different economies, one ' plantation ' and the other ' peasant ', to a more integrated economy based on industry as well as on agriculture? Is the class structure the rigid one of the plantation and colonial period or is the society more open, one in which individuals can move up or down, each one finding his place according to his talents and not on the basis of face or skin-colour? Finally, we will consider the 'national' aspect. What is the evidence that the West Indian colonies have become, or are in the process of becoming communities? To what extent do they make the crucial decisions about themselves and their policies? In our relationship with other countries and in our own artistic and cultural life do we act as a nation with an identity of its own?

We will consider first social integration and political organisation and leadership. In the period between 1930 and 1950 especially, the number of societies and associations increased substantially. Primary producers, including banana growers, nutmeg producers, citrus growers, rice growers, cane farmers and others formed associations to protect and enlarge their markets, negotiate for better prices, set higher standards and improve methods of production. Small producers and middle class urban workers founded savings unions, credit unions, co-operative societies. Professional men, merchants and industrialists established societies, chambers of commerce, manufacturers associations and the like. One of the oldest of these groups, and one of the most active, was the West Indies Sugar Manufacturers Association which negotiated for long-term contracts on the British and Commonwealth sugar markets, encouraged research into better varieties of sugar-cane and improved methods of production. Groupings and associations like those that we have mentioned showed that West Indian society was developing a number of centres of cohesion.

The most significant and dramatic evidence, however, of social integration was the rapid growth of trade unions, a labour movement and political parties in the decade after the riots of 1936–8. Bain Alves, Cipriani, Thorne and other labour leaders had blazed a path; but up to 1937 trade unions counted for little in West Indian life and there was no labour movement. Then there came a bush-fire change. Antigua registered its first trade union in 1940. Soon union membership there rose to 12,000. In 1938 Jamaica had 1089 trade union members. By 1947 the number stood at 57,000 and at 67,000 in 1950. The introduction of universal adult suffrage enfranchised the masses and as a result trade unions gained political power, and trade union leaders dominated the legislature. Some foreign advisers frowned on the close link between the political parties and labour unions, but there is no doubt that, whatever the disadvantages, this intimate relationship involved the people quickly and comprehensively in the political process. The names prove the point: Vere Bird, Bradshaw, Grantley Adams, Walcott, Gairy, Jagan, Bustamante, Manley. The trade union was labour organised to protect its security and to improve the conditions of the working class. The political parties, which were often rooted in the labour movement, represented a wider coalition of interests. Within a decade the colonial system of narrow class representation and ineffectual legislative councils in which non-official members spoke only as individuals was replaced by assemblies made up of elected members who, in almost every instance, belonged to parties. In many countries two party systems developed, evidence that these new societies were able to accommodate their political differences within a framework of national loyalty. The role of the opposition in a developing country was defined by Norman Manley in these terms:

> there must be a constant presentation of the fact that there is an alternative to the existing Government... But it must be a real alternative, and that implies two quite different things. First of all, it implies that both parties accept in a general way the foundations of their society, so that neither consciously desires or intends or will be forced to destroy the other. Democratic socialism is a real alternative to conservatism simply because it accepts the principles of parliamentary democracy and believes in the essential importance and value of the individual man. On the other hand communism is not a real alternative either to liberalism or to conservatism because it rejects the principle of parliamentary government and is prepared to undertake the radical and total alteration of the society to which we belong... both parties must stand on some set of shared fundamentals... the party in opposition must present a clear alternative in

terms of policy and aim so that there is a real stimulus to its
followers and a real challenge to the future.

The development of trade unions, of political parties and of
party-government marked the rise of modern West Indian
countries; for one of the chief characteristics of a ' modern '
society is that it has within itself procedures or mechanisms for the
orderly transfer of political power.

When we look at the process of economic development we find
evidence in every part of the region of vigorous action by governments and by private enterprise. Once a sleepy neglected district, the region around Corozal in Belize has been transformed
by private investors into a major sugar-producing centre. A
thousand miles away in the north-eastern Caribbean, Tortola's
capital, Road Town, has developed a modern port and marina.
The Leewards and Windwards have improved harbours and
airports, extensive resort development and new light industries.
Barbados, with a new deep water harbour, has maintained a
steady rate of economic growth. New hotels line Tobago's
beaches, and new petro-chemical industries add strength to
Trinidad's economy. Guyana increased its rate of industrial
development. In Jamaica, Kingston and other urban areas
grew rapidly as a result of increasing industrialisation. The
governments used a variety of methods to stimulate production.
They passed laws that gave special incentives to overseas investors, set up national banks to control the flow of money, established industrial and agricultural corporations and promoted
tourism. Some countries also gained special benefits from the
emigration of their people to the United Kingdom during the
1950's.

Another development that benefitted Jamaica especially was
the expansion of its bauxite industry, an expansion that enabled
the island to achieve a high rate of growth during the 1950's.

Growing up in the midst of these changes, we take them for
granted. If we were to look at a film showing the landscape of
the 1930's, the chief occupations of the people and their way of
life, we would be struck by the change from a ' rural life style '
based on export and cash crops to an ' urban life style ' based on
growing cities, industry and on the development of procedures for
settling disputes and finding solutions to difficulties by agreement.

If we could watch the growth in production, the increasing flow of visitors from other lands, ships and aeroplanes bringing and carrying away cargo, an increase in spending power and gleaming supermarkets replacing dingy groceries, we would see that many of our countries have entered the industrial age. Watching our film, we would see a flow of talent into managerial positions and the chief posts in the government; and we would find the change marked in colour, with a flow of browns and blacks into areas once reserved for whites. We would observe also, in the second half of the 1960's, efforts at regional cooperation that were very different in kind from the ill-fated attempt at political federation in 1958–62. The search for economic security has led to regional cooperation and to the establishment of links with the larger American community.

By 1968, under the spur of economic necessity, the West Indian governments—now the countries of the Commonwealth Caribbean—began defining areas where national needs could be met by regional cooperation. They established a Caribbean Free Trade Area (CARIFTA) in 1968, with its Secretariat in Georgetown. Under the agreement, most of the items of trade between member countries entered free of duty. Some items were placed on a reserve list, customs duties on them being phased out over a five year period in the most developed countries and over a ten year period in those less developed. The CARIFTA Agreement was an important first step, and by 1972 there were encouraging signs that the larger market had begun to stimulate production and was resulting in more regional trade. However, the agreement was not sufficiently far reaching to produce basic changes in the economy. An important second step was taken in 1969 when the West Indian countries established a Caribbean Development Bank to finance development in member countries and, where possible to coordinate production. The regional contacts widened with the admission of Barbados, Jamaica and Trinidad and Tobago in the Organisation of American States, hitherto made up wholly of Latin American countries and the United States. Time was to show how the Organisation would adjust to the membership of black Caribbean states. The difference in point of view was made clear when, in 1972, Jamaica, Barbados and Trinidad and Tobago objected strongly to the sending of an

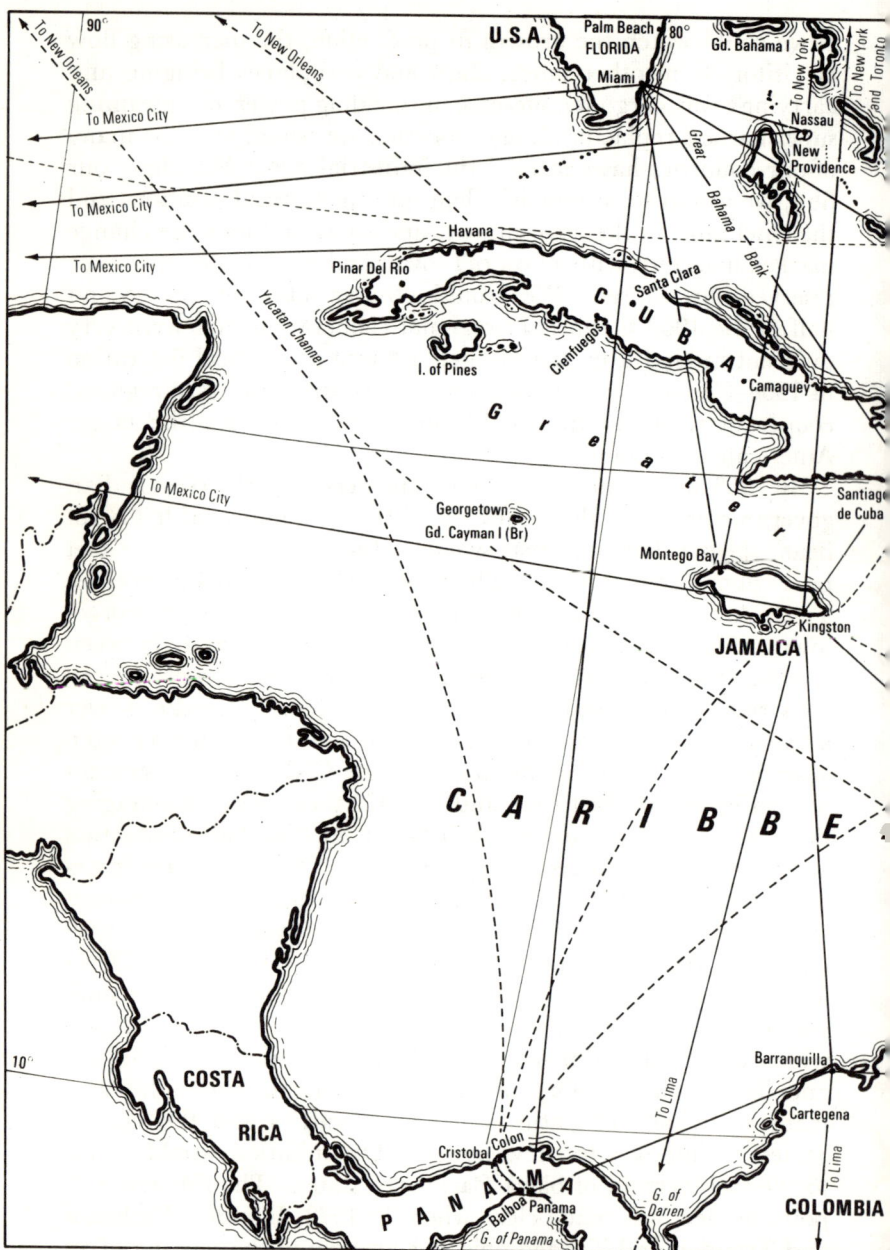

Present Day Caribbean showing main transport routes

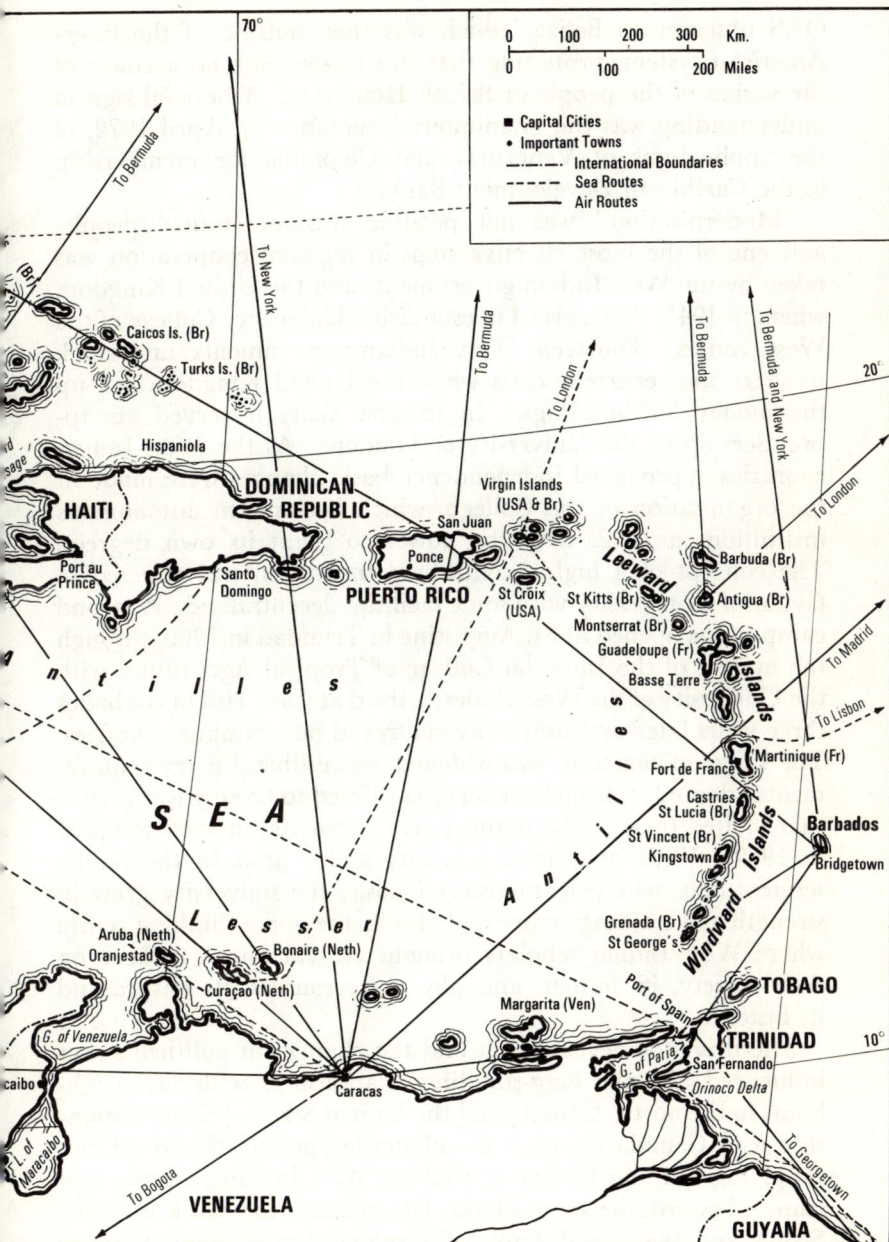

70°

0 100 200 300 Km.
0 100 200 Miles

■ Capital Cities
● Important Towns
---- International Boundaries
--- Sea Routes
— Air Routes

To Bermuda

To New York

To Bermuda

To London

To Bermuda and New York

20°

To London

Caicos Is. (Br)

Turks Is. (Br)

Hispaniola

DOMINICAN
REPUBLIC

Virgin Islands
(USA & Br)

HAITI

San Juan

Leeward

Barbuda (Br)

Port au
Prince

Ponce

Santo
Domingo

PUERTO RICO

St Croix
(USA)

St Kitts (Br)

Antigua (Br)

Montserrat (Br)

Guadeloupe (Fr)

To Madrid

Basse Terre

Antilles

Islands

To Lisbon

SEA

Martinique (Fr)

Fort de France

Antilles

Castries
St Lucia (Br)

St Vincent (Br)
Kingstown

Barbados

Bridgetown

Lesser

Grenada (Br)
St George's

Windward Islands

Aruba (Neth)
Oranjestad

Bonaire (Neth)

Curaçao (Neth)

Margarita (Ven)

Port of Spain

TOBAGO

G. of Venezuela

TRINIDAD

10°

caibo

San Fernando

G. of Paria

L. of Maracaibo

Caracas

Orinoco Delta

To Georgetown

To Bogota

VENEZUELA

GUYANA

331

OAS observer to Belize, which was then outside of the inter-American system, protesting that this action took no account of the wishes of the people of British Honduras. A hopeful sign of understanding was the unanimous acceptance, in April 1972, of the applications of Venezuela and Colombia for membership in the Caribbean Development Bank.

' Modernisation ' was not possible without trained people, and one of the most effective steps in regional cooperation was taken by the West Indian governments and the United Kingdom when, in 1945, they agreed to establish a University College of the West Indies. Fourteen West Indian governments undertook to share the recurrent costs while the United Kingdom put up the money for buildings. In its first years it served an apprenticeship to the University of London. As the West Indian countries approached independence basic changes were made in the organisation of the College, which became an autonomous institution in 1962, with the power to grant its own degrees. The concept of a highly centralised institution was rejected in favour of a university with some facilities decentralised. A second campus was opened at St. Augustine in Trinidad in 1960, through the merger of the Imperial College of Tropical Agriculture with the University of the West Indies; a third at Cave Hill in Barbados three years later and university centres in non-campus countries. The range of teaching was widened, more liberal entry requirements adopted, consultative services offered to those governments that invited them. The numbers rose from 700 in 1960 to 6,300 in 1972. With its alumni reaching senior posts in the public services and achieving ministerial posts, the university grew in strength as a training centre and also as a regional thinking centre where West Indian scholars brought critical minds to bear on their society, its human and physical resources, its nature and its history.

The drive for development and the changes in political status influenced also the long-standing relationships with the neighbours to the north, Canada and the United States. The relationship with Canada began in the plantation period, the Maritimes supplying fish and timber and taking West Indian molasses and rum. Toward the close of the last century the Bank of Nova Scotia and the Royal Bank of Canada started doing business

Canadian Trade With The Commonwealth Caribbean

(thousands of dollars Canadian)

	Canadian Exports			Canadian Imports		
	1938	1964	1971	1938	1964	1971
JAMAICA	4,442·4	29,450	39,172	6,192·4	47,858	28,551
TRINIDAD & TOBAGO	3,714·3	18,040	20,321	2,352·4	20,738	7,717
BARBADOS	1,077·4	7,070	11,197	2,131·7	3,851	2,451
GUYANA	1,397·9	7,292	6,595	7,113·5	35,653	25,123
BRITISH HONDURAS	279·6	983	1,557	102·2	1,858	3,478
LEEWARD & WINDWARD ISLANDS	1,777·6	8,036	9,718	2,382·8	1,026	2,405
TOTAL	12,689·2	70,871	89,160	20,275·0	110,984	69,725

Source: Dominion Bureau of Statistics. Trade of Canada.

in the West Indies and banking became one of the chief areas of Canadian enterprise. Another was life insurance. Canadian Insurance Companies established themselves in the region with the result that about one half of all Life Insurance Companies doing business in the region are Canadian owned or Canadian subsidiaries. The discovery of bauxite in Guyana and in Jamaica further increased Canadian investment in those two countries. In recent years the popularity of West Indian beaches and sunshine increased the flow of Canadians to the islands. This in turn attracted Canadian capital into resort development. Canadian aid money went into the improvement of transport facilities and school construction and Canadian volunteers gave valuable service in all the countries of the Commonwealth Caribbean.

For one reason or another, however, the Canadian presence in the West Indies has not grown to the measure that might have been expected. The Canada-West Indies trade treaties of 1912, 1920 and 1925 did not result in any marked increase in trade and although the absolute value of trade between the two countries has increased, Canada's relative position in the over-all West India market has deteriorated.

Two areas of sensitivity developed in the post-independence period. One was migration, and this involved questions of race and of a brain-drain; and the other was the bauxite industry. Canada imports people, but up to 1962 the number of West Indians who went there was less than 1,000 a year, an insignificant proportion of the total number of Canadian immigrants. The chief reason for this was that Canadian immigration regulations were designed to attract European immigrants. Their transportation across the Atlantic was subsidised and the regulations for their entry were liberal. West Indians had to be sponsored by close relatives, though in 1955 this rule was eased in order to permit the entry of a small number of female domestic workers. An important change was made in 1962 when West Indians were permitted to enter Canada on the same terms as Europeans—that is, on the basis of skill, education and training. In the following years there was evidence that although the regulations were non-discriminatory, there was in practice a measure of discrimination. Levitt and McIntyre in a recent study of *Canada—West Indies Economic Relations* showed that a larger proportion of professional workers were admitted from the West Indies than from a number of European countries (more than twice the number as from Italy, for example) whereas a larger proportion of non-professional workers were admitted from Europe than from the West Indies. Though West Indians were concerned at this heavy brain drain, they were much more concerned at the fact that there appeared to be discrimination against the non-professional West Indian worker and in favour of the European non-professional worker. As a result, the Canadian Government, in a White Paper presented at the Ottawa Conference in 1966, stated that as a matter of principle immigration policies ' must involve no discrimination by reason of race, colour or religion.' This declaration was welcomed but the White Paper was generally criticised as being too restrictive and Canada thereupon relaxed the regulation in several important respects. The changes made in 1962 and 1966 had the effect of increasing the flow of West Indians to Canada, but the problem of the brain drain remained, as the figures show.

There was sensitivity also over capital investment. This was not limited to Canada but extended to every foreign country with large investments in the West Indies, whether in sugar, oil, petro-chemicals, resorts or insurance companies or bauxite. Indeed, the problem concerned many developed countries as well. Canada, for example, has been concerned about the size of United States investment in its industries and about the extent to which American financial interests might influence Canadian government policy and Canadian national development. The problem is acute in many third world countries. It has given concern to the new nations of the West Indies, because their resources are so limited, their rate of unemployment so high, their economy so dependent on overseas markets, their need for capital so urgent. The questions that have arisen over the bauxite industry in Guyana and in Jamaica illustrate the point; but they do not arise only in connection with this industry. In the riots in Trinidad in 1970 the militants charged the government with being in the power of overseas investors, and claimed that political independence had not given Trinidad the power to make critical decisions in financial matters. The questions that were being asked more and more widely in the West Indies were: How does

Immigration to Canada from West Indies by intended occupation 1965 & 1971

Intended Occupation	Jamaica		Trinidad and Tobago		Guyana		Others		Total	
	1965	1971	1965	1971	1965	1971	1965	1971	1965	1971
Managerial	8	56	13	105	7	72	6	29	34	252
Professional	184	194	206	265	52	164	119	86	561	709
Clerical	198	485	107	704	108	420	205	340	618	1949
Transportation	4	28	1	10	3	2	5	8	13	48
Communications	2	11	—	8	5	4	3	3	10	26
Commercial	9	64	7	127	14	94	11	48	41	333
Financial	5	21	1	18	3	7	6	15	15	61
Service	220	565	62	210	28	74	264	187	574	1036
Farming	3	22	2	13	—	9	11	3	16	47

Immigration to Canada from West Indies by intended occupation 1965 & 1971

Intended Occupation	Jamaica 1965	Jamaica 1971	Trinidad and Tobago 1965	Trinidad and Tobago 1971	Guyana 1965	Guyana 1971	Others 1965	Others 1971	Total 1965	Total 1971
Construction	42	173	9	99	11	51	28	57	90	380
Manufacturing & Mechanical	118	643	74	588	44	277	100	188	336	1696
Labourers	14	35	3	26		13	16	11	37	85
Others		47		155		67		76		345
Total Workers	807	2344	485	2328	279	1254	774	1054	2345	6980
Total Non-Workers	407	1599	295	1821	330	1130	278	575	1310	5125
Total Immigration	1214	3903	775	4149	609	2384	1052	1626	3655	12062

Source: Department of Citizenship and Immigration

a small developing country attract investment without coming under the power of the investor? By what means can it attract capital without in the long run becoming an exporter of capital in the dividends that have to be paid out? In what ways can nationals participate in the profits and share in the management of enterprises financed by foreign companies? Bearing these questions in mind, let us turn to the bauxite industry.

The pioneer companies in the development of the industry in Guyana and Jamaica were the Aluminium Company of Canada (ALCAN) which worked in Guyana through a subsidiary, the Demerara Bauxite Company (DEMBA) incorporated in 1916, and Alcan Jamaica, established in 1942; and the Reynolds Bauxite Company, through its subsidiary Reynolds Jamaica Mines. Both these companies knew that open cast mining presented the perfect picture of destructive exploitation and they took steps from the beginning to correct the image by their work in cattle raising, afforestation, rehabilitation of mined land and the encouragement of smallholdings. At a later stage, in Jamaica, three other American companies began work; Alcoa, Revere Copper and the Kaiser Bauxite Company. Production was stepped up to the point where in 1968 Jamaica was producing twenty per cent of the world's bauxite. But a country benefits about threefold if its bauxite is processed into alumina locally; and it is important to note that Revere Copper, Alcoa and Alumina Partners Jamaica, have committed themselves to the production of alumina in the island. There has also been discussion about the possibility of establishing a smelter to make the alumina into aluminium. But how could a country with bauxite get the maximum benefit from the industry? Prime Minister Forbes Burnham of Guyana said in 1966, that ' aluminium in a few years would have to be Guyanese if Demba is to play her proper role in an independent Guyana, Guyana took over Demba in 1970. That was one way of dealing with the problem. In Jamaica, after the Peoples National Party won the general election of February 1972, the Prime Minister, Mr. Michael Manley appointed a National Bauxite Commission to look into existing arrangements with the Companies and to make proposals that would ensure that the country got the greatest possible benefit from the industry.

It was the United States whose presence grew to mighty proportions in the Caribbean in this century. Her overwhelming power and wealth were evident on every hand, in second world war military bases in Guyana, Trinidad, St. Lucia, Antigua and Jamaica; in a flow of American visitors throughout the year, new plants and industries financed by American aid money, schools and roads and ports built with American help, Peace Corps workers in villages and towns, radio and television programmes that took American events and American personalities into West Indian homes. West Indians had moved out of the metropolitan orbit of the United Kingdom into the American orbit, and they both welcomed and resented the fact. They have always had a 'love-hate' relationship with the country that was for so many West Indians a land of opportunity and a land where they met insults and discrimination; where in Claude McKay's phrase, they were fed 'bread of bitterness.'

Africa had been present in the Caribbean from the days of the early Spanish colonists, but it was a presence rarely mentioned, hardly ever asserted. In recent years Garvey of Jamaica, Padmore and James of Trinidad, have emphasised the African connection. So have Cuban and Haitian writers who rejected Europe and turned to Africa. Mussolini's invasion of Ethiopia had roused West Indian blacks, and the rise of new African nations, especially of Ghana, Nigeria, and Sierra Leone have built into the West Indian community a sense of black achievement and of black history. On attaining independence, West Indian leaders not only took the beaten path to London but also went on voyages of discovery and goodwill to the African states. The 1950's and 1960's witnessed a growing identification of the West Indian with Africa, and also with other new world blacks.

Our history shows the hard road by which we have travelled to this present time. Tomorrow holds out no bright hope of ease. The social restructuring of our society has yet to be accomplished. Our economy has yet to be made secure. The living standards of the great mass of our people have yet to be improved. Chronic unemployment has yet to be conquered. In the last analysis, our resource lies in the quality of the West Indian people. The years that open before us will test that quality as we seek to stand on our own feet, to make our own way in the world.

Appendix

Appendix

CARIBBEAN COUNTRIES

Country	Area (sq Kms)	Population (in thousands)	Density (per sq Km)	Language	Status	Capital
BARBADOS	400	254	635·0	English	Indep.	Bridgetown
CUBA	115,000	8,250	71·7	Spanish	,,	Havana
DOMINICAN REPUB.	49,000	4,174	85·2	,,	,,	St. Domingo
GUYANA	215,000	742	3·5	English	,,	Georgetown
HAITI	28,000	4,768	170·3	French	,,	Pt-au-Prince
JAMAICA	11,000	1,959	178·1	English	,,	Kingston
TRINIDAD & TOBAGO	5,000	1,040	208·0	,,	,,	Pt-of-Spain
BAHAMAS	11,000	195	17·7	,,	Aut.	Nassau
BELIZE	23,000	120	5·2	,,	,,	Belize
CAYMAN ISLDS.	300	12	40·0	,,	,,	Georgetown

Country	Area (sq Kms)	Population (in thousands)	Density (per sq Km)	Language	Status	Capital
Windward & Leeward Islands						
ANTIGUA & BARBUDA	400	63	157·5	English	A.S.	St. Johns
DOMINICA	800	74	92·5	,,	,,	Roseau
GRENADA	300	105	350·0	,,	,,	St. Georges
MONTSERRAT	100	15	150·0	,,	Aut.	Plymouth
ST. KITTS-NEVIS ANGUILLA	400	56	140·0	,,	A.S.	Basseterre
ST. LUCIA	600	110	183·3	,,	,,	Castries
ST. VINCENT	400	95	237·5	,,	,,	Kingstown
BR. VIRGIN IS.	200	9	45·0	,,	Col.	Road Town
TURKS & CAICOS IS.	400	6	15·0	,,	Col.	Grand Turk.
NETHERLAND ANTILLES	1,000	218	218·0	Dutch	Kingdom of Holland	Willemstad
SURINAM	163,000	389	2·4	Dutch	,,	Paramaribo

Windward & Leeward Islands

Country	Area (sq Kms)	Population (in thousands)	Density (per sq Km)	Language	Status	Capital
GUADELOUPE & Dependencies	2,000	323	161·5	French	Dept. of France	Basse-Terre
FRENCH GUIANA	91,000	48	0·53	,,	,,	Cayenne
MARTINIQUE	1,000	332	332·0	,,	,,	Fort de France
PUERTO RICO	9,000	2,754	306·0	Spanish & English	Commonwealth (U.S.A.)	San Juan
AM. VIRGIN ISLANDS	300	60	200·0	English	Colony (U.S.A.)	Charlotte Amalie

Suggestions for Further Reading

The books listed are easily available.

Fuller bibliographies including primary sources, are given in:

J. H. Parry and
P. M. Sherlock: *Short History of the West Indies* (Macmillan, London, 3rd edition 1971).

E. Williams: *From Columbus to Castro:* (Deutsch, London, 1971).

CHAPTERS 1–4

S. E. Morison: *Christopher Columbus, Admiral of the Ocean Sea* (Boston 1942).

C. Sauer: *The Early Spanish Main* (University of California Press, 1966).

C. H. Haring: *The Spanish Empire in America,* (New York, 1947).

J. H. Parry: *Europe and a Wider World,* (Hutchinson, London).

CHAPTERS 5–9

R. Oliver and
J. D. Fage: *Short History of Africa* (Penguin African Library, London 1962).

J. H. Parry and
P. M. Sherlock: *Short History of the West Indies* (Chapters 3–4 Macmillan, London).

B. Davidson: *African Past* (Penguin African Library, London, 1964).

V. T. Harlow: *History of Barbados,* 1625–1682 (Oxford, 1926).

A. P. Newton: *The European Nations in the West Indies* (London 1933).

R. Sheridan: *Development of the Plantations to 1750* (Caribbean Universities Press, 1972).
An Era of West Indian Prosperity (Caribbean Universities Press, 1972).

CHAPTERS 10–13

J. F. Ajaye and
Ian Espie (eds): *A Thousand Years of West African History* (Ibadan University Press, 1965).

W. E. B. du Bois: *The World and Africa* (International Publishers, New York, 1965).

M. Heskovits: *Myth of the Negro Past* (New York, 1941).

J. H. Parry and
P. M. Sherlock: *Short History of the West Indies* Chapters 4–7.

W. E. F. Ward: *History of Ghana*, (Allen & Unwin, London 1958).

E. Williams: *Capitalism and Slavery*, (Chapel Hill, N.C. 1944).
From Castro to Columbus: (Deutsch, London 1971).

CHAPTERS 14–18

E. Brathwaite: *Creole Society in Jamaica, 1770–1820*, (Oxford).

P. D. Curtin: *The Atlantic Slave Trade*, (Wisconsin University Press, 1969).

E. Goveia: *Slave Society in the British Leeward Island*, (New Haven 1965).

R. Guerra y Sanchez: *Sugar and Society in the Caribbean*, trans. Margery M. Urquidi (New Haven 1964).

C. L. R. James: *Black Jacobins*, 2nd ed. (New York, 1963).

D. P. Mannix: *Black Cargoes*, (London 1962).

R. Pares: *West India Fortune*, (London, 1950).

O. Patterson: *Sociology of Slavery*: (McGibbon & Kee, London 1967).

E. Williams: *Capitalism and Slavery*, (London, 1964).

E. Williams: *From Columbus to Castro*, (London, 1965).

CHAPTERS 18-25

E. Clarke: *My Mother Who Fathered Me*, (London, 1957).

W. E. B. du Bois: *Suppression of the African Slave Trade*, (Schocken, N. Y. 1969).

D. Hall: Free Jamaica, 1838–1865, (Yale University Press 1959).

F. R. Hart: *Life of George William Gordon*: (Institute of Jamaica).

G. K. Lewis: *Growth of the Modern West Indies*, (London, 1968).

D. Lowenthal: *West Indian Societies*, (Oxford, 1972).

J. Mordecai: *The West Indies, The Federal Negotiations*, (London, 1968).

I. A. Wright (ed.): *Lady Nugent's Journal*, (Institute of Jamaica, 1972).

G. R. Coulthard: *Race & Colour in the Caribbean* (Oxford University Press).

R. M. Nettleford: *Mamley and the New Jamaica* (Longman).

O. Jefferson: *Post War Development of Jamaica* (Institute of Social & Economic Research. University of West Indies 1972).

W. K. Marshall: *Peasant Development in West Indies* (I.S.E.R. University of West Indies).

GENERAL WORKS

Augier, Gordon, Hall and Reckord: *Making of the West Indies*, (Longmans, London, 1960).

F Cassidy: *Jamaica Talk* (Macmillan, London 1961).

Franklin & Starr (ed.): *Negroes in 20th Century America* (New York).

M. Horowitz: *People and Cultures of the Caribbean*. (New York.)

J. G. Leyburn: *The Haitian People* (New Haven).

J. H. Parry and P. M. Sherlock: *Short History of the West Indies*. (Macmillan, London, 1956. 3rd ed. 1971).

K. Ramchand: *West Indian Narrative*, (London 1966).

G. Roberts: *Population of Jamaica*, (Cambridge University Press, 1957).

HISTORIES OF INDIVIDUAL COUNTRIES

C. V. Black:	*History of Jamaica* (Collins, London 1968).
D. G. H. Hall:	*Five of the Leewards 1834–70* Caribbean Universities Press 1971).
F. A. Hoyos:	*Barbados Our Island Home,* (Macmillan, London, Rev. ed. 1970).
G. W. Roberts:	*Population of Jamaica* (Cambridge University Press, 1957).
P. M. Sherlock:	*Junior History of Jamaica,* (London).
P. M. Sherlock:	*Junior History of Belize,* (London).
M. Swan:	*British Guiana* (London).
D. A. G. Waddell:	*British Honduras,* (Oxford University Press, 1961).
E. Williams:	*History of the People of Trinidad and Tobago,* (Deutsch 1964).

Index

Esquivel, Juan de, 16
Essequibo, 67, 148, 149, 165, 169, 205, 217, 247
estancias, 30
Ethiopia, 62, 61
ethnic groupings, 241
Europe since Napoleon (Thomson), 227
European Economic Community, 305, 307
Eyre, E. J., Governor of Jamaica, 259–60

Fajardo, Luis, 69
Falconbridge, Capt., 123–4
Family Compact (1761), 162
family structure, 196
famine, 170, 188
Fanon, Frantz, 308–9, 310
Fante, the, 100, 105
Federation of British West Indies, 292–5
Ferdinand and Isabella, 18, 29, 33, *see also* Isabella, Queen
Fermin, Antenor, 309
Ferre, Luis, 315
Ferres Galley, voyage of, 200
Fire Next Time, The (Baldwin), 265
Florida, 17, 38, 43, 46, 156, 163: Channel, 44–6
Flota, the, 37
folk culture, 187
Fon people, the, 106–7, 199
Fonseca, Juan Rodriquez de, 26
Foster, William, 223
France, 43, 66–8, 216–17, 306–10: corsairs, 43–4; foothold in Eastern Caribbean, 72; Code Noir, 133, 181, 208; slave trade, 154, 221; sugar, 165–7; Crown control of colonies, 176, and revolt in St. Domingue, 208–15; abolition of slavery, 220, 229–30
Franciscans, the, 38
Franklin, Benjamin, 173
Franklin, John Hope, 62, 64
Free African immigrants, 242, 246, 249–51: and the land, 252–5; health services, 255; education, 255–8
Free Ports Act (1766), 167, 170
French Guiana, 115, 127, 165, 306
French Guinea Company, 154
French Revolutions, 163, 165, 183, 222: and revolt in St. Domingue, 208–10

Freyre, Gilberto, 53
friendly societies, 279
Friends of the Blacks, 209
From Columbus to Castro (Williams), 277
From Slavers to Freedom (Franklin), 62

Gairy, Eric, 269, 327
galleons fleet, 37–8
Gambia river, 49, 101, 102
Garvey, Marcus, 268, 279–81, 284, 288, 309, 339
General History of the French Antilles (du Tertre), 76
Georgetown, 245, 253, 279
Georgia, 156, 168
Gilbert, Nathaniel, 223
Gladstone, John, 245
Gold Coast, 100, 102, 105, 107, 116, 118, 135, 204, 205
Gordon, Edward George, 258–60
Goree, 70, 115
Goslinga, Professor, 243, 244
Goveia, Dr. Elsa, 7, 77, 130, 141, 178, 182
government systems, 174–8, 233–6, 285–6
Grant, Sir John Peter, 235
Great Ardrah, 106, 107
Grenada, 70, 116, 124, 136, 163, 165, 169, 178, 211, 225, 250, 252, 256, 272, 274, 281: sugar, 128, 147, 148; ceded to Britain (1763), 128, 147, 162, 206, 233; government, 234, 236, 295; small holdings, 261, 262; and Federation, 293
Grenadines, the, 147
Grey, Lord, 257
Groenewegen, Capt., 67, 71
gros blancs, 173
Growth of the Modern West Indies, The (Lewis), 280
Guadeloupe, 72, 91, 115, 147, 160–2, 165, 183, 184, 210, 211, 215–17, 206, 307: and slave trade, 126, 127; sugar, 144, 161, 215–16
Guantanamo (Cuba), 320
Guarionex, 22, 25
Guatemala, 4, 18, 22, 34
Guerra y Sanchez, 30, 230
Guillaume, President, 318
Guillén, Nicholas, 95, 231–3
Guinea coast, 41, 49, 52, 54, 102, 114, 116, 117
Guinea grass, 146
Guyana (Guiana), 6, 57, 63, 67–8, 70,

128, 145, 206, 226, 229, 240-2
244-6, 271, 274, 282, 300, 328, 339:
sugar, 52, 219; slave risings, 201,
220, 222; East Indian labour, 219;
mortality rates, 244-5; small farming, 247; free Africans, 249, 253-4;
population, 269, 270, 299; bauxite,
271, 274-5, 282, 334, 335, 338, *see also*
British Guiana and French Guiana

hacienda, the, 138, 139
Hague, Treaties of the: (1595), 47;
(1673), 84
Hailes, Lord, 294
Haiti, 5, 55, 63, 87, 116, 125, 137, 192,
194, 199, 202, 316-19: Revolution
(1800-04), 163, 207, 209-16, 219,
220, 222, 230, 232, 267; writers,
309, 339; and USA, 318-19
Harcourt, Robert, 67
Harlan, Justice, 266-7
Harris, Lord, 235, 257-8
Havana, 16, 30, 36-8, 44-7, 78, 80,
162, 165, 248, 322
Hawkins, Sir John, 41-5, 52, 66
Hawkins, William, 41
Health services, 255, 275
Henry the Navigator, Prince, 12, 52
herring trade, 69
Herskovits, Melville, 58-9, 107, 188
Heureaux, Ulises, 316
Hill, Richard, 258
Hilton, Anthony, 78
Hindu rites, 258, 259
Hispaniola, 5, 8, 14, 17, 21-7, 37, 38,
41-2, 44, 49, 50, 52, 65, 76, 77, 79-
81, 93, 145, 149, 201, 217, 230
History of Barbados (Ligon), 88
History of Dominica (Attwood), 130
History of Slavery (Saco), 232
*History of the People of Trinidad and
Tobago* (Williams), 247
History of Trinidad (de Verteuil), 108
History of the West Indies (Edwards),
138—41
Honduras, 4, 22, 37, 76, 78, 138, 163,
270, 317
Honduras, Bay of, 18, 156, 207
Hood, Admiral, 169
Houel, Charles, 88
Howard, John, 165
Huggins, Edward, slave owner, 179-
80
Huguenots, the, 79
Hugues, Victor, 211, 216, 217

hurricanes, 160, 170, 183, 188, 270,
275

Ibibio, the, 107, 109
Ibo, the, 100, 107, 109, 134, 135, 192,
205
Imperial College of Tropical Agri-
culture, 274, 332
Incas, the, 40
indenture system, 73-4, 129, 139, 192,
219, 246, 248
indigo, 75, 126, 144, 146, 156, 174,
209
Indonesians, 241, 243, *see also* Javanese
Inquisition, the, 38-9, 43, 68
Introduction to Jamaican Creole (Le
Page), 157
Isabella of Castile, Queen, 13, 14, 49
Isasi (Ysassi), Cristobel de, 80, 201
Ivory Coast, 49, 107

Jacobin Commissioners in West Indies,
210, 211, 216
Jagan, Dr. Cheddi, 292, 296, 327
Jakin, 106, 107
Jamaica, 16, 24, 27, 28, 30, 37, 55, 57,
62, 63, 65, 75, 81-4, 86, 91-3, 124,
134, 136, 145, 147, 153, 159, 161,
162, 167, 168, 174, 175, 177, 178,
183, 189, 192-5, 210, 211, 217, 218,
223, 224, 237, 242, 271, 274, 283,
302, 317, 326, 328, 339: annexed by
England, 30, 80, 81, 201; sugar, 52,
126, 127, 154, 166, 167, 172, 208,
238, 272; plantations, 84, 93, 115-
16, 124, 135, 139-40, 142-6, 159,
165, 179, 220, 230, 300; cocoa, 92,
93, 126, 170; slave trade, 126-8,
157; hurricanes, 170, 188, 270, 275;
famine, 170, 188; provision grounds,
190, 191; slave risings, 201-2, 204-
5, 220, 222; and emancipation,
225-6, 229; 'Baptist War', 226-7;
government, 233, 234, 237, 285,
289; break-up of estates, 238; free
Africans, 250, 252-6; unrest and
rising of 1865, 259-60; peasant
holdings, 261, 262, 300; population,
269-71, 300; bananas, 271, 274,
282; death rate, 275; constitutional
change, 291-2; and Federation, 293,
294; independence, 295; disorders
(1966-8), 303; bauxite, 328, 334,
335, 338; in OAS, 329
Jamaica Acts: (1702), 177; (1674),
178-9